How to Interpret Financial Statements for Better Business Decisions

How to Interpret Financial Statements for Better Business Decisions

Barry E. Miller and
Donald E. Miller

amacom

American Management Association

Library of Congress Cataloging-in-Publication Data

Miller, Barry E.
    How to interpret financial statements for better business
decisions / Barry E. Miller and Donald E. Miller.
        p.   cm.
    Includes index.
    ISBN 0-8144-5940-4
    1. Financial statements.   2. Ratio analysis.   3. Business—
Decision making.   I. Miller, Donald E.   II. Title.
HF5681.B2M46   1991
658.15'12—dc20   90-55206
                                                       CIP

Printing number

10   9   8   7   6   5   4   3   2   1

Contents

Preface

This book is designed for rapid learning, in-depth understanding, and long-term reference. *You do not need to read every chapter in order to become proficient in the analysis of financial statements, a highly important management skill in today's competitive business environment.* In fact, even if you have no previous knowledge of accounting and financial management, the first 135 pages will provide you with the essential information you need to make effective use of cause-and-effect ratio analysis for better business decisions.

Based on two generations of financial management experience, this book will show you how to transform an income statement and balance sheet into a source of vital information about any company's competitive strengths and weaknesses.

How to Interpret Financial Statements for Better Business Decisions is actually three books in one because it serves three important purposes:

1. *Rapid learning.* By the time you have completed Parts I through IV, you will be able to identify the comparative financial advantages and disadvantages of any company. In other words, you do *not* have to read the entire book to obtain significant benefit from the cause-and-effect ratio approach. For a fast start, you may wish to examine Chapter 22 ("Impact of the Seven Causal Ratios on the Nine Ratios That Measure Effect") and Chapter 23 ("The Three Most Common Reasons for Management Review of Financial Statements") and then select further reading from the Table of Contents and the Index.

2. *In-depth understanding.* To help you acquire a more complete working knowledge of the cause-and-effect ratio method in a variety of common business situations, four extensive case studies are presented in Part V, followed by ten examples of practical problem solving through ratio analysis in Part VI. The last two chapters of Part V, Chapter 28 ("Ratio Analysis: A Tool for Making Policy Decisions") and Chapter 29 ("Measures to Restore Financial Health"), are particularly useful to company owners and managers. Part VII provides guidance in identifying appropriate benchmark data for more accurate analysis.

3. *Long-term reference.* For detailed explanations of such important topics as working capital vulnerability, coverage of interest and long-term liabilities, measuring management performance, sustainable growth, potential for bankruptcy, business valuation, and investors' perspective of cash flow relative to invested capital, you should consult Appendix A. Appendix B covers other vital

business issues in operating analysis and profit planning: key operating ratios, break-even analysis, cash flow analysis, gross margin return on inventory, and value added. Appendix C is a particularly helpful guide to understanding how statistical methods affect comparative data. Even the most experienced accountant, financial analyst, or strategic planner will find the discussions of these issues valuable.

This is a practical book, which draws its strength from nearly five decades of business application by company owners and managers, accountants, bank loan officers, credit managers, corporate financial officers, merger and acquisition specialists, business brokers, valuation experts, and trade association executives. Through constant testing and refinement in the real world, the critical relationships between the key factors on the financial statement have been identified, organized, and explained for immediate use. Whether you are approaching the analysis of financial statements for the first time or have an interest in advancing your existing knowledge of this important decision-making technique, you will find the cause-and-effect ratio approach to be a highly effective skill-building tool.

The basic cause-and-effect methodology was developed by Donald E. Miller in hundreds of practical business situations between 1942 and 1965. Because so many of the underlying concepts are attributable to his pioneering work, he is properly recognized as coauthor of this book. Throughout his career as Eastern Area credit manager of Crown Zellerbach Corporation and during his voluntary service as chairman of the National Association of Credit Management's Credit Interchange Board of Governors, he worked unrelentingly to design and improve analytical tools for company owners and officers, as well as for credit grantors.

Acknowledgments

Since assisting my father, Donald E. Miller, as editor and technical contributor in the preparation of *The Meaningful Interpretation of Financial Statements* (first published by AMACOM in 1966), I have served as a consultant to business decision makers and national trade associations. Through nearly twenty-five years of additional experience—in conducting association surveys and producing industry ratio reports, presenting management seminars, providing confidential counseling to company owners and managers, appearing in court as an expert witness, and preparing more than 2,000 individualized financial management reports—I have used, discussed, and continually refined the ideas in this book.

In this endeavor, I have been privileged to receive more than a little help from my friends.

My wife, Karen, enabled this book to evolve from a manuscript of *The Meaningful Interpretation of Financial Statements* (which she typed in our dining room throughout a hot Philadelphia summer without the benefit of air conditioning during our first year of marriage) to the present publication. Her loving support for all these years has been essential.

Elizabeth Jensen, who has worked with me to develop an expert system for preparing individualized financial management reports based on the cause-and-effect ratio approach, made numerous important editorial contributions while participating in the production of the manuscript. Kathleen J. McNally not only played a key role in preparing the text and tables from the first rough page through the completion of the final manuscript but provided good counsel concerning style and grammar. Without their special skills, this book would not exist.

Through the years, numerous colleagues, particularly Elizabeth Muller and Martin B. Beckerman, have advanced useful ideas for explaining and applying the cause-and-effect method.

Because so many association executives have also contributed to the development of the concepts in this book, restricting the acknowledgments is a difficult task. I would, however, like to make special mention of suggestions and encouragement from Robert A. Gale, president of the American Machine Tool Distributors' Association, who was instrumental in convincing me to apply the cause-and-effect approach to the improvement of industry ratio reports; John A. Bell, who helped to make these ideas available to thousands of business owners and managers during his tenure with the National Tooling and Machining Association;

C. Christopher Kelly, controller of the National Machine Tool Builders' Association, who has directed the development of new management tools for addressing today's important financial issues; and Francis Mason, former controller of the National Machine Tool Builders' Association, who aided greatly in introducing a particularly effective format for presenting financial ratios to trade association members.

The insightful observations and suggestions by John J. Hampton, provost and professor of finance at the College of Insurance, and Cecilia L. Wagner, assistant professor of finance at Seton Hall University, greatly improved the organization and structural integrity of the final manuscript. Likewise, the genial and enthusiastic guidance of Myles Thompson from concept through written word and the patient, yet insistent, direction of Richard Gatjens during the conversion from typed pages to a readable book were immensely valuable.

For all this help I am deeply appreciative.

The ideas in this book, applied in the world of business for almost half a century, reflect the work of those acknowledged and many more.

Barry E. Miller

Part I

The Importance of Understanding the Basics of Financial Management

A company's success depends upon management awareness. Every businessperson must know the full potential of his company and be thoroughly aware of the means by which this potential can be realized before he can guide his organization to ultimate success. And no company owner or manager can consider himself entirely informed about the position of his business, his competitors, or his industry unless he understands financial statements and the information they contain. General impressions of financial structure or vague notions of the competitive climate do not provide an adequate background for making the specific decisions that successful operations demand. Sound financial knowledge is absolutely essential, knowledge that is within the grasp of every business decision maker who understands and applies the principles of *cause-and-effect ratio analysis*. In companies where owners and executives do not have an organized approach to financial management based on a solid understanding of the basics, serious difficulties are likely to limit the growth and profitability that determine business success.

The analytical system known as the *cause-and-effect ratio approach* was originally developed to help independent business owners and their top managers make better financial decisions. It was designed to enable individuals with no formal training in accounting or finance to understand the fundamental factors that determine a company's competitive position. For 25 years, the cause-and-effect ratio approach has also proved highly valuable to accountants, bankers, credit managers, consultants, and business brokers because it serves as a concise summary of important financial principles—a focal point in the sea of numbers generated today. Because each key financial relationship can be explained through a step-by-step logical process, this approach helps financial professionals communicate more effectively with their business clients. For the same reason, executives and managers in some of our country's largest corporations have found this system useful in directing attention to the key financial elements in business competition and testing the validity of assumptions in internal reports and projections such as budgets and cash flow analyses.

In Part I, we study the present state of financial management in small and medium-size companies and consider how business owners and managers with no previous training in accounting or finance can acquire fundamental financial skills. We also take a brief look at the important elements of the financial statement, which is the raw material for cause-and-effect ratio analysis.

Chapter 1

A Method to Improve Financial Management

Even the most experienced businessperson can improve his or her understanding of financial management through the cause-and-effect ratio approach. By providing an organized structure for evaluating the specific relationships between the key factors on the financial statement, this method enables the business decision maker to identify his company's competitive strengths and weaknesses with greater ease and assurance. The individual who possesses little or no familiarity with financial analysis will find the cause-and-effect approach particularly useful. Because it clearly points out factors that cause changes in a company's financial structure—and distinguishes them from the factors that simply measure effect—this method helps beginning analysts (business owners and managers, as well as investors and students) to gain rapid understanding of the fundamentals of financial management.

Before examining the specifics of improving financial management, however, let us present briefly the challenges faced by small and medium-size companies in this critical area of management expertise.

Financial Management in Small and Medium-Size Companies

Small businesses, in the words of the U.S. Small Business Administration, "have been leaders in America's evolution." Many of the recent advances in the service sector, in particular, have come from small companies. And even as the U.S. economy has been shifting from manufacturing to services and information providers (with large manufacturers reporting a net loss of 100,000 jobs between the mid-1970s and the mid-1980s), small manufacturers increased their net employment by 1.3 million workers during that same period.

Yet every day the doors of hundreds of companies close forever. Tax lien notices are posted; "for sale" or "for rent" signs appear; business owners undergo examination in bankruptcy or receivership courts. These daily failures mount to a staggering annual loss, measured not only in dollars and cents but in the disappointment of those whose efforts and hopes were once placed in companies that have collapsed. Many of these business disasters could have been averted. Countless other companies struggle along; they neither attain success nor succumb to failure, but hover constantly at a level far short of their goals and their real potential. Still other businesses appear reasonably successful when they are compared with many firms in their line; yet they do not achieve all that is within their capabilities. These companies are not failing, but they can certainly improve their performance. In all of these cases, the application of cause-and-effect ratio analysis can markedly enhance financial understanding and be a key factor in profit improvement and business success.

Large and complex business organizations, the giants of industry, are staffed with numerous specialists who supply policymakers and line officers with documented information regarding virtually every phase of operations—the kind of information that leads to detailed planning and improves the probability of arriving at sound decisions. The small business with limited funds and relatively few employees must, on the other hand, count on management to furnish both background and decisions. The manager in a small concern cannot turn to the tax department, purchasing agent, legal staff, production planning manager, personnel officer, or credit manager for background information. The management of the small or moderate-size concern generally consists of five or fewer officers; this group must supply comprehensive management skills if the company is to prosper. Balanced management is not easily secured, because the majority of officers and executives in small companies come from either the ranks of sales or production personnel. Far too few managers have a really comprehensive background in the financial aspect of the business that is also essential to success.

Such companies clearly have qualities and problems quite dissimilar from those of the relatively few concerns employing 1,000 or more or possessing net worth greater than $10 million. Unfortunately, the bulk of today's financial material is written about and for large corporations and their specialists. Decision makers in smaller companies generally require more basic information, for they themselves must provide comprehensive management, either as a team of individuals with diverse experience and skills or by acquiring the necessary talents through education and self-improvement.

Evidence that many owners and managers could benefit from improved knowledge can be seen in the rapid turnover of the business population. According to the latest study by the Small Business Administration,* one of every four new companies in the United States ceases operations or undergoes a change in ownership within two years, and if recent trends continue, more than half of today's business start-ups will close their doors within four years. Long-established companies also fail. Sound management can greatly reduce this toll, and sound management is an acquired technique.

Far too many businesses, particularly relatively small ones, suffer from inadequate financial management. In a great number of these concerns, the treasurer's function is merely to keep the *books* in balance. But the skilled

*Bruce Phillips, "Analysis of New Firm Survival and Growth," Office of Economic Research, U.S. Small Business Administration, May 1988.

financial officer must do a great deal more than that; he or she must keep the *business* in balance as well. What a difference in approach this demands! The books will balance with red ink; they will even balance in bankruptcy court. But surely neither of these results represents the objectives of the owners.

Excessive concentration on sales contributes to the financial difficulties encountered by so many small companies. The primary danger to a business directed predominantly by sales or production people is the strong inclination of management to assume that a business is formed to produce and sell or to buy and sell and that, if these functions are performed, the success of the company is assured. Often no real thought is given to the effects a particular operating or marketing move will have on the financial stability and growth potential of the enterprise. Certainly a competent sales or production person can become a very fine financial officer, but to attempt to develop and refine financial talent through trial and error is risky at best. Unless the owners can hire someone with financial skill to become a part of the company's management team, they themselves must acquire fundamental knowledge of finance to give the business the balance and guidance it needs.

Financial proficiency is not an inherited trait; it can be acquired—and hundreds of hours of university courses or professional lessons are not needed to master the essentials. Some companies have even acquired their management education in the bankruptcy courts, although this is hardly recommended. A renowned bankruptcy referee, who has presided over some 5,000 cases in his long career, says that more than half the companies that have come before him— under the most difficult circumstances—have succeeded in reorganizing and thriving after initial payment problems. Those that achieved financial stability after discharge from bankruptcy undoubtedly reversed their former unsuccessful practices not simply because they were freed from court domination but because the court and the creditors' committee taught them some sound financial management techniques. If a bankrupt company can surmount its difficulties, how much more easily can a struggling but still independent and free concern do so? Owners' and officers' interest in learning how to diagnose their own problems is the first— and most important—step toward solving the difficulties that inevitably arise in business competition.

Acquiring Financial Skill

To assume responsibility for the financial affairs of your company, you need not be an accountant or an auditor, nor must you have a university degree in finance. You can master the fundamentals of finance and make major policy decisions with assurance if you take the time to understand two relatively simple aspects of business management: (1) the meaning of each asset and liability on your company's balance sheet and the significance of each major item appearing on the income statement; and (2) the cause-and-effect ratio method of analyzing a financial statement so that you can accurately assess your company's essential trends and draw meaningful conclusions when comparing the results of your company with typical operating performance and financial structure in its industry.

You don't need a formal education in accounting or bookkeeping to learn the meaning of financial statement items. Bookkeepers and accountants are hired to make all of the various debit and credit entries that culminate in the end products: the balance sheet, the income statement, various expense schedules, funds flow statements, and reconciliation of net worth. Auditors and public accounting firms are brought in to check the accuracy of the internal records, to verify certain assets and liabilities, and to certify the validity of the closing statement prepared for the owners. It is not necessary for you, as a manager, to follow a particular figure from its derivation all the way through to its entry on the books, but you must be aware of the meaning of each item that appears on the statement. The "how"—the mechanics of bookkeeping—is of secondary interest only. But the "what," the "why," the "when," and the "where" should hold your interest, for in the answers to these questions rests the future of your company. The term *current assets*, for instance, should be immediately understood by the business owner or manager. If not, you need to devote a small amount of time each week to study Chapter 3. Similarly, if you make the company's important financial decisions, you should instantly recognize the term *fixed assets* and what it represents, even though your comprehension of the computation of depreciation reserves may be somewhat cloudy. You should know what is meant by *accounts payable*, without necessarily knowing the specific debit and credit entries posted to the subsidiary ledgers. Although routine entries are not ordinarily a matter of management concern, the information produced from those entries is very much within the scope of the owner's and manager's responsibility. That end product consists of the financial statement, which the business decision maker must be able to read with understanding. The entire future of the company hinges on the ability of the owner or manager to identify and evaluate relevant financial data as a means of planning profitable moves.

Ratio Analysis

Ratio analysis, the second vital element in mastering financial management, is not new. For many years, a variety of analysts—credit grantors, accountants, university professors, and business consultants—have attempted to add meaning to financial statement figures by comparing different items through the use of ratios, dividing one item by another to obtain a proportionate relationship. For instance, the *current ratio*, the proportion of current assets to current liabilities, is somewhat familiar to many businesspeople. Unfortunately, earlier attempts to relate important elements of the financial statement through key financial ratios have suffered from a lack of systematic application because of an unawareness of the fundamental principle of cause and effect. Most analysts have essentially given equal weight and equal value to all ratios—simply creating a "laundry list" of calculations with no indication of which ratios might be most important. Ratios are not equal in importance any more than people are equal in ability or wealth or power. Some ratios lead and others follow; some represent cause and some, effect. As we see in the following pages, the impact of specific causal ratios varies from one line of business to another, depending on credit terms, the presence and extent of inventory, the commitment of funds to fixed assets, and the availability of credit from suppliers and banks. We shall also see that, regardless of a company's business activity, certain key factors are primary, causing changes in the other important measures of a company's operating performance and basic financial structure.

Even when analysts have attempted to assign greater weight to certain ratios and reduce the importance of others, their methods have seldom been effectively applied in practice, because the formulas do not explain why particular ratios deserve greater consideration than others. Moreover, the importance of comparing an individual company's ratios with those of concerns of similar size in the same line of business activity during the same fiscal period has not always been well recognized. In fact, the special characteristics of small and moderate-size businesses have frequently been ignored in academic studies and publications on financial management. All of these aspects of financial management are stressed in the cause-and-effect ratio approach. Once the cause-and-effect technique is well understood, fundamental financial statement analysis becomes comparatively easy for every company decision maker, whether his background happens to be in finance or in some other business area.

The Ratio

The *ratio*, the mathematical relationship between two quantities, is of major importance in financial analysis because it injects a qualitative measurement and demonstrates in a precise manner the adequacy of one key financial statement item relative to another. The 16 ratios that have proved themselves to be of greatest value in actual business decision making are described and applied in detail in the following chapters. But the cause-and-effect technique cannot be understood in bits and pieces; it must, instead, be viewed as a complete system of financial analysis. Knowing the exact dollar amount of a company's assets is, in and of itself, of little value to management even though the accuracy of that figure may be confirmed without qualification by the best firm of certified public accountants. Suppose you learn from your company's financial statement that cash and short-term investments stand at $100,130 at year-end, while accounts receivable have reached $624,965, inventory is $748,500, and other current assets total $24,290. These are intimate facts about the business, but do they reflect sound financial management? To answer that question, you require additional information and systematic cause-and-effect analysis.

What is the company's sales volume, its cost of sales, and its net profit? What are the amounts of its current liabilities and working capital? How much money does the company have committed to fixed assets and miscellaneous assets? What level of long-term liabilities has it incurred? And what is the company's net worth (its owners' equity or shareholders' equity)? From these relatively few additional facts, a person familiar with cause-and-effect ratio analysis can calculate the key measures of financial management and identify any unusual characteristics. By obtaining the same facts from earlier periods and computing just 16 ratios, he can readily see whether the company's operating results and financial structure are becoming more favorable or are revealing potentially dangerous trends. And by comparing the company's important ratios with industry standards derived from the financial statements of concerns of similar size in the same line of activity, the analyst can determine the company's comparative strengths and weaknesses, the key factors which determine its competitive position within the industry.

Even if management is concerned only about inventory at this particular time, that asset item must be related to other key financial elements in order to be understood in a manner that will lead to better business decisions. *Cost of Sales to Inventory* provides vital information about the "turnover" of inventory, a major measure of asset management. Computing the ratio is very simple, but taking this basic analytical step requires the involvement of another item on the financial statement: cost of sales. Gaining a complete understanding of the impact of inventory on a company's financial structure and competitive position also depends on calculating those ratios affected by inventory turnover (such as *Current Assets to Current Liabilities* and the *Quick Ratio*) and relating the dollar amount of inventory to the company's working capital. Through a few simple calculations, both the management and the influence of inventory can be evaluated. This, then, is the significance of ratios: By relating one financial statement item to another, they impart meaning or reason (*ratio* means "reason" in Latin) to those numbers.

Cause-and-Effect Analysis

Cause-and-effect ratio analysis is based on 16 key financial relationships expressed as mathematical proportions between major balance sheet and income statement items. Each of the 16 ratios demonstrates a significant connection between two important elements of a company's financial structure. An almost infinite number of other ratios can, of course, be calculated by pairing financial statement entries at random, and certain of these additional ratios are useful in specialized operations. But the 16 ratios of cause-and-effect analysis have been applied and tested as a unified system in thousands of business situations and have demonstrated that, taken together, they provide the fundamental financial understanding needed by business managers, credit grantors, and independent analysts.

All of life is subject to cause and effect. If a rock is thrown at a plate glass window with sufficient force, the window breaks. The throwing of the stone is the cause; the shattering of the glass is the effect. One could hardly believe the reverse—that the breaking of the glass caused the rock to be thrown. Applying the basic principle of cause and effect, we recognize that a business organization ordinarily finds itself in a particular financial position because of one or two primary causes, but may occasionally be in substantial difficulty due to a multiplicity of causes. The immediate situation is the effect; the cause or causes must be sought.

A company's financial balance, measured through ratios, is clearly subject to the principle of cause and effect. Some ratios are basic, fundamental, primary. Others are resultant, secondary, derivative. The seven ratios discussed in the next part are causal; they are the keys to financial balance.

Knowledge of the meaning of each ratio is, by itself, not sufficient to provide anyone with the ability to use the ratio analysis technique effectively. Nor can reference to individual industry standards yield complete understanding; no company can be expected to adhere strictly to industry norms in all respects. The analyst will likely find a company deficient in several areas, but above the comparative standard in others. What then can he conclude about the company's performance? On balance, is the company's financial structure favorable or unfavorable or somewhere between these extremes? Is the degree of deviation from normal a reasonable basis for separating the sheep from the goats?

An understanding of the cause-and-effect factors in ratio analysis provides the answers to these questions. Developed nearly 50 years ago—but made even more useful today through continual testing and refinement—the cause-and-effect system of analysis has been used to assist many thousands of business owners and managers since that time. It has served numerous business decision makers as the key to quick and accurate detection of basic financial problems and has thus guided many companies to practical solutions and ultimate success.

Chapter 2

Financial Statements: The Raw Material of Ratio Analysis

The soundness of management decisions depends, of course, upon the accuracy of financial data. Unfortunately, financial statements vary significantly with respect to quality and scope. In any analysis of a company's financial position, the type of statement from which the figures are derived must be considered. Financial statements may be broadly classified in the following manner.

1. *The Audited Statement.* The audited statement covers a specific period, generally the fiscal year. Prepared by certified public accountants, audited statements are normally quite reliable—subject, of course, to the degree of competence and true independence of the auditor. Accompanying every audited financial statement is a declaration in which the accounting firm may (1) express an unqualified opinion that the statement presents fairly the financial position and results of operations of the subject company during the accounting period, (2) limit the scope of the opinion because of incomplete examination or confirmation of accounts, (3) set forth an adverse opinion based upon the company's failure to adhere to generally accepted accounting principles, or (4) state that certain factors preclude an expression of opinion regarding the overall adequacy of the financial statement. The analyst must read the accountant's opinion with care, for only through such scrutiny can he determine the degree of reliance to be placed on the figures presented.

2. *The Unaudited Year-End Statement.* Many small companies do not have their year-end statements audited. They often engage an accountant to compile the statement from their records, but some prepare the statement themselves. Such unaudited statements may be either signed by a company officer or unsigned. Audits performed on insolvent concerns all too often disclose that the compiled statements upon which management had been relying were far from representative of the actual operations and financial condition—a fact learned too late to permit corrective action.

3. *The Interim Statement.* Depending upon management's needs, interim figures may be prepared monthly, quarterly, or semiannually. Because interim

statements are seldom audited, some inaccuracies may find their way into the figures. The interim statement is, nevertheless, of substantial aid to the business-person who is interested in evaluating results periodically to determine adherence to targeted performance and to detect incipient problems. The analyst must recognize that interim figures are subject to radical year-end adjustments; hence these statements should be viewed with some reservations.

4. *The "Estimated" Statement.* Only the most naive businessperson would base management decisions upon estimated figures. Successful competitive moves cannot be approximate; they must be clearly defined and precisely executed. One cannot buy an estimated piece of machinery, hire an estimated salesperson, or invoice customers at an estimated final price. Approximations can lead business managers—and their creditors—into dangerously erroneous beliefs regarding the company's financial position.

Although an independent verification of the amounts contained in the financial statement can be exceedingly valuable to both management and outside analysts, it is important to remember that the auditor is not a valuer or appraiser. He or she may establish that the accounts receivable of the XYZ Company are $1,411,512.26 through 100% verification, but confirmation of book value in no manner indicates the collectibility of those receivables. A good auditor will classify them according to length of time outstanding and create an appropriate reserve of bad debts, but the final interpretation of the auditor's figures, and the decisions based upon them, are the responsibility of the business owner or manager. Nor does the auditor attempt to determine whether a company's receivables balance is appropriate for its volume of sales or whether working capital can support its sales activity. Qualitative measurement of quantitative figures is performed by the financial analyst—the business decision maker, a credit grantor, an investor, or an industry consultant.

The analyst who has access to financial statements from previous fiscal periods should be especially alert to major year-to-year changes in the dollar amount of items on the income statement and the balance sheet. Such shifts in the composition of financial statement items, which will be signaled by the key financial ratios, ordinarily indicate actual differences in operations and financial structure. Naturally, such differences should be investigated in assessing a company's competitive position and its prospects. In some cases, however, ratio differences from one year to the next will reflect changes in accounting procedures or a revaluation of the company's assets. Whenever a noticeable change in the financial ratios is blithely explained by management as simply a matter of accounting differences, a thorough evaluation of the circumstances is needed. The underlying reasons for changes in accounting methods or in the valuation of assets may be highly significant.

Before discussing the details of ratios and the cause-and-effect approach, we should note briefly the broad categories of financial statement items with which we will be dealing. Items from both the income statement and the balance sheet are used in ratio analysis. The cause-and-effect approach is designed to highlight the factors that reveal a company's fundamental operating effectiveness and its basic financial structure—factors that are common to all lines of business activity.

The cause-and-effect approach is not primarily intended as a method of studying operating expenses (although detailed suggestions for using ratio analysis in evaluating cost patterns will be found in Appendix B). Consequently, net sales, cost of sales, and net profit are the only three items from the income statement that serve as components of the 16 key financial ratios for all industries. These three factors are, however, so important that they are included in six of the seven primary ratios that determine a company's competitive strengths and weaknesses. The balance sheet is represented by a larger number of individual items, each a significant element of a company's total financial composition as portrayed by cause-and-effect ratio analysis. A definition and description of each asset and liability that might appear on a company's balance sheet is purposely omitted because this important and detailed matter of classification has been covered in excellent fashion in numerous accounting texts. Moreover, business owners and managers should already know the meaning of such terms as *accounts receivable* and *mortgages payable*. If they do not, they should certainly consult with their own accountants to gain an understanding of each item appearing on their financial statement. Primarily as a review, then, the major categories of financial statement items used in cause-and-effect ratio analysis are outlined in the following paragraphs.

The Balance Sheet

The *balance sheet* represents, in dollars, the resources owned by a company, its *assets*, versus the amount of money it owes to others, its *liabilities*. The difference, which makes the balance sheet balance, is *net worth*, the owners' equity in the company.

Assets

Assets can be divided into four distinct categories: (1) current assets, (2) fixed assets, (3) intangible assets, and (4) miscellaneous assets.

Current assets consist of cash plus those items that the company plans to convert to cash in the course of its normal manufacturing or marketing process. The theory is that current assets can be turned into cash within a relatively short time, certainly within one year (although in a few industries the full cash cycle extends beyond one year). In actual business practice, the two largest items classified as current assets—accounts receivable and inventory—are subject to delays in moving through the cash cycle and may yield actual amounts that are significantly less than the dollar figures shown on the financial statement. Detecting the potential for such problems is one of the primary aims of ratio analysis.

Fixed assets, briefly, are the tangible, physical facilities utilized by the company in performing its avowed business function. These assets ordinarily represent a permanent investment in such items as land, buildings, machinery, autos and trucks, computer equipment, furniture and fixtures, and leasehold improvements. The important distinction between fixed assets and current assets is that fixed assets are not sold in the normal day-to-day operation of the business, although they obviously can be converted to some amount of cash in distress situations. Plant and equipment tend to lose value through age, use, or obsolescence and hence are subject to periodic downward adjustment in value through either depreciation or amortization charges (in some extractive industries, through depletion as well). Many leases that have characteristics similar to outright ownership are capitalized and reported on the balance sheet, although other (operating) leases are not. Fixed assets include only facilities owned directly by the company and do not extend to any investments in subsidiaries or affiliated concerns. Investment in a subsidiary or affiliate constitutes a miscellaneous asset.

Intangible assets are difficult to define in a single phrase because in some cases they represent definite money value, while in most others their cash value can only be estimated. Within this category are found patents, franchises, and licenses, as well as items of even less definable value such as organizational expense and goodwill. As a rule, intangible assets are not available for payment of debts of a going concern. Sometimes, however, they can be converted to cash; for instance, some companies have sold certain of their franchises or patents as a means of extricating themselves from temporary problems. Intangible assets seldom have value if the company itself is liquidated, but this is not universally true. A large independent soft drink bottler, for example, may possess exclusive franchises which retain their market value despite the company's insolvency. The difficulty of assigning an accurate monetary value is, however, the characteristic which distinguishes intangible assets. This characteristic, in turn, suggests that analysts should reduce net worth by the book value of intangible assets when analyzing financial statements. Financial ratios developed for bank credit officers are based on tangible net worth only, but most financial reports prepared for industry trade associations include intangible items in miscellaneous assets and use the net worth amount shown on the balance sheet without adjustment.

Miscellaneous assets are identified through the process of elimination. If the asset is tangible, is not intended for conversion into cash in the normal operation of the business, and is not a part of the physical facilities by means of which the business function is performed, it falls automatically into the miscellaneous category. Included among miscellaneous assets are such items as the cash-surrender value of life insurance (although its liquidity makes a strong argument for classification as a current asset); investments in subsidiaries; money due from officers, directors, and employees; deferred charges; and prepaid expenses.

Liabilities

Turning now to the right-hand side of the balance sheet, we find the sources that support a company's assets: (1) current liabilities, (2) long-term liabilities, and (3) net worth (owners' equity or shareholders' equity).

Current liabilities are those obligations that mature within one year from the closing date of the financial statement; this category includes demand notes, which have no fixed maturity date. Within current liabilities are accounts payable, notes payable to banks and trade suppliers, trade acceptances payable, the portion of long-term loans that must be paid within the next 12 months, tax liabilities or reserves, accrued items (such as rent and wages), customers' deposits and advance payments, dividends declared but unpaid, and reserves for contingencies (which are established as claims to be paid but which may be subject to court appeal or some other deferment or possible nullification).

The sole distinction between current and *long-term liabilities* is the time element. Any obligation due within one year from statement date is current; any claim falling due beyond one year is long-term. Certain company obligations, of course, include both long-term and current elements—for example, scheduled long-term debt, serial notes, mortgages, debentures, and other types of bonds of which specific portions come due within one year and the balance of which mature at clearly defined dates in subsequent years. A company may list among its long-term liabilities "notes payable, officers" for some stated amount, but fail to show the maturity dates of the notes. Investigation may disclose that these notes are payable on demand, and, despite the avowed intention of the note holders not to press their claims "until the company can afford to repay," such notes should be reclassified as current liabilities. If, however, the maturities are clearly indicated, and the due dates extend beyond one year, the notes may properly be treated as long-term indebtedness despite their being payable to the owners. The analyst should acquaint himself with some of the more common forms of long-term debt and should know the nature and extent of the assets that serve as collateral for secured borrowing in specific instances.

Throughout this book, as in most financial management publications, the terms "debt" and "liabilities" are used interchangeably. In the investment community, however, "debt" is often restricted to interest-bearing obligations and, in some cases, this term is meant to apply only to actual debt securities (corporate bonds versus a bank line of credit). When referring to other publications, particularly sources of comparative data, the analyst should make a specific effort to review the precise definition of each term.

The final category on the right-hand side of the balance sheet is *net worth*, the excess of total assets over total debt (current and long-term). In effect, net worth is what the business owners hold as their equitable share after the claims of creditors have been subtracted from the book value of total assets. A proprietorship or partnership statement normally shows the difference between assets and liabilities as simply "net worth" (in some cases, "capital accounts"), while the corporate statement is generally more complicated and may subdivide net worth ("shareholders' equity") among any or all of the following: preferred stock, common stock, capital surplus, and earned surplus.

One additional balance sheet term with which the analyst should be familiar is *working capital*. The amount of this item is found very simply by deducting current liabilities from current assets. The significance of working capital will be explored in later pages as the actual use of ratios is explained.

The Income Statement

The *income,* or *profit-and-loss, statement* (now often called the *operating statement*) has received less attention from financial analysts than has the balance sheet, for several reasons. Outside analysts, particularly credit grantors, are ordinarily more interested in the company's fundamental financial position, as revealed by the 16 key ratios, than in detailed company operations. In addition, expense categories necessarily differ from industry to industry. Manufacturing encompasses process industries and producers of standard components or complete consumer items, as well as custom producers and contract manufacturers ("job shops"), each sector having its own terminology and emphasis. The income statements of wholesalers, distributors, retailers, and service firms also differ widely with respect to specific details.

Income statement items are, by their nature, far less standardized than those on the balance sheet. The level of detail required for meaningful interpretation of balance sheet items is well established, but business owners and managers often disagree about the usefulness of separating expense categories—such as inside sales commissions, outside sales commissions, sales service compensation, sales administration, marketing administration, advertising, promotion, telemarketing, travel, and entertainment—into even greater detail in the chart of accounts and on the income statement. Some companies combine these costs into three or four major items. Company size is one factor in that decision, but some comparatively large organizations find that highly detailed income statement data are not particularly useful to top management.

Development of Industry Standards

Whatever the merits of these arguments from one line of business to the next, the fact that owners and managers disagree about the level of detail on the income statement has been an impediment to the development of industry standards in this area. Nevertheless, ongoing effort is required because management can gain great benefit from clearly defined, accurate, meaningful facts about performance in the company's specific line of business. Analysis of the income statement, the study of each individual expense item in relation to industry benchmarks, will demonstrate why one company attained an outstanding profit percentage while a competing company recorded a loss. Companies in virtually every line of business now have, through their respective trade associations, the opportunity to obtain the guidance of industrywide cost figures. Of course, each industry group necessarily develops its own presentation of expense items, some more detailed than others, according to the particular characteristics and needs of that line of business activity.

Only through standardized reporting of financial statement items can the key financial ratios and detailed expense percentages be sufficiently comparable to serve as meaningful analytical tools. Many trade associations have taken the lead in setting forth for their members uniform standards governing the classification of assets, liabilities, and expense entries. Companies need not, of course, keep their books in complete agreement with the industry method; but in reporting annual figures to the association for the compilation of industry norms, each company must make any necessary reclassifications to conform with common practice. In other words, like items must be related to like items if industry ratios and operating percentages are to provide reliable standards for evaluating the company's position in relation to its competitors. This important aspect of cause-and-effect ratio analysis is examined in greater detail later in this book.

Part II

The Seven Causal Ratios

In the following pages, each of the sixteen key financial ratios is considered in detail. Part II is devoted to a study of the seven primary, or causal, ratios, those relationships that determine a company's entire financial structure. The nine secondary ratios, those that yield important information about the company's fundamental financial condition and its competitive position but do not indicate causes of comparative strength or weakness, are presented in Part III.

To achieve a true working knowledge of the cause-and-effect ratio method, you must not only read about ratios but also apply them to business problems. Hypothetical cases, composites of actual company situations, have been used in the text to help you gain familiarity with cause-and-effect ratio analysis. The comparative ratios—termed the *industry standards* in these examples—are a blend of actual values drawn from several lines of business familiar to the authors. In presentations of composite ratios for a group of companies in a specific line of business activity, the median (the middle value in a set of ratios arrayed from lowest to highest) is ordinarily used to represent the typical response. That convention is followed throughout this book. As described in detail in Appendix C, the extreme values that often occur in the calculation of certain key ratios exert much less influence on the group median than they would in determining the average of the same data.

In Part II, we examine the seven primary, or causal, ratios:

1. *Net Profit to Net Sales*
2. *Net Sales to Total Assets*
3. *Collection Period of Accounts Receivable*
4. *Cost of Sales to Inventory*
5. *Net Sales to Fixed Assets*
6. *Net Sales to Net Worth*
7. *Long-Term Liabilities to Total Noncurrent Assets*

The method of computation and the significance of each of these primary ratios, as well as their interaction, is explained and illustrated.

As emphasized throughout this book, the ratios derived from any company's financial statement must be related to past performance, as well as to averages or norms for the industry in which that concern is engaged. Only in this way can deviations—either good or bad—be detected. In later discussions of individual ratios, specific sources of comparative statistical data will be cited.

Ratio Summaries

For the ratio summaries that appear at the ends of the following chapters, we use the terms *favorable* and *unfavorable* in a conservative context. Of the two extremes, the favorable side is characterized by high profit, low debt, and high liquidity. Actually, for relatively small companies, the most favorable financial structure may be near the middle of the competitive pack. The underlying assumption is that most firms gain their greatest advantage from concentrating on their special talents—toolmaking, designing and manufacturing furniture, distributing electrical equipment, wholesaling produce, selling men's clothing, exterminating pests, marketing and installing cable television—or whatever their business purpose may be. From this perspective, financial management, clearly a critical element in business success, is seen as a means of keeping a company out of trouble and enabling management to sleep better at night. For credit grantors, financial analysis is viewed as the most effective means of avoiding problems—and, of course, sleeping better too.

Unless a company's decision makers are familiar (and comfortable) with techniques of financial management and specific means of achieving a comparative advantage, maintaining the business's financial structure in line with that of typical competitors is generally a good idea. Particularly with respect to working capital sufficiency and financial leverage, experimentation with a novel financial approach can be dangerous. By following common industry practice in most financial matters, management can concentrate on achieving excellence in the business's basic operations: attaining a high level of profit and outstanding officers'/owners' compensation through superior performance in the company's specific areas of expertise. Only one ratio, *Net Profit to Net Sales*, is regarded as having a consistently favorable direction: the higher the better. But even this ratio must be viewed with some caution. High *Net Profit to Net Sales* may be the result of a disinvestment strategy that cannot be sustained—a strategy of short-term cost minimization that will penalize the company's competitive position in the future.

As a practical matter, financial management involves balancing risk and reward. If management has reason to consider a comparatively high-debt, low-liquidity, or low-profit strategy for well-defined operational or strategic purposes, ratio analysis will be helpful in evaluating both the potential risk and the likely reward. On the other hand, this book does not advocate taking unusual financial risks as a means of increasing monetary return. Caution is especially advised in the areas of debt and working capital. Focusing attention on the manipulation of financial leverage to boost the rate of return on owners' equity is the preserve of investment professionals and outright gamblers.

Beyond recommending a middle-of-the-road approach, this book is conservative at a second level. When a company's financial structure is significantly different from that of its typical competitor (as reflected in industry ratios for companies of similar size in similar business activities), a low-debt, high-liquidity strategy is assumed to be preferable to a high-debt, low-liquidity strategy. Business owners and managers seeking to maximize profits through an aggressive financial approach are advised to obtain guidance from a professional in the field and concentrate their own energies on providing a better product or service.

Whenever available, the range of common experience is displayed in the summary for each ratio to alert the analyst to the values most frequently encountered by bank credit officers and other financial professionals. Although all serious financial practitioners recognize that the specific figures for any company must be compared with typical values in that company's particular line of business activity, there is a natural tendency to develop a sense of "normal" or expected values based on cumulative experience. Such predispositions or expectations can, as a practical matter, cause experienced lenders to react with vague suspicion to values that are unusual even though they may be directly in line with common practice for the specific industry in which the company operates. For that reason, the analyst should make an effort to identify any such uncommon values—and be prepared to discuss the reasons why the company's ratios (and, if applicable, the industry's ratios) lie outside the range of common experience—before entering into loan negotiations or other important transactions with financial professionals who have occasion to review these measures on a regular basis.

Some ratios, such as *Long-Term Liabilities to Total Noncurrent Assets*, have a narrow range of common experience because of the nature of the relationship they represent. Borrowing only a small proportion of the purchase price of fixed assets and other noncurrent assets is not ordinarily a wise practice; on the other hand, few lenders are willing to advance funds in excess of 80% or 90% of book value. Consequently, this ratio is generally found in the 0.5 to 0.7 range. The values for *Net Sales to Fixed Assets*, on the other hand, vary widely from industry to industry. Obviously, the amount of sales volume that can be generated per dollar of fixed assets by a petroleum refinery is likely to be different from that among appliance repair shops, wholesale florists, cable companies, restaurants, or tire manufacturers. The range of common experience for *Net Sales to Fixed Assets* is 6.8 to 22.4, but industry norms may be as low as 1.0 (for recreation clubs and refrigerated warehouses) or as high as 100.0 (for cotton wholesalers). The median—the middle value—of all manufacturing industries is approximately 9.0, while wholesaling industries report a median of near 30.0 and retailing lines have a median somewhat above 20.0. Interestingly, the values for *Net Sales to Fixed Assets* in service industries center near 5.0, noticeably lower than the other classifications, because this business category contains more capital-intensive lines of activity (such as motels, bowling centers, car washes, amusement parks, and outdoor advertising firms) than those with relatively little need for extensive fixed assets (such as temporary help agencies, building maintenance establishments, computer programming companies, and accounting firms).

A relatively high or low ratio for a particular industry is not necessarily favorable or unfavorable; it simply reflects industry conditions. Machine tool distributors, for instance, are typically able to operate with *Current Assets to Current Liabilities* between 1.2 and 1.3 because their assets are extremely liquid, consisting largely of accounts receivable and cash. In that line of business, a 1.4 *Current Assets to Current Liabilities* ratio is comparatively strong. Some industries are characterized by significant year-to-year changes in the key financial ratios, with almost all companies reporting very poor performance at certain points in the national economic cycle. In the worst case, a continuing deterioration of the ratios may indicate that most members of that industry are no longer competitive in the international economy. The analyst must be alert to industry trends, as well as to changes in an individual company's performance; but if he has basic confidence in the survival of the industry itself, he can ordinarily accept the norms for that line of business as reasonable representations of adequate operating results and financial structure for member companies. A 60-day median *Collection Period of Accounts Receivable* in an industry characterized by net 30-day terms clearly indicates that the firms in that line are experiencing difficulty in convincing customers to pay their bills when due—or, more likely, that most companies are actually offering some special terms or conditions. Although this case definitely warrants investigation, a company operating in that industry must, nonetheless, consider those competitive conditions when evaluating its credit policy and collection performance. If company management has reason to believe that the 60-day industry norm accurately reflects the current experience of other concerns—taking into account the influence of their customers, suppliers, and bankers—then expecting payment of most invoices within 30 to 40 days may be unrealistic. If customers' purchases are determined to any significant extent by credit terms, the industry norm (however deficient it may appear to an outside analyst) must be carefully regarded by the company's decision makers. Lax asset management or timid credit-and-collection policies should not be encouraged through slavish adherence to mediocre practices; otherwise, unwise decisions made by the majority, and reflected in the industry norms, will become self-fulfilling prophecies. On the other hand, typical performance should not be ignored in formulating company strategy.

Chapter 3

Net Profit to Net Sales

Every company has as its goal the realization of profit from each dollar of sales. *Net Profit to Net Sales* measures the success any given company has achieved in meeting this objective.

Net Profit to Net Sales (also known as the *Return on Sales Ratio*) is computed very simply by dividing net profit by net sales for the same fiscal period and then multiplying the result by 100 (or pressing the % key on a calculator) to express this measure as a percentage. By achieving a profit of $150,000 on sales of $5 million, Company B shows a *Net Profit to Net Sales* ratio of 3.0%, as displayed in Table 3-1, later in the chapter.

Profit may be expressed in many ways: after income taxes (the ultimate "bottom line"), before income taxes (to afford direct comparison of firms within the same industry by eliminating the impact of current tax liabilities, which may be influenced by special credits and carry-forwards from previous years), before nonoperating and nonrecurring items (to focus on return from operations), before interest (to eliminate the influence of investment adequacy and debt structure), and before owners' compensation (recognizing that the amount of salaries and bonuses paid to owners, while often somewhat arbitrary, is a major determinant of a company's reported profit). In the remaining pages, *Net Profit to Net Sales* will be considered on a pre-tax basis, which conforms with most industry studies and enables the most effective company-to-company comparison.

Unless a company profits—at least marginally—from selling its goods or services, it has little reason to exist. For every dollar of sales, the successful company finds a number of pennies in profit flowing back into its coffers. The more pennies per dollar, the greater the opportunity for growth, and through growth those pennies may accumulate to become quarters or dollars. A company losing pennies per sales dollar must reverse that trend, or it will obviously meet with extinction at some date in the future.

Profit retained in the business bolsters working capital, adds to net worth, and aids in restoring balance to any ratios that may be deficient. Conversely, losses on sales aggravate any financial imbalance, for they strike directly at both working capital and net worth and automatically distort any ratios that relate to those two vital areas, as shown in the following chapters.

Reported profit, particularly in the short run, does not necessarily reflect a company's productivity or management's proficiency in creating shareholder value. A successful business strategy may make provision for reduced profit—or even a temporary loss—in order to achieve a clearly defined long-term objective. Nevertheless, a reasonable *Net Profit to Net Sales* is necessary over any extended period in order to satisfy the desire of owners to obtain a financial reward for their investment of funds. In addition, every growing company must bolster owners' equity through retained earnings to maintain a sound financial structure, including a satisfactory balance between debt and net worth. Adequate *Net Profit to Net Sales* is also important in providing a margin of protection against price-cutting tactics by competitors.

Comparison of Four Companies

To become more familiar with the comparative aspect of ratio analysis, let us briefly observe the performance of Companies A, B, C, and D with respect to *Net Profit to Net Sales*, as presented in Table 3-1. Company A's *Net Profit to Net Sales* ratio is definitely favorable and can be used to strengthen every element of the concern's financial structure—provided that a major portion is retained in the business. Management must be alert, however, to the possibility of making greater market penetration and generating a higher return on owners' equity through the expansion of sales at a somewhat lower margin. If the company's financial structure is sufficient to support increased business activity at the same net worth without incurring a burdensome level of debt, sales of $2 million at a 4.5% return will produce more total revenue than sales of $1,500,000 at 5.0%. It is possible, of course, that some new product, process, or marketing concept has temporarily given Company A a superior profit position that can be fully exploited now at a 5.0% or even higher return but is likely to be dissipated as others in the industry introduce competitive products or ideas. A few companies, however, manage to maintain a consistent advantage in profitability as a result of innovation, modernization, training, process control, and well-informed cost containment.

For the present, at least, Company A is benefiting from each dollar of sales to a greater extent than the industry in general and is to be commended. The

Table 3-1.   *Net Profit to Net Sales* **for four companies.**

	Company A	Company B	Company C	Company D
Net profit	$ 76,000	$ 150,000	$ 150,000	$ 950,000
Net sales	1,500,000	5,000,000	12,500,000	50,000,000
Net Profit to Net Sales				
Company	5.1%	3.0%	1.2%	1.9%
Industry standard	3.2%	3.2%	3.2%	3.2%

initiative shown in gaining the company's current position indicates sound management, and such leadership may very well guide Company A to even further future advantages over its less imaginative competitors. The analyst should never be alarmed by profitability—unless, of course, such profit is fraudulently or ignorantly created by inflating sales, concealing potential asset write-offs in accounts receivable, inventory, or fixed assets, or failing to provide for contingent liabilities related to pending product claims or known environmental hazards. These observations also assume that owners' compensation has not been artificially reduced to generate a higher net profit, although the company's financial structure will benefit from retained earnings, regardless of their basis.

Company B is near the industry norm with respect to *Net Profit to Net Sales*. To the extent that it retains an average portion of profit in the business, Company B's other financial ratios will benefit no more and no less than those of its typical competitor.

Company C earned a small profit on each dollar of sales, and even this minimal amount will aid in attaining its overall objectives. By failing to keep pace with the average business in its line, Company C is losing some ground within the industry, but its internal financial balance will not be adversely affected. Suppose, however, that sales volume for companies within the industry is typically rising at a faster rate than Company C can increase net worth through retained earnings. If Company C attempts to keep pace with the competition, a problem will arise. In that case, as we see in Parts III and IV, several of Company C's key financial ratios will be penalized by the comparatively low *Net Profit to Net Sales* ratio. In any event, Company C's management should be far from satisfied with its present profitability and should study the concern's entire cost pattern to determine why the company is unable to match the attainment of the typical concern with which it competes.

Company D's *Net Profit to Net Sales* is also somewhat weak, but it provides some opportunity for sales expansion while holding total liabilities within a manageable level—by increasing net worth through retained earnings. We will see, in a step-by-step study in Parts III and IV, how *Net Profit to Net Sales* affects every one of the secondary ratios. At that time the relationship between sales, profit, net worth, and debt will become clear.

Factors Affecting Net Profit to Net Sales

The *Net Profit to Net Sales* ratio is affected by several factors: pricing (whether based on accurate cost information, market pressure, or guesswork), sales volume (a reflection of customer demand, as influenced by workmanship and service, merchandising or estimating policies and price levels, as well as intangibles, such as location and reputation), and cost control. The analyst's ability to detect the basis for a company's net profit advantage or disadvantage will depend on available sources of information. For an officer or an employee assigned the task of evaluating the company's operating performance and financial structure, detailed year-to-year comparisons of all major cost items should be entirely possible. If that information is now considered the domain of the company's accountant, management should take prompt action to see that responsibility for detailed cost analysis is assigned to a key employee or assumed by the owner. Converting each expense and profit item to a percentage of net sales for each year will reveal exactly how the company's cost pattern has changed—for better or for worse—over time.

For comparisons with other companies in the industry, however, the analyst is limited to published data. Most multi-industry reports, such as those described in detail in Part VII, provide percentages for cost of sales, selling and administrative expenses, all other income/expense (net), and net profit, as well as officers' compensation and depreciation. Several national trade associations provide far more detailed expense breakdowns in their operating ratio reports. They typically display such cost items as direct labor, indirect labor, employee benefits, utilities, sales compensation, advertising, and bad debts as percentages of net sales. These reports frequently contain additional background information that enables a creative evaluator to develop special-purpose operating ratios, such as: indirect labor to direct labor; sales and profit per square foot of production area or selling space; sales per employee; annual costs related to physical facilities (plant and equipment) per employee; and net profit per employee. Some industry reports are sufficiently detailed to permit reasonable estimates of fixed costs versus variable costs, important classifications in break-even analysis. Because the level of available operating detail varies so widely from one industry to another, general-purpose suggestions are difficult to provide. This issue is, however, more thoroughly explored in Part VII and Appendix B1.

Summary: Net Profit to Net Sales

Popular names	*Return on Sales Ratio; Net Profit Margin; Profit Percentage; The Bottom Line*
Purpose	Measures a company's ability to generate profit on its average sales dollar.
Calculation	Divide net profit by net sales, then multiply result by 100, converting ratio to a percentage.
Example	Your company's net profit was $32,000 and your net sales were $1 million during your last fiscal year. What was your return on sales?
	Solution: $32,000 \div 1,000,000 = .032$; then $.032 \times 100 = 3.2\%$
Financial impact	A *high* percentage exerts a *favorable* influence: It in-

creases return on equity and tends to decrease financial leverage.

Operational impact A *high* ratio tends to reduce interest cost (provided that earnings are retained to reduce debt) and promote greater operating freedom; however, a high ratio may indicate a disinvestment or "harvesting" strategy that cannot be sustained.

Definition Net profit *before taxes* is ordinarily used by bankers and other credit grantors as the basis for measuring comparative profitability (versus previous performance or external standards). Net profit *after taxes* is the true "bottom line," but the effect of state and local income taxes, as well as federal income tax credits and carrybacks, can distort comparative performance. Net profit *from operations* (before nonoperating income, nonoperating expense, and extraordinary items) and net profit *before officers'/owners' compensation* are also useful measures.

Special reminder *Net Profit to Net Sales* is expressed as a percentage, not as a simple ratio.

Critical value A *negative* percentage, which shows a net loss for the period, causes a negative return on equity and tends to increase interest cost and financial leverage.

Range of common experience 2.3% to 4.4% (before income taxes).

Chapter 4

Net Sales to Total Assets

Net Sales to Total Assets measures a company's ability to generate sales volume on the financial and physical resources it employs. This ratio is a primary, or causal, factor at the most fundamental level of financial structure. If this ratio is substantially out of line with common industry practice, all major elements of the income statement and the balance sheet will be affected. This measure is unique among the causal ratios because it performs two functions: It summarizes other causal ratios and it has an important effect in its own right.

Computed by dividing a company's net sales by its total assets (including fixed assets at book or depreciated value), *Net Sales to Total Assets* is expressed in "times." Company B, reporting annual net sales of $5 million and total assets of $2 million at year-end, has a ratio of 2.5, as shown in Table 4-1, later in the chapter.

Net Sales to Total Assets (also known as the *Asset Utilization Ratio*) summarizes the combined sales-generating efficiency of the assets acquired by management. Accounts receivable (measured by the *Collection Period of Accounts Receivable*), inventory (measured by *Cost of Sales to Inventory*), and facilities and equipment (measured by *Net Sales to Fixed Assets*)—plus cash and short-term investments, other current assets, and other noncurrent (miscellaneous) assets—all affect a company's *Net Sales to Total Assets*.

A company that maintains relatively high *Net Sales to Total Assets* is able to conduct business with comparatively little invested capital (net worth), while incurring debt no greater than that of its typical competitors. The rate of return on owners' equity in the company is also strongly influenced by *Net Sales to Total Assets*. By achieving only ordinary *Net Profit to Net Sales*, a company with a high *Net Sales to Total Assets* ratio is able to attain a relatively high-percentage return on owners' equity. And through superior *Net Profit to Net Sales*, such a company is able to produce a very high rate of return on the owners' investment—while still holding debt to a moderate level.

Net Sales to Total Assets can be increased by improving the component ratios: reducing the *Collection Period of Accounts Receivable*, increasing *Cost of Sales to Inventory*, or increasing *Net Sales to Fixed Assets*. Reducing the level of cash and short-term investments, other current assets, and miscellaneous assets will also contribute to an increase in the *Net Sales to Total Assets* ratio.

Although low *Net Sales to Total Assets* tends to have an unfavorable impact on the balance sheet from a conservative viewpoint, some companies successfully pursue a strategy involving unusually high commitment to assets in relation to sales. They aim to achieve superior *Net Profit to Net Sales* in order to compensate for the greater investment by owners that is required to support the high level of assets.

Turning to Table 4-1, we see that Company A has made a comparatively small financial commitment to total assets in relation to net sales. Company A's relatively high *Net Sales to Total Assets* may be a sign of efficient asset management, or it may suggest the need for greater investment to remain competitive. Reference to the other asset ratios will be needed to make that judgment. In any case, the immediate impact of Company A's *Net Sales to Total Assets* is favorable from a conservative point of view.

Company B's balance between net sales and total assets is essentially in line with the industry standard. Nevertheless, this moderate *Net Sales to Total Assets* may conceal offsetting factors, such as a short *Collection Period of Accounts Receivable* compensating for a low *Cost of Sales to Inventory*. As a summary factor, however, Company B's *Net Sales to Total Assets* has a moderating effect on the company's basic financial structure.

Company C, on the other hand, reports relatively low *Net Sales to Total Assets*. At first impression, the difference between the company's 1.9 ratio and the 2.4 industry standard may not appear to be highly significant. In reality, it translates into an additional $1,440,000 in total assets that must be supported by debt or by increased owners' equity. Instead of $6,650,000 in total assets, Company C would have only $5,210,000 of combined liabilities and equity tied up in accounts receivable, inventory, fixed assets, and other asset items. (Dividing Company C's $12,500,000 in net sales by the 2.4 median *Net Sales to Total Assets* for the comparison group yields total assets of approximately $5,210,000, the amount that the company would have reported if asset utilization had been equal to the industry norm.) Unless Company C's additional assets are known to be producing greater profit or meeting a clearly defined competitive aim, the analyst must conclude that the concern's asset management needs improvement.

The very high *Net Sales to Total Assets* ratio shown by Company D is a

Table 4-1.   *Net Sales to Total Assets* for four companies.

	Company A	Company B	Company C	Company D
Net sales	$1,500,000	$5,000,000	$12,500,000	$50,000,000
Total assets	536,000	2,000,000	6,650,000	11,400,000
Net Sales to Total Assets				
Company	2.8 times	2.5 times	1.9 times	4.4 times
Industry standard	2.4 times	2.4 times	2.4 times	2.4 times

strong indication that the company is working with almost fully depreciated fixed assets or is leasing a substantial portion of its facilities. In fact, such a high ratio in comparison with industry practice suggests unusually low levels of accounts receivable and inventory, as well. Extraordinarily high *Net Sales to Total Assets* is often a sign that the company is attempting to compensate for inadequate owners' equity (very low net worth) by severely restricting assets in order to hold down debt.

The influence of *Net Sales to Total Assets* on the secondary ratios will be seen throughout Part III.

Summary: Net Sales to Total Assets

Popular names	*Asset Utilization Ratio; Asset Management Ratio*
Purpose	Measures a company's ability to generate sales volume on the assets it employs or, from another perspective, its ability to control assets in relation to sales. Summarizes the combined influence of the individual asset utilization ratios—particularly *Collection Period of Accounts Receivable, Cost of Sales to Inventory,* and *Net Sales to Fixed Assets*.
Calculation	Divide net sales by total assets.
Example	Your company's net sales during your last fiscal year were $1 million, and your total assets at year-end were $400,000. What was your *Net Sales to Total Assets*?
	Solution: 1,000,000 ÷ 400,000 = 2.5
Financial impact	A *high* ratio exerts a *favorable* influence: It reduces financial leverage and/or increases return on equity.
Operational impact	A *high* ratio tends to reduce interest cost.
Range of common experience	1.9 times to 2.8 times.

Chapter 5

Collection Period of Accounts Receivable

A company's credit terms and standards, its collection program, and the competence of its credit manager together exert direct influence on three critical financial factors: sales attainment, profit, and need for borrowing.

The *Collection Period of Accounts Receivable*, which is a tool to aid in the analysis of a company's trade receivables, is computed according to several different formulas, depending on the specific circumstances. For purposes of comparing a company with other concerns in its industry, this ratio is better defined as "days of net sales in accounts receivable." Most industry studies compute the *Collection Period of Accounts Receivable* by a shortcut method:

1. Multiply accounts receivable at year-end by 365.
2. Divide the result by net sales for the year.
3. Express the ratio as a whole number (days).

This formula does not take into account sales (possibly the majority of sales) that may have been conducted on a cash basis—and also offers little understanding of the important relationships represented by this ratio. As shown in Table 5-2 (later in this chapter), Company B has accounts receivable of $625,000 and net sales of $5 million. By the shortcut method, the analyst would first multiply 625,000 by 365 to obtain 228,125,000 and then divide that amount by 5 million to yield a *Collection Period of Accounts Receivable* of 46 days (rounded up from the calculated figure of 45.625).

To gain a better understanding of this key financial ratio, an alternative formula may be helpful:

1. Divide net sales for the year by 365 to obtain average daily net sales.
2. Divide accounts receivable at year-end by that result.
3. Express the ratio as a whole number (days).

In effect, however, this approach also treats all sales for the period as if they were conducted on a credit basis. By this method, Company B would show average daily net sales of $13,700. When the dollar amount of accounts receivable—

29

$625,000—is divided by $13,700, the resulting *Collection Period of Accounts Receivable* is also 46 days (45.625 rounded to a whole number).

Since information about cash sales versus credit sales is not generally available in industry financial statistics, calculation of the days of net sales in accounts receivable—instead of a true *Collection Period of Accounts Receivable*—must suffice for comparative purposes. Nevertheless, the analysis of a specific company's trends in credit management is best accomplished by computing the *Collection Period of Accounts Receivable* in the following manner:

1. Determine total *credit* sales for the company. If all business is transacted on credit terms, then the net sales figure for the year as taken from the company's operating (profit-and-loss) statement will be identical with the total credit-sales figure. If, however, any significant portion of sales are conducted on a cash basis, these sales must be subtracted, because they do not involve any credit risk, and their inclusion would thus be misleading in determining the true condition of the company's receivables. Suppose, for example, that total sales for the year were $1 million, of which 20% represented cash sales. The company's annual credit sales then would be only $800,000.

2. Calculate credit sales per day by dividing the dollar amount of credit sales for the year by 365. If annual net sales are $1 million, all on credit, then credit sales per day amount to $2,740. Or, if 20% of these sales were for cash, credit sales per day would be $2,192 ($800,000 divided by 365).

3. Add together all trade receivables—accounts receivable, notes receivable, trade acceptances receivable—arising from regular merchandise transactions. Assume that these amount to $103,500.

4. Divide the total receivables ($103,500) by the credit sales per day (either $2,740 or $2,192). The resulting figure is the *Collection Period* reckoned in days. If sales are on a straight credit basis, the company has roughly 38 days outstanding. If 20% of sales are for cash, the *Collection Period* is approximately 47 days.

A Measure of Internal Credit-and-Collection Efficiency

The *Collection Period of Accounts Receivable* is designed to accomplish several specific objectives. First, it measures the internal credit-and-collection efficiency of the company. Second, it determines the probability that bad-debt write-offs may be lurking among the concern's receivables. Finally, it measures the company's receivables position relative to the accomplishments of its own industry, provided that you remember to take into consideration the extent to which the company's selling terms differ from those which characterize its competitors.

We shall initially consider *Collection Period of Accounts Receivable* from the standpoint of internal credit-and-collection efficiency. Assume that Company C's terms of sale are stated as "1–10–30" (indicating that a 1% discount may be taken for remittance within 10 days and that, otherwise, payment of the full amount is expected within 30 days) and that the *Collection Period of Accounts Receivable* is found to be 61 days. Is this good or bad? How good or how bad? By any standard, a 61-day *Collection Period of Accounts Receivable* is definitely on the high side, within the highest quarter of all companies in most manufacturing lines. The company has two months' sales on its books; this undoubtedly hampers bill-paying ability and may forecast credit losses that will, some time in the future, adversely affect the company's profit picture. You would be wise to study an aging schedule of Company C's receivables to see for yourself just how seriously overdue some of the balances might be.

Suppose that in this instance the statement date is December 31 and that the aging schedule shows the exposures, by month of billing, indicated in Table 5-1. Viewing the foregoing results, you would have every reason to be alarmed. Company C appears to be building up a heavy percentage of deadwood on its books. These slow-paying items represent an abnormally high potential bad-debt loss. Such charge-offs are, of course, business expenses, which must be deducted from the company's profit. Even if the company is able eventually to collect most of these receivables, it will probably have to resort to drastic action to do so. Such an effort may necessitate expenditures for attorney fees, litigation costs, and collection-agency charges, all of which would have to be absorbed before any profit could be realized.

Referring again to the 61-day *Collection Period of Accounts Receivable* but assuming for the moment that no aging schedule has been compiled, consider one factor that might justify such an extremely high figure—the seasonal element. If the bulk of annual sales are concentrated in November and December, because of the nature of Company C's product and its regular selling pattern, then 61 days is a far from calamitous *Collection Period of Accounts Receivable*. But you should bear in mind that any such significant deviation must be thoroughly studied.

Now let us consider that Company D has a *Collection Period of Accounts Receivable* of 21 days on 1–10–30 terms. This record is not necessarily favorable. On the contrary, such a performance in all likelihood reflects an uncommonly severe and restrictive credit-and-collection approach on the part of Company D. In its fear of bad-debt losses, the company has evidently limited its salespeople

Table 5-1. Aging schedule of accounts receivable for Company C.

December 31, 1989		
December	$1,054,000	50.4%
November	466,000	22.3
October	188,000	9.0
September	94,000	4.5
Prior	288,000	13.8
	$2,090,000	100.0%

to soliciting orders from prime credit risks only. Management may even insist upon discounting performance from its customers. Such a negative sales outlook is anything but profit-minded, for not only is volume lost, but so is the higher profit attainment that is possible from undiscounted sales to small firms and perhaps even marginal credit risks. The presence of a seasonal factor, accounting for an ebb in receivables at Company D's closing date, would, of course, tend to mitigate this harsh judgment. So, too, would the discovery, through more complete analysis, that Company D has resorted to stringent control of accounts receivable to compensate for a severely undercapitalized condition, one that requires extremely high asset utilization to keep debt from totally breaking the company's financial structure.

The Company in Relation to Its Industry

In addition to measuring a company's credit-and-collection performance against its own selling terms, you must compare the concern's attainment with that of its industry. If we find, for example, that a company has a 32-day collection period on 1–10–30 terms, then its receivables appear to be quite efficiently administered. Naturally, some customers will discount, most others will pay according to terms, and a smaller percentage will be slow payers. A 32-day collection period, then, seems to be a good overall accomplishment for the company—an accomplishment reflecting the influence of each of the three broad types of accounts to which it sells. If, however, the industry average should prove to be 48 days in contrast to the company's 32 days, you must investigate the possibility that the industry sells on substantially longer terms than does the company under study. Do competitors extend perhaps 60-day net terms, with discount privilege for 30-day payment? Or could they be granting "1% 10th prox, net 30th prox" terms (allowing a 1% discount until the 10th day of the next month and otherwise expecting payment by the end of the next month)? Or on the other hand, is the company simply more efficient than the industry in general with respect to credit management? Once these points are resolved, you must probe further and determine the answers to the following questions.

1. Has the company lost valuable accounts and sales volume as a result of its restrictive credit policy?
2. Can the company afford the increased receivables exposure that would result from terms liberalization to match those offered by other companies in the same line? Would this limit the company's ability to pay its own bills or add a financing burden to support receivables?
3. Is a change desirable or necessary, or is the company doing well on its present basis? While there may be "general" terms for an industry, successful operation of an individual business does not require strict adherence to such "general" policy.

The *Collection Period of Accounts Receivable* thus provides you with two significant measurements of receivables. You can initially test a company's *Collection Period of Accounts Receivable* against its own selling terms to determine the collectibility of receivables and to measure credit-and-collection efficiency. Then you can gauge the company's ratio against the industry standard to ascertain the concern's competitive strengths and weaknesses relative to competing credit terms and overall financial accomplishment.

A noticeable increase in a company's *Collection Period of Accounts Receivable* from one year to the next (or from one quarter to the next) may indicate a concerted attempt to stimulate sales—and reduce inventory—by extending more liberal credit terms, offering sales incentives (such as discounts or rebates), or otherwise exerting unusual sales pressure shortly before the end of the accounting period. Such an occurrence should cause management (and outside investors) to examine carefully the company's prospects for sales and profit in the immediate future—after the effects of such promotional efforts have subsided.

Comparison of a Key Ratio Among Competitors

To see the benefit of comparing one company's value for a key financial ratio with the results achieved by competitors, let us examine Companies A, B, C, and D, all in the same industry and all selling on 1–10–30 terms. The *Collection Period of Accounts Receivable* for each of these four companies is shown in Table 5-2. Without knowing additional facts about the other three organizations, you might logically conclude that Company D has a far too rigid and unimaginative approach to credit sales. One can assume that profitable sales are being lost. The company's negativism may be holding overall sales volume well below the company's potential, possibly to levels inadequate to cover expenses. Company D is apparently in no jeopardy from bad-debt losses, but its management may very well be in danger of losing the entire business through such extreme credit wariness. At the same time, it is possible that a very short *Collection Period of Accounts*

Table 5-2. *Collection Period of Accounts Receivable* for four companies.

	Company A	Company B	Company C	Company D
Net sales	$1,500,000	$5,000,000	$12,500,000	$50,000,000
Accounts receivable	152,000	625,000	2,090,000	2,850,000
Collection Period of Accounts Receivable				
Company	37 days	46 days	61 days	21 days
Industry standard	44 days	44 days	44 days	44 days

Receivable reflects a desperate effort to collect receivables as rapidly as possible because of a cash shortage due to undercapitalization, inventory build-up, or a major investment in fixed assets.

By contrast, the performance of Company A—other factors being equal—indicates that management is neither too cautious nor too blindly trusting. Its *Collection Period of Accounts Receivable* is less than that of the typical company in its comparison group, but it is generally in line with stated terms. Company B's *Collection Period of Accounts Receivable* is only slightly higher than the industry norm, but management should evaluate the reasons that the average customer pays more than 15 days beyond the net period. Perhaps such liberality is required by competitive conditions, but management may find that the *Collection Period* is being needlessly lengthened by slowness in sending invoices as a result of incomplete paperwork or office inefficiencies, errors in billing, partial or incorrect shipments, inadequate follow-up, or delays in depositing receipts.

As we noted before, Company C may have significant collection trouble facing it, and you can assume—without knowledge of any other segment of the financial statement—that its cash flow will be tight, its debt heavy and pressing, and its potential collection fees and bad-debt losses abnormally high. If Company C should become a failure statistic, the epitaph on its financial gravestone might appropriately read, "Underlying cause of failure: receivables difficulties."

Summary: Collection Period of Accounts Receivable

Popular names	*Collection Period*; *Days' Sales in Receivables*
Purpose	Measures a company's control of accounts receivable in relation to net sales volume; indicates the average number of days required to convert accounts receivable to cash.
Calculation	Multiply accounts receivable by 365, then divide result by net sales; express ratio as whole number.
Example	Your company's accounts receivable were $125,000 at year-end, and net sales for your last fiscal year were $1 million. What was your *Collection Period of Accounts Receivable*?
	Solution 1 (for the calculator): $125,000 \times 365 = 45,625,000$; then $45,625,000 \div 1,000,000 = 46$ days
	Solution 2 (for greater understanding): average daily net sales $= 1,000,000 \div 365 = 2,740$; then $125,000 \div 2,740 = 46$ days of net sales outstanding as accounts receivable
Financial impact	A *low* ratio exerts a *favorable* influence: It increases

	asset utilization, reduces financial leverage, and/or increases return on equity.

Operational impact   A *low* ratio tends to reduce record keeping and verification costs and also lowers the probability of loss due to bad debts (customer insolvency or unwillingness to pay); on the other hand, a *low* ratio may also indicate an unduly restrictive credit-and-collection policy that is reducing potentially profitable sales to otherwise creditworthy customers.

Range of common experience   24 days to 48 days.

Chapter 6

Cost of Sales to Inventory

Cost of Sales to Inventory (the *Inventory Turnover Ratio*) serves as an indicator of the purchasing, production, and/or merchandising efficiency of a company. Generally speaking, the faster the movement of inventory, the better the company is performing with respect to scheduled and balanced buying and inventory control. A low *Cost of Sales to Inventory* ratio points out the likelihood that some unsalable material is included in the book figure for inventory and the possibility that a write-off will result.

    Cost of Sales to Inventory is computed by dividing cost of sales (also known as cost of goods sold or factory cost of shipments in certain manufacturing industries) for the year by the book value of inventory at year-end. Cost of sales is used as the numerator instead of net sales, since inventory is ordinarily carried on the books at cost (or, occasionally, market value when that amount is lower). Some analysts prefer to calculate this ratio on an average inventory figure taken from the beginning and ending balances. A particularly valuable adjustment in seasonal industries is to base the denominator on a quarterly or monthly average, which helps to eliminate the effect of the highly variable inventory levels that will occur at different fiscal year closing dates. Realistically, however, industry statistics are based on less detailed data than that available to the internal analyst; thus, we use the simplified ratio of cost of sales for the year divided by ending inventory. Company B, with cost of sales of $3,775,000 and inventory of $750,000, has a *Cost of Sales to Inventory* ratio of 5.0, as shown in Table 6-2 later in this chapter.

    For some contract (make-to-order) manufacturers, inventory is composed almost entirely of work-in-process, but other custom producers have a significant inventory of raw material, components, and subassemblies as well. In the first case, the *Cost of Sales to Inventory* ratio actually measures inventory throughput, which indicates the efficiency of scheduling (material, manpower, and machinery) and shop floor control. In the second case, more traditional purchasing practices relating to quantities on hand are also measured. With respect to make-to-stock manufacturers, *Cost of Sales to Inventory* indicates the efficiency of the entire spectrum of activities—from purchasing and production through selling and final distribution. On the other hand, some contract manufacturers are essentially service operations, producing parts from material supplied by customers, and carry little or no inventory.

Although some distribution lines that sell almost exclusively on a drop-ship basis also carry virtually no inventory, most wholesalers and retailers pay extremely close attention to *Cost of Sales to Inventory*. In fact, inventory is frequently their largest asset item. For them, the "turn and earn" relationship—inventory turnover multiplied by gross margin (net sales minus cost of sales)—is an important measure of merchandising efficiency. Unfortunately, many companies in wholesaling and retailing focus their entire attention on purchasing, marketing, and sales, forgetting that the other fundamentals of financial management, such as collecting their accounts receivable in a timely manner and maintaining adequate capital investment to support sales, have an equally strong bearing on ultimate financial survival and prosperity.

For pure service industries, such as insurance firms or travel agencies, *Cost of Sales to Inventory* has no application. On the other hand, many companies in the service category actually have a large stock of repair parts or other items for resale. In those business lines, merchandise cost of sales is divided by merchandise inventory to determine *Cost of Sales to Inventory*.

While *Cost of Sales to Inventory* clearly does not represent an actual physical turnover of inventory, it is the best general measure available to indicate the manner in which a company's inventory is moving through the cash cycle. Inventory represents a mix of actual goods, including some that move in and out of the system very quickly and others that may have been on hand for a considerable period. In this respect, *Cost of Sales to Inventory* represents only an average efficiency measure. As inventory turnover declines, the likelihood of losses due to damage, obsolescence, or simple unsalability increases.

LIFO and FIFO Methods of Accounting for Inventory

In large manufacturing companies, the method of accounting for inventory—LIFO (last-in, first-out) or FIFO (first-in, first-out)—can have a significant impact on *Cost of Sales to Inventory*. The FIFO method closely approximates actual practice in a company that manages its physical inventory well; the first items put into inventory are ordinarily the first items withdrawn for conversion or sale. The LIFO method, which is the record-keeping equivalent of taking inventory from the front of the shelf instead of rotating stock, is a device for reducing taxes by increasing the cost of sales and decreasing reported profits during periods of rapid inflation. The cumulative effect of this method is to hold a portion of the book value of inventory to its lower, pre-inflation value. FIFO, by contrast, gradually raises the book value of inventory toward current price levels. Industry statistics rarely distinguish between companies on LIFO and those on FIFO, and further investigation of these methods should be pursued in books devoted to accounting or inventory management.

For analysts who may desire to review the significance of LIFO and FIFO, Table 6-1 illustrates the effect of these two methods on the amount of profit and

Table 6-1.   Effect of LIFO and FIFO on profit and inventory.

Opening inventory	625	units @ $100	$ 62,500
First purchase	500	units @ $102	51,000
Second purchase	1100	units @ $105	115,500
Third purchase	1400	units @ $110	154,000
Fourth purchase	750	units @ $116	87,000
Fifth purchase	250	units @ $120	30,000
Sixth purchase	250	units @ $122	30,500
	4875		$530,500
Closing inventory	650		
Units sold	4225		
FIFO (first-in, first-out)			
Units sold	625	units @ $100	$ 62,500
	500	units @ $102	51,000
	1100	units @ $105	115,500
	1400	units @ $110	154,000
	600	units @ $116	69,600
	4225		
Cost of sales			$452,600
Net profit			$ 20,000*

inventory shown on a company's financial statement. Although this is a somewhat extreme example, based on a price rise of 22% in a single year, businesspeople responsible for management of critical material in the late 1970s will recognize the situation. By their own admission, however, most small-business owners and managers are less concerned about LIFO and FIFO than two other inventory methods that will come into being without proper controls: FISH (first-in, still-here) and OSWO (oh-s———, we're-out).

In utilizing available industry averages to study *Cost of Sales to Inventory*, you may encounter a warning that a high ratio is indicative of a perilous condition which can lead to loss of sales "through lack of adequate inventories in stock and failure to offer proper depth of selection to customers." This admonition should be carefully considered, but it is generally applicable only to severely undercapitalized companies, particularly start-ups. Other special situations that may produce unusually high *Cost of Sales to Inventory* are those involving converters or distributors whose primary supplier requires cash in advance because of failure to meet credit requirements. Most business owners are sufficiently sales-minded that they will stock at least the items customers desire, and, unfortunately, often more.

Obviously, as the company meets its merchandising objectives with increas-

Closing inventory	150	units @ $116	$ 17,400
	250	units @ $120	30,000
	250	units @ $122	30,500
	650		$ 77,900

LIFO (last-in, first-out)

Units sold	250	units @ $122	$ 30,500
	250	units @ $120	30,000
	750	units @ $116	87,000
	1400	units @ $110	154,000
	1100	units @ $105	115,500
	475	units @ $102	48,450
	4225		
Cost of sales			$465,450
Net profit			$ 7,150†
Closing inventory	25	units @ $102	$ 2,550
	625	units @ $100	62,500
	650		$ 65,050

*Actual profit reported using FIFO method
†Calculated net profit using LIFO method; cost of goods sold $12,850 greater under LIFO, reducing net profit from $20,000 under FIFO to $7,150 under LIFO

ing effectiveness, it should succeed in boosting sales while limiting the growth of inventory. If an inadequate stock of goods causes sales volume to fall, then *Cost of Sales to Inventory* will begin to decline. Ironically, an extreme drop in sales would cause *Cost of Sales to Inventory* to be moderately low, unless the shelves are bare. The reduction of inventory to a level inadequate to support sales almost invariably results from other conditions such as suspended credit lines due to insufficient working capital, which in turn may be traced to factors indicated by the other causal ratios presented in this part.

Clearly, however, inventory does influence sales. Many companies have lost business because of the following inventory-related problems that will be reflected in the *Cost of Sales to Inventory* ratio:

1. Inefficient purchasing practices that lead to work-in-process bottlenecks in manufacturing or low customer satisfaction and unbalanced stock in wholesaling and retailing.
2. Curtailment of credit by certain prime suppliers because of improper management of the cash cycle: purchasing, sales, and collection of accounts receivable. Such restriction can result in disruption of production and merchandising until new sources of supply are established or until existing suppliers are satisfied.

3. Insolvency of principal suppliers or their inability to meet scheduled delivery.

But such developments frequently result in low—rather than high—inventory turnover rates, for in such cases large quantities of certain parts or items are often on hand, even as other out-of-stock conditions or production delays cause customers to send orders to the firm's competitors.

A Measure of Working Capital

The function of the *Cost of Sales to Inventory* ratio is quite similar to that of the *Collection Period of Accounts Receivable*; both ratios measure the quality of working capital. Just as receivables become subject to shrinkage through bad debts and, indirectly, through heavy attorney and collection agency fees as outstanding accounts reach advanced age, so inventory is susceptible to possible writedown in value for a variety of reasons:

1. Physical deterioration through age and natural forces.
2. Softening of prices of the material comprising inventory.
3. Obsolescence, change in customer preference, or the introduction of new materials or improved products.
4. The seasonal influence and annual style or model changes.
5. Overvaluation—intentional or unintentional. Despite the many refinements in valuation techniques developed by the accounting profession, the validity of inventory figures still depends in large measure upon the honesty, integrity, and good sense of the manager who submits them.
6. Purchase or retention of unusable materials.
7. Failure to verify book figures through periodic physical count.

A steep decline in the value of an excessive inventory can completely wipe out a tight working capital position. And if the company is operating on a slim margin of profit, the write-off of inventory could easily throw its year's total into red ink. Slowdown of inventory turnover can, of course, hinder a company's ability to meet its short-term obligations and can also affect its profit, through physical handling and recordkeeping costs, loss of purchase discounts, and additional interest expense that may result from diminished cash flow. The analyst should be alert to a sudden decline in *Cost of Sales to Inventory* (particularly if, for a manufacturing company, detailed information indicates that the inventory build-up is attributable to finished goods), because such a development strongly suggests the possibility that recent sales volume has not met management expectations.

Table 6-2. *Cost of Sales to Inventory* **for four companies.**

	Company A	Company B	Company C	Company D
Cost of sales	$1,110,000	$3,775,000	$9,750,000	$40,000,000
Inventory	170,000	750,000	2,500,000	4,900,000
Cost of Sales to Inventory				
Company	6.5 times	5.0 times	3.9 times	8.2 times
Industry standard	5.1 times	5.1 times	5.1 times	5.1 times

Comparison of Inventory Control

Let us now consider how Companies A, B, C, and D compare with respect to inventory control, as measured by *Cost of Sales to Inventory* in Table 6-2. Company A's *Cost of Sales to Inventory* indicates superior management of inventory in relation to sales volume. Keeping inventory at a relatively low level that is consistent with meeting customer demand offers many advantages to Company A: lower handling and carrying costs, decreased risk of writedowns, and improved working capital balance. Company B's *Cost of Sales to Inventory* is near the middle of the competitive pack with regard to inventory control: The company has no apparent advantage, but no obvious disadvantage either. Company C's *Cost of Sales to Inventory* is noticeably below the industry standard. From this ratio alone, you have reason to believe that Company C may be suffering from problems associated with sluggish inventory, particularly periodic cash flow squeezes and reduced profit. Company D shows *Cost of Sales to Inventory* well above the comparison group median. While a high ratio ordinarily exerts a favorable effect on basic financial structure, the possibility exists that Company D's decidedly high ratio in relation to the industry norm is an indication of inadequate owners' equity, requiring extremely tight control of the company's assets to hold down liabilities.

The causal effect of *Cost of Sales to Inventory* on the key secondary ratios is described in Part III and further illustrated through detailed case studies in Part V and brief examples of management decision making through ratio analysis in Part VI.

Summary: Cost of Sales to Inventory

Popular name   *Inventory Turnover Ratio*

Purpose   Measures a company's control of inventory in relation to cost of sales; indicates how many times inventory "turns" in a year.

Calculation	Divide cost of sales by inventory.
Example	Your company's cost of sales during your last fiscal year was $750,000, and your inventory at year-end was $150,000. What was your *Cost of Sales to Inventory*?
	Solution: 750,000 ÷ 150,000 = 5.0
Financial impact	A *high* ratio exerts a *favorable* influence: It increases asset utilization, reduces financial leverage, and/or increases return on equity.
Operational impact	A *high* ratio tends to reduce storage, record-keeping, verification, and interest costs and lowers the probability of loss due to physical deterioration or obsolescence; however, in wholesaling, retailing, and make-to-stock manufacturing, a *high* ratio also tends to increase ordering costs and raises the probability of stock-outs and customer dissatisfaction because of limited product selection. This ratio is not applicable to distributors and service industries that do not maintain inventory.
Range of common experience	4.1 times to 8.2 times.

Chapter 7

Net Sales to Fixed Assets

Net Sales to Fixed Assets is a measure of the extent to which a company is utilizing its investment in physical facilities—land, plant, equipment, furniture, fixtures, vehicles, and so forth—to generate sales volume. You must keep in mind that an abnormally high ratio usually indicates very old, nearly fully depreciated fixed assets or the leasing of property and equipment.

Computed by dividing a company's net sales by the book or depreciated value of fixed assets, this ratio is expressed in "times." Company B, with annual net sales of $5 million on fixed assets of $500,000 at year-end, has *Net Sales to Fixed Assets* of 10.0, as illustrated in Table 7-1.

Since fixed assets are acquired to further the sales progress of a company by increasing production and service or by reducing costs, the utilization of these assets is measured by reference to sales activity. The management of plant and equipment, expressed in dollars of net sales to dollars of fixed assets, must be evaluated in order to determine present conditions and future needs in this area. In general, high *Net Sales to Fixed Assets* (also called the *Fixed Assets Activity Ratio*) reflects efficient use of money invested in plant and in other productive or capital assets. If this ratio is well above the industry average, you must consider that plant, machinery, trucks, and other fixed assets have not only a theoretical but an actual capacity. As this capacity is reached, profitable business may be lost because of inadequate facilities for conducting sales, insufficient distribution resources, or the company's lack of ability to increase production due to limitations in plant size or available equipment. On the other hand, a rapid decline in *Net Sales to Fixed Assets* from one year to the next may indicate that significant capital expenditures have occurred during recent months, or that the company has suffered a recent drop in sales volume.

Refer to Companies A, B, C, and D in Table 7-1 to see how *Net Sales to Fixed Assets* is applied. (Part VI explores total cause-and-effect ratio analysis, but for the present it is desirable to concentrate solely on this primary ratio before seeing how it relates to the other key financial measures, both primary and secondary.) In the case of Company A, we find a picture of comparatively efficient use of plant and equipment: The company has been able to achieve approximately 20% more net sales per dollar of fixed assets than has its typical competitor. Through its success in limiting fixed assets, Company A has potentially freed a greater amount of funds for working capital purposes. Also, the

Table 7-1.   *Net Sales to Fixed Assets* for four companies.

	Company A	Company B	Company C	Company D
Net sales	$1,500,000	$5,000,000	$12,500,000	$50,000,000
Fixed assets	124,000	500,000	1,400,000	2,450,000
Net Sales to Fixed Assets				
Company	12.1 times	10.0 times	8.9 times	20.4 times
Industry standard	10.3 times	10.3 times	10.3 times	10.3 times

company's per unit charges against sales income to cover depreciation and other fixed costs attributable to plant and equipment are, in all probability, comparatively low, giving management still further operating freedom. In a period of intense competition, such advantages enhance management's ability to meet possible price-cutting tactics of competitors, assuming that the company's financial structure is otherwise in line with the norm for the industry. The ability of Company A to boost its *Net Sales to Fixed Assets* is, of course, subject to an upper limit; for even though the business might resort to 24-hour-a-day activities, the total physical capacity of existing facilities must ultimately be reached. As this point nears, Company A will be obliged to consider additional capital goods acquisition, which, unless sales keep pace, will bring *Net Sales to Fixed Assets* closer to the industry average.

Company B's *Net Sales to Fixed Assets* is similar to that of the typical concern in its comparison group, indicating fixed asset utilization in line with general industry practice. Company C's ratio is less attractive, as its investment in fixed assets has not yet been justified by the level of net sales attained. To achieve standard performance reported by its industry group, Company C would need to increase its volume to $14,420,000—nearly $2 million more than present sales activity. (Multiplying Company C's fixed assets of $1,400,000 by the 10.3 median *Net Sales to Fixed Assets* yields net sales of $14,420,000 needed to equal the industry norm for the utilization of plant and equipment.) The company might well find that its comparatively high level of fixed assets in relation to net sales has caused one or more of the following problems:

1. A drain on working capital
2. Greater than normal debt pressure, either short-term or long-term in nature
3. Reduced profit stemming from comparatively high fixed costs on each unit of sales

In order to evaluate Company C's present fixed asset commitment, you must know the dates of acquisition of the major components of plant and equipment and the company's sales volume for the preceding two or three years. If the investment in fixed assets proves to be relatively recent, quite possibly Company C made a carefully considered move to expand facilities somewhat beyond its immediate needs. While the company might feel temporary financial strain, such advance planning might indeed become a future advantage. You must take care not to judge the significance of a financial statement item entirely by figures recorded on a single date. If sales are moving upward at an appreciable rate, this trend would tend to minimize the dangers of the concern's present deficiency in fixed asset activity. Assume, for example, that Company C's net sales are:

19X7	$ 7,500,000
19X8	8,750,000
19X9	10,500,000
19X0	12,500,000

These figures indicate that, although the company's dollar amount of fixed assets may now be something of a burden to Company C, continuation of the present trend in sales will very soon justify the outlay.

Conversely, if a declining sales pattern is discovered, Company C's commitment in fixed assets requires closer attention. If a recent investment in fixed assets has been made in the face of a downward sales trend, then the comparatively low ratio of 8.9 times may indicate an error in judgment on the part of management. On the other hand, the benefits of the recent acquisition may be reflected in reduced costs rather than increased sales. It is possible, too, that improvements in productive facilities will take several years to reverse a sales decline of long duration. If, however, no substantial additions to fixed assets have been made recently, Company C's problem may be serious indeed. Since fixed assets are annually reduced in book value through depreciation charges, low *Net Sales to Fixed Assets* based on older facilities indicates either substantial over-investment in the past or sharply declining sales volume.

A high level of fixed assets relative to net sales is likely to have an adverse effect on net profit. Other factors being equal, Company C's annual depreciation charges will be a higher percentage of net sales than will those of its competitors. Property taxes, insurance, and interest expense are in all likelihood also higher than the industry norm and together exercise further downward pressure on profit. Repairs and maintenance and a variety of other charges might, likewise, also enter into the picture at a higher than normal rate per sales dollar.

On the other hand, modernization of facilities may actually produce a net reduction in total costs. Shipping and receiving, material handling and display, repairs and maintenance, tools and supplies, utilities, and other expenses related to physical operations may be lowered significantly through automation or improved facilities. Of greater importance, Company C may be able to increase prices, provide a greater degree of customer satisfaction (possibly reducing selling costs), and boost productivity, thereby lowering other cost percentages significantly. Although we have previously found that Company C's profit performance is substandard at this time, further investigation may reveal that profit improvement has in fact been achieved by virtue of investment in fixed assets.

In the case of Company D, a quick glance might prompt the conclusion that the business is a tremendously efficient operator—that it has achieved peak net sales performance from each dollar invested in fixed assets. With Company D's ratio nearly twice as great as the industry standard, however, further investigation would almost surely disclose that the company is financing a substantial part of its fixed assets through rental arrangements and operating leases or is conducting business with antiquated facilities.

As we will see in Part III, *Net Sales to Fixed Assets* has an influence on all nine of the secondary ratios.

Summary: Net Sales to Fixed Assets

Popular name	*Fixed Assets Activity Ratio*
Purpose	Measures a company's control of fixed assets in relation to net sales volume or, from another perspective, indicates a company's ability to produce net sales from use of its fixed assets (land, buildings, leasehold improvements, machinery, equipment, furniture, fixtures, and vehicles).
Calculation	Divide net sales by fixed assets.
Example	Your company's net sales during your last fiscal year were $1 million, and your fixed assets at year-end were $200,000. What was your *Net Sales to Fixed Assets?*
	Solution: 1,000,000 ÷ 200,000 = 5.0
Financial impact	A *high* ratio exerts a *favorable* influence: It increases asset utilization, also reduces financial leverage, and/or increases return on equity.
Operational impact	A *high* ratio tends to reduce depreciation and interest costs; however, it also tends to increase costs related to operating leases (by substituting leased facilities and equipment for acquired assets), personnel (due to lack of automation, crowded sales space, etc.), and travel or delivery expenses (when less costly facilities are acquired in outlying areas).
Range of common experience	6.8 times to 22.4 times.

Chapter 8

The Effect of Three Other Asset Factors on Net Sales to Total Assets

In addition to the three major asset items represented by the *Collection Period of Accounts Receivable*, *Cost of Sales to Inventory*, and *Net Sales to Fixed Assets*, three other asset factors may exert an influence on the *Net Sales to Total Assets* ratio: cash and short-term investments, other current assets (those current assets that are not cash and short-term investments or accounts receivable or inventory), and miscellaneous assets (those noncurrent assets that are not classified as fixed assets). Each of these asset categories may have a significant impact on *Net Sales to Total Assets* and also cause noticeable changes in the nine key ratios that measure financial effect, but those occurrences are comparatively infrequent. Because they help to explain the financial structure of comparatively few firms, the special ratios that are used to analyze these three—ordinarily minor—asset items rarely appear in industry studies. Nevertheless, the experienced analyst will find that cash and short-term investments, other current assets, or miscellaneous assets (or all three in combination) will, from time to time, be major causal factors—occasionally the primary explanation of financial imbalance. For that reason, the ratios that measure these three asset items are included in this section describing the key causal ratios.

Days' Sales in Cash and Short-Term Investments

Days' Sales in Cash and Short-Term Investments is seldom published in industry reports, but it can occasionally explain an otherwise puzzling financial structure. Even when industry comparisons are not available, tracking a company's trend for this ratio over several years can reveal the reason for changes in other important ratios. *Days' Sales in Cash and Short-Term Investments* does not ordinarily have a major impact on financial structure. Nevertheless, it can act as a causal ratio that, from time to time, exerts a highly important influence on several other key financial ratios. This measure is not enumerated as one of the seven causal ratios because of its comparative rarity in a significant causal role.

The easiest method of computing this ratio is as follows:

1. Multiply cash and short-term investments at year-end by 365.
2. Divide the result by net sales for the year.
3. Express the ratio as a whole number (days).

To reinforce your understanding of the underlying logic, you may prefer to calculate this ratio by an alternative formula:

1. Divide net sales for the year by 365 to obtain average daily net sales.
2. Divide cash and short-term investments at year-end by that result.
3. Express the ratio as a whole number (days).

Most companies attempt to maintain the lowest level of cash and short-term investments needed to cover expected demands for funds. In fact, many concerns manage cash so closely that they invest excess balances daily. As a result, industry norms for *Days' Sales in Cash and Short-Term Investments* are ordinarily very low. Consequently, a company with an extremely small amount of cash and short-term investments in relation to net sales rarely differs from the industry norm to any significant extent. On the other hand, a company with a very high level of cash and investments may find that this item exerts an important influence on the company's entire financial structure.

Of course, an abundance of cash and short-term investments rarely represents a problem from a conservative viewpoint. Nevertheless, the presence of an inordinate amount of cash and investments raises questions about the company's strategic plan (or, in less formal terms, its sense of direction). Does management expect to use these highly liquid assets to fund the replacement of other assets or to support sales growth? On the other hand, should cash be withdrawn from the company or otherwise invested in more profitable endeavors? Depending on the specific manner of holding cash and investing other available funds, such balances may actually depress a company's return on shareholders' equity. Excess liquidity will also tend to reduce *Net Sales to Total Assets*. Some firms attempt to maximize income from investments by pushing suppliers' invoices to the furthest point short of losing credit privileges altogether and earning interest on the difference. Despite their high cash and investment balances, these companies may also show a comparatively high level of debt in relation to net worth. Unfortunately, management does not recognize that most suppliers will find a way to compensate for their customers' delayed payments by raising prices or reducing services—resulting in hidden costs that often exceed the interest income gained from the temporary investment of those delayed payments.

Turning to Table 8-1, we find that Company A's cash and short-term investment balance, at 13 days of net sales, is noticeably higher than the 9-day industry standard. As a practical matter, however, this difference reflects only a somewhat conservative financial approach, not a clear commitment to excessive holdings of

Table 8-1.   Three asset factors affecting asset utilization for four companies.

	Company A	Company B	Company C	Company D
Net sales	$1,500,000	$5,000,000	$12,500,000	$50,000,000
Cash and short-term investments	52,000	100,000	100,000	100,000
Other current assets*	24,000	25,000	50,000	550,000
Other noncurrent (miscellaneous) assets†	14,000	0	510,000	550,000
Days' Sales in Cash and Short-Term Investments				
Company	13 days	7 days	3 days	1 day
Industry standard	9 days	9 days	9 days	9 days
Days' Sales in Other Current Assets				
Company	6 days	2 days	1 day	4 days
Industry standard	4 days	4 days	4 days	4 days
Days' Sales in Other Noncurrent (Miscellaneous) Assets				
Company	3 days	0 days	15 days	4 days
Industry standard	3 days	3 days	3 days	3 days

*Current assets other than cash and short-term investments, accounts receivable and inventory
†Noncurrent assets other than fixed assets

cash and near-cash items. Company B is, once again, generally in line with the industry norm. Both Company C and, especially, Company D show very low cash balances in relation to net sales. Perhaps *Days' Sales in Cash and Short-Term Investments* for these firms indicates extremely careful cash management on a continuing basis. It may, however, simply reflect a "window dressing" effort to pay down current liabilities at year-end.

Days' Sales in Other Current Assets

Days' Sales in Other Current Assets is rarely a major factor affecting a company's basic financial structure. When it does have such an impact, however, the situation frequently baffles even experienced financial analysts, because this factor is not separately identified in most discussions of financial management. Although *Days' Sales in Other Current Assets* is not listed among the seven causal ratios, this measure can occasionally exert an important influence on the nine secondary ratios.

For quick calculation, the best approach is as follows:

1. Multiply other current assets at year-end by 365.
2. Divide the result by net sales for the year.
3. Express the ratio as a whole number (days).

On the other hand, the underlying logic of this measure is best understood by:

1. Dividing net sales for the year by 365 to obtain average daily net sales
2. Dividing other current assets at year-end by that result
3. Expressing the ratio as a whole number (days)

A number of special circumstances cause other current assets to represent a notable proportion of total assets. Accounting procedures relating to progress payments and to the percentage-of-completion method of reporting work-in-process may result in a very large amount in this asset classification. Although prepaid expenses and deferred charges are often included in other current assets, most industry studies classify these items as other noncurrent (miscellaneous) assets.

When a high level of other current assets is encountered, you must inquire about the composition of the item. In some cases, a portion or all of other current assets should be transferred to another category. In certain manufacturing companies, for example, other current assets that are attributable to progress payments against inventory should ordinarily be added back to inventory in order to permit a more accurate comparison of both inventory and other current assets.

Table 8-1 reveals that not one of the four companies we have been following is noteworthy with respect to *Days' Sales in Other Current Assets*.

Days' Sales in Other Noncurrent (Miscellaneous) Assets

Days' Sales in Other Noncurrent (*Miscellaneous*) *Assets* identifies the presence of assets that are not employed in the cash cycle (current assets) and are not physical facilities (fixed assets) that support sales and then measures those miscellaneous assets in relation to sales activity. When this ratio is comparatively high, it prompts an important question: Are the company's assets being properly used to generate sales and profit?

To calculate this ratio by the most direct method:

1. Multiply miscellaneous assets at year-end by 365.
2. Divide the result by net sales for the year.
3. Express the ratio as a whole number (days).

Many analysts prefer to use a different process in order to improve their understanding of this key financial ratio:

1. Divide net sales for the year by 365 to obtain average daily net sales.
2. Divide miscellaneous assets at year-end by that result.
3. Express the ratio as a whole number (days).

Miscellaneous assets include all noncurrent assets that are not considered fixed assets. In other words, if an asset is not classified as ''current''—cash and all items (such as accounts receivable and inventory) expected to turn to cash or be otherwise expended in the next year—and is not classified as ''fixed''—land, buildings, equipment, vehicles, furniture, fixtures, computers, and the like—it is, by process of elimination, a miscellaneous asset.

The assets most frequently classified as miscellaneous include:

- Money due from officers, directors, or employees (representing loans or advances from the company).

- Investments in or advances to subsidiaries or affiliated companies (usually firms related through mutual ownership).

- Prepaid expenses and deferred charges. Accountants differ regarding the classification of these items as either current or miscellaneous assets. The most widely circulated source of industry averages excludes ''prepaid and deferred'' from current assets, and since comparison is meaningless unless ratios are derived from uniformly classified figures, this item is included here as a component of miscellaneous assets. An industry preparing its own ratios can categorize figures according to any generally accepted accounting method, provided, of course, that the assignment of these items is made clear to those reviewing the industry averages.

- Any long-term receivables, such as a mortgage receivable.

It is true that such miscellaneous assets do not constitute a prominent part of the typical balance sheet, and in perhaps only one case out of 15 does *Days' Sales in Other Noncurrent (Miscellaneous) Assets* indicate the basic cause of a company's financial imbalance. But, if we are to have a ratio approach that assures the analyst of reasonable certainty in his final determination of cause and cure, we cannot afford even a 5% or 10% percent margin of error. Although *Days' Sales in Other Noncurrent (Miscellaneous) Assets* is not listed among the seven primary ratios, it should be reviewed at any time that the status of the nine secondary ratios is not fully explained by the seven causal measures. By the end of Part III, you will know when such additional investigation is required.

Every company has a limited amount of invested capital with which to achieve its objectives. Commitment of an inordinate proportion of this capital to miscellaneous assets restricts working capital and productive fixed assets and may concurrently increase the company's debt position.

A general lack of industry norms makes the evaluation of *Days' Sales in Other Noncurrent (Miscellaneous) Assets* difficult. Moreover, effective analysis of miscellaneous assets depends on further information about the exact composition of this item, but these details are seldom available on an industrywide basis. To make specific recommendations to company management, the analyst would benefit from knowing whether excess exposure in this area is, for example, the result of borrowings by officers and employees or the result of investment in companies controlled by the owners or their families. Although *Days' Sales in Other Noncurrent (Miscellaneous) Assets* is considered only briefly here, it is nevertheless recommended for inclusion in any statistical presentation by individual industries.

This ratio indicates the fundamental cause of any difficulty only infrequently, but it must be considered in any discussion of the causal ratios. If owners have borrowed heavily from the business, such withdrawals will be reflected in a depressed *Current Ratio* or in elevated debt ratios. The same result will follow from substantial diversion of funds into other noncurrent assets making up this miscellaneous category. In the case of officers' or owners' borrowing, creditors are the parties that should be most concerned. At the same time, owners should scrutinize their own actions, for it is always possible to "kill the goose that laid the golden egg." It has been done all too often.

Miscellaneous assets are especially vulnerable to write-off or markdown from book figures. Money lent to officers is, in many cases, never repaid. Amounts shown as invested in or lent to a subsidiary or affiliate are only as good as the company that received the funds. The owners of the business would be wise to show realistic values on the balance sheet, for, otherwise, they are simply deceiving themselves. Credit grantors must investigate the companies to which funds have been channeled to ascertain that book figures reflect true worth. If, for example, a company has invested in or lent to its subsidiary a sum of $250,000 and that subsidiary is on the verge of bankruptcy with deficit net worth, can this asset properly be shown at the full $250,000 figure? To the extent that any miscellaneous asset must be scaled down in value or written off, the recognition of such nonrecurring charges can easily throw otherwise profitable operations into a net loss for the year. In this event, all ratios relating to net profit (or loss) and net worth will be adversely influenced.

Reference to Companies A, B, C, and D in Table 8-1 indicates that only Company C, with *Days' Sales in Other Noncurrent (Miscellaneous) Assets* of 15 days versus the 3-day industry norm, requires special comment. Company C has clearly diverted a significant amount of total resources into this asset category. The result is necessarily a tightening of working capital. Profitable expansion of the company's operations may be hampered, for substantial funds that might otherwise be used to support such growth are tied up in miscellaneous assets. Company C is likely to be passing up cash discounts, and slowness in trade payment is also a distinct possibility. Further research into the makeup of this asset item is clearly important to anyone making a serious analysis of Company C's financial condition. If such research reveals a major investment in a subsidiary company, an analysis of the financial soundness of the subsidiary would clearly be in order. The actual market value of any other miscellaneous assets should also be investigated.

If advances to officers and employees represent a large proportion of miscellaneous assets, the analyst must discover to which individuals loans were granted, how widespread the practice of borrowing from the company has become, the terms or understanding with respect to repayment, and the company's means of collecting its advances. There have actually been cases—involving substantially higher percentages than in this example—in which money was being carried on the books as due from employees who had terminated their association with the company a year or two before, whose whereabouts were unknown, and from whom there was no evidence of, or admission of, debt. These reported assets turned out to be 100% losses for the benevolent employer who had so freely and generously lent the money. Whether or not the stated value of the miscellaneous assets on Company C's books is well supported, additional investment in this area must be carefully scrutinized. In fact, management should consider initiating an effort to redirect some of the outstanding funds to more active use in the regular operation of the business.

Summary: Days' Sales in Cash and Short-Term Investments, in Other Current Assets, and in Other Noncurrent (Miscellaneous) Assets

Days' Sales in Cash and Short-Term Investments

Purpose	Measures a company's level of cash and short-term investments in relation to its net sales volume.
Calculation	Multiply cash and short-term investments by 365, then divide the result by net sales; express ratio as whole number.

Days' Sales in Other Current Assets

Purpose	Measures a company's level of other current assets (current assets other than cash and short-term investments, accounts receivable, and inventory) in relation to its net sales volume.
Calculation	Multiply other noncurrent assets by 365, then divide the result by net sales; express ratio as whole number.

Days' Sales in Other Noncurrent (Miscellaneous) Assets

Purpose	Measures a company's level of other noncurrent (miscellaneous) assets in relation to its net sales volume.
Calculation	Multiply other noncurrent assets by 365, then divide the result by net sales; express ratio as whole number.
Example	Your company's net sales were $1 million for the year, and your cash and short-term investments were $20,000, your other current assets were $5,000, and your other

noncurrent (miscellaneous) assets were zero at year-end. What was your company's value for each of these three asset management ratios?

Solution: Days' Sales in Cash and Short-Term Investments: 20,000 × 365 = 7,300,000; then 7,300,000 ÷ 1,000,000 = 7 days

Days' Sales in Other Current Assets: 5,000 × 365 = 1,825,000; then 1,825,000 ÷ 1,000,000 = 2 days

Days' Sales in Other Noncurrent (Miscellaneous) Assets: 0 × 365 = 0; then 0 ÷ 1,000,000 = 0 days

Financial impact

In all three cases, a *low* ratio is ordinarily a *favorable* influence: It increases asset utilization, reduces financial leverage, and/or increases return on equity. Possible exceptions are short-term or long-term investments that generate a higher rate of return than that produced by primary operations.

Range of common experience

Insufficient industry data.

Chapter 9

Net Sales to Net Worth

Net Sales to Net Worth measures the extent to which a company's sales volume is supported by owners' equity. A ratio substantially higher than the industry norm depicts the overtrader, a company that is attempting to stretch each invested dollar to its maximum capacity. The overtrader's statement, as we shall see, is generally burdened by heavy debt. In extreme cases, the company's survival hinges on the long-term continuation of optimum internal and external conditions. The undertrader, on the other hand, has capital resources in excess of the company's needs or, from another perspective, inadequate sales to justify the level of investment by the owners. The undertrading concern is less likely to be debt-ridden than is the overtrader (unless asset utilization is so poor that a high level of total liabilities is necessary to supplement net worth); its most pressing need is to boost sales to a level that produces an adequate return on owners' equity.

Many companies simply exist, paying the owners an income no higher than they would receive as employees elsewhere, and providing a return on invested capital far below interest rates on savings accounts. A reasonable balance must be maintained between the two extremes of overtrading and undertrading; *Net Sales to Net Worth* measures the degree to which a company has attained this balance.

Net Sales to Net Worth (also known as the *Investment Adequacy Ratio*) is computed by dividing a company's annual sales by its net worth. Company B, with annual sales of $5 million and net worth of $750,000, has *Net Sales to Net Worth* of 6.7, as illustrated in Table 9-1.

The calculation of this key financial measure requires special explanation. Ratios that involve both the income statement and the balance sheet traditionally use the income statement item—in this case, net sales—as the numerator, which is then divided by the balance sheet item. A calculation of this kind can cause some confusion when we are focusing our analysis on the balance sheet item (net worth). For *Net Sales to Net Worth*, a *high* ratio means that the amount of net worth available to support net sales is relatively *low*. As this ratio increases, it shows a decline in net worth relative to sales volume.

Clearly, the objective of commercial ventures is to realize a profit, which can be accomplished only by selling goods or services in adequate quantities at proper price levels. Since the majority of businesses are started by salespeople, the driving force in most concerns is to sell as much as possible, subject only to the limit of the hours comprising the business day. The greater the number and the dollar amount of orders, the greater the profit; that seems to be the predominant philosophy. The playwright Arthur Miller has, in his various literary efforts, expressed the view that the salesman, more than any other professional group, epitomizes modern American society.

In many ways, the push to "sell, sell, sell" has much to commend it. Every company must reckon with daily costs of both fixed and variable nature. And fixed costs, of course, continue without interruption, whether the plant operates or is idle, whether a single item moves off the shelf. Only by achieving a level of sales adequate to offset fixed costs (such as rent, office salaries, and equipment expenses) after covering variable expenses (such as material or goods for resale, hourly labor, and office supplies) can any company hope to break even, let alone realize profit. As sales exceed the break-even level, the company's profit percentage rises faster than the increase in sales volume (if we assume that a fairly consistent level of prices is maintained). So management may logically expend strenuous effort to achieve even higher sales in the hope of obtaining ever greater profit.

Owners' Equity as Basis for Sales Volume

But every company possesses a limited amount of owners' equity—its net worth—upon which attainment of its sales goals must be based. The two factors— sales and equity—are necessarily linked, whether the company likes it or not, for sales must look to net worth for support. Only so much sales activity can be derived from each dollar of equity capital without incurring debt that is beyond the company's ability to service—unless the company develops one or more compensating advantages.

The company might shorten its terms of sale or initiate more rigid enforcement of existing terms, whereby its *Collection Period of Accounts Receivable* would become substantially lower than industry average. Management might reduce inventory to increase cash flow. Or the company might attempt to secure a sale-and-lease-back agreement covering its plant and equipment, thus freeing cash for working capital purposes. Many companies have successfully built such competitive advantages into their financial structure on a permanent basis so that they are able to offset capital deficiencies through superior asset management.

Management could, of course, attempt to attract additional equity capital from outside investors. The injection of new capital may solve immediate problems, but for many small businesses this would mean the weakening or even the loss of management control.

A company that has reached the limit of sales volume that can be supported by owners' equity may choose to reduce sales or, while holding the line on sales, add to net worth through retention of all earnings in the business. Selective selling, the elimination of less profitable or even unprofitable customers, may actually improve profit percentage while reducing sales volume. Retaining all earnings in the business and forgoing dividends or executive bonuses will, in time, bring the relationship between sales and net worth into balance, provided that profit is earned.

A significant rise in *Net Sales to Net Worth* may be attributable to an important change in owners' equity, rather than to an increase in sales volume. The reduction of net worth through operating losses or as the result of a writedown of assets would be immediately apparent from the bottom line of the income statement. Excessive dividends (or withdrawals from an unincorporated business) or the purchase of minority shareholdings, however, would not appear on the income statement and might escape the analyst's notice if he or she does not have the benefit of a reconciliation of net worth or a statement of changes in financial position. A rise in *Net Sales to Net Worth* would, nevertheless, direct attention to such changes in net worth, particularly if net sales showed a steady or declining trend.

Let us study the relative position of Companies A, B, C, and D with respect to *Net Sales to Net Worth*, displayed in Table 9-1. Company A's ratio reflects the company's conservative philosophy: Support net sales with a comparatively high level of owners' equity. Whether or not the owners fully understand ratio analysis, they have found from experience that a relatively great net worth contributes to a reduction of debt and enables them to sleep better. While somewhat low, Company A's *Net Sales to Net Worth* does not indicate actual undertrading to the extent that profit on owners' equity is being severely impaired. Company B's management has succeeded in steering a middle course, maintaining *Net Sales to Net Worth* very close to the industry standard. This important causal ratio is neither a favorable nor an unfavorable factor with respect to Company B's financial structure.

Company C is somewhat more aggressive in generating sales volume on net worth, but the concern is certainly not a severe overtrader. Its comparatively high *Net Sales to Net Worth* will tend to increase total debt while also tending to boost the rate of return on owners' equity.

Table 9-1. *Net Sales to Net Worth* for four companies.

	Company A	Company B	Company C	Company D
Net sales	$1,500,000	$5,000,000	$12,500,000	$50,000,000
Net worth	254,000	750,000	1,540,000	1,550,000
Net Sales to Net Worth				
Company	5.9 times	6.7 times	8.1 times	32.3 times
Industry standard	6.8 times	6.8 times	6.8 times	6.8 times

Company D is definitely an overtrader. Investigation of this situation reveals that the company was recently transferred to key employees in a leveraged buyout. Very high *Net Sales to Net Worth* most frequently results from expanding sales far more rapidly than net worth can be increased through retained earnings or as a consequence of operating losses which erode net worth. During the late 1980s, however, a significant number of overtrading situations were created by leveraged buyouts. In Company D's case, management must maintain exceedingly careful control of cash flow and avoid any mistakes that would result in the need for additional financing, which would make management even more dependent on the company's ever-present creditors. In an emergency situation, however, the extreme commitment of creditors to the company's future may impel them to extend additional funds in order to protect their position, unless they have reason to believe that they would fare better by simply cutting their losses and salvaging what they can.

Ill Effects of Overtrading

Either *overtrading* (conducting excessive sales on limited owners' equity) or *undertrading* (generating such a low level of sales that owners receive an inadequate return on their investment) is, in itself, an unfavorable condition and requires thorough scrutiny. From a conservative viewpoint, however, overtrading is certainly the less desirable course of action. The thinner the overtrading concern stretches its invested dollar, the more vulnerable it becomes to some sudden and unexpected calamity. The overtrading company is much like an army that has penetrated deeply into enemy territory at a pace too rapid for its line of supply. A breakdown in the flow of material at the height of battle can place the army at the mercy of its foe. The overtrader involved in a prolonged strike finds its income cut off; but bills must be paid, and generally these bills are staggeringly high and of a short-term nature. Or it may lose several of its major accounts, either to competitors or through the insolvency of those customers. With already heavy inventory on hand and advance orders placed, such a loss of sales could create a situation that might not be solvable outside the bankruptcy courts. A price war can be devastating to the overtrader's income and to its financial balance, which is generally so encumbered by debt that ability to meet changing conditions is almost nonexistent.

Statistics indicating the percentage of business failures directly attributable to overtrading are, understandably enough, not available. The death blow is not dealt directly by the fact of overtrading, but instead is the result of one of the weaknesses caused by overtrading: a breakdown in the perfect meshing of all financial gears that is required for successfully conducting sales on inadequate owners' equity. In the postmortem, the failure of an overextended company might be blamed on "receivables difficulties" or "inventory difficulties," but in the final analysis the true cause was overtrading, which in time placed the company in such an inflexible position that it was not able to respond to unexpected developments.

Unsecured creditors generally lose more in an overtrading failure than in any other type of business suspension. By definition, the overtrader requires more and more goods for sale or conversion and ever greater lines of credit. When some unexpected development upsets the delicate balance that the overtrading company must maintain between asset management and creditor relations, the concern's liabilities are generally exceedingly high in relation to the "cushion" provided by owners' equity. By the time unsecured creditors recognize the severity of the problem, the company has often resorted to every conceivable type of financing—and the more severe the level of overtrading, the more inclined banks and some major suppliers are to request security for their advances. Although the assets shown on the overtrader's books may be large, assets have a tendency to shrink a great deal in the courts or under the auctioneer's hammer, while liabilities and expenses flourish there and are augmented by administrative costs and attorney fees. Frequently, bankruptcy cases involving overtraders terminate as total losses to unsecured creditors as well as to owners.

The number of overtraders appears to have grown—hand in hand with increased competition and, in many industries, accompanied by a continually lessening rate of profit return per dollar of sales—over the past 15 or 20 years. Given a narrower profit margin, the typical company must sell more to achieve even its former rate of return on invested capital; this fact provides the impulse to overtrade, but it can be a dangerous impulse and it must be watched carefully.

Undertrading

A company may conduct too little sales volume on its owners' equity as well as too much, but undertrading becomes perilous only if sales are inadequate to cover operating costs. If this is the case, the company's operations are thrown into a loss situation. There are many instances where sales are normal with respect to receivables, inventory, and fixed assets, but operations are nevertheless in the red. Under these circumstances, further examination of expenses is clearly dictated. Undertrading is defined as low *Net Sales to Net Worth*, not as inadequate income related to expenses.

If a company has substantial equity capital with only modest sales to match, danger of loss to creditors is minimal. The owners, however, are not receiving full value on their investment and might profitably divert the excess portion into an area that will bring them a greater return. Among small or mid-size companies, overcapitalization was once a relatively rare phenomenon. Today, however, a large number of firms established between 1945 and 1960 are owned by founders who are approaching retirement age. Many of these companies are now in an undertrading situation because of a conservative financial philosophy combined with a diminished interest in sales growth.

Occasionally, *Net Sales to Net Worth* takes an ironic turn. Some companies have been undertrading to such an extent that operating losses have drained net worth to an extremely low level over an extended period. These concerns can suddenly become technical overtraders when their diminishing net worth becomes extremely small, even in relation to their low level of net sales. If net worth falls from $200,000 to $100,000 and then to $10,000 because of major losses in two successive years, constant sales of $1 million would produce *Net Sales to Net Worth* of 5.0 at the end of the first year and 100.0 only two years later.

Best Measure of Financial Leverage

Net Sales to Net Worth is closely related to financial leverage, the effort to obtain the highest return on owners' equity by using debt to multiply the profit achieved on sales and on total assets. In certain respects, *Net Sales to Net Worth* may be the best measure of financial leverage, since it is the multiplication factor that links return on sales with return on equity, a concept we will examine in detail in Part III. The equation is simple: *Net Profit to Net Sales* multiplied by *Net Sales to Net Worth* equals *Net Profit to Net Worth*, the ratio that measures return on equity, an important concept discussed throughout Chapter 12. If a company's profit percentage on net sales remains constant, its return on equity will increase as *Net Sales to Net Worth* increases.

Summary: Net Sales to Net Worth

Popular names	*Investment Adequacy Ratio*; *Trading Ratio*
Purpose	Measures the adequacy of a company's net worth in support of its net sales volume or, from another perspective, the multiplier effect of "trading on equity" to achieve a higher percentage return on shareholders' investment.
Calculation	Divide net sales by net worth.
Example	Your company's net sales during your last fiscal year were $1 million, and your net worth at year-end was $150,000. What was your *Net Sales to Net Worth*?
	Solution: 1,000,000 ÷ 150,000 = 6.7
Financial impact	A *low* ratio exerts a *favorable* influence in one respect: It reduces financial leverage. However, a *low* ratio is *unfavorable* in another respect: It reduces return on equity.
Operational impact	A *low* ratio tends to reduce interest cost.

Definition	Net worth, called ''owner's equity'' in a sole proprietorship (IRS Schedule C), ''partners' capital'' in a partnership (IRS Form 1065), and ''stockholders' equity'' or ''shareholders' equity'' in a corporation (IRS Form 1120, 1120-A, or 1120S), equals total assets minus total liabilities.
Special reminder	A *low* ratio shows a *high* level of net worth to support net sales.
Critical value	When total liabilities are greater than total assets, net worth will be in a deficit position and a meaningful ratio cannot be calculated. In such a case, treat *Net Sales to Net Worth* as a very large number for comparative purposes. Deficit net worth is a serious condition that warrants close management attention.
Range of common experience	4.8 times to 8.4 times.

Chapter 10

Long-Term Liabilities to Total Noncurrent Assets

Long-Term Liabilities to Total Noncurrent Assets measures a company's use of long-term borrowing to finance its acquisition of fixed assets and other noncurrent (miscellaneous) assets. This ratio illustrates the important concept of matching long-term financing to noncurrent, that is, long-term, assets. Surprisingly, *Long-Term Liabilities to Total Noncurrent Assets* is included in very few published ratio studies. Reasonable approximations can, however, often be derived from available reports.

This causal measure is calculated by dividing long-term liabilities by the sum of fixed assets and miscellaneous (other noncurrent) assets. In Table 10-1, the asset side of Company B's balance sheet shows fixed assets of $500,000 and a zero amount for miscellaneous assets, while long-term liabilities of $250,000 appear on the other side of the ledger. Dividing the $250,000 of long-term debt by the $500,000 of total noncurrent assets produces a ratio of *Long-Term Liabilities to Total Noncurrent Assets* of 0.5.

A low ratio is considered a favorable indicator from a conservative viewpoint, but a ratio below the industry norm also means that the company is financing a relatively large proportion of its noncurrent assets from current liabilities and net worth, or by reducing current assets, thereby lowering working capital. In fact, very low *Long-Term Liabilities to Total Noncurrent Assets* can cause major cash flow difficulties.

Table 10-1. *Long-Term Liabilities to Total Noncurrent Assets* **for four companies.**

	Company A	Company B	Company C	Company D
Fixed assets	$124,000	$500,000	$1,400,000	$2,450,000
Other noncurrent (miscellaneous) assets	14,000	0	510,000	550,000
Long-term liabilities	62,000	250,000	1,330,000	4,450,000
Long-Term Liabilities to Total Noncurrent Assets				
Company	0.4 times	0.5 times	0.7 times	1.5 times
Industry standard	0.5 times	0.5 times	0.5 times	0.5 times

Such a problem most often arises in highly seasonal businesses or in industries subject to large swings in sales volume resulting from changes in general economic conditions. As sales decline, either seasonally or during an economic downturn, accounts receivable and inventory also decline. The difference becomes cash. At this point, management may decide to purchase new equipment or vehicles with the "excess" cash on hand rather than incur the interest costs associated with long-term financing. When the next sales upturn occurs, however, the company may not have sufficient working capital to support the increased activity. At the least, the company pays a price in the form of passed trade discounts, interest on the use of its credit line, or the extra costs of refinancing noncurrent assets. For a cyclical business, the expansion phase ordinarily follows a period of weak (or even dismal) operating performance, making financing of any kind relatively difficult to obtain. Under these circumstances, the company may be forced to forgo profitable sales and possibly lose valuable customers for lack of sufficient working capital.

Very low *Long-Term Liabilities to Total Noncurrent Assets* also occurs in well-established companies that have become overcapitalized through slow growth and the accumulation of retained earnings. This condition is often found in companies whose owners are nearing retirement age. Noncurrent assets are purchased for cash because the funds are available, and, in many cases, because the company's return on invested capital is lower than the interest rate on long-term financing. For such companies, the decision to acquire equipment and vehicles for cash makes sense within a very narrow focus. A broader view, however, suggests that the owner should diversify his personal investment portfolio by means of funds that could be withdrawn from the company (as compensation or dividends, depending on the circumstances). He should certainly question the wisdom of retaining such a large amount of personal wealth in the company, where it is exposed to the ongoing risks of business competition, in order to receive a return so low that purchasing fixed assets for cash actually appears more advantageous.

Unusually high *Long-Term Liabilities to Total Noncurrent Assets* often indicates a leveraged buy-out based on anticipated earnings or a major refinancing based on an appraised value of fixed assets well above their stated value on the books.

Table 10-1 shows *Long-Term Liabilities to Total Noncurrent Assets* and its balance sheet components for Companies A, B, C, and D. Company A's ratio is slightly lower than the industry standard, tending to reduce working capital. Consequently, cash flow will be relatively vulnerable to problems caused by variability of sales volume, inventory turnover, and collection of accounts receivable unless management has made either of two compensating moves:

1. Increased its investment adequacy by maintaining a comparatively high level of owners' equity in relation to net sales (reflected in comparatively low *Net Sales to Net Worth*)

2. Raised the utilization of fixed assets and held miscellaneous assets to a relatively low level (reflected in high *Net Sales to Fixed Assets* and low *Days' Sales in Miscellaneous Assets*)

In view of Company A's consistently favorable rating with respect to the other causal ratios, there is good reason to believe that the company's comparatively low *Long-Term Liabilities to Total Noncurrent Assets* is also a favorable influence in this case. As a practical matter, Company A requires relatively little long-term financing and incurs relatively little interest expense.

Company B's *Long-Term Liabilities to Total Noncurrent Assets* is directly in line with the industry standard, while Company C has used long-term borrowing to finance a relatively large proportion of its long-term (noncurrent) assets, thereby boosting working capital.

Company D's extremely high *Long-Term Liabilities to Total Noncurrent Assets* suggests that the business has recently been purchased on a leveraged basis, with the expectation that earnings will be used to pay long-term creditors (very likely the previous owners). Another possibility is that Company D has encountered serious cash flow difficulties due to operating losses, major bad debts, or inventory write-offs and that a bank or leasing company has agreed to provide new long-term financing, using the noncurrent assets as security, because an appraisal shows market value of those assets to be far greater than their book value. Land and buildings, as well as other noncurrent assets such as patents and licenses, frequently rise in market value over time, while certain equipment holds its market value well above book value (net of depreciation). Consequently, lenders may agree to refinancing on a long-term basis in preference to forcing the company into liquidation—provided, of course, that management has proposed a plan of corrective action and has demonstrated a reasonable probability that interest and principal payments can be met.

Summary: Long-Term Liabilities to Total Noncurrent Assets

Popular name	*Long-Term Financing Ratio*
Purpose	Measures a company's use of long-term borrowing to finance acquisition of fixed assets and other noncurrent (miscellaneous) assets.
Calculation	Divide long-term liabilities by total noncurrent assets.
Example	Your company's long-term liabilities were $50,000, your fixed assets were $100,000, and your other noncurrent assets were zero at year-end. What was your *Long-Term Liabilities to Total Noncurrent Assets*?
	Solution: Total noncurrent assets = 100,000 + 0 = 100,000; then 50,000 ÷ 100,000 = 0.5

Financial impact	A *high* ratio increases working capital sufficiency and tends to increase working capital balance. From a conservative viewpoint, high debt is ordinarily an unfavorable condition; but for this ratio, the benefit of strengthening working capital must be considered.
Operational impact	A *high* ratio may increase or decrease interest cost, depending on two factors: (1) the company's need for short-term bank borrowing, and (2) short-term versus long-term interest rates.
Critical value	A ratio *greater* than 1.0 shows long-term borrowing in excess of the book value of fixed assets and other noncurrent assets.
Range of common experience	0.5 times to 0.7 times.

Chapter 11

The Seven Causal Ratios: Review and Concise Summary of Basic Principles

Through our examination of the seven causal ratios (and the three related measures of asset utilization), we find that Company A's performance is consistently superior to the industry standard, while Company C shows evidence of difficulty in almost every key area. When we turn to the secondary ratios in Part III, we expect to find that Company A is operating with relative freedom from creditor pressure while producing an outstanding return on the owners' investment. Company C, on the other hand, is likely to be in a highly disadvantageous position with respect to financial leverage, working capital, and return on equity because of the influence of the causal ratios. Company B, which has shown such close adherence to the industry norm in managing its causal relationships, will undoubtedly appear near the middle of the group in the secondary measurements.

But what can we predict about Company D's secondary ratios? The seven causal ratios have proved to be a mixed bag for Company D:

1. *Net Profit to Net Sales* is comparatively low, a fundamentally unfavorable influence on the secondary ratios.
2. *Net Sales to Total Assets* is very high, a favorable factor from a conservative point of view because it reduces debt and strengthens working capital.
3. The *Collection Period of Accounts Receivable* is very low, contributing to Company D's high asset utilization rating.
4. *Cost of Sales to Inventory* is very high, also tending to increase total asset utilization.
5. *Net Sales to Fixed Assets* is very high, a third positive influence on asset utilization.
6. *Net Sales to Net Worth* is extremely high, showing an unusually low level of owners' equity to support sales volume, an unfavorable condition which increases debt and weakens working capital.
7. *Long-Term Liabilities to Total Noncurrent Assets* is very high, tending to strengthen working capital by substituting long-term debt for current obligations.

Importance of Secondary Ratios

When the causal ratios are at such extremes, some favorable and others unfavorable, the combined influence on the secondary ratios is difficult to predict. That is precisely why the secondary ratios are such an important part of cause-and-effect ratio analysis. If every company could be classified as either favorable or unfavorable in all causal areas, there would be no need for further analysis; the secondary ratios would simply confirm what we already knew about the causal ratios. In the real world, however, the vast majority of companies have at least one distinctly favorable causal factor and at least one that can be quickly identified as unfavorable. Often, one or more causal ratios that are far from the industry norm will more than offset the influence of four or five moderately favorable or unfavorable measures. Also, depending on the relative importance of the underlying financial statement item (such as accounts receivable) in the company's line of business, a single highly favorable or unfavorable ratio (in this case, the *Collection Period of Accounts Receivable*) may have a profound impact on the company's entire financial structure. On the other hand, the influence of a specific causal ratio may be diminished by the relative dollar amount of the other financial factors. The *Collection Period of Accounts Receivable*, for example, exerts comparatively little influence in certain industries characterized by major investments in plant, production equipment, and inventory. Part III shows how the conflicting forces among Company D's causal ratios have shaped the nine ratios that measure effect.

As background for gaining a solid understanding of the concept of cause and effect in ratio analysis, a summary of the basic financial principles represented by the primary ratios may be helpful at this point.

The Causal Ratios: Summary of Basic Financial Principles

1. *Maintain an adequate profit percentage on sales volume.* High *Net Profit to Net Sales* affords protection against losses in the event of increased price competition or a general decline in demand. As a causal ratio, it also increases return on equity and tends to reduce financial leverage (depending on management policy with respect to retention of earnings).
2. *Manage total assets carefully in relation to sales volume.* High *Net Sales to Total Assets* tends to reduce costs associated with asset management (bad debts, inventory handling costs, inventory writedowns, depreciation, insurance, property taxes, and interest expense). As a causal ratio, it also reduces financial leverage and/or increases return on equity.
3. *Collect accounts receivable at least as rapidly as competitors—unless there is profitable advantage in extending special terms.* Low (short) *Collection Period of Accounts Receivable* tends to reduce bad debts, collection costs, and interest expense. As a causal ratio, it also strengthens

working capital balance, reduces financial leverage, and/or increases return on equity.

4. *Hold inventory to the same or lower level (in relation to cost of sales) as competitors—unless there is a profitable advantage in maintaining a greater variety of stock on hand, carrying more raw material, or accepting orders that involve slower throughput (higher work-in-process).* High *Cost of Sales to Inventory* tends to reduce occupancy costs, handling costs, inventory writedowns, insurance, local and state taxes (in some jurisdictions), and interest expense. As a causal ratio, it also strengthens working capital balance, reduces financial leverage, and/or increases return on equity.

5. *Achieve a comparatively high level of net sales in relation to fixed assets—unless there is a profitable advantage in greater modernization, automation, a prestige location, or an unusual array of mechanical capabilities.* High *Net Sales to Fixed Assets* tends to reduce depreciation, occupancy costs, insurance, property taxes, and interest expense. As a causal ratio, it also strengthens working capital sufficiency and balance, reduces financial leverage, and/or increases return on equity.

6. *Maintain an adequate level of net worth (owners' equity) to support sales volume.* Low *Net Sales to Net Worth* tends to reduce interest expense. As a causal ratio, it also reduces financial leverage and tends to strengthen working capital sufficiency and working capital balance (depending on management policy with respect to accounts receivable and inventory versus fixed assets). On the other hand, low *Net Sales to Net Worth* tends to reduce return on equity.

7. *Finance fixed assets and other noncurrent assets with long-term liabilities.* High *Long-Term Liabilities to Total Noncurrent Assets* may increase interest expense (depending on the availability of "free" money, such as accounts payable, and on long-term versus short-term interest rates). A high ratio, however, exerts a favorable influence on the secondary ratios by improving working capital sufficiency and strengthening working capital balance.

If all seven causal ratios are equal to their respective industry medians, the nine secondary ratios will also be in line with the industry norms.

Part III

The Nine Secondary Ratios That Measure Effect

We have examined seven of the sixteen ratios upon which total cause-and-effect analysis is based. Having developed familiarity with the seven causal measures and having acquired some facility in computing and applying them, you are now ready to explore the nine secondary, or resultant, ratios. Of course, no skill can be mastered on the first performance, but thoughtful handling of practice cases—real or hypothetical—will refine techniques and clarify the significance of all the ratios.

By studying the nine secondary ratios, you will gain a clear comprehension of *cause and effect*, the most important concept in the effective use of ratio analysis. An understanding of the cause-and-effect element allows you to examine any financial statement and, within minutes, pinpoint the precise nature of any lack of balance reflected in that statement. Ignorance of cause and effect will leave you jousting with windmills, concentrating on entirely incidental factors.

One important aspect of financial management is represented by each of the nine secondary ratios. By definition, these measures are not as influential as the seven causal ratios, but they are entirely necessary for gaining a sound understanding of a company's basic financial structure. Improvement in operating performance and financial structure can only be achieved through changes in the seven causal ratios, but the extent of that improvement is measured by the nine secondary ratios. In fact, certain of the secondary measures—particularly *Current Assets to Current Liabilities*, *Total Liabilities to Net Worth*, and *Net Profit to Net Worth*—are among the first ratios examined by credit grantors and investors because they serve as highly convenient summaries of a company's competitive strengths and weaknesses. The interest of outside analysts in the secondary ratios is, in itself, good reason for management to become familiar with these key financial measures.

In Part III, we examine the nine ratios that measure effect:

1. *Net Profit to Net Worth*
2. *Total Liabilities to Net Worth*
3. *Current Liabilities to Net Worth*
4. *Net Sales to Working Capital*
5. *Current Assets to Current Liabilities*
6. *Cash and Short-Term Investments plus Accounts Receivable to Current Liabilities* (the *Quick Ratio*)
7. *Total Noncurrent Assets to Net Worth*

8. *Long-Term Liabilities to Working Capital*
9. *Net Profit to Total Assets*

Each of these secondary ratios is explained and illustrated by reference to our friends, Companies A, B, C, and D. In addition, the examples trace the influence of the seven causal ratios on each secondary measure.

Chapter 12

Net Profit to Net Worth

Net Profit to Net Worth (also known as the *Return on Equity Ratio*) measures the percentage of profit produced on owners' equity, the reward for assumption of ownership risk. An individual will seldom volunteer to face the perils that are involved with the operation of his own business unless he has reason to believe that his daring and his efforts will provide him with an adequate, and continuing, reward. He expects, in time, to earn superior personal compensation and a reasonable profit on his financial stake—both his original investment and the earnings that have been retained in the company. Moreover, no business can provide for future growth without supplementing net worth through income from operations. Nor can a company attract additional investment, if required to support rapid sales expansion, without a substantial return on present and past investments or at least the prospect of future profit attainment.

These considerations must, however, be conditioned by the recognition that *Net Profit to Net Worth* is a secondary measure of both net profit and net worth. You must be alert to the fact that when a company's capital account is abnormally low, even a substandard return on sales dollars (as measured by *Net Profit to Net Sales*) will appear as a sensational return on owners' equity and create a very misleading impression of success.

Net Profit to Net Worth is computed by dividing a company's net profit by its net worth and then multiplying the result by 100 or pressing the % key on a calculator. A profit of $30,000 on net worth of $150,000 produces a ratio of 20.0%. The same $30,000 profit on net worth of $250,000 would yield *Net Profit to Net Worth* of 12.0%. Industry statistics published for the benefit of bank loan officers and other credit grantors often subtract intangible assets from net worth—in order to obtain tangible net worth—before computing this ratio. Most financial management reports prepared under the sponsorship of national trade associations, however, use the book value of owners' equity (net worth) as the denominator without adjustment.

As we saw in our study of the causal ratio *Net Profit to Net Sales*, profit can be expressed in many forms: profit from operations (before income taxes and nonoperating items), profit before income taxes, profit after income taxes, and profit before income taxes and owners' compensation, among others. From an outside investor's viewpoint, after-tax profit as a percentage of net worth is the most relevant measure of return on owners' equity. As a practical matter, an investor will receive an actual return—directly through dividends or indirectly through earnings retained in the company—only after taxes have been paid. Nevertheless, for comparative purposes, pre-tax *Net Profit to Net Worth* is ordinarily used to measure a company's fundamental return on equity, because of the special (and frequently temporary) circumstances that can affect the current year's tax liability of a small company.

Another, often more important consideration in selecting the best measure of return on equity is the fact that owners often recover a portion of their investment of time and money in the business through salaries and bonuses that reduce net profit. Consequently, owners generally look at pre-tax return on equity as one key basis for determining whether additional compensation may be appropriate. The outside analyst will gain additional insight into the company's true profitability—particularly in comparison with the return earned by other firms in the industry—by adding back officers'/owners' compensation to net profit and dividing the sum by net worth. A reasonable industry standard can be calculated by multiplying pre-tax *Net Profit to Net Worth* by an adjustment factor (the sum of pre-tax net profit plus officers'/owners' compensation divided by pre-tax net profit).

Ability to Support Sales Growth

In analyzing a small or mid-size company, *Net Profit to Net Worth* is most valuable as an indication of ability to support sales growth. As sales volume expands, total assets will ordinarily increase in approximately the same proportion as sales. If sales volume doubles, accounts receivable will necessarily double unless customer accounts are collected more rapidly than before. In actual business practice, receivables often grow at a faster rate than sales, since slower-paying accounts may be added during times of expansion. Rapid sales growth, which is often accompanied by inefficient inventory management, can cause work-in-process and stock on hand to build up more rapidly than the increase in sales. Through the combined effects of depreciation and inflation (which reduce the book value of older assets and increase the cost of current acquisitions), a small expansion of total physical capacity may result in a significant rise in the book value of fixed assets. Greater total assets will require a proportionate increase in net worth to avoid a rise in financial leverage—*Total Liabilities to Net Worth*. In fact, unless net worth is increased at a rate equal to or greater than the growth of net sales, total debt will rise at an even faster pace, causing a rapid build-up of pressure from creditors. This increase in net worth would ordinarily be expected to come from retained earnings. Therefore, return on equity—*Net Profit to Net Worth*—is directly related to a company's ability to support sales growth without increasing debt at a faster rate than owners' equity.

In the analysis of stock of publicly traded corporations, *Net Profit to Net Worth* is often included as a key measure of company performance. For small privately held companies, however, the profit reported for tax purposes is strongly influenced by the compensation of owners. This compensation is, of course, determined by the owners themselves, often in an essentially arbitrary manner. A rise in cash on hand, personal tax considerations, or the individual requirements of owners may cause compensation to be significantly increased or decreased, thus affecting the company's net profit. In fact, tax considerations cause most business owners to obtain both their compensation for personal work and their return on investment in the company in the form of salaries, bonuses, and fringe benefits—instead of retained earnings and dividends—whenever possible. Consequently, *Net Profit to Net Worth* (after subtracting owners'/officers' compensation) is usually a poor measure of actual shareholders' return on equity.

When profit has been realized after paying the company's executives their base salary and when the company's cash position is adequate, bonuses are normally granted to shareholders active in the company. Dividends may also be distributed to all shareholders, including outside investors and family members with no role in day-to-day management. Prudence is important in this regard, since the retention of earnings determines the rate at which sales can be comfortably expanded. Future growth, supported by today's retained earnings, may well produce a return to shareholders far greater than any current distribution.

A Test of Net Worth

Net Profit to Net Worth serves to test net worth as well as profit. An abnormally high ratio may very well indicate an inadequate profit coupled with even more inadequate net worth. This aspect of *Net Profit to Net Worth* is often ignored by those who think in terms of the typical well-capitalized company listed on a stock exchange. Many small and mid-size companies, however, have a very low level of owners' equity in relation to net sales, some because of inadequate initial capitalization, others because of extremely rapid sales growth, which has outstripped retained earnings; and still others because of the erosion of owners' equity through operating losses or asset writedowns. During the 1980s, a significant number of publicly traded companies also entered the ranks of low equity-to-sales firms (reflected in high *Net Sales to Net Worth* and high *Total Liabilities to Net Worth*), primarily as a result of leveraged buy-outs. Poorly capitalized companies, small and large, are able to show a spectacular *Net Profit to Net Worth* through a modest *Net Profit to Net Sales*. Adverse developments in company operations, interest rates, or general economic conditions can, however, easily turn a very high profit on net worth into a loss that wipes out owners' equity in a short time.

Let us now return to Companies A, B, C, and D for comparative analysis of *Net Profit to Net Worth*. Table 12-1 shows that Company A has once again achieved a relatively favorable result. Based on our knowledge of this company's consistently outstanding financial position, as shown by the causal ratios summa-

Table 12-1. *Net Profit to Net Worth* **for four companies.**

	Company A	Company B	Company C	Company D
Net profit	$ 76,000	$150,000	$ 150,000	$ 950,000
Net worth	254,000	750,000	1,540,000	1,550,000
Net Profit to Net Worth				
Company	29.9%	20.0%	9.7%	61.3%
Industry standard	21.6%	21.6%	21.6%	21.6%
Causal factors				
Net Profit to Net Sales				
Company	5.1%	3.0%	1.2%	1.9%
Industry standard	3.2%	3.2%	3.2%	3.2%
Net Sales to Net Worth				
Company	5.9 times	6.7 times	8.1 times	32.3 times
Industry standard	6.8 times	6.8 times	6.8 times	6.8 times

rized in Chapter 11, we would expect each secondary measure to reflect the positive influence of those primary relationships. From a conservative viewpoint, Company A's comparatively high *Net Profit to Net Worth* was attained in the most favorable manner: high *Net Profit to Net Sales* coupled with low *Net Sales to Net Worth*, which indicated relatively high investment adequacy. Low *Net Sales to Net Worth* tends to reduce debt pressure on the company, but it also has the effect of depressing *Net Profit to Net Worth*. Company A's comparatively high *Net Profit to Net Sales* more than compensated for the influence of its conservative *Net Sales to Net Worth*.

Company B once again reported a ratio similar to the industry standard. *Net Profit to Net Sales* and *Net Sales to Net Worth* were both close to the comparison group norm, producing *Net Profit to Net Worth* in line with the group median. Company C, however, reported an unfavorable *Net Profit to Net Worth*. The company's relatively low *Net Profit to Net Sales* was entirely responsible for its low *Net Profit to Net Worth*. The other causal factor, *Net Sales to Net Worth*, was actually comparatively high, tending to increase Company C's *Net Profit to Net Worth*. Because of the company's low profit percentage in relation to net sales, Company C shows a comparatively unfavorable position in all three respects, with low *Net Profit to Net Worth*, low *Net Profit to Net Sales*, and high *Net Sales to Net Worth* (indicating low investment adequacy).

Company D demonstrates the achievement of remarkably high *Net Profit to Net Worth*, strictly as a result of undercapitalization. Company D's *Net Profit to Net Sales*, at 1.9%, was actually very low in relation to the industry standard. In fact, the company's *Net Profit to Net Sales* ratio was not much above that of Company C. Nevertheless, Company D's extremely high *Net Sales to Net Worth*—showing a very low level of owners' equity to support sales volume—propelled its *Net Profit to Net Worth* to a rarefied 61.3%. It should now be obvious that the underlying reasons for any reported return on equity, particularly an unusually high number, should always be carefully analyzed.

Even for companies that once maintained a highly conservative structure, the concept of aggressive financial leverage—using liabilities, instead of owners' equity, to support the largest portion of the company's asset base—has become an increasingly popular concept in recent years. As a result, an ever greater number of publicly traded corporations now report a *Net Profit to Net Worth* that conforms to the expectations of investors even while generating a lackluster *Net Profit to Net Sales*. Through the multiplier effect of higher *Net Sales to Net Worth*, which results from substituting debt for equity, *Net Profit to Net Worth* can be maintained or even increased at the same time that *Net Profit to Net Sales* is in moderate decline. On the other hand, more rapid reductions in *Net Profit to Net Sales*, especially as a result of rising interest rates, would also become magnified by the rise in *Net Sales to Net Worth*. Unless the national economy becomes more stable than ever before, *Net Profit to Net Worth* may begin to show increasingly great swings between ebullient earnings and staggering losses.

Summary: Net Profit to Net Worth

Popular name	*Return on Equity*
Purpose	Measures a company's ability to produce profit on owners' investment (original investment plus retained earnings) and to increase net worth for future sales growth.
Calculation	Divide net profit by net worth, then multiply result by 100, converting ratio to a percentage.
Example	Your company's net profit was $30,000 for the year, and your net worth was $150,000 at year-end. What was your *Net Profit to Net Worth*?
	Solution: 30,000 ÷ 150,000 = .200; then .200 × 100 = 20.0%
Financial impact	A *high* ratio is a *favorable* result: It shows a comparatively high rate of return on owners' equity, which, in turn, tends to decrease financial leverage. However, a high ratio may be a symptom of low investment adequacy.
Operational impact	A *high* ratio tends to reduce interest cost over time; however, a high ratio may occur when both total debt and interest cost are on the high side.
Definitions	Net profit *before taxes* is ordinarily used by bankers and other credit grantors as the basis for measuring comparative profitability (versus previous performance or exter-

nal standards). Net profit *after taxes* is the true "bottom line," but the effect of state and local income taxes, as well as federal income tax credits and carrybacks, can distort comparative performance. Net profit *from operations* (before nonoperating income, nonoperating expense, and extraordinary items) and net profit *before officers'/owners' compensation* are also useful measures.

Net worth—called "owner's equity" in a sole proprietorship (IRS Schedule C), "partners' capital" in a partnership (IRS Form 1065), "stockholders' equity" or "shareholders' equity" in a corporation (IRS Form 1120, 1120-A, or 1120S)—equals total assets minus total liabilities.

Special reminders   Net profit is expressed as a percentage, not as a simple ratio relative to net worth.

Net worth is stated at book value, not market value, which is often significantly higher. Consequently, *Net Profit to Net Worth* at actual market value may be substantially lower than *Net Profit to Net Worth* at book value.

Critical values   A *negative* percentage, which shows a net loss for the period, tends to increase *financial leverage*. When total liabilities are greater than total assets, net worth will be in a deficit position and a meaningful ratio cannot be calculated. In such a case, treat *Net Profit to Net Worth* as a very large number for comparative purposes. Deficit net worth is a serious condition that warrants close management attention.

Range of common experience   15.2% to 21.3% (before income taxes).

Chapter 13

Total Liabilities to Net Worth

The operating freedom of every company is conditioned by the relative stake creditors have in the business in contrast with the investment of the owners. The company with comparatively low *Total Liabilities to Net Worth*—which denotes a strong ownership position in proportion to the liabilities that have been incurred by the business—enjoys relative freedom from creditors' demands for repayment of debts or lenders' attempts to impose their interests on the company's management decisions. Conversely, if this ratio is higher than the industry norm, management must be more apprehensive and may be compelled by creditors (or by management's assumption of creditor attitudes) to take courses of action that would rob the company of valuable initiative and innovation.

Total Liabilities to Net Worth (also known as the *Financial Leverage Ratio* or the *Debt-to-Equity Ratio*) is computed by dividing total liabilities by net worth. A company with total liabilities of $250,000 and net worth of $150,000 has a *Total Liabilities to Net Worth* ratio of 1.67, rounded to 1.7. If that same company should increase its total assets from $400,000 (supported by $250,000 in total liabilities and $150,000 in net worth) to $450,000 while holding net worth constant, the ratio *Total Liabilities to Net Worth* would rise to 2.0 ($300,000 in total liabilities divided by $150,000 in net worth).

Because the typical value for *Total Liabilities to Net Worth* ranges rather widely from one industry to another, no universal "rule of thumb" can be used with any degree of confidence. As emphasized throughout this book, you must locate an appropriate standard (preferably including the range of common experience as well as the median) for the particular line of business in which a company operates before attempting to assess its competitive strength or weakness. Bank credit officers frequently refer to the *RMA Annual Statement Studies*, published by Robert Morris Associates, the national association of bank loan and credit officers, to obtain comparative industry values for *Total Liabilities to Net Worth* and the other key financial measures. This multi-industry data source is described, together with other published reports containing comparative norms, in Chapter 35. Regardless of the industry standards used, bankers and other creditors become concerned when *Total Liabilities to Net Worth* is substantially above the norm for the company's line of business. As lenders of other people's money placed in their care by depositors and shareholders, creditors are understandably concerned about the margin of safety they enjoy in the worst case—

liquidation. When owners have only a comparatively small stake in the enterprise, creditors are more vulnerable to bad-debt losses, inventory writedowns, and losses on the sale of fixed assets. In fact, when the owners' equity represents an unusually small amount relative to the interests of creditors, management initiative may be diminished by creditor pressure, or management judgment may be impaired by a sense of urgency to "hit the lottery," resulting in imprudent moves as the company attempts to throw off the shackles of indebtedness.

Wider Variances in Secondary Ratios

To gain a better understanding of *Total Liabilities to Net Worth*, we turn to selected dollar figures and financial ratios for Companies A, B, C, and D, which show considerable difference with respect to the proportion of debt to owners' equity. Key financial data for all four companies are displayed in Table 13-1. In many of our previous examples, the variances of these businesses from the industry standard appeared to be rather subtle distinctions. *Net Sales to Net Worth* of 2.8 versus the 2.4 industry standard does not, at first, seem all that important. Now, however, the accumulated differences in the causal ratios begin to appear with full force in the secondary, or effect, ratios.

Company A's comparatively low *Total Liabilities to Net Worth* provides considerable latitude for management in making business plans. In fact, Company A could begin a rapid sales expansion that would double outstanding debt (to support larger facilities, more inventory, and a higher level of accounts receivable) almost overnight—and still remain within an acceptable range for *Total Liabilities to Net Worth* in this industry. Company B is, as usual, in a comfortable position near the middle of its peers. This company does not enjoy any special advantages,

Table 13-1. *Total Liabilities to Net Worth* **for four companies.**

	Company A	Company B	Company C	Company D
Total liabilities	$282,000	$1,250,000	$5,110,000	$9,850,000
Net worth	254,000	750,000	1,540,000	1,550,000
Total Liabilities to Net Worth				
Company	1.1 times	1.7 times	3.3 times	6.4 times
Industry standard	1.8 times	1.8 times	1.8 times	1.8 times
Causal factors				
Net Sales to Total Assets				
Company	2.8 times	2.5 times	1.9 times	4.4 times
Industry standard	2.4 times	2.4 times	2.4 times	2.4 times
Net Sales to Net Worth				
Company	5.9 times	6.7 times	8.1 times	32.3 times
Industry standard	6.8 times	6.8 times	6.8 times	6.8 times

but it is able to compete on the fundamental basis of product, service, and management skill—the very reason for its existence in the eyes of most business owners—without nagging concerns about debt.

Companies C and D, however, face creditor pressure at all times, as evidenced by their comparatively high readings for *Total Liabilities to Net Worth*: 3.3 and 6.4, respectively. In the case of Company C, both of the causal ratios, *Net Sales to Total Assets* and *Net Sales to Net Worth*, were unfavorable from a conservative point of view. Actually, neither of these primary measures looks terribly out of line at first glance (1.9 versus 2.4 and 8.1 versus 6.8), but together they have driven Company C's *Total Liabilities to Net Worth* to nearly twice that of its typical competitor.

Company D's situation is simply a case of undercapitalization or substandard investment adequacy. While the typical business in Company D's comparison group is conducting $6.80 in net sales on every dollar of owners' equity (net worth), Company D is attempting to support $32.30 in net sales. Even while achieving a remarkable level of asset utilization—*Net Sales to Total Assets* of 4.4 versus 2.4 for the industry standard—Company D finds itself deeply in debt. When one causal ratio is exceedingly weak, even a heroic effort in other causal areas cannot always right the balance.

Pressure of Debt

Debt pressure or the fear of pressure may cause management to forgo profitable growth opportunities and even defer spending in basic areas (such as maintenance, modernization, and training) that are critical to long-term competitiveness and survival. A business under creditor pressure is much like a poker player going into a sky's-the-limit game with only $50 or $100 in his pocket. For fear of losing his limited capital and facing his wife's recriminations if he returns home with empty pockets, he folds his cards on many a winning hand. His wealthier competitors can easily run bluffs on him because they lack his trepidation. Timing is all-important in the development and implementation of major business decisions, and a certain amount of imagination and daring is also helpful. If the owners know that certain actions are beyond their reach, or are fearful that creditors may effectively veto management's plans by withholding further credit or accelerating demands for payment, owners and officers can easily lose both their drive and their vision.

In our present example, Company A has initiative in its grasp, for, as a practical matter, it is under little or no obligation to anyone other than the owners. Total liabilities exceed owners' equity, as is the case in most lines of business activity today, but Company A's comparatively low *Total Liabilities to Net Worth* indicates that trade credit and bank financing are readily available. Conversely, Company D's freedom of action is undoubtedly limited, subject to the concurrence of a variety of creditors whose views of any planned management gambit might necessarily be influenced by the element of risk rather than by potential profit. A negative opinion, or even the thought of being turned down by their banker or a major supplier, might well deflate the ambitions of the officers of Company D. Management can ill afford a negative or frightened frame of mind.

The ability of the debt-heavy company to exist and function is often limited by the extent of grace given it by understanding and lenient creditors whose satisfaction is highly contingent upon uninterrupted production, sales, and collections. Heavy indebtedness is often a characteristic of overtrading, as in the case of Company D: The ability to survive the pressures that accompany this situation is dependent on prolonged optimum operating conditions. If, however, an unexpected difficulty should arise, few resources could be called upon to support the company. A strike at a customer's plant may suddenly occur, shutting down orders from an important source of cash. Worse yet, a major customer may go bankrupt. Plant and inventory will lie idle, but suppliers' bills will continue to come due, and the heavily extended company with a minimal working capital cushion and already restless creditors to satisfy may collapse under the strain. Even retailers with walk-in business may suddenly feel the impact of the unexpected, such as construction of new sewers and sidewalks along the entire block, or a six-month shutdown of a nearby parking garage for repair and expansion.

Financial Leverage

Financial publications today carry numerous stories about creative financial leverage: the practice of using debt to attain higher return on equity, fend off a hostile takeover, or achieve some other objective of professional managers, investors, or greenmail artists. These articles often suggest that *Total Liabilities to Net Worth* is actually a causal factor, an element of business strategy to be consciously manipulated. In reality, this ratio largely reflects fundamental financial factors represented by the causal ratios. To a certain extent, these stories regarding the maneuverings of publicly traded corporations correctly show that publicly traded corporations often have considerable latitude in designing their financial leverage. On the other hand, the reports often ignore basic operating realities, particularly the asset utilization factors that directly influence financial leverage even before other management moves can be considered. Both inadequate asset management (low *Net Sales to Total Assets*) and operating losses (negative *Net Profit to Net Sales*) have the effect of increasing *Total Liabilities to Net Worth*, regardless of other management intentions concerning financial leverage. Unusually high *Total Liabilities to Net Worth* is not necessarily more desirable or less burdensome, because it can be traced to purposeful manipulation instead of uncontrolled causes.

For relatively small, privately held companies, however, financial leverage—represented by *Total Liabilities to Net Worth*—is almost always the *result* of sales growth, profit performance, asset management, and available equity. Creative financial leverage is seldom the issue. The essential problem facing management in a small company is frequently quite the opposite: how to manage assets and retain sufficient earnings to support sales growth, to increase net profit dollars (and personal compensation) while staying out of trouble with creditors. In the real world of small and mid-size business, financial leverage results from the interaction of three ratios: *Net Sales to Total Assets* and *Net Sales to Net Worth*, which are the immediate causal factors, and *Net Profit to Net Sales*, which plays a major role in determining the growth of owners' equity.

Total Liabilities to Net Worth represents the fact that other people's money can be obtained to supplement owners' equity in conducting business. Provided that those funds are either interest free (as in the case of trade credit) or, in the aggregate, carry an interest rate less than the company's pre-interest return on assets, using those funds will enable owners to increase the rate of return on their investment in the company. Of course, borrowed funds—whether interest-free trade credit or advances from a bank—add an element of risk, since they have to be paid back.

As noted briefly in Chapter 9, *Net Sales to Net Worth* is, in some respects, the best measure of financial leverage because that primary ratio represents the direct multiplier of *Net Profit to Net Sales*, which results in *Net Profit to Net Worth*. Why, then, has *Total Liabilities to Net Worth* become the most widely recognized measure of financial leverage? This secondary ratio has been popularized primarily by lenders, who are particularly concerned with the "cushion" provided by net worth in relation to a company's outstanding liabilities. It is well suited to that purpose, but it does not directly show the return-on-equity multiplier effect. High *Total Liabilities to Net Worth* may simply indicate poor asset management, an excessive accumulation of assets that require support from creditors. In this case, the comparatively high ratio, which presumably shows financial leverage, does nothing to improve the percentage of profit on owners' equity. Only an increase in *Net Sales to Net Worth* will translate directly into a higher *Net Profit to Net Worth*. Nevertheless, *Total Liabilities to Net Worth* is generally regarded as the *Financial Leverage Ratio*.

Interest Expense

High *Total Liabilities to Net Worth* does not necessarily result in high interest cost as a percentage of net sales. Some companies are better able to obtain extended terms, either formally or by means of unchallenged late payments, from their suppliers, particularly if they are comparatively large customers (by virtue of actual size or concentration of orders with one company). In many cases, suppliers are able to recover the cost of extended terms through subtle price increases or other charges. Nevertheless, interest cost, as such, will not reflect these expenses. Consequently, a company with high *Total Liabilities to Net Worth* may actually show interest cost as a low to moderate percentage of net sales.

There is a second, often more important, reason why a company that reports *Total Liabilities to Net Worth* above the norm may not exhibit a high level of interest expense in relation to net sales. Efficient asset utilization, demonstrated by comparatively high *Net Sales to Total Assets*, reduces the need for both total liabilities and net worth to support total assets. If $500,000 in total assets is typically required to support net sales of $1 million, and a company can conduct the same level of sales with only $400,000 in assets, then that company can operate with $100,000 less in total liabilities and net worth combined. Even if management had diverted all of the $100,000 difference (from lowering total assets) into personal compensation, the company's total liabilities would be no greater than those of the typical concern. Assuming that net worth had been reduced by the $100,000 decrease in total assets, *Total Liabilities to Net Worth* would be significantly higher than the industry standard—and may have become astronomically high by any standard, depending on the original *Total Liabilities to Net Worth*. Nevertheless, total liabilities and interest expense would have remained moderate, as a proportion of net sales, in comparison with the industry norm for companies of similar size. Since total liabilities would be no higher than the typical proportion of net sales, interest expense would also remain moderate, despite higher *Total Liabilities to Net Worth*.

Summary: Total Liabilities to Net Worth

Popular names	*Financial Leverage Ratio; Debt-to-Equity Ratio; Debt-to-Worth Ratio*
Purpose	Measures a company's funds from creditors (suppliers, banks, and other lenders) against the investment of owners (original investment plus retained earnings); indicates the pressure of total debt (current and long-term) relative to equity.
Calculation	Divide total liabilities by net worth.
Example	Your company's total liabilities were $250,000, and your net worth was $150,000 at year-end. What was your *Total Liabilities to Net Worth?*
	Solution: $250,000 \div 150,000 = 1.7$
Financial impact	A *low* ratio is a *favorable* condition from a conservative perspective: It shows comparatively little dependence on outside sources in relation to owners' equity. However, a low ratio may be unfavorable in another respect: It may be related to a low return on equity.
Operational impact	A *low* ratio tends to reduce interest cost and lower the probability of disadvantageous changes in credit terms or interference in management prerogatives by creditors.

Definition

Net worth—called "owner's equity" in a sole proprietorship (IRS Schedule C), "partners' capital" in a partnership (IRS Form 1065), "stockholders' equity" or "shareholders' equity" in a corporation (IRS Form 1120, 1120-A, or 1120S)—equals total assets minus total liabilities.

Critical value

When total liabilities are greater than total assets, net worth will be in a deficit position and a meaningful ratio cannot be calculated. In such a case, treat *Total Liabilities to Net Worth* as a very large number for comparative purposes. Deficit net worth is a serious condition that warrants close management attention.

Range of common experience

1.4 times to 2.1 times.

Chapter 14

Current Liabilities to Net Worth

Current Liabilities to Net Worth shows the stake of short-term creditors (suppliers, banks, and others to whom money is due within one year) versus the amount of investment by owners. This ratio measures the pressure of current liabilities, including the portion of long-term debt payable within the next 12 months, relative to owners' equity (net worth).

Dividing the dollar amount of current liabilities by the amount of net worth on the balance sheet will produce *Current Liabilities to Net Worth*. For Company B in Table 14-1, current liabilities of $1 million divided by net worth of $750,000 yields a ratio of 1.3.

Because of its early maturity, a preponderance of debt due within 12 months or less carries with it more immediate danger to the company's operating freedom. In fact, some current debt may have been due yesterday. From the time standpoint, *Current Liabilities to Net Worth* obviously represents more pressing obligations than does *Total Liabilities to Net Worth*. On the other hand, long-term debt has its own demand on management attention since it is, in most cases, exactly fixed as to maturity and may involve certain stated requirements with respect to the company's financial condition. Moreover, the repayment of long-term obligations is usually more enforceable because it is ordinarily backed by the pledge of specific collateral.

A company with relatively high *Total Liabilities to Net Worth* is likely to have comparatively high *Current Liabilities to Net Worth* as well. This relationship, however, may be altered by differences in fixed asset activity (and, in some cases, the level of miscellaneous assets) relative to the management of current assets, as well as the arrangements made with respect to long-term financing of noncurrent assets. A company with substantial physical facilities in relation to the sales volume it generates (shown by comparatively low *Net Sales to Fixed Assets*) may be able to maintain relatively low *Current Liabilities to Net Worth*, if the company arranges to finance a comparatively high proportion of those fixed assets on a long-term basis. Other firms compensate for the acquisition of fixed assets by reducing current assets and also show a comparatively low level of current debt in relation to owners' equity. Of course, if a company uses long-term debt to fund only a relatively small amount of its fixed assets (resulting in

Table 14-1. *Current Liabilities to Net Worth* **for four companies.**

	Company A	Company B	Company C	Company D
Current liabilities	$220,000	$1,000,000	$3,780,000	$5,400,000
Net worth	254,000	750,000	1,540,000	1,550,000
Current Liabilities to Net Worth				
Company	0.9 times	1.3 times	2.5 times	3.5 times
Industry standard	1.4 times	1.4 times	1.4 times	1.4 times
*Causal factors**				
Total Liabilities to Net Worth				
Company	1.1 times	1.7 times	3.3 times	6.4 times
Industry standard	1.8 times	1.8 times	1.8 times	1.8 times
Total Noncurrent Assets to Net Worth				
Company	0.5 times	0.7 times	1.2 times	1.9 times
Industry standard	0.7 times	0.7 times	0.7 times	0.7 times
Long-Term Liabilities to Total Noncurrent Assets				
Company	0.4 times	0.5 times	0.7 times	1.5 times
Industry standard	0.5 times	0.5 times	0.5 times	0.5 times

*At the most fundamental level, causal factors include the influences on *Total Liabilities to Net Worth* (*Net Sales to Total Assets* and *Net Sales to Net Worth*) and on *Total Noncurrent Assets to Net Worth* (*Net Sales to Fixed Assets, Days' Sales in Miscellaneous,* and *Net Sales to Net Worth*).

comparatively low *Long-Term Liabilities to Total Noncurrent Assets*), its *Current Liabilities to Net Worth* may be unusually high, even if its *Total Liabilities to Net Worth* is moderate.

Looking at Table 14-1, we find that Company A has maintained its usual conservative position by holding *Current Liabilities to Net Worth* to a comparatively low level. If Company A's reduction of current liabilities is the result of holding down interest-bearing debt (for example, by maintaining accounts payable at a constant level while reducing short-term bank credit), this strategy may be largely beneficial from a conservative standpoint. Likewise, the company may be taking prompt-payment discounts, which also has the effect of reducing current liabilities, thereby bolstering *Net Profit to Net Sales*. On the other hand, Company A may not be making full use of trade credit, which carries no interest expense. Unless the organization is gaining identifiable financial or service benefits from suppliers by paying its bills earlier than required (or expected), Company A's owners will receive a lower rate of return on their equity when trade credit is not used to its fullest.

Company B's *Current Liabilities to Net Worth* is similar to the group median, while Companies C and D show current debt decidedly higher than the industry standard in proportion to net worth. Without a comparatively high level of long-term debt, which has the effect of reducing *Current Liabilities to Net Worth,*

Company C would be under strong pressure from current creditors. To hold down current liabilities, the business has obtained more long-term debt per dollar of noncurrent assets than has the typical company in its comparison group. In addition, Company C's long-term debt is based on a very high level of noncurrent assets relative to net worth. Even with this heavy reliance on long-term financing, Company C has relatively high *Current Liabilities to Net Worth*, showing implied if not formal restrictions on operating freedom. Company D, as we learned earlier, is carrying an extremely heavy debt load, both current and long-term, as the result of a leveraged buy-out. There is no doubt that its management actions are under continuing scrutiny by short-term creditors. Although Company D's *Current Liabilities to Net Worth* is very high indeed, it is comparatively less disadvantageous than *Total Liabilities to Net Worth* because of the special circumstances that allowed for an extraordinary level of long-term debt.

Summary: Current Liabilities to Net Worth

Popular names	*Current-Debt-to-Equity Ratio*; *Current-Debt-to-Worth Ratio*
Purpose	Measures a company's funds from short-term creditors (ordinarily trade suppliers and banks) plus the current portion of long-term debt in relation to the investment of owners (original investment plus retained earnings); indicates the pressure of current debt relative to equity.
Calculation	Divide current liabilities by net worth.
Example	Your company's current liabilities were $200,000, and your net worth was $150,000 at year-end. What was your *Current Liabilities to Net Worth*?
	Solution: $200,000 \div 150,000 = 1.3$
Financial impact	A *low* ratio is a *favorable* condition from a conservative perspective: It shows comparatively little dependence on short-term obligations in relation to owners' equity. However, a low ratio may be unfavorable in another respect: It may be related to a low return on equity.
Operational impact	A *low* ratio tends to reduce interest cost and lower the probability of disadvantageous changes in credit terms or interference in management prerogatives by creditors.
Definition	Net worth—called "owner's equity" in a sole proprietorship (IRS Schedule C), "partners' capital" in a partnership (IRS Form 1065), "stockholders' equity" or "shareholders' equity" in a corporation (IRS Form 1120, 1120-A, or 1120S)—equals total assets minus total liabilities.

Critical value

When total liabilities are *greater* than total assets, net worth will be in a deficit position and a meaningful ratio cannot be calculated. In such a case, treat *Current Liabilities to Net Worth* as a very large number for comparative purposes. Deficit net worth is a serious condition that warrants close management attention.

Range of common experience

Insufficient industry data.

Chapter 15

Net Sales to Working Capital

Net Sales to Working Capital indicates the demands made upon working capital in supporting the sales volume of a business concern. The principle that a company's net sales volume requires a certain amount of working capital is sound. The higher the level of net sales in relation to available working capital, the greater the strain a company encounters in satisfying trade and bank creditors while meeting payroll, taxes, and other regular obligations. In cases where this ratio appears disproportionately high, it serves to point out working capital deficiencies in dramatic fashion.

Working capital is found by subtracting current liabilities from current assets. Then the amount of net sales is simply divided by working capital to derive *Net Sales to Working Capital*, which is expressed in "times." In Table 15-1 (shown later in the chapter), Company B, reporting $5 million in net sales during the year, together with current assets of $1,500,000 and current liabilities of $1 million at year-end, has a ratio of 10.0 times: 5 million divided by the difference between 1,500,000 and 1 million.

High Ratio as Indication of Low Working Capital

The calculation of this ratio requires a special reminder. As we noted earlier, ratios that involve both the income statement and the balance sheet traditionally use the income statement item—in this case, net sales—as the numerator, which is then divided by the balance sheet item. This type of calculation can cause some confusion when the analysis is primarily focused on the balance sheet item (working capital). For *Net Sales to Working Capital*, a *high* ratio means that the amount of working capital available to support net sales is relatively *low*. As this ratio declines, it demonstrates that working capital is being strengthened in relation to net sales.

When *Net Sales to Working Capital* (also known as the *Working Capital Sufficiency Ratio*) is high—indicating a small amount of working capital to support net sales—a company is more vulnerable to cash shortages in the event of a temporary sales slowdown, a delay in customer payments, or an unexpected change in suppliers' credit terms. A company with comparatively thin working capital must manage its cash flow with greater precision than its competitors—and hope to avoid unpleasant surprises.

On the other hand, very low *Net Sales to Working Capital* suggests that the company is pursuing an unnecessarily conservative strategy. An unusually high level of working capital in relation to net sales provides a high degree of operating freedom and a strong base for sales expansion, but it also indicates that long-term debt or owners' equity may be greater than needed to maintain the company's sales volume. If, however, current assets, particularly accounts receivable and inventory, are high in relation to net sales, relatively low *Net Sales to Working Capital* will be needed to maintain proper balance between current assets and current liabilities.

Value Determined by Four Causal Factors

Net Sales to Working Capital exerts an influence on *Current Assets to Current Liabilities* and the *Quick Ratio (Cash and Short-Term Investments plus Accounts Receivable to Current Liabilities),* which we examine in the following chapters. As a practical matter, however, *Net Sales to Working Capital* is a secondary ratio because its value is determined by three primary ratios: *Net Sales to Net Worth, Net Sales to Fixed Assets,* and *Long-Term Liabilities to Total Noncurrent Assets,* in combination with *Days' Sales in Other Noncurrent (Miscellaneous) Assets,* a causal factor (described in Chapter 8) which occasionally exerts a significant influence on working capital. A low level of owners' equity (net worth) in proportion to net sales—high *Net Sales to Net Worth*—tends to reduce working capital. If owners have only a small investment in the company, that will provide only a small spread between current assets and current liabilities (unless the company incurs a very high level of long-term liabilities in proportion to total noncurrent assets). A high level of fixed assets in proportion to net sales—low *Net Sales to Fixed Assets*—also tends to reduce working capital. If net worth is largely used to acquire fixed assets, that will reduce the spread between current assets and current liabilities. A high level of miscellaneous assets—high *Days' Sales in Other Noncurrent (Miscellaneous) Assets*—will also have the effect of reducing working capital.

The impact of comparatively high commitment to fixed assets and miscellaneous assets can be offset to some degree by long-term borrowing. On the other hand, relatively low *Long-Term Liabilities to Total Noncurrent Assets* will tend to reduce working capital on a comparative basis.

For comparative analysis of the key financial factors that influence *Net Sales to Working Capital*, see Table 15-1, which displays selected figures from Companies A, B, C, and D, all engaged in the same industry. Company A shows a conservative 8.4 *Net Sales to Working Capital* ratio, versus the 10.2 industry standard, as a result of comparatively high owners' equity in relation to sales (relatively low *Net Sales to Net Worth*) and comparatively low commitment to plant and equipment (relatively high *Net Sales to Fixed Assets*). Company B's primary and secondary ratios are all similar to the comparison group norm. Consequently, *Net Sales to Working Capital* is in line with the industry median.

Table 15-1. *Net Sales to Working Capital* **for four companies.**

	Company A	Company B	Company C	Company D
Net sales	$1,500,000	$5,000,000	$12,500,000	$50,000,000
Current assets	398,000	1,500,000	4,740,000	8,400,000
Current liabilities	220,000	1,000,000	3,780,000	5,400,000
Working capital	170,000	500,000	960,000	3,000,000
Net Sales to Working Capital				
Company	8.4 times	10.0 times	13.0 times	16.7 times
Industry standard	10.2 times	10.2 times	10.2 times	10.2 times
Causal factors				
Net Sales to Net Worth				
Company	5.9 times	6.7 times	8.1 times	32.3 times
Industry standard	6.8 times	6.8 times	6.8 times	6.8 times
Net Sales to Fixed Assets				
Company	12.0 times	10.0 times	8.9 times	20.4 times
Industry standard	10.3 times	10.3 times	10.3 times	10.3 times
Days' Sales in Other Noncurrent (Miscellaneous) Assets				
Company	3 days	0 days	15 days	4 days
Industry standard	3 days	3 days	3 days	3 days
Long-Term Liabilities to Total Noncurrent Assets				
Company	0.4 times	0.5 times	0.7 times	1.5 times
Industry standard	0.5 times	0.5 times	0.5 times	0.5 times

For Company C, three of the four causal ratios affecting working capital sufficiency are unfavorable from a conservative point of view. As a result, *Net Sales to Working Capital* is relatively high, showing a low level of working capital in support of net sales. The causes of this situation are high *Net Sales to Net Worth* (a low level of net worth relative to net sales), high *Days' Sales in Other Noncurrent (Miscellaneous) Assets*, and low *Net Sales to Fixed Assets* (a high level of fixed assets relative to net sales). A comparatively high level of long-term borrowing in relation to noncurrent assets (high *Long-Term Liabilities to Total Noncurrent Assets*) pulls *Net Sales to Working Capital* toward the industry standard. Nevertheless, this measure is substantially above the norm, indicating working capital weakness in relation to sales volume and suggesting that Company C experiences periodic cash flow difficulties unless accounts receivable and inventory are especially well managed.

Company D illustrates the interaction of extreme ratios, a situation that actually occurs rather frequently. While *Net Sales to Working Capital*, at 16.7, is definitely on the high side in relation to the 10.2 industry median, it is not especially unusual. *Net Sales to Working Capital* ratios of 20.0, 50.0, 100.0, or even 1,000.0—indicating a very thin working capital position—will often be found within any large group of companies. In fact, an infinitely high ratio will occur when working capital is in a deficit position (when current liabilities are greater than current assets).

Company D's *Net Sales to Working Capital* reflects one unfavorable causal factor partially offset by two favorable causal factors (observed, as usual, from a conservative point of view). The company's extremely high *Net Sales to Net Worth* shows that very little owners' equity was available to provide a positive working capital position. On the other hand, Company D's very high *Net Sales to Fixed Assets* demonstrates that the book value of physical facilities was comparatively small in relation to sales volume, leaving a comparatively large proportion of financial resources to increase working capital. In addition, *Long-Term Liabilities to Total Noncurrent Assets* is extremely high, providing a major boost to working capital. As noted in the earlier explanation of the causal ratio *Long-Term Liabilities to Total Noncurrent Assets*, a ratio greater than 1.0 strongly suggests that the company has undergone a leveraged buy-out or made some other special financial arrangement. For Company D, the two favorable factors fall short of counterbalancing the one major unfavorable factor (low investment adequacy), but the company's *Net Sales to Working Capital* has been prevented from becoming outrageously high.

In the Event of Added Receivables

Now let us suppose that each of these companies has just been notified that one of its major accounts is unable to meet a payment covering nearly one week's average sales. Instead of remitting within the usual 15 days of billing, this customer cannot be expected to pay for at least one month, possibly two, or perhaps even longer. Companies C and D may well encounter considerable difficulty as a result of this unexpected development, which will cause accounts receivable to mount by $240,000 (one week's sales on annual volume of $12,500,000) in Company C's case and by $962,000 for Company D (which has annual sales four times greater than those of Company C). Because of Company D's tight working capital position, the increase in trade credit or short-term bank borrowing that will be needed to support additional receivables may not, in fact, be readily available to the concern. Thus, Company C, and especially Company D, may be required to reduce sales or to secure outside investment. Neither Company A nor Company B will likely find the temporary buildup of accounts receivable burdensome.

We see, then, that as a measure of the amount of net sales supported by each dollar of working capital, *Net Sales to Working Capital* is highly useful in the total analysis of a company's financial structure.

Summary: Net Sales to Working Capital

Popular name	*Working Capital Sufficiency Ratio*
Purpose	Measures the sufficiency of a company's working capital—the excess of current assets over current liabilities—in support of its net sales volume.
Calculation	Subtract current liabilities from current assets to obtain working capital, then divide net sales by working capital.
Example	Your company's net sales were $1 million during your last fiscal year, your current assets were $300,000, and your current liabilities were $200,000 at year-end. What was your *Net Sales to Working Capital*?
	Solution: Working capital = 300,000 − 200,000 = 100,000; then 1,000,000 ÷ 100,000 = 10.0
Financial impact	A *low* ratio is a *favorable* condition from a conservative perspective: It shows a comparatively large spread between current assets and current liabilities in relation to net sales.
Operational impact	A *low* ratio tends to reduce the probability of bill-paying difficulty from irregularities in cash flow; however, a low ratio may increase interest costs if comparatively high long-term liabilities are used to increase working capital.
Definition	Working capital equals current assets minus current liabilities.
Special reminder	A *low* ratio shows a *high* level of working capital to support net sales.
Critical value	When current liabilities are greater than current assets, working capital will be in a deficit position and a meaningful ratio cannot be calculated. In such a case, treat *Net Sales to Working Capital* as a very large number for comparative purposes. Deficit working capital is a serious condition that warrants close management attention.
Range of common experience	8.6 times to 25.3 times.

Chapter 16

Current Assets to Current Liabilities

Current Assets to Current Liabilities (also known as the *Current Ratio*) measures the margin of safety provided for paying short-term debts in the event of a reduction in the value of current assets. It also furnishes a general picture of the adequacy of a company's working capital and of its ability to meet day-to-day payment obligations. This is not a ratio which can stand alone; the story it tells is conditioned by the quality of the major components of current assets—receivables and inventory. To the extent that receivables and inventory can be established as *liquid*—convertible to cash at full stated value—*Current Assets to Current Liabilities* assumes importance as a specific measure of a company's capacity to cover its short-term operating requirements.

Current Assets to Current Liabilities is computed by dividing total current assets by total current liabilities. In Table 16-1, Company B, with $1.5 million in current assets and $1 million in current liabilities, has a 1.5 *Current Assets to Current Liabilities* ratio.

A Venerated Ratio

In historical terms, *Current Assets to Current Liabilities* is the patriarch among ratios. At one time it commanded such widespread respect that many business-people regarded it as being endowed with the infallibility of nature's laws—a law of gravity applied to the balance sheet. A 2–to–1 value became the inflexible standard, the minimum value that analysts thought this ratio should have in a properly operating concern. Financial analysis surely owes something to the creator of the *Current Assets to Current Liabilities* ratio, for at least he recognized the importance of relative values in preference to isolated figures. Using this ratio, the credit manager or lending officer could put away his "flipping coin" and could instead make decisions based on some degree of logic and accuracy. Prompting inquiry into other financial relationships, *Current Assets to Current Liabilities* has played a significant part in the evolution and general acceptance of a reasonably objective approach to financial analysis.

In the long run, however, the originator of the 2–to–1 theory has done more

Table 16-1. *Current Assets to Current Liabilities* **for four companies.**

	Company A	Company B	Company C	Company D
Current assets	$398,000	$1,500,000	$4,740,000	$8,400,000
Current liabilities	220,000	1,000,000	3,780,000	5,400,000
Current Assets				
to Current Liabilities				
Company	1.8 times	1.5 times	1.3 times	1.6 times
Industry standard	1.5 times	1.5 times	1.5 times	1.5 times
Causal factors				
Net Sales to Working				
Capital				
Company	8.4 times	10.0 times	13.0 times	16.7 times
Industry standard	10.2 times	10.2 times	10.2 times	10.2 times
Collection Period				
of Accounts Receivable				
Company	37 days	46 days	61 days	21 days
Industry standard	44 days	44 days	44 days	44 days
Cost of Sales				
to Inventory				
Company	6.5 times	5.0 times	3.9 times	8.2 times
Industry standard	5.1 times	5.1 times	5.1 times	5.1 times

*At the most fundamental level, causal factors include the influences on *Net Sales to Working Capital* (*Net Sales to Net Worth, Net Sales to Fixed Assets, Days' Sales in Other Noncurrent Assets,* and *Long-Term Liabilities to Total Noncurrent Assets*).

disservice than can be imagined. An alarming number of credit grantors and business owners look for easy solutions to problems, and what could be easier than to resolve all doubt by one simple test? A credit manager appears, on the surface, to be quite professional when he or she says, "Yes, we can accept the order from XYZ Company, for I have analyzed its statement, and the company is liquid; it has a 2.78–to–1 *Current Assets to Current Liabilities* ratio." Or, "I don't see my way clear to go along with XYZ on its present $75,000 order, for its *Current Assets to Current Liabilities* has slipped to 1.89–to–1 and is now in the danger zone." Similarly, some business owners have pointed with pride to their better than 2–to–1 *Current Assets to Current Liabilities* as evidence of prosperity, even though they may be in constant conflict with their suppliers over their inability to pay within terms of sale. Blind reliance on a 2–to–1 standard for this ratio is an indication of the ongoing groping for certitude by credit grantors and businesspeople who do not possess financial understanding. This sort of oversimplification is not only an impediment to profitable business decisions, it often leads directly to financial disaster.

At the very outset, the 2–to–1 theory fell far short of original expectations. This arbitrary standard implied that any company with a 2–to–1, or better, *Current Assets to Current Liabilities* ratio was a sheep and could be admitted to the credit fold. Companies that fell below that all-important dividing line were goats; the door was barred against them, or very stringent conditions of sale were imposed. Strangely enough, it was discovered that many 2–to–1s—or even 3–to–1s or better—experienced difficulty meeting current obligations; in fact, a surprisingly large number wound up in the bankruptcy courts or in some form of insolvency. On the other hand, an impressive number of goats, companies with *Current Assets to Current Liabilities* less than 2–to–1 and occasionally even less than 1–to–1, found the path to success and often were able to discount their bills while the presumed sheep were dodging creditors.

How could this happen? In theory, two dollars in current assets should be adequate to cover one dollar in current liabilities. The answer is, quite simply, that *Current Assets to Current Liabilities* tests quantity, not quality. The ratio measures only total dollars' worth of assets and total dollars' worth of liabilities. There is an underlying question: How good are those assets and liabilities? The quality of liabilities involves no doubt. They are very real and worth every dollar of debt shown on the balance sheet. Liabilities are rarely subject to shrinkage. But current assets, which generally consist in large measure of cash, accounts receivable, notes receivable, and inventory, may indeed decline in value. If a company's books are loaded with doubtful receivables or with slow-moving and unsalable inventory, then not only is its short-term ability to pay greatly impaired, but its long-term solvency may be threatened. Experience has shown that *Current Assets to Current Liabilities* is subject to further questioning, for the margin of error involved in blind reliance on a 2–to–1 figure has proved to be too great.

In their various endeavors to improve the ratio, financial analysts logically focused on the component parts of current assets; they concentrated initially on the influence of inventory. Because inventory once represented a much larger dollars-and-cents figure than did accounts receivable, its impact on liquidity and debt-paying ability was much greater than it is today. Then, too, methods of valuation of inventory were not well defined, nor were there perpetual inventory systems or any of the modern refinements in purchasing and inventory control. The early analyst had seen inventory values rise and fall in rhythm with economic cycles and thus had considerable reason to view inventory as the element that caused the 2–to–1 *Current Assets to Current Liabilities* yardstick to prove so unreliable.

The Acid Test Ratio

The first major refinement of *Current Assets to Current Liabilities* was the *Acid Test Ratio: Cash and Short-Term Investments plus Accounts Receivable to Current Liabilities* (now known as the *Quick Ratio*). Its name implied that absolute certainty would now reign, making the analyst's life serene by eliminating all doubt surrounding future decisions. If inventory was the stumbling block that had so often thwarted the infallibility of the 2–to–1 *Current Assets to Current Liabilities* ratio in the past, then it seemed logical that inventory could simply be eliminated from evaluations of liquidity. That line of reasoning suggested that if there was one dollar in cash and receivables for every dollar in current liabilities, the credit grantor was taking no chances. Accordingly, the 1–to–1 *Acid Test Ratio* became the vogue and is still regarded by some adherents as an important indicator of financial health. (As described in detail in the following chapter, the *Quick Ratio* is calculated by adding cash and short-term investments to accounts receivable and then dividing the sum by current liabilities.)

Experience revealed, however, that the basic weakness that caused *Current Assets to Current Liabilities* to falter as a single definitive test plagued the *Acid Test Ratio* as well, perhaps explaining its change of name. It, likewise, proved to be a quantitative rather than a qualitative standard. While the *Quick Ratio* eliminates concern about the value and liquidity of inventory, it remains susceptible to possible uncollectibility of accounts receivable. In fact, on a proportionate basis, the *Quick Ratio* will decline more rapidly than *Current Assets to Current Liabilities* in the event of a major bad-debt loss. Ultimately, serious practitioners of financial analysis came to realize that an array of key financial ratios, some identified as causal measures and some reflecting the effect of those causal ratios, was necessary to explain a company's competitive strengths and weaknesses.

Qualifications

Current Assets to Current Liabilities has not diminished in significance, nor has it lost its place in the meaningful interpretation of today's financial statement. However, you must bear three points in mind:

1. *Current Assets to Current Liabilities* must be subjected to qualitative tests. The major components of current assets, receivables and inventory, must be carefully assessed to determine their value in relation to the amount shown on the balance sheet and to ascertain the likelihood that they can be converted to cash on a regular basis; otherwise, the ratio may be grossly misleading.

2. The ratio is subject to the influence of other financial forces that can depress or revive it dramatically overnight. Not only does the movement of receivables and inventory cause it to fluctuate, but it responds to the acquisition of fixed assets and other noncurrent assets, to sales, and to profit or loss as well.

3. The 2–to–1 *Current Assets to Current Liabilities* ratio must be abandoned as a reference point. Each industry has its own peculiar problems reflected in its own specific averages. *Current Assets to Current Liabilities* of 1.3 is perfectly acceptable in some lines of business activity, whereas a ratio greater than 2.0 is typical of other commercial and industrial classifications. In fact, *Current Assets to Current Liabilities* now centers near 1.5 for the entire spectrum of business activity.

Keeping these qualifications in mind, let us examine current assets and current liabilities, and, more importantly, the *working capital balance* (*Current Assets to Current Liabilities*) that results from the relationship between these two items for the four companies we have been analyzing. Table 16-1 shows the applicable financial statement figures. All other factors being equal, the higher a company's *Current Assets to Current Liabilities*, the greater its likelihood of meeting day-to-day operating expenses without interruption. A company with a comparatively high ratio is better able to take in stride unforeseen emergencies while remaining relatively free from creditor pressure.

Company A, with *Current Assets to Current Liabilities* substantially above the benchmark for its industry comparison group, is in a relatively strong position to withstand any major slowdown or outright loss in converting accounts receivable and inventory to cash. Assuming that Company A's *Net Sales to Working Capital, Collection Period of Accounts Receivable*, and *Cost of Sales to Inventory* are similar or superior to the industry norm, the company is in a highly favorable position with respect to liquidity and operating freedom.

Company B's *Current Assets to Current Liabilities* is directly in line with the group median, while Company C finds itself with relatively low working capital balance. Company C is clearly more susceptible to bill-paying difficulties in the event of a significant delay in receiving funds from a major customer, a temporary sales decline with resulting inventory sluggishness, or actual write-offs of accounts receivable or inventory. Company D's *Current Assets to Current Liabilities* is slightly higher than the industry standard, indicating a slightly larger than normal cushion between current assets and current liabilities.

Current Assets to Current Liabilities is as important to creditors as the actual amount of working capital in relation to net sales. If for some reason each of the four companies were to suffer a 25% decline in the value of both receivables and inventory, the resulting impact on working capital would be as illustrated in Table 16-2. While such an occurrence may seem farfetched, write-offs or markdowns of this magnitude do in fact occur for a variety of reasons, ranging from the sudden

Table 16-2. The effect of loss through write-off on working capital for four companies.

	Company A	Company B	Company C	Company D
Accounts receivable	$152,000	$ 625,000	$2,090,000	$3,000,000
Inventory	170,000	750,000	2,500,000	4,900,000
Current Assets	378,000	1,500,000	4,740,000	8,400,000
Current liabilities	220,000	1,000,000	3,780,000	5,400,000
Working capital	178,000	500,000	960,000	3,000,000
Loss through write-off	80,000	345,000	1,150,000	1,975,000
Remaining working capital (or deficit)	98,000	155,000	(190,000)	1,025,000

insolvency of a major customer to rapid reverses in the local economy. Company C, with the lowest *Current Assets to Current Liabilities*, would actually incur a working capital deficit. With current liabilities greater than current assets after the write-off, Company C would obviously experience great difficulty in meeting obligations as they come due. Company A, with the highest *Current Assets to Current Liabilities*, would still enjoy a comfortable cushion between current assets and current liabilities even after an otherwise startling loss. This exercise demonstrates that the relative position of current assets to current liabilities (the *Current Assets to Current Liabilities* ratio) is highly important in judging a company's competitive position and prospects for survival and growth.

A Specific Measure of Working Capital

Current Assets to Current Liabilities initially presents a general picture of the adequacy of a company's working capital position. If, through later tests of receivables and inventory, the analyst finds that these two asset items are normal with regard to collectibility and turnover, then *Current Assets to Current Liabilities* assumes importance as a specific measure of the working capital position. An adequate cushion between current assets and current liabilities, together with the management flexibility it provides, is clearly essential to the achievement of many company objectives.

Returning to Table 16-1, we see how Company A has achieved comparatively high *Current Assets to Current Liabilities*. Three other ratios exert a major influence. As described previously, *Net Sales to Working Capital* measures the actual amount of working capital available to a company in support of its sales volume. When this ratio is low, indicating a high level of working capital in relation to net sales, it tends to increase *Current Assets to Current Liabilities*. In fact, Company A's relatively low *Net Sales to Working Capital* has done just that. We can see that *Current Assets to Current Liabilities* is directly dependent on the amount of working capital available to support net sales. As mentioned earlier, *Net Sales to Working Capital* is not considered a causal ratio, despite its effect on *Current Assets to Current Liabilities*, because it primarily reflects the interaction of other, more fundamental, ratios.

In addition to the influence of *Net Sales to Working Capital*, Company A's comparatively short *Collection Period of Accounts Receivable* and its relatively rapid inventory turnover (shown by its *Cost of Sales to Inventory* higher than the group standard) also increased the company's *Current Assets to Current Liabilities*. Because accounts receivable and inventory are the key components of current assets, it may seem strange that a relatively low level of accounts receivable and inventory would contribute to comparatively high *Current Assets to Current Liabilities*. The resolution of this seeming paradox is actually quite simple: The cash freed from a planned, orderly decrease in accounts receivable and inventory is ordinarily used to reduce current liabilities. Decreases due to charge-offs or writedowns have a very different result, as we have seen. Since current liabilities are smaller than current assets (in a solvent company), current liabilities are actually reduced at a faster rate than current assets; consequently, *Current Assets to Current Liabilities* rises. On the other hand, an increase in accounts receivable and inventory will cause the ratio to decline (assuming that long-term liabilities and net worth remain essentially the same).

Company B, which was similar to the group median with respect to *Current Assets to Current Liabilities* and all three causal factors, can be used to illustrate how an orderly decrease in accounts receivable and inventory, and a similar reduction in current liabilities, produces a higher *Current Assets to Current Liabilities*. The effect of changes in current assets and current liabilities on *Current Assets to Current Liabilities* is seen in the following table.

	Today	After decrease	After increase
Current assets	$1,500,000	$1,000,000	$2,000,000
Current liabilities	1,000,000	500,000	1,500,000
Working capital	500,000	500,000	500,000
Current Assets to Current Liabilities	1.5 times	2.0 times	1.3 times

This table is based on the assumption that the $500,000 decrease in accounts receivable and inventory reflects an orderly move to speed up collection of receivables and increase inventory turnover. In other words, the reduction in accounts receivable and inventory resulted in increased cash, which was applied to the reduction of current liabilities.

Company C's comparatively low *Current Assets to Current Liabilities* is traceable to the unfavorable influence of all three causal factors: high *Net Sales to Working Capital*, high *Collection Period of Accounts Receivable,* and low *Cost of Sales to Inventory*.

Company D has a somewhat unusual, but by no means extraordinary, financial structure. Its *Current Assets to Current Liabilities* is slightly on the high side, indicating moderate-to-strong working capital. Yet Company D's *Net Sales to Working Capital*, at 16.7, is much higher than the industry standard, showing relatively weak working capital. How can this be? Whenever there are contradictory indications from these two ratios, the difference is traceable to the turnover of current assets. Specifically, whenever *Current Assets to Current Liabilities* is moderate or strong (high) and *Net Sales to Working Capital* is weak (high), the *Collection Period of Accounts Receivable* will be comparatively short, *Cost of Sales to Inventory* will be high, or both conditions will be present. This is precisely Company D's situation: An unusually short *Collection Period of Accounts Receivable* and very high *Cost of Sales to Inventory* relative to the industry norm have enabled this business, with comparatively weak working capital in support of net sales, to achieve a moderate-to-strong *Current Assets to Current Liabilities* ratio. On the other hand, a company with moderate *Net Sales to Working Capital* could show low *Current Assets to Current Liabilities* because of a high *Collection Period of Accounts Receivable* or low *Cost of Sales to Inventory*.

Summary: Current Assets to Current Liabilities

Popular name	*Current Ratio*
Purpose	Measures a company's ability to cover its current liabilities (obligations due within one year) from its current assets (cash and short-term investments plus the other assets, accounts receivable and inventory, expected to turn into cash within one year); indicates a company's ability to meet day-to-day obligations within terms and to withstand operating difficulties or possible writedowns of inventory or accounts receivable.
Calculation	Divide current assets by current liabilities.
Example	Your company's current assets were $300,000, and your current liabilities were $200,000 at year-end. What was your *Current Assets to Current Liabilities?*
	Solution: $300,000 \div 200,000 = 1.5$
Financial impact	A *high* ratio is a *favorable* condition from a conservative perspective: It indicates a comparatively great margin of safety for payment of current liabilities from the conversion of current assets into cash (in the course of normal operations or in the event of liquidation of assets).
Operational impact	A *high* ratio tends to increase operating freedom and reduce the probability of bill-paying difficulty from write-downs of accounts receivable or inventory.
Range of common experience	1.3 times to 1.7 times.

Chapter 17

Cash and Short-Term Investments plus Accounts Receivable to Current Liabilities (the Quick Ratio)

Cash and Short-Term Investments plus Accounts Receivable to Current Liabilities is more commonly known as the *Quick Ratio* because it measures a company's ability to cover its current liabilities from *quick*, or relatively liquid, assets (and is easier to say). For brevity's sake, we refer to it as the *Quick Ratio* throughout this book.

The *Quick Ratio* is similar in concept to *Current Assets to Current Liabilities*, but it recognizes the possibility that inventory may not be salable at its stated value, particularly in the event of liquidation. Therefore, this ratio shows the extent to which a company can cover its short-term obligations (due within the next year) without the need to convert inventory to cash. The *Quick Ratio* also eliminates other current assets, such as deferred and prepaid items, as well as special items related to progress payments and the percentage-of-completion method of accounting, in judging a company's liquidity.

The *Quick Ratio* is calculated by adding cash and short-term investments to accounts receivable and dividing the total by current liabilities. Company B, for example, has total quick assets of $725,000: cash and short-term investments of $100,000 plus accounts receivable of $625,000, as shown in Table 17-1 later in this chapter. When that $725,000 total is divided by the company's $1,000,000 in current liabilities at year-end, the *Quick Ratio* is found to be 0.725, which rounds to 0.7.

As described earlier, the *Quick Ratio* was once known as the *Acid Test Ratio*, suggesting that it was the single definitive measure of a company's solvency. Through unfortunate experiences, however, analysts learned that like *Current Assets to Current Liabilities*, the *Quick Ratio* is subject to the influence of the asset utilization ratios, particularly the *Collection Period of Accounts Receivable*. *Current Assets to Current Liabilities* and the *Quick Ratio* are both important measures of effect, but the cause must be sought elsewhere.

Table 17-1. *Cash and Short-Term Investments plus Accounts Receivable to Current Liabilities (Quick Ratio)* **for four companies.**

	Company A	Company B	Company C	Company D
Cash and short-term investments	$ 52,000	$ 100,000	$ 100,000	$ 100,000
Accounts receivable	152,000	625,000	2,090,000	2,850,000
Current liabilities	220,000	1,000,000	3,780,000	5,080,000
Cash and Short-Term Investments plus Accounts Receivable to Current Liabilities (Quick Ratio)				
Company	0.9 times	0.7 times	0.6 times	0.5 times
Industry standard	0.7 times	0.7 times	0.7 times	0.7 times
Causal factors				
Current Assets to Current Liabilities				
Company	1.8 times	1.5 times	1.3 times	1.6 times
Industry standard	1.5 times	1.5 times	1.5 times	1.5 times
Net Sales to Working Capital				
Company	8.4 times	10.0 times	13.0 times	16.7 times
Industry standard	10.2 times	10.2 times	10.2 times	10.2 times
Collection Period of Accounts Receivable				
Company	37 days	46 days	61 days	21 days
Industry standard	44 days	44 days	44 days	44 days
Cost of Sales to Inventory				
Company	6.5 times	5.0 times	3.9 times	8.2 times
Industry standard	5.1 times	5.1 times	5.1 times	5.1 times

*At the most fundamental level, causal factors include the influences on *Net Sales to Working Capital* (*Net Sales to Net Worth, Net Sales to Fixed Assets, Days' Sales in Other Noncurrent Assets,* and *Long-Term Liabilities to Total Noncurrent Assets*).

The arbitrary 1–to–1 standard for the then-called *Acid Test Ratio* failed to pass its own acid test, for there were far too many companies with 1.0 or better ratios that ended in failure and too many "substandard" companies (below the 1.0 threshold) that performed beautifully and became outstandingly successful organizations. The trouble lay in oversimplification: Analysts failed to recognize that working capital does not simply exist but is influenced by other forces within the financial structure of a company. Working capital ebbs and flows to the extent that these forces, which are measurable from the financial statement, are kept in balance or are allowed to drift out of control.

Qualifying Test

Like *Current Assets to Current Liabilities*, the *Quick Ratio* must be subjected to an important qualitative test: the *Collection Period of Accounts Receivable*. If the *Collection Period of Accounts Receivable* is noticeably longer than the company's net terms or the industry standard, a significant portion of receivables may not be readily collectible or may be subject to total write-off. And if the *Collection Period of Accounts Receivable* is substantially longer than the terms offered by suppliers, periodic late payment of the company's obligations is a possibility even if the *Quick Ratio* is comparatively high.

The *Quick Ratio* clearly cannot be relied upon to resolve all of the financial analysts' uncertainties, but it does help to focus attention on the importance of *liquidity*, the ability to convert current assets to cash. In combination with *Current Assets to Current Liabilities*, it also emphasizes the extent to which a shift from cash and accounts receivable into inventory may impair bill-paying ability. Although such a shift within current asset items would not be reflected in *Current Assets to Current Liabilities*, the *Quick Ratio* will decline if cash and accounts receivable are reduced to support an inventory build-up.

The *Quick Ratio* for each of our old friends, Companies A, B, C, and D, is displayed in Table 17-1. Once again, Company A represents a conservative financial structure, showing a *Quick Ratio* of 0.9, compared with the 0.7 industry standard. While the industry norm is well below the once-hallowed 1.0 acid-test value, the majority of business lines typically show a *Quick Ratio* between 0.6 and 0.9.

Company B's *Quick Ratio* is directly in line with the industry standard, while Company C shows a *Quick Ratio* slightly lower than the norm. Company D, which reported the second highest *Current Assets to Current Liabilities*, has the lowest *Quick Ratio*, noticeably below the median for the industry comparison group.

Determining Causal Factors

The causal factors that determine the numerical value of the *Quick Ratio* have a comparatively complex relationship. In fact, the influence of *Collection Period of Accounts Receivable*, *Cost of Sales to Inventory*, *Days' Sales in Cash and Short-Term Investments* (a causal factor that occasionally exerts a significant influence on basic financial structure, as described in Chapter 8), *Net Sales to Working Capital*, and *Current Assets to Current Liabilities* forms a very intricate pattern that is difficult to trace without extensive calculation. There are, however, a few basic comparisons with *Current Assets to Current Liabilities* and *Net Sales to Working Capital* that make the *Quick Ratio* especially useful in financial analysis:

1. When *Current Assets to Current Liabilities* is comparatively high and the *Quick Ratio* is comparatively low, as in the case of Company D, cash and accounts receivable represent a relatively low proportion of current assets. You must then ask other questions. Is the company's *Collection Period of Accounts Receivable* unusually short? If so, why? Is the company's *Cost of Sales to Inventory* unusually low? If so, why? Does an unusual level of cash or "other current assets"—shown by low *Days' Sales in Cash and Short-Term Investments* or high *Days' Sales in Other Current Assets* (another causal factor that, on comparatively rare occasions, has a major impact on financial structure, as described in Chapter 8)—contribute to the company's relatively low *Quick Ratio*?

2. As *Current Assets to Current Liabilities* falls, cash and accounts receivable must increase as a proportion of current assets to hold the *Quick Ratio* constant.

3. As *Net Sales to Working Capital* rises (as the increase in working capital lags behind the increase in sales volume), cash and accounts receivable must increase as a proportion of current assets to avoid a decrease in the *Quick Ratio*.

Even in the absence of a detailed analysis of the contributory factors, comparing a company's *Quick Ratio* for several years may reveal a decline (or an increase) in the ability to meet current obligations from liquid assets. Similarly, a comparison of the company's most recent *Quick Ratio* with the appropriate industry standard will disclose any comparative advantage or disadvantage in the company's capacity to cover current debt without the need to convert inventory to cash.

Summary: Cash and Short-Term Investments plus Accounts Receivable to Current Liabilities (Quick Ratio)

Popular names	*Quick Ratio; Acid Test Ratio*
Purpose	Measures a company's ability to cover its current liabilities (obligations due within one year) from its liquid assets (cash and short-term investments plus accounts receivable); indicates a company's ability to meet day-to-day obligations within terms without the need to convert inventory to cash and to withstand operating difficulties or possible writedowns of accounts receivable.
Calculation	Add cash and short-term investments to accounts receivable, then divide the sum by current liabilities.
Example	Your company's cash and short-term investments were $20,000, your accounts receivable were $125,000, and your current liabilities were $200,000 at year-end. What was your *Quick Ratio*?

Solution: Liquid assets = 20,000 + 125,000 = 145,000; then 145,000 ÷ 200,000 = 0.7

Financial impact

A *high* ratio is a *favorable* condition from a conservative perspective: It indicates comparatively little dependence on the salability of inventory to meet current obligations.

Operational impact

A *high* ratio tends to increase operating freedom and lower the probability of bill-paying difficulty from write-downs of accounts receivable.

Range of common experience

0.6 times to 1.0 times.

Chapter 18

Total Noncurrent Assets to Net Worth

The operations of every solvent company are supported to some extent by the investment of owners, termed *proprietor's equity, partners' capital,* or *shareholders' equity*, depending on the business's form of legal organization. This *net worth*, which includes the owners' original investment plus earnings retained in the company, must be put to effective use in order for the concern to perform its business purposes: assuring the company's survival, allowing for future growth, and providing a reasonable return to the proprietor, partners, or shareholders. To accomplish these ends, management must make decisions regarding the apportionment of net worth among current assets, fixed assets, and miscellaneous (other noncurrent) assets. *Total Noncurrent Assets to Net Worth* measures the extent to which a company's invested capital or net worth is tied up in nonliquid, permanent, depreciable assets together with other assets that are not expected to be converted to cash during the next 12 months. From another perspective, it measures the amount of owners' equity that remains for acquisition of current assets, thereby increasing working capital.

The sum of fixed assets plus miscellaneous assets divided by net worth yields *Total Noncurrent Assets to Net Worth*, which is expressed in "times." As shown in Table 18-1, because Company B reported zero miscellaneous assets, total noncurrent assets are equal to fixed assets: $500,000. Dividing this amount by the company's $750,000 in net worth at year-end produces a ratio of 0.667, rounded to 0.7. If Company B had acquired $175,000 in miscellaneous assets while maintaining the same level of fixed assets and net worth, the concern's *Total Noncurrent Assets to Net Worth* would have climbed to 0.9.

A disproportionately large commitment of net worth to fixed assets and miscellaneous assets places a burden on the company because it limits current assets, increases total liabilities, and may depress net profit through heavy fixed costs. You must, however, be aware that a comparatively high value for this ratio does not automatically prove that noncurrent assets are excessive. Every ratio serves as a measure of both halves of the fraction. *Total Noncurrent Assets to Net Worth* can be distorted by inadequate net worth, as well as by a high level of fixed assets and miscellaneous assets. A company's ratio can also become substantially higher than the industry standard through the combination of total

Table 18-1. *Total Noncurrent Assets to Net Worth* **for four companies.**

	Company A	Company B	Company C	Company D
Fixed assets	$124,000	$500,000	$1,400,000	$2,450,000
Miscellaneous assets	14,000	0	510,000	550,000
Total noncurrent assets	138,000	500,000	1,910,000	3,000,000
Net worth	254,000	750,000	1,540,000	1,550,000
Total Noncurrent Assets to Net Worth				
Company	0.5 times	0.7 times	1.2 times	1.9 times
Industry standard	0.7 times	0.7 times	0.7 times	0.7 times
Causal factors				
Net Sales to Fixed Assets				
Company	12.0 times	10.0 times	8.9 times	20.4 times
Industry standard	10.3 times	10.3 times	10.3 times	10.3 times
Days' Sales in Miscellaneous Assets				
Company	3 days	0 days	15 days	4 days
Industry standard	3 days	3 days	3 days	3 days
Net Sales to Net Worth				
Company	5.9 times	6.7 times	8.1 times	32.3 times
Industry standard	6.8 times	6.8 times	6.8 times	6.8 times

noncurrent assets somewhat above the norm coupled with net worth somewhat on the low side. Whenever the analyst finds that *Total Noncurrent Assets to Net Worth* has undergone a significant year-to-year change or is noticeably different from the industry standard, he should refer to *Net Sales to Net Worth*, *Net Sales to Fixed Assets,* and *Day's Sales in Other Noncurrent (Miscellaneous) Assets* to identify the cause or causes.

Table 18-1 offers another comparison of Companies A, B, C, and D. As usual, Company A, with *Total Noncurrent Assets to Net Worth* of 0.5 versus the 0.7 industry average, appears definitely favorable from a conservative viewpoint. Because a comparatively low proportion of Company A's net worth has been committed to total noncurrent assets, a relatively high proportion of owners' equity is available to increase current assets and boost working capital. Company B's position with respect to *Total Noncurrent Assets to Net Worth* is equal to the norm for the industry.

Company C is in a comparatively difficult financial position. Its investment in noncurrent assets, greater than its owners' equity and nearly twice the industry norm as a proportion of net worth, has subjected Company C to substantially greater working capital pressure than that felt by the typical company in its line. The fact that Company C's ratio exceeds 1.0 shows that the business must rely on long-term financing in order to maintain positive working capital (hold current liabilities below current assets). Company D's situation is even more extreme: With $3 million in total noncurrent assets and only $1,550,000 in net worth, the owners must borrow more than $1,450,000 (nearly equal to all of owners' equity) on a long-term basis just to have any working capital whatever.

Value Determined by Three Causal Measures

With respect to its influence on working capital, *Total Noncurrent Assets to Net Worth* acts much like a primary, or causal, ratio. It is not classified as a primary ratio, however, because its numerical value is determined by three other truly causal measures: *Net Sales to Fixed Assets* and *Net Sales to Net Worth*, two of the seven primary ratios, together with *Days' Sales in Other Noncurrent (Miscellaneous) Assets*, a causal factor that occasionally exerts a significant influence on basic financial structure, as described in Chapter 8. In other words, *Total Noncurrent Assets to Net Worth* results from management decisions relating to the acquisition and utilization of fixed assets, financial commitment to miscellaneous assets, and the balance between net sales and the net worth required to support that level of activity.

Company A's comparatively low *Total Noncurrent Assets to Net Worth*, a favorable condition from a conservative viewpoint, is traceable to a high level of fixed asset activity (comparatively high *Net Sales to Fixed Assets*), a moderate commitment to miscellaneous assets, and a high level of investment adequacy (shown by comparatively low *Net Sales to Net Worth*). Company C evidences just the opposite characteristics. Its high *Total Noncurrent Assets to Net Worth* is attributable to low fixed asset activity (a high level of fixed assets in relation to net sales), a very large commitment to miscellaneous assets, and low investment adequacy (a low level of net worth in relation to net sales). Company D's situation is inconsistent: very high fixed asset activity, but extremely low investment adequacy, resulting in very high *Total Noncurrent Assets to Net Worth*.

Summary: Total Noncurrent Assets to Net Worth

Popular name	*Noncurrent-Assets-to-Equity Ratio*
Purpose	Measures a company's ability to support its acquisition of fixed assets and miscellaneous (other noncurrent) assets by means of owners' investment (original investment plus retained earnings).
Calculation	Divide total noncurrent assets by net worth.
Example	Your company's fixed assets were $100,000, your miscellaneous assets were zero, and your net worth was $150,000 at year-end. What was your *Total Noncurrent Assets to Net Worth*?

Solution: Total noncurrent assets = 100,000 + 0 = 100,000; then 100,000 ÷ 150,000 = 0.7

Financial impact

A *low* ratio exerts a *favorable* influence from a conservative perspective: It increases working capital sufficiency and tends to increase working capital balance. However, a *low* ratio may be *unfavorable* in another respect: It may be related to a low return on equity.

Operational impact

A *low* ratio tends to reduce interest costs.

Definition

Net worth—called "owner's equity" in a sole proprietorship (IRS Schedule C), "partners' capital" in a partnership (IRS Form 1065), "stockholders' equity" or "shareholders' equity" in a corporation (IRS Form 1120, 1120-A, or 1120S)—equals total assets minus total liabilities.

Critical values

When total liabilities are *greater* than total assets, net worth will be in a deficit position and a meaningful ratio cannot be calculated. In such a case, treat *Total Noncurrent Assets to Net Worth* as a very large number for comparative purposes. Deficit net worth is a serious condition that warrants close management attention.

A ratio *greater* than 1.0 shows that net worth is not sufficient to fund fixed assets and miscellaneous (other noncurrent) assets. Consequently, long-term liabilities are required to achieve a positive working capital position.

Range of common experience

0.5 times to 1.3 times.

Chapter 19

Long-Term Liabilities to Working Capital

The extent to which *working capital*, the excess of current assets over current liabilities, depends on long-term financing is measured by *Long-Term Liabilities to Working Capital*. From another perspective, this ratio indicates a company's ability to repay long-term liabilities by reducing working capital. As we saw earlier, the spread between current assets and current liabilities is a critical factor in enabling a company to meet its financial obligations as they come due, and the analyst will benefit from understanding the relationship between working capital and the amount of long-term debt that supports it.

The preferred method of repaying long-term debt is by means of net cash flow, the funds made available by after-tax net profit plus depreciation (a noncash charge). Alternatively, cash can be generated by decreasing current assets or increasing current liabilities and then applying those funds to the payment of long-term obligations, reducing working capital in the process. In actual practice, new long-term liabilities are often substituted for existing obligations when new fixed assets and other noncurrent assets are acquired. In some cases, long-term debt, such as mortgages and equipment loans, can be refinanced. When a company's *Long-Term Liabilities to Working Capital* is higher than the comparison group median, it indicates that working capital would suffer a comparatively large reduction if it became necessary to repay long-term liabilities from that source alone.

Working capital is found by subtracting current liabilities from current assets. Then, to compute *Long-Term Liabilities to Working Capital*, divide long-term liabilities (those maturing more than one year from statement date) by working capital. In Table 19-1, Company B, with current assets of $1,500,000 and current liabilities of $1 million at year-end, has working capital of $500,000. When long-term liabilities of $250,000 are divided by this amount, the company has a ratio of 0.5. *Long-Term Liabilities to Working Capital* is expressed in "times." A company with no long-term indebtedness has a ratio of zero regardless of the amount of its working capital.

Long-term liabilities, as determined earlier, consist of any indebtedness payable more than one year from the date of the financial statement, including intermediate financing, such as two- or three-year term loans or chattel mort-

Table 19-1. *Long-Term Liabilities to Working Capital* **for four companies.**

	Company A	Company B	Company C	Company D
Current assets	$398,000	$1,500,000	$4,740,000	$8,400,000
Current liabilities	220,000	1,000,000	3,780,000	5,400,000
Working capital	178,000	500,000	960,000	3,000,000
Long-term liabilities	62,000	250,000	1,330,000	4,450,000
Long-Term Liabilities to Working Capital				
Company	0.3 times	0.5 times	1.4 times	1.5 times
Industry standard	0.6 times	0.6 times	0.6 times	0.6 times
Causal factors				
Net Sales to Fixed Assets				
Company	12.1 times	10.0 times	8.9 times	20.4 times
Industry standard	10.3 times	10.3 times	10.3 times	10.3 times
Days' Sales in Miscellaneous Assets				
Company	3 days	0 days	15 days	4 days
Industry standard	3 days	3 days	3 days	3 days
Net Sales to Net Worth				
Company	5.9 times	6.7 times	8.1 times	32.3 times
Industry standard	6.8 times	6.8 times	6.8 times	6.8 times
Long-Term Liabilities to Total Noncurrent Assets				
Company	0.4 times	0.5 times	0.7 times	1.5 times
Industry standard	0.5 times	0.5 times	0.5 times	0.5 times

gages, as well as real estate mortgages. You must remember, however, that any portion of such long-term obligations that falls due within the year following the statement date is considered among the current liabilities of the company.

Companies ordinarily require long-term financing to supplement owners' equity (net worth) when acquiring fixed assets. By matching long-term financing to noncurrent assets, they avoid the decrease in working capital that would result from reducing current assets or increasing current liabilities to pay for plant and equipment. Such borrowing, of course, obligates the company to generate sufficient cash from operations to meet interest and principal installments. Although the amount reported as depreciation expense on the operating statement may be applied to the repayment of principal, a positive net profit (after depreciation and interest expense) will be needed to maintain and increase working capital.

Some companies resort to long-term borrowing to reinforce their working capital position when bill-paying ability has become impaired through operating losses or the accumulation of sluggish receivables or inventory. In many cases, cash for meeting current obligations may be obtained by refinancing fixed assets. Otherwise, a personal guarantee of the owners and a pledge of collateral security may be required. If the company's decision makers have properly analyzed the company's problems and have taken steps to prevent their recurrence (and eventually to restore proper balance), they may find long-term financing of immeasurable aid during the period of return to liquidity. But money alone is not the answer. Borrowing commitments should not be made unless and until the underlying cause of the working capital deficiency has been identified and a corrective program instituted, or unless the purpose for borrowing is such that funds for repayment will be generated through improved profit, for both the principal and the interest of any such loan will have to be repaid. Thus, if the borrowed funds are utilized to camouflage fundamental operating losses that remain uncorrected, the same financial ghosts will return to haunt the company with even greater vengeance.

Effect of Causal Factors

Long-Term Liabilities to Working Capital is determined by the same causal factors that influence *Net Sales to Working Capital*: *Net Sales to Net Worth*, *Net Sales to Fixed Assets*, and *Long-Term Liabilities to Total Noncurrent Assets*, together with *Days' Sales in Other Noncurrent (Miscellaneous) Assets*, a measure that occasionally exerts a significant influence on basic financial structure, as described in Chapter 8. The effect of three of the causal factors is the same in both cases. High *Net Sales to Net Worth*, low *Net Sales to Fixed Assets,* and high *Days' Sales in Other Noncurrent (Miscellaneous) Assets* have the unfavorable effect of reducing working capital. In other words, when owners' equity is decreased and noncurrent assets are increased, working capital falls, and the potential for cash flow difficulties becomes greater. Consequently, these three causal factors increase both *Net Sales to Working Capital* and *Long-Term Liabilities to Working Capital*.

The fourth causal factor, *Long-Term Liabilities to Total Noncurrent Assets,* ordinarily affects these two working capital ratios in opposite ways. As long-term debt increases in proportion to plant, equipment, and other noncurrent assets, *Long-Term Liabilities to Working Capital* will increase (an unfavorable development from a conservative perspective) whenever its original value is less than 1.0. At the same time, *Net Sales to Working Capital* will decline (a favorable trend from a conservative point of view) when *Long-Term Liabilities to Total Noncurrent Assets* is increased for the purpose of reducing current liabilities or boosting current assets. In other words, working capital will rise in relation to net sales through long-term borrowing, but the proportion of working capital required to repay long-term liabilities will also be increased (when *Long-Term Liabilities to Working Capital* is below 1.0). Somewhat ironically, once this ratio exceeds 1.0, increasing long-term debt to strengthen working capital will result in a lower numerical value for *Long-Term Liabilities to Working Capital*.

Let us now examine Companies A, B, C, and D to learn more about the significance of *Long-Term Liabilities to Working Capital*. Comparative values for this ratio, together with the dollar components and the causal factors that determine those values, are displayed in Table 19-1.

Company A's *Long-Term Liabilities to Working Capital*, at 0.3, is only half as great as the industry standard. A comparatively low level of fixed assets in relation to sales volume (comparatively high *Net Sales to Fixed Assets*), coupled with a comparatively high level of owners' equity in relation to net sales (comparatively low *Net Sales to Net Worth*), has enabled Company A to hold long-term liabilities to a relatively small proportion of working capital.

Company B has pursued a middle-of-the-road policy: moderate fixed assets, miscellaneous assets, and net worth in relation to sales volume, and moderate long-term debt in proportion to noncurrent assets. Consequently, *Long-Term Liabilities to Working Capital* is moderate, as well.

Company C, however, has required a very high level of long-term debt in relation to working capital. There are three causes: a high level of fixed assets in relation to net sales (low *Net Sales to Fixed Assets*), a high level of miscellaneous assets in relation to net sales (high *Days' Sales in Miscellaneous Assets*), and a low level of net worth in relation to net sales (high *Net Sales to Net Worth*). A comparatively high proportion of fixed and miscellaneous assets was financed on a long-term basis in order to boost working capital. The net result was high *Long-Term Liabilities to Working Capital*, showing that Company C would suffer a comparatively great reduction of working capital if net cash flow is insufficient to meet current maturities of long-term debt—unless those long-term liabilities are periodically refinanced. In fact, because this ratio is greater than 1.0, any reduction in long-term liabilities attributable to decrease in working capital would cause a greater proportionate decline in working capital than in long-term liabilities, pushing this ratio to a still higher level.

Company D's high *Long-Term Liabilities to Working Capital* is entirely traceable to its very low net worth in support of its present sales volume (as evidenced by its extremely high *Net Sales to Net Worth*). Company D has held its fixed assets to an extraordinarily low level in relation to net sales and has made only a modest financial commitment to miscellaneous assets. Nevertheless, management has found it necessary to incur long-term debt greater than the company's total noncurrent assets (in a leveraged buyout) in order to maintain a positive working capital position. Consequently, Company D is under extreme pressure to produce a positive net profit in order to meet interest payments, retire principal from current earnings, and boost working capital. No opportunity for refinancing is evident, and short-term creditors, as well as long-term debt holders, will expect to be paid. *Long-Term Liabilities to Working Capital* greater than 1.0 may be an indication that current maturities of long-term debt are greater than annual depreciation charges, requiring the company to operate at a profitable level in order to repay long-term debt from earnings and avoid reducing working capital for that purpose.

In considering the significance of *Long-Term Liabilities to Working Capital*, you must bear in mind that it is entirely possible for existing long-term debt to be re-funded indefinitely. Nevertheless, the conservative view of a company's financial structure allows for the possibility that working capital may eventually may be reduced by the amount of long-term borrowing.

Summary: Long-Term Liabilities to Working Capital

Popular name   *Working Capital Dependency Ratio*

Purpose   Measures the extent to which a company's working capital is dependent on long-term liabilities; from another perspective, measures a company's ability to repay long-term liabilities by reducing working capital.

Calculation   Subtract current liabilities from current assets to obtain working capital, then divide long-term liabilities by working capital.

Example   Your company's current assets were $300,000, your current liabilities were $200,000, and your long-term liabilities were $50,000 at year-end. What was your *Long-Term Liabilities to Working Capital*?

                      Solution: Working capital = 300,000 − 200,000 = 100,000; then 50,000 ÷ 100,000 = 0.5

Financial impact   A *low* ratio is a *favorable* condition from a conservative perspective: It indicates comparatively low dependence on long-term debt to hold current liabilities below current assets.

Operational impact A *low* ratio tends to decrease interest cost.

Critical values   When current liabilities are greater than current assets, working capital will be in a deficit position, and a meaningful ratio cannot be calculated. In such a case, treat *Long-Term Liabilities to Working Capital* as a very large number for comparative purposes. Deficit working capital is a serious condition that warrants close management attention.

                      A ratio greater than 1.0 shows that long-term borrowing was required to achieve a positive working capital position (due to total noncurrent assets greater than net worth).

Range of common   Insufficient industry data.
experience

Chapter 20

Net Profit to Total Assets

Net Profit to Total Assets (also known as the *Return on Assets Ratio*) measures a company's ability to produce profit on the assets it uses. This relationship is of interest to the analyst because assets are ordinarily increased with the intention of boosting profit. For example, more liberal credit terms may be extended to customers (with a resulting rise in accounts receivable) in order to increase profitable sales, or additional equipment may be acquired with the expectation of reducing costs and improving net profit. *Net Profit to Total Assets* indicates the effectiveness of such moves; that is, whether profit has in fact kept pace with sales growth.

The calculation of this ratio is a simple procedure: Divide net profit by total assets and multiply the result by 100 (or press the % key on a calculator). As noted earlier, most comparative studies use net profit before income taxes (but after interest expense) as the numerator and use all assets (including intangibles) as the denominator. In Table 20-1, for Company B, pre-tax net profit of $150,000 divided by total assets of $2 million yields *Net Profit to Total Assets* of 7.5% (after converting .075 to a percentage). Of course, you must be alert to the possibility of a negative value for net profit.

Table 20-1. *Net Profit to Total Assets* **for four companies.**

	Company A	Company B	Company C	Company D
Net profit	$ 76,000	$ 150,000	$ 150,000	$ 950,000
Total assets	536,000	2,000,000	6,650,000	11,400,000
Net Profit to Total Assets				
Company	14.2%	7.5%	2.3%	8.3%
Industry standard	7.7%	7.7%	7.7%	7.7%
Causal factors				
Net Profit to Net Sales				
Company	5.1%	3.0%	1.2%	1.9%
Industry standard	3.2%	3.2%	3.2%	3.2%
Net Sales to Total Assets				
Company	2.8 times	2.5 times	1.9 times	4.4 times
Industry standard	2.4 times	2.4 times	2.4 times	2.4 times

Rate of Interest Expense

This ratio takes into account the interest expense incurred in financing the company's assets. Because interest expense is subtracted before calculating *Net Profit to Total Assets*, this ratio is a good measure of management's effectiveness in coordinating operations, assets, and debt structure to generate a net profit. On the other hand, because the amount of interest expense is strongly influenced by *investment adequacy* (owners' equity available to support sales volume) and by the balance between trade credit and interest-bearing debt, this ratio is not exclusively a measure of operating control and asset management. Consequently, it is ordinarily not an appropriate measure of the performance of a general manager or other employee unless that person controls the company's borrowing arrangements and its basic financial structure. The combined effectiveness of operating control and asset management is, in most companies, best evaluated by adding back interest expense to net profit and then dividing by total assets. Many large corporations measure the effectiveness of divisional performance by comparing net profit before interest expense against *net assets employed*, total assets after subtracting all non-interest-bearing liabilities, such as trade credit and accruals, and, in some cases, further subtracting cash and short-term investments, since these assets will lower *Net Profit to Total Assets* for a company with highly profitable operations.

A Way to Evaluate Owners' Equity

Net Profit to Total Assets serves as a means of evaluating *Net Profit to Net Worth*. As we see in the following chapters, *Net Profit to Total Assets* helps management determine the extent to which the percentage return on owners' equity is attributable to:

1. Profitability on the assets used by the business
2. Financial leverage, substituting liabilities for a portion of owners' equity

If, for example, *Net Profit to Net Worth* is significantly higher than the industry median and *Net Profit to Total Assets* is low or moderate, the superior return on equity would be traceable to comparatively high *Total Liabilities to Net Worth*, not to unusually profitable utilization of assets.

Table 20-1 shows how *Net Profit to Total Assets* compares for Companies A, B, C, and D. Company A has achieved superior *Net Profit to Total Assets* because of the favorable influence of the two causal ratios that determine the outcome: *Net Profit to Net Sales* is comparatively high, and *Net Sales to Total Assets* is also on the high side. Company A enjoys both a relatively high percentage return on each sales dollar and a comparatively high level of asset utilization, producing superior *Net Profit to Total Assets*.

Company B evidences middle-of-the-road performance, with *Net Profit to Total Assets* of 7.5% versus the 7.7% industry standard. *Net Profit to Net Sales* and *Net Sales to Total Assets* are both similar to the figures reported by the typical company in the comparison group. Company C's ability to generate profit on assets used in the business is comparatively low. The poor performance of Company C in this regard is traceable to low *Net Sales to Total Assets* as well as substandard *Net Profit to Net Sales*.

Company D achieved *Net Profit to Total Assets* somewhat higher than the comparison group standard, despite *Net Profit to Net Sales* that was well below the norm. In fact, Company D's *Net Profit to Net Sales* was not much above that of Company C. For Company D, however, extremely high *Net Sales to Total Assets*, 4.4 versus the 2.4 industry median, boosted *Net Profit to Total Assets* to a comparatively high level.

Summary: Net Profit to Total Assets

Popular name	*Return on Assets*
Purpose	Measures a company's ability to produce profit on assets employed.
Calculation	Divide net profit by total assets, then multiply result by 100, converting ratio to a percentage.
Example	Your company's net profit was $30,000 for the year, and your total assets were $400,000 at year-end. What was your *Net Profit to Total Assets*?
	Solution: $30,000 \div 400,000 = .075$; then $.075 \times 100 = 7.5\%$
Financial impact	A *high* ratio is a *favorable* result: It indicates a comparatively high rate of return on assets employed.
Operational impact	A *high* ratio tends to reduce interest cost over time.
Definition	Net profit *before taxes* is ordinarily used by bankers and other credit grantors as the basis for measuring comparative profitability (versus previous performance or external standards). Net profit *after taxes* is the true "bottom line," but the effect of state and local income taxes, as well as federal income tax credits and carrybacks, can distort comparative performance. Net profit *from operations* (before nonoperating income, nonoperating expense, and extraordinary items) and net profit *before officers'/owners' compensation* are also useful measures.
Special reminder	Net profit is expressed as a percentage, not as a simple ratio.
Critical value	A *negative* percentage shows that operating policy and asset management resulted in a net loss for the period.
Range of common experience	5.3% to 9.0% (before income taxes).

Chapter 21

The Nine Secondary Ratios: Review and Concise Summary of Basic Principles

Our study of the nine secondary ratios has revealed that our predictions about the financial structure of Companies A, B, and C were entirely correct. When the causal ratios are overwhelmingly favorable, as in the case of Company A, the effect ratios will necessarily follow suit. And, as expected, Company C's substandard performance in the causal areas has resulted in relative weakness in all of the secondary ratios. Also predictably, Company B's middle-of-the-road management of the causal ratios has kept the secondary measures in line with the industry standard. Company D, however, has provided some interesting surprises as a result of the conflicting forces among the concern's causal ratios:

■ Despite low *Net Profit to Net Sales*, the company reports very high *Net Profit to Net Worth* because of its very low investment adequacy, reflected in very high *Net Sales to Net Worth*.

■ Although Company D shows very high *Current Liabilities to Net Worth*, its *Current Assets to Current Liabilities* is slightly higher than the industry norm. This unusual relationship does *not* suggest that current assets are very high. In fact, we know that accounts receivable are comparatively low (indicated by a relatively low *Collection Period of Accounts Receivable*) and that inventory is also low (shown by high *Cost of Sales to Inventory*). The primary reason for the unusual relationship between *Current Assets to Current Liabilities* and *Current Liabilities to Net Worth* is Company D's extremely low level of net worth (owners' equity) in relation to sales volume, as reflected in very high *Net Sales to Net Worth*.

■ The two secondary ratios that measure working capital are on opposite sides: *Current Assets to Current Liabilities* slightly above the industry norm indicates a favorable working capital balance, while relatively high *Net Sales to Working Capital* shows that Company D's working capital is insufficient to support the concern's present sales volume. These seemingly contradictory results actually demonstrate that Company D's management has used two compensating advantages—rapid collection of accounts receivable and the high rate of inventory turnover—to speed up the cash cycle, hold down current liabilities, and thereby maintain favorable *Current Assets to Current Liabilities*. Whether such stringent control of accounts receivable and inventory can be maintained for long is a valid question, which we investigate in Chapter 27, but at the moment Company D's balance between current assets and current liabilities is essentially favorable.

■ *Total Liabilities to Net Worth* reflects the most direct clash between two causal ratios: Company D's very high asset utilization (shown by very high *Net Sales to Total Assets*) tends to reduce debt, while the concern's extremely low investment adequacy (indicated by very high *Net Sales to Net Worth*) tends to cause a rise in total liabilities. In this case, even extraordinarily high asset utilization could not offset extremely low investment adequacy, and Company D's *Total Liabilities to Net Worth* stands far above the industry standard, indicating unusually high financial leverage and concomitant pressure from creditors.

By reviewing the comparative performance of these four companies for a single year, we have become familiar with the basic cause-and-effect relationships. In Part V, we observe how more comprehensive ratio analysis is performed. There we will also consider the importance of trend as we review the financial history of Companies A, B, C, and D.

The Secondary Ratios: Summary of Basic Financial Principles

1. Reinvest sufficient *profit* in relation to *net worth* (in order to support future *sales* volume).

   ■ High *Net Profit to Net Worth* enables a company to increase owners' equity at a comparatively rapid pace for the purpose of supporting sales growth. The actual percentage increase in net worth depends on the effective tax rate, as well as management policy with respect to retaining net profit. If owners' equity is expanded at a more rapid rate than sales volume, *Total Liabilities to Net Worth* will decline at an even faster rate than *Net Sales to Net Worth*.

   ■ *Net Profit to Net Worth* can be increased through changes in two causal ratios: boosting *Net Profit to Net Sales* and/or raising *Net Sales to Net Worth*.

2. Manage *financial leverage* in relation to *return on equity*.

   ■ Although high *Total Liabilities to Net Worth* reflects relatively great pressure from creditors, it also tends to increase *Net Profit to Net Worth* (depending on the availability of "free" money, such as accounts payable, as well as the rate of interest on any funds borrowed from commercial lenders). Management must determine the extent to which the advantage of a higher percentage of profit on owners' equity is offset by actual or implied restrictions on management's operating freedom.

- *Total Liabilities to Net Worth* can be reduced through changes in two causal ratios: lowering *Net Sales to Net Worth* and/or increasing *Net Sales to Total Assets*. If high *Net Sales to Total Assets* is coupled with high *Net Profit to Net Sales*, a company may enjoy low financial leverage as well as high return on equity.

3. Maintain sufficient *working capital* to support *sales* volume.

- Low *Net Sales to Working Capital* indicates that cash flow problems are relatively unlikely. On the other hand, achieving a high degree of operating freedom by maintaining a high level of working capital in relation to sales volume tends to reduce *Net Profit to Net Worth*.
- *Net Sales to Working Capital* can be reduced (showing stronger working capital in relation to net sales) by changes in three causal ratios: lowering *Net Sales to Net Worth* (which lowers return on equity), increasing *Long-Term Liabilities to Total Noncurrent Assets* (which may reduce return on equity, depending on interest rates on short-term debt versus long-term debt and the availability of non-interest-bearing trade credit), and increasing *Net Sales to Fixed Assets* (which will have a positive effect on return on equity if such higher fixed asset activity reflects improved asset management, but may have a negative effect on return on equity if the increase results from failure to modernize and a willingness to operate with obsolete, nearly fully depreciated facilities).

4. Maintain an adequate balance between *current assets* and *current liabilities*.

- High *Current Assets to Current Liabilities* shows a comparatively great ability to absorb possible bad-debt losses or writedowns of inventory without failing to meet current obligations. Nevertheless, achieving such a favorable balance from a conservative perspective may result in a reduction of return on equity.
- A company with low *Net Sales to Working Capital* will automatically enjoy high *Current Assets to Current Liabilities* if other key financial factors are equal. (The causal ratios that determine the secondary measure *Net Sales to Working Capital* were identified in Chapter 15.) With no change in *Net Sales to Working Capital*, *Current Assets to Current Liabilities* may be increased through changes in two causal ratios: reducing the *Collection Period of Accounts Receivable* (which will have a positive effect on return on equity if the decrease in accounts receivable

reflects improved credit policies and collection procedures, but may have a negative effect if the reduction results from restricting sales to fast-paying accounts) and/or increasing *Cost of Sales to Inventory* (which may have a positive or negative impact on return on equity, depending on improvements in inventory management versus reductions of stock on hand or restrictions on production). In fact, a company with low working capital sufficiency—high *Net Sales to Working Capital*—can achieve high *Current Assets to Current Liabilities* by means of a very low *Collection Period of Accounts Receivable* and/or very high *Cost of Sales to Inventory*.

Part IV

Two Important Reference Guides

Many company owners and managers use the cause-and-effect ratio approach just once each year to evaluate their business's annual financial statement. Although a regular, or at least an annual, assessment of competitive position is highly recommended, other business-people review the key financial ratios only on those infrequent occasions when a significant problem becomes apparent in day-to-day operations or in their relations with credit grantors. A busy executive, whether he or she constitutes the entire management team or is responsible for a single administrative area, cannot expect to remember all of the finer points of ratio analysis, or even recall each of the 16 ratios, from one year to the next. The company owner or manager simply cannot devote the time needed to absorb all of the information that proves valuable to the professional financial analyst. Accordingly, the reference guides in Chapter 22 and Chapter 23 have been developed to assist every individual, particularly the active businessperson, who may, from time to time, require a summary of the essential elements in identifying a company's competitive strengths and weaknesses. Accountants, credit grantors, investors, and other financial professionals who are experienced in the analysis of financial statements might also benefit from a periodic review of these important points, much as a veteran airline pilot is regularly scheduled for refresher training.

Chapter 22

Impact of the Seven Causal Ratios on the Nine Ratios That Measure Effect

The seven causal ratios exert a predictable influence on the nine ratios that measure effect. A comparatively low *Collection Period of Accounts Receivable* will, for example, reduce *Total Liabilities to Net Worth* and increase *Current Assets to Current Liabilities*. In many companies, however, the impact of one causal ratio will be favorable, while a second causal ratio will push the business in an unfavorable direction. The net result, which is always reflected in the nine secondary ratios, will depend on the relative importance of each of the causal ratios within the company's financial structure. The concern's comparative standing will also be affected by the importance of the components of each ratio in relation to the other financial statement items for the typical company in its line of business activity. A wide numerical variation from the industry norm with respect to *Cost of Sales to Inventory* may, for example, have only a minimal impact on the secondary ratios of a company when it operates within an industry that is generally characterized by a very small inventory level in relation to net sales. On the other hand, a seemingly minor difference in *Net Sales to Fixed Assets* may have a noticeable influence on several of the nine ratios that measure effect whenever the company's line of business activity involves major investment in physical facilities and equipment. Because the importance of specific financial factors differs from one industry to another, you must examine each causal ratio known to have a bearing on any of the secondary measures you may identify as being significantly different from the industry norm. To make this investigation easier, the following outline is provided for your consideration.

Causal Ratio: Net Profit to Net Sales

If the other causal ratios remain unchanged at the same sales volume, an *increase* in *Net Profit to Net Sales* will have the following impact on the secondary ratios:

Net Profit to Net Worth   Increase: greater return on equity because of rise in net profit

Total Liabilities to Net Worth	Decrease: lower financial leverage because of expansion of net worth*
Current Liabilities to Net Worth	Decrease: lower current liabilities in relation to net worth because of expansion of net worth*
Current Assets to Current Liabilities	Increase: greater cushion between current assets and current liabilities because of rise in current assets and/or reduction of current liabilities†
Cash and Short-Term Investments plus Accounts Receivable to Current Liabilities (Quick Ratio)	Increase: greater coverage of current liabilities from liquid assets because of rise in cash and accounts receivable and/or reduction of current liabilities†
Net Sales to Working Capital	Decrease: greater working capital sufficiency in relation to net sales because of rise in current assets and/or reduction of current liabilities†
Total Noncurrent Assets to Net Worth	Decrease: lower proportion of net worth used to support fixed assets because of expansion of net worth*
Long-Term Liabilities to Working Capital	Decrease: lower dependence of working capital on long-term liabilities because of rise in working capital†
Net Profit to Total Assets	Increase: greater return on assets because of rise in net profit

Causal Ratio: Net Sales to Total Assets

If the other causal ratios remain unchanged at the same sales volume, an *increase* in *Net Sales to Total Assets* will have the following impact on the secondary ratios:

Net Profit to Net Worth	Increase: greater return on equity (assuming a net profit) because less owners' equity is required to support a lower level of assets; interest-bearing debt may be reduced, increasing net profit
Total Liabilities to Net Worth	Decrease: lower financial leverage because reduced assets require less borrowing; decrease based on assumption that total liabilities would be paid down at a faster rate than net worth would be reduced through dividends or other distribution of equity

*Assuming retention of at least some portion of the additional profit.
†Assuming that a portion of retained earnings will be used to increase cash and short-term investments or other current assets—or to reduce current liabilities.

Current Liabilities to Net Worth	Decrease: lower current liabilities in relation to net worth due to (1) reduced current assets (assuming that current liabilities would be paid from at least a portion of funds released) and/or (2) smaller current maturities of long-term debt used to finance fixed assets*
Current Assets to Current Liabilities	Increase: (1) greater coverage of current liabilities by current assets because current liabilities would be reduced at a faster rate than current assets and/or (2) greater cushion between current assets and current liabilities by virtue of lower current maturities of long-term debt*
Cash and Short-Term Investments plus Accounts Receivable to Current Liabilities (Quick Ratio)	Increase likely, but depends on asset items responsible for increase in *Net Sales to Total Assets,* as well as whether *Quick Ratio* is greater or less than 1.0*
Net Sales to Working Capital	Decrease likely, but depends on asset items responsible for increase in *Net Sales to Total Assets**
Total Noncurrent Assets to Net Worth	Decrease likely, but depends on asset items responsible for increase in *Net Sales to Total Assets**
Long-Term Liabilities to Working Capital	Decrease likely, but depends on asset items responsible for increase in *Net Sales to Total Assets**
Net Profit to Total Assets	Increase: greater return on assets (assuming net profit) because of lower asset base

Causal Ratio: Collection Period of Accounts Receivable

If the other causal ratios remain unchanged at the same sales volume, a *decrease* in the *Collection Period of Accounts Receivable* will have the following impact on the secondary ratios:

Net Profit to Net Worth	Increase: greater return on equity (assuming a net profit) because less owners' equity is required to support a lower level of assets; interest-bearing debt may be reduced, increasing net profit
Total Liabilities to Net Worth	Decrease: lower financial leverage because reduced assets require less borrowing; decrease based on assumption that total liabilities would be paid down at a faster rate than net worth would be reduced through dividends or other distribution of equity

*NOTE: A review of the next three causal ratios—the *Collection Period of Accounts Receivable, Cost of Sales to Inventory,* and *Net Sales to Fixed Assets*—will provide more specific guidance with respect to influences on these secondary measures.

Current Liabilities to Net Worth	Decrease: lower current liabilities in relation to net worth because reduced assets require less borrowing; decrease based on assumption that current liabilities would be paid down at a faster rate than net worth would be reduced through dividends or other distribution of equity
Current Assets to Current Liabilities	Increase: greater coverage of current liabilities by current assets because current liabilities would be reduced at a faster rate than current assets (assuming that this ratio is greater than 1.0 and that a portion of the cash generated by the reduction in accounts receivable would be applied to lowering current liabilities)
Cash and Short-Term Investments plus Accounts Receivable to Current Liabilities (Quick Ratio)	Depends whether the ratio is greater or less than 1.0: increase (greater coverage of current liabilities from liquid assets) will result if the ratio is greater than 1.0 because current liabilities would be reduced at a faster rate than liquid assets; decrease (reduced coverage of current liabilities from liquid assets on a proportionate basis) will result if the ratio is less than 1.0 because current liabilities would be reduced at a slower rate than liquid assets
Net Sales to Working Capital	No change (assuming that a portion of the reduction in accounts receivable would be applied to lowering current liabilities)
Total Noncurrent Assets to Net Worth	No change
Long-Term Liabilities to Working Capital	No change
Net Profit to Total Assets	Increase: greater return on assets (assuming a net profit) because of lower asset base

Causal Ratio: Cost of Sales to Inventory

If the other causal ratios remain unchanged at the same sales volume, an *increase* in *Cost of Sales to Inventory* will have the following impact on the secondary ratios:

Net Profit to Net Worth	Increase: greater return on equity (assuming a net profit) because less owners' equity is required to support a lower level of assets; interest-bearing debt may be reduced, increasing net profit

Total Liabilities to Net Worth	Decrease: lower financial leverage because reduced assets require less borrowing; decrease based on assumption that total liabilities would be paid down at a faster rate than net worth would be reduced through dividends or other distribution of equity
Current Liabilities to Net Worth	Decrease: lower current liabilities in relation to net worth because reduced assets require less borrowing (and also assuming that current liabilities would be paid down faster than net worth would be decreased through dividends or other distribution of equity)
Current Assets to Current Liabilities	Increase: greater coverage of current liabilities by current assets because current liabilities would be reduced at a faster rate than current assets (assuming that this ratio is greater than 1.0 and that a portion of the cash generated by the reduction in inventory would be applied to lowering current liabilities)
Cash and Short-Term Investments plus Accounts Receivable to Current Liabilities (Quick Ratio)	Increase: greater coverage of current liabilities from liquid assets because of lower current liabilities (assuming that current liabilities would be lowered by a portion of the reduction in inventory)
Net Sales to Working Capital	No change (assuming that a portion of the reduction in inventory would be applied to lowering current liabilities)
Total Noncurrent Assets to Net Worth	No change
Long-Term Liabilities to Working Capital	No change
Net Profit to Total Assets	Increase: greater return on assets (assuming a net profit) because of lower asset base

Causal Ratio: Net Sales to Fixed Assets

If the other causal ratios remain unchanged at the same sales volume, an *increase* in *Net Sales to Fixed Assets* will have the following impact on the secondary ratios:

Net Profit to Net Worth	Increase: greater return on equity (assuming a net profit) because less owners' equity is required to support a lower level of assets; interest-bearing debt may be reduced, increasing net profit

Total Liabilities to Net - Worth	Decrease: lower financial leverage because reduced assets require less borrowing; decrease based on assumption that total liabilities would be paid down at a faster rate than net worth would be reduced through dividends or other distribution of equity
Current Liabilities to Net Worth	Decrease: lower current liabilities in relation to net worth because of (1) smaller current maturities of long-term debt used to finance fixed assets and/or (2) reduction of short-term debt
Current Assets to Current Liabilities	Increase: greater cushion between current assets and current liabilities because of lower current debt
Cash and Short-Term Investments plus Accounts Receivable to Current Liabilities (Quick Ratio)	Increase: greater coverage of current liabilities from liquid assets because of lower current debt
Net Sales to Working Capital	Decrease: greater working capital sufficiency in relation to net sales because of reduction in amount of funds shifted from working capital to fixed assets
Total Noncurrent Assets to Net Worth	Decrease: lower proportion of net worth used to support fixed assets because of reduction in fixed assets
Long-Term Liabilities to Working Capital	Decrease: lower dependence of working capital on long-term liabilities because of (1) greater working capital, due to reduction of funds shifted from working capital to fixed assets and (2) lower long-term debt used to support fixed assets
Net Profit to Total Assets	Increase: greater return on assets (assuming net profit) because of lower asset base

Causal Ratio: Net Sales to Net Worth

If the other causal ratios remain unchanged at the same sales volume, a *decrease* in *Net Sales to Net Worth* will have the following impact on the secondary ratios:

Net Profit to Net Worth	Decrease: lower return on equity (assuming a net profit) because of greater owners' equity (net worth)*
Total Liabilities to Net Worth	Decrease: lower financial leverage because of the rise in net worth
Current Liabilities to Net Worth	Decrease: lower current liabilities in relation to net worth because of the rise in net worth

*Unless the increase in net worth is used to pay off liabilities with an effective interest rate greater than pre-interest and pre-tax return on assets.

Current Assets to Current Liabilities	Increase: greater cushion between current assets and current liabilities because of lower current liabilities†
Cash and Short-Term Investments plus Accounts Receivable to Current Liabilities (Quick Ratio)	Increase: greater coverage of current liabilities from liquid assets because of lower current liabilities†
Net Sales to Working Capital	Decrease: greater working capital sufficiency in relation to net sales because of lower current liabilities†
Total Noncurrent Assets to Net Worth	Decrease: lower proportion of net worth used to support fixed and other noncurrent assets because of the rise in net worth
Long-Term Liabilities to Working Capital	Decrease: lower dependence of working capital on long-term liabilities because of greater working capital†
Net Profit to Total Assets	Indeterminate: depends on the substitution of net worth for interest-bearing debt versus reduction of interest-free funds, such as accounts payable; however, any reduction of interest-bearing debt would increase this ratio, assuming that all other causal ratios remain unchanged at the same sales volume

Causal Ratio: Long-Term Liabilities to Total Noncurrent Assets

If the other causal ratios remain unchanged at the same sales volume, an *increase* in *Long-Term Liabilities to Total Noncurrent Assets* will have the following impact on the secondary ratios:

Net Profit to Net Worth	Indeterminate: depends on the substitution of liabilities (interest-bearing debt for interest-free funds, such as accounts payable), as well as the current interest rate, interest coverage, and the relationship between return on assets and return on equity
Total Liabilities to Net Worth	No change*
Current Liabilities to Net Worth	Decrease: lower current liabilities in relation to net worth*
Current Assets to Current Liabilities	Increase: greater cushion between current assets and current liabilities because of lower current liabilities*

†Assuming that a portion of the increase in net worth would be used to reduce current liabilities.
*Assuming that the increase in long-term debt is used to reduce current liabilities.

Cash and Short-Term Investments plus Accounts Receivable to Current Liabilities (Quick Ratio)	Increase: greater coverage of current liabilities from liquid assets because of lower current liabilities*
Net Sales to Working Capital	Decrease: greater working capital sufficiency in relation to net sales because of lower current liabilities*
Total Noncurrent Assets to Net Worth	No change*
Long-Term Liabilities to Working Capital	Depends whether the ratio is greater or less than 1.0: increase (proportionately greater dependence of working capital on long-term liabilities) will result if the ratio is less than 1.0, because long-term liabilities would be increased at a faster rate than working capital; decrease (proportionately less dependence of working capital on long-term liabilities) will result if the ratio is greater than 1.0, because long-term liabilities would be increased at a slower rate than working capital
Net Profit to Total Assets	Indeterminate: depends on the substitution of liabilities (interest-bearing debt for interest-free funds, such as accounts payable)

*Assuming that the increase in long-term debt is used to reduce current liabilities.

Chapter 23

The Three Most Common Reasons for Management Review of Financial Statements

Owners and managers have many occasions to analyze their company's financial statement. In my experience, however, almost all of them are closely related to the three situations most likely to prompt a detailed financial review: (1) cash flow difficulties, (2) the prospect of rapid growth in the immediate future, and (3) pending bank negotiations. The analytical steps appropriate to making better business decisions in each of these situations are set forth in the following checklist.

1. Cash Squeeze; Problem Paying Bills

    ☐ Slow collection of customer invoices: high *Collection Period of Accounts Receivable**
    ☐ Sluggish inventory: low *Cost of Sales to Inventory**
    ☐ Insufficient working capital: high *Net Sales to Working Capital*; causes:

    ☐ Inadequate owners' equity: high *Net Sales to Net Worth**
    ☐ Poor utilization of fixed assets (tending to draw funds from working capital to fixed assets): low *Net Sales to Fixed Assets**
    ☐ Diversion of working capital into miscellaneous assets: high *Days' Sales in Miscellaneous Assets**
    ☐ Poor matching of long-term debt to noncurrent assets (thereby penalizing working capital): low *Long-Term Liabilities to Total Noncurrent Assets**

2. Rapid Growth Planned: Possible Danger Signs

    ☐ High financial leverage: high *Total Liabilities to Net Worth*; causes:

    ☐ Inadequate owners' equity: high *Net Sales to Net Worth**
    ☐ Substandard asset utilization: low *Net Sales to Total Assets*;* causes:

    ☐ Slow collection of customer invoices: high *Collection Period of Accounts Receivable**

*Causal ratio.

☐ Sluggish inventory: low *Cost of Sales to Inventory**
☐ Poor utilization of fixed assets: low *Net Sales to Fixed Assets**

☐ Weak working capital balance (small cushion in coverage of current liabilities from current assets): low *Current Assets to Current Liabilities*; causes:

☐ Slow collection of customer invoices: high *Collection Period of Accounts Receivable**
☐ Sluggish inventory: low *Cost of Sales to Inventory**
☐ Insufficient working capital: high *Net Sales to Working Capital*; causes:

☐ Inadequate owners' equity: high *Net Sales to Net Worth**
☐ Poor utilization of fixed assets (tending to draw funds from working capital to fixed assets): low *Net Sales to Fixed Assets** (although this problem may be reduced by sales expansion if excess capacity at present time)
☐ Diversion of working capital into miscellaneous assets: high *Days' Sales in Miscellaneous Assets**
☐ Poor matching of long-term debt to noncurrent assets (thereby penalizing working capital): low *Long-Term Liabilities to Total Noncurrent Assets**

☐ Poor return on equity (tending to limit ability to increase net worth from retained earnings): low *Net Profit to Net Worth*; causes:

☐ Deficient profit margin on sales: low *Net Profit to Net Sales** (low *Net Sales to Net Worth*, the other factor that can produce low *Net Profit to Net Worth*, is not a likely problem with respect to potential sales growth)

☐ Inadequate owners' equity: high *Net Sales to Net Worth** (this condition may cause a problem, even if *Total Liabilities to Net Worth* is not now high, because it requires the company to maintain high *Net Sales to Total Assets* in order to avoid high *Total Liabilities to Net Worth* in the future)
☐ Deficient profit margin on sales: low *Net Profit to Net Sales** (this condition may cause a problem, even if *Net Profit to Net Worth* is not low, because it makes the company vulnerable to price competition, particularly if the expansion plans call for significant investment in fixed assets)

3. Bank Negotiations Pending: Possible Danger Signs That May Require Explanation

☐ High financial leverage: high *Total Liabilities to Net Worth*; causes:

☐ Inadequate owners' equity: high *Net Sales to Net Worth**
☐ Substandard asset utilization: low *Net Sales to Total Assets*;* causes:

☐ Slow collection of customer invoices: high *Collection Period of Accounts Receivable**
☐ Sluggish inventory: low *Cost of Sales to Inventory**
☐ Poor utilization of fixed assets: low *Net Sales to Fixed Assets**

*Causal ratio.

☐ Weak working capital balance (small cushion in coverage of current liabilities from current assets): low *Current Assets to Current Liabilities*; causes:

   ☐ Slow collection of customer invoices: high *Collection Period of Accounts Receivable**
   ☐ Sluggish inventory: low *Cost of Sales to Inventory**
   ☐ Insufficient working capital: high *Net Sales to Working Capital*; causes:

      ☐ Inadequate owners' equity: high *Net Sales to Net Worth**
      ☐ Poor utilization of fixed assets (tending to draw funds from working capital to fixed assets): low *Net Sales to Fixed Assets**
      ☐ Diversion of working capital into miscellaneous assets: high *Days' Sales in Miscellaneous Assets**
      ☐ Poor matching of long-term debt to noncurrent assets (thereby penalizing working capital): low *Long-Term Liabilities to Total Noncurrent Assets**

☐ Subnormal coverage of current liabilities from liquid assets: low *Cash and Short-Term Investments plus Accounts Receivable to Current Liabilities* (*Quick Ratio*); causes:

   ☐ Weak working capital balance (small cushion in coverage of current liabilities from current assets): low *Current Assets to Current Liabilities*; causes: See "Weak working capital balance," listed earlier.
   ☐ Sluggish inventory: low *Cost of Sales to Inventory**

Even for owners and managers of companies experiencing no evident difficulties in operating performance or basic financial structure, using this checklist to analyze the company's position on an annual basis may reveal trends that foreshadow future problems. If certain causal factors are found to be less than satisfactory, you may wish to refer to Chapter 29, which describes possible corrective measures.

*Causal ratio.

Part V

Application of the Causal Ratios

Now that we have examined the sixteen ratios that together form the financial picture of a company and have seen that changes in the seven primary ratios necessarily affect the nine secondary ratios, a question arises regarding the order of importance of the causal measures. How do we ascertain cause or promote cure of a business ill if two of the seven primary ratios are at wide variance with industry norms? Or if four are out of line? And if all seven are distorted, what is their rank of importance? The answer to these questions is that no relative weight can arbitrarily be assigned among the primary ratios. Although no strict rule exists for distinguishing the comparative importance of each primary ratio in a situation where more than one differ significantly from industry standards, the application of fundamental logic will enable you to assess the role of each, as we see in the following chapters.

In many cases, fortunately, only one of the causal ratios is distorted relative to the industry norm, and your problem is then quite simple. Occasionally, all seven causal measures contribute to a company's plight; under such extreme circumstances, the business under analysis may be beyond redemption. Before you pass judgment on a company's future prospects, however, it is necessary to evaluate each specific problem identified through ratio analysis and to consider the corrective measures that may be realistically undertaken. A careful review of the comparative condition and influence of each causal ratio will indicate the nature of changes that should be made. If the analyst is an owner or officer of the company—or, as a professional advisor or major creditor, is able to influence the thinking of a top decision maker in the firm—he or she can establish a plan of constructive action to strengthen the company's financial structure. To illustrate this point, we review the year-to-year changes in the causal factors that have brought our now familiar Companies A, B, C, and D to their present circumstances, as reflected in the secondary ratios we have studied. In the next four chapters, we will see how the key financial ratios can be used to identify fundamental financial management problems and guide the analyst to practical solutions.

As we have previously observed, Companies A, B, C, and D are in the same line of business, which permits direct comparison with a single set of industry standards. In many industries, however, statistical norms are compiled for several size categories (ordinarily separated by the dollar amount of net sales or total assets). When such detailed information can be obtained, it should obviously be used; but, in the following examples, one composite financial profile is assumed to be the only comparative data available. For purposes of illustration, composite financial figures from several contract manufacturing lines have been compiled and treated as a single industry. Contract (make-to-order) manufacturing firms were selected because of their comparative flexibility with respect to sales and marketing strategy, their distribution of assets (between accounts receivable, inventory, and fixed assets), and their vulnerability to cyclical changes in the economy. Examples of the cause-and-effect ratio technique in standard manufacturing, wholesaling, distribution, retailing, and service industries are found in Part VI.

Chapter 24

Company A: A New Strategy to Avert Disaster

Company A, which has been our most consistent example of a profitable firm with a conservative financial structure, was not always in that position. In fact, this company's financial characteristics had been far different only three years earlier.

The management crisis that occurred at Company A in early 19X7 was more than unpleasant, but it resulted in new life for a dying family business. When Jim Palumbo, Company A's general manager, learned that his father, the sole owner, had been in a major auto accident and would be unable to return to work for weeks or possibly months, his first concern was his father's health. Within one day, however, he was more worried about keeping the family business—actually his father's business—alive. For nearly five years, Jim (known as Jim Junior to most of the shop employees and called The Kid by the older machinists) had made loud but futile attempts to convince his father to change Company A's method of operating: to modernize and become more aggressive in finding new customers. Jim Senior, who had founded the company in the 1950s and had run it more for his personal creative satisfaction than for big profits, could not see the need for change. Even a loss for the year 19X7, the first red ink in the company's history, had not convinced The Big Boss that a new strategy was in order.

Less than one week after the accident, Jim Junior told his mother that his father must give him power of attorney for all transactions of Company A or he would quit before the end of the month. He was working countless hours, but virtually all of his time was spent shuttling between the business and the hospital, just carrying orders to the plant and bringing back bad news: We're out of this, our biggest customer wants that, our best steel supplier wants to know when we'll send a check. Jim Junior had, in effect, made many of the day-to-day decisions for years but had always needed his father's approval to give the final word. The company's basic business approach (which was not an actual plan or coherent strategy) had, however, always been the domain of Jim Senior. This emergency situation made Jim Junior painfully aware of the waste of time involved in seeking approval for decisions he had already made. More than that, he knew that the company's very existence was in immediate peril from the cumulative effects of a method of operation (a nonstrategy in reality) that was no longer appropriate for today's conditions.

When he stood at the foot of the hospital bed and stated his ultimatum, Jim Junior was met with bitter recriminations. Forty-eight hours later, he held the power of attorney. The personal details are not important.

Need for Fundamental Analysis

Jim Junior immediately set to work with Cliff Kelly, his shop supervisor, to discuss a course of action for the next three months. By the end of the first evening, both Jim and Cliff realized that short-term moves must be tied to a long-term strategy based on a fundamental analysis of the company's competitive position. They were both convinced that Company A needed major modernization of its equipment in order to eliminate production bottlenecks, reduce costs, and compete more effectively for new, more profitable business. But could the company afford such a move? Because Jim Junior knew that cash was extremely tight, he suggested to Cliff that they defer any discussion of equipment acquisition until morning.

To begin his analysis of Company A's competitive position and its feasible alternatives, Jim went to the shelf where his father had neatly placed—unread—all of the annual industry studies he had received from his trade association over the years. The latest report, for the previous year (19X6), had just arrived. Fortunately, the study had been prepared by a consultant familiar with cause-and-effect ratio analysis, so that Jim was able to calculate Company A's key financial ratios by following a few simple instructions. (The dollar figures for 19X6 are shown in the first column of Table 24-1.) He then wrote Company A's ratios in the margin next to the published figures for the appropriate sales volume category. The key ratios for Company A and its comparison group are displayed in Table 24-2.

Jim immediately found verification of his belief that Company A's investment in equipment was inadequate: *Net Sales to Fixed Assets* was much higher than the industry standard. Such a result could also indicate highly efficient use of modern equipment, but Jim knew that this was not the case. High *Net Sales to Fixed Assets* can also occur when a large portion of the company's equipment is leased on an operating basis, but that was not a factor for Company A. Consequently, the increase in fixed assets advocated by both Jim and Cliff seemed, at first impression, to be a reasonable move.

Comparatively high *Net Sales to Fixed Assets* tends to increase total asset utilization and thereby produce relatively high *Net Sales to Total Assets*. After reading that observation in the industry report, Jim compared Company A's *Net Sales to Total Assets* with the group median and found just the opposite: Company A's asset utilization was actually very low in relation to the results achieved by its competitors. Obviously, other factors were influencing this summary ratio. Further reading suggested a review of *Cost of Sales to Inventory* and the *Collection Period of Accounts Receivable*.

Table 24-1. Income statement and balance sheet for Company A for four years.

	19X6	19X7	19X8	19X9
Income statement				
Net sales	$1,300,000	$1,100,000	$1,300,000	$1,500,000
Cost of sales	1,066,000	846,000	976,000	1,110,000
Selling & administrative expenses	222,000	240,000	264,000	296,000
Net profit before interest expense	12,000	14,000	60,000	94,000
Interest expense	64,000	32,000	30,000	18,000
Net profit before taxes	(52,000)	(18,000)	30,000	76,000
Income taxes	(18,000)	(6,000)	10,000	26,000
Net profit after taxes	$ (34,000)	$ (12,000)	$ 20,000	$ 50,000
Depreciation expense	$ 10,000	$ 34,000	$ 24,000	$ 24,000
Balance sheet				
Cash & short-term investments	$ 10,000	$ 30,000	$ 40,000	$ 52,000
Accounts receivable	256,000	120,000	140,000	152,000
Inventory	344,000	164,000	164,000	170,000
Other current assets	10,000	20,000	22,000	24,000
Current assets	620,000	334,000	366,000	398,000
Fixed assets	62,000	172,000	148,000	124,000
Other noncurrent assets	78,000	14,000	14,000	14,000
Total assets	$ 760,000	$ 520,000	$ 528,000	$ 536,000
Current liabilities	$ 544,000	$ 224,000	$ 236,000	$ 220,000
Long-term liabilities	20,000	112,000	88,000	62,000
Total liabilities	564,000	336,000	324,000	282,000
Net worth	196,000	184,000	204,000	254,000
Total liabilities & net worth	$ 760,000	$ 520,000	$ 528,000	$ 536,000

Jim had assumed that inventory turnover (actually inventory throughput in the case of contract manufacturing) would be comparatively low for Company A and would tend to depress total asset utilization. Comparing Company A's *Cost of Sales to Inventory* revealed that Jim was right again: Company A was far below the industry norm. Relative to its sales activity, the business obviously had a tremendous amount of money tied up in inventory, a problem that Jim believed could be greatly reduced through modernization.

Following the suggestion in the industry report, he also took a quick look at the *Collection Period of Accounts Receivable*—and was startled by what he saw. Other companies in the industry were typically collecting their money in only 42 days, one month faster than Company A. How could that be? Jim Senior, who handled credit-and-collection activities for all the major customers, had often said that he would like to see the money come in faster, but slow payment was just

Table 24-2.   Primary and secondary ratios for Company A over four years.

	19X6	*19X7*	*19X8*	*19X9*
Primary (causal) ratios				
Net Profit to Net Sales				
Company	(4.0)%	(1.6)%	2.3%	5.1%
Industry standard	2.7%	1.0%	2.1%	3.2%
Net Sales to Total Assets				
Company	1.7 times	2.1 times	2.5 times	2.8 times
Industry standard	2.5 times	2.4 times	2.5 times	2.4 times
Collection Period				
of Accounts Receivable				
Company	72 days	40 days	39 days	37 days
Industry standard	42 days	44 days	43 days	44 days
Cost of Sales to Inventory				
Company	3.1 times	5.2 times	6.0 times	6.5 times
Industry standard	5.7 times	5.3 times	5.5 times	5.1 times
Net Sales to Fixed Assets				
Company	20.1 times	6.4 times	8.8 times	12.1 times
Industry standard	10.5 times	10.0 times	10.5 times	10.3 times
Net Sales to Net Worth				
Company	6.6 times	6.0 times	6.4 times	5.9 times
Industry standard	6.9 times	6.7 times	6.9 times	6.8 times
Long-Term Liabilities				
to Total Noncurrent				
Assets				
Company	0.1 times	0.6 times	0.5 times	0.4 times
Industry standard	0.5 times	0.5 times	0.5 times	0.5 times
Secondary (effect) ratios				
Net Profit to Net Worth				
Company	(26.5)%	(9.8)%	14.7%	29.9%
Industry standard	18.6%	6.7%	14.5%	21.6%
Total Liabilities				
to Net Worth				
Company	2.9 times	1.8 times	1.6 times	1.1 times
Industry standard	1.7 times	1.8 times	1.8 times	1.8 times
Current Liabilities				
to Net Worth				
Company	2.8 times	1.2 times	1.2 times	0.9 times
Industry standard	1.4 times	1.4 times	1.4 times	1.4 times
Net Sales				
to Working Capital				
Company	17.1 times	10.0 times	10.0 times	8.4 times
Industry standard	10.9 times	11.1 times	10.9 times	10.2 times
Current Assets				
to Current Liabilities				
Company	1.1 times	1.5 times	1.6 times	1.8 times
Industry standard	1.5 times	1.4 times	1.4 times	1.5 times

	19X6	19X7	19X8	19X9
Cash and Short-Term Investments plus Accounts Receivable to Current Liabilities (Quick Ratio)				
Company	0.5 times	0.7 times	0.8 times	0.9 times
Industry standard	0.7 times	0.7 times	0.7 times	0.7 times
Total Noncurrent Assets to Net Worth				
Company	0.7 times	1.0 times	0.8 times	0.5 times
Industry standard	0.7 times	0.7 times	0.7 times	0.7 times
Long-Term Liabilities to Working Capital				
Company	0.3 times	1.0 times	0.7 times	0.3 times
Industry standard	0.5 times	0.6 times	0.5 times	0.6 times
Net Profit to Total Assets				
Company	(6.8)%	(3.5)%	5.7%	14.2%
Industry standard	6.9%	2.4%	5.2%	7.7%

one of the problems of this line of business. Jim Junior suddenly realized that Company A had been acting as a charitable banker, a source of free money for its customers. At the same time, he was aware that chronic late delivery by Company A made attempts to collect past-due accounts more difficult.

> High *Net Sales to Fixed Assets* increases *Net Sales to Total Assets*. That beneficial effect, however, can be more than offset by a high *Collection Period of Accounts Receivable* or low *Cost of Sales to Inventory*.

For the next hour, Jim calculated how much cash he could squeeze out of inventory and accounts receivable if he could get *Cost of Sales to Inventory* and *Collection Period of Accounts Receivable* in line with industry standards. The company could pay for new equipment with the new-found funds. But, of course, there was one catch: Company A needed that money, and possibly more, for equipment in order to improve inventory throughput (and reduce costs in the process) and thereby offer more reliable delivery as an inducement for more rapid payment by customers. After 25 years in small business, Jim knew that changing the payment habits of customers is not an easy matter. Just the same, he was confident that after a few months of improved operations he could convince Company A's customers to pay more rapidly.

Meeting With a Banker

The next morning, he called Company A's banker for an appointment the following day. Armed with his handwritten projections, which showed that

Company A could easily pay for $150,000 of new equipment from a reduction of accounts receivable and inventory, Jim approached the meeting with unbridled optimism. Within minutes after sitting down in the bank conference room, however, Jim learned that he had an unexpected problem. Art Weber, a mid-level bank officer who was a long-time friend of Jim's father, told him that the bank was worried about "the company's undercapitalized situation" and might have to restrict use of its credit line. The banker cited the company's very high *Total Liabilities to Net Worth* and its very low *Current Assets to Current Liabilities* as evidence of undercapitalization. In view of the company's recent operating loss, Art suggested that Jim should invest $100,000 or $150,000 in the business as a means of reducing debt. He offered to meet again in one week to discuss what the bank might be willing to do if that condition could be met.

Realizing that he had not done all his homework, Jim went back to the plant to ponder what his banker had said. First of all, investing $100,000 or more was out of the question. He didn't have the money to put into the company because his father continued to pay him just enough to maintain an adequate middle-class existence. More than that, Jim instinctively believed that the company wasn't really undercapitalized. His father had always plowed back any profits into the company, apparently to support the high level of accounts receivable and inventory. Jim was determined to read the rest of the industry report that night and find out more about capitalization and any other factors that would give him a better sense of direction.

From his earlier study of the causal ratios, Jim remembered that the report had referred to undercapitalization as relatively high *Net Sales to Net Worth*. He also seemed to recall that Company A's ratio was slightly on the low side. After rechecking his calculations, he reconfirmed that Company A was not undercapitalized in the strictest sense: There was, in fact, sufficient owners' equity (net worth) to support sales volume. Why, then, did the *Total Liabilities to Net Worth* ratio emphasized by the banker look so bad?

Following the logic of the industry report, Jim saw that the problem had to be low *Net Sales to Total Assets*, the only other possible cause of high *Total Liabilities to Net Worth*. The report also noted that, although bankers are primarily interested in repayment from future earnings, they are also concerned about downside risk. Consequently, lenders often pay particular attention to *Total Liabilities to Net Worth*, which shows how much debt a company has incurred in relation to owners' equity (net worth). The higher the *Total Liabilities to Net Worth* ratio, the lower the cushion against adverse developments, such as continuing losses, bad debts, or writedowns of inventory. From that single perspective, Company A could be considered "undercapitalized," although the cause was clearly low asset utilization rather than inadequate investment adequacy. Whatever the terminology, Jim now realized that an even swap between lower accounts receivable and inventory and higher fixed assets would not be satisfactory to the banker. Company A needed to increase its total *Net Sales to Total Assets* ratio.

A high *Total Liabilities to Net Worth* ratio does not necessarily mean that a company is undercapitalized. It may be caused by low *Net Sales to Total Assets* as well as by high *Net Sales to Net Worth*. High *Net Sales to Net Worth*, which shows a small amount of owners' equity (net worth) supporting net sales, is the best measure of capitalization.

Art Weber, the banker, had also talked about Company A's low *Current Assets to Current Liabilities*. When Jim referred to the industry standard, he saw that Art had a valid point: Company A's *Current Assets to Current Liabilities* was well below the norm. In fact, current assets barely exceeded current liabilities. He could see why Art was worried—and began to worry a little himself. The industry report showed that *Current Assets to Current Liabilities* can be pulled down by a high *Collection Period of Accounts Receivable*, low *Cost of Sales to Inventory*, or high *Net Sales to Working Capital*. Jim had already discovered that the two causal ratios—the *Collection Period of Accounts Receivable* and *Cost of Sales to Inventory*—were unfavorable; he soon learned that *Net Sales to Working Capital*, an important secondary ratio, was also on the unfavorable side, indicated by a comparatively high value in relation to the industry norm.

According to the industry report, three ratios ordinarily had the largest influence on *Net Sales to Working Capital*: *Net Sales to Fixed Assets* (already identified as favorable in terms of basic financial structure), *Net Sales to Net Worth* (known to be slightly on the favorable side), and *Long-Term Liabilities to Total Noncurrent Assets*. Although a low level of debt is usually considered a favorable factor from a conservative viewpoint, low *Long-Term Liabilities to Total Noncurrent Assets* also tends to reduce working capital. A low ratio shows that the company has not matched long-term debt to its long-term (noncurrent) assets. In Company A's case, however, that one ratio did not seem far enough out of line to cause such high (unfavorable) *Net Sales to Working Capital*.

Low *Long-Term Liabilities to Total Noncurrent Assets* reduces working capital because current assets are decreased or current liabilities are increased, on a relative basis, to pay for noncurrent assets. Lower working capital in support of sales volume (shown by high *Net Sales to Working Capital*) increases the likelihood of cash flow difficulties. This situation also lowers *Current Assets to Current Liabilities*, providing lenders with a smaller cushion against bad-debt losses and inventory writedowns.

Move to Reduce Accounts Receivable and Inventory

The industry report mentioned the possibility that a high level of miscellaneous (other noncurrent) assets, such as investments in affiliated companies, might also reduce working capital and produce high *Net Sales to Working Capital*. Determined to prepare a solid financial plan, Jim checked out this lead and discovered that the amount of miscellaneous assets on the company's books was actually greater than the depreciated value of its fixed assets. All those little investments in cousin Tony's business over the years had grown to a substantial amount that was now hurting Company A's working capital to a major extent. In view of Tony's recent success, Jim was sure that the company could turn $60,000 in loans and promises of stock into cash within a short time—an important step toward paying bills and improving Company A's basic financial position. Such a move would immediately increase working capital, lower *Net Sales to Working Capital*, and boost *Current Assets to Current Liabilities*. The most fundamental objective, however, would be to reduce accounts receivable and inventory in order to decrease current liabilities. *Current Assets to Current Liabilities* would then rise and *Total Liabilities to Net Worth* would fall, both favorable signs to a banker.

> Although not ordinarily a major financial factor, miscellaneous assets (all noncurrent assets other than fixed assets) can occasionally have a significant impact on a company's financial structure. Most industry reports do not publish information concerning the relationship between miscellaneous assets and net sales; consequently, comparative standards are difficult to locate. In most lines of business, however, a level of miscellaneous assets greater than 10 days of net sales would be definitely on the high side. A high level of miscellaneous assets reduces working capital and increases debt.

A New Plan

With his new understanding of financial ratios, Jim began to develop a two-step plan for realizing his vision of a more modern, more efficient, more competitive, and more profitable Company A. He would make it his highest priority to work with Cliff Kelly to improve internal efficiency and inventory throughput within the limits of the company's existing equipment; he would personally attempt to speed collection of the most overdue accounts; and he would use $10,000 of the money expected from cashing in the loans/investment in Tony's business as a down payment on $50,000 of equipment that would help to relieve two critical production bottlenecks and thereby add greatly to the inventory reduction effort. Jim knew that he should propose this transaction to the banker before proceeding, but he decided that successful implementation would argue more eloquently than any plans he might put on paper.

    In their meeting the following week, Jim thanked Art Weber for pointing out the problems with *Total Liabilities to Net Worth* and *Current Assets to Current Liabilities* and outlined his strategy for reducing accounts receivable and inventory. Then he asked for a commitment from Art. If Company A could reduce its *Total Liabilities to Net Worth* from its present level of 2.9 to 2.3 within six months or less—and also increase its *Current Assets to Current Liabilities* from 1.1 to 1.3, half the way back to the industry standard of 1.5—would the bank be willing to finance $100,000 of equipment needed to make Company A fully competitive? Art hesitated, observed Jim's determination, and then signaled his agreement with an outstretched hand.

A Stronger Financial Structure

Four months later, Jim returned to Art's office to report that both goals for the ratios had been met, but not without related problems. One major customer, accounting for more than 10% of 19X6 sales, had stopped ordering two months ago when Jim pressed for payment on overdue bills. Most of the outstanding amount had been paid in the meantime, but total income for the current year would be reduced from previous projections. In fact, a small loss for 19X7 appeared likely. A few other customers were expressing displeasure with the change in policy, but most were expected to adjust without undue difficulty. Art appeared a bit uneasy about the drop in sales and another loss year, but he honored his commitment to finance the needed equipment. By the end of 19X7, Company A's basic financial structure was much stronger, despite lower total sales, a net loss, and a substantial boost in fixed assets.

Jim realized in retrospect that he may have pushed too hard and too fast in reducing accounts receivable, but Company A had surpassed its goals for the year in restoring financial balance. Although *Net Sales to Fixed Assets* had fallen well below the industry standard because of the rapid modernization program, the reduction of the *Collection Period of Accounts Receivable* and the increase in *Cost of Sales to Inventory* boosted *Net Sales to Total Assets* toward the industry norm. The critical factor was Company A's slightly favorable *Net Sales to Net Worth* at the inception of the new strategic plan, a condition attributable to Jim Senior's conservative financial viewpoint. It is questionable whether Company A could have recovered from the combined effect of four unfavorable causal ratios— low (actually negative) *Net Profit to Net Sales*, high *Collection Period of Accounts Receivable*, low *Cost of Sales to Inventory*, and low *Long-Term Liabilities to Total Noncurrent Assets* (as well as a high level of miscellaneous assets relative to net sales)—without such a solid investment base.

The years 19X8 and 19X9 saw Company A return to prosperity and an unusually solid financial structure. The company has not shown spectacular growth or monumental profitability (at least not yet), but it is clearly a stable enterprise as of 19X9. In fact, it serves as an excellent example of a profitable and conservatively managed company relative to the industry standard. Jim Senior, now a semi-retired consultant to the firm which he sold to his son in 19X8, shows grudging respect for the turnaround.

With experience, you will begin to recognize the interplay between causal ratios, not only as they influence the secondary ratios, but also as they affect one another. In the case of Company A, the apparently favorable utilization of fixed assets (shown by the firm's very high *Net Sales to Fixed Assets*) during 19X7 was actually exerting an unfavorable influence on profit margin, the collection of accounts receivable, and inventory turnover. As a practical matter, every causal ratio that is significantly different from common industry practice requires investigation. In some situations, further analysis will reveal that a competitive advantage can be strengthened; in others, you will find that the apparently favorable effect of an extremely high or low ratio is actually detrimental to one or more of the other causal factors. There is no doubt that Company A's very high *Net Sales to Fixed Assets* tended to increase total asset utilization and thereby reduce total debt. Those beneficial effects were, however, far outweighed by the operating loss, the torpid collection of accounts receivable, and the sluggish inventory that were attributable, at least in part, to Company A's nearly obsolete facilities.

High Financial Leverage and Undercapitalization

Greater experience with the cause-and-effect ratio approach will enable the analyst to distinguish two important, and often related, conditions: high financial leverage and undercapitalization. All too many bankers, accountants, and consultants make the mistake of assuming that abnormally high financial leverage (*Total Liabilities to Net Worth* significantly above the industry standard) is, in and of itself, proof of undercapitalization. In reality, undercapitalization is properly defined as inadequate owners' equity to support sales volume: high *Net Sales to Net Worth*.

As we have seen in the case of Company A, poor asset utilization is often the basic cause of excessive financial leverage (a comparatively high ratio of *Total Liabilities to Net Worth*). Consequently, in a few exceptional cases, a chronically low asset utilization ratio makes high *Total Liabilities to Net Worth* an accurate indicator of undercapitalization. A company with moderate *Net Sales to Net Worth* might be properly identified as undercapitalized if a low level of asset utilization is inherent in the company's strategic position, involving, for example, an extraordinarily great ongoing commitment to costly plant and equipment or extremely slow inventory throughput by virtue of the complexity of the product. Under such circumstances, where there is essentially no hope of bringing asset utilization in line with the industry norm, an unusually high level of owners' equity would certainly be required to hold financial leverage within the range of common experience. Thus, it might be argued that, in this specific instance, *Total Liabilities to Net Worth* can be used to measure both financial leverage and the adequacy of capitalization. Nevertheless, such situations are relatively rare, and you should use the causal ratio, *Net Sales to Net Worth*, as an indicator of investment (or capitalization) adequacy, not the secondary ratio, *Total Liabilities to Net Worth*.

Ordinarily, such fine distinctions and issues of semantics do not arise in cause-and-effect ratio analysis. The causal factors are usually quite apparent, and the resultant factors are easily identified. With respect to financial leverage and capitalization, however, the terminology is often used imprecisely or incorrectly. Press reports of leveraged buy-outs have, for example, done much to suggest that high financial leverage is necessarily a matter of low capitalization. Nevertheless, as long as the conscientious analyst recognizes the causal nature of *Net Sales to Net Worth* (measuring investment adequacy) as distinguished from the resultant characteristics of *Total Liabilities to Net Worth* (measuring financial leverage), he will reach the right conclusion.

Chapter 25

Company B: Steps Toward the Comfort Level

Throughout our comparison of operating results and financial structure by means of the key ratios, Company B has been our middle-of-the-road example, close to the industry standard in virtually every respect during 19X9. But this was not always the case.

Until 19X6, Company B's owner, Matt Leonardziak, had taken extreme pains to avoid owing money for anything but major equipment purchases, and even then, he had always been careful to make a big down payment. He wanted to concentrate on production, which he liked and understood. Financial leverage and other approaches to maximizing return on investment were of no interest to Matt, who had turned a garage-based business into a solid money-making enterprise. Nevertheless, Matt had felt increasing money pressure for several years, and by 19X6 he knew that something was wrong. When he received his financial statement for that year, he asked his financial advisor to review the numbers for ideas about improving the firm's basic structure. Company B's dollar figures are shown in Table 25-1, and the sixteen key financial ratios are displayed in Table 25-2.

Lacking understanding of cause-and-effect ratio analysis, Matt's financial advisor calculated the six ratios he considered most appropriate for Company B, compared them with industry standards he found in the trade association report that Matt had given him, and concluded that Company B was in solid financial shape at the end of 19X6. His brief report made the following observations:

1. *Net Profit to Net Sales* was similar to the industry standard, showing an adequate profit margin.
2. *Net Sales to Total Assets* was somewhat higher than the industry standard, indicating satisfactory asset utilization.
3. The *Collection Period of Accounts Receivable* was very low, demonstrating prompt payment by customers.
4. *Cost of Sales to Inventory* was very high, showing efficient purchasing and rapid throughput (low work-in-process).
5. *Total Liabilities to Net Worth* was below the group median, indicating relatively low financial leverage.

Table 25-1. Income statement and balance sheet for Company B for four years.

	19X6	19X7	19X8	19X9
Income statement				
Net sales	$4,250,000	$4,500,000	$4,750,000	$5,000,000
Cost of sales	3,200,000	3,390,000	3,575,000	3,775,000
Selling & administrative				
expenses	860,000	1,020,000	1,085,000	1,000,000
Net profit				
before interest expense	190,000	90,000	90,000	225,000
Interest expense	90,000	75,000	67,500	75,000
Net profit before taxes	100,000	15,000	22,500	150,000
Income taxes	30,000	5,000	7,500	50,000
Net profit after taxes	$ 70,000	$ 10,000	$ 15,000	$ 100,000
Depreciation expense	$ 175,000	$ 175,000	$ 75,000	$ 100,000
Balance sheet				
Cash & short-term				
investments	$ 0	$ 50,000	$ 75,000	$ 100,000
Accounts receivable	350,000	510,000	550,000	625,000
Inventory	400,000	500,000	600,000	750,000
Other current assets	25,000	25,000	25,000	25,000
Current assets	775,000	1,085,000	1,250,000	1,500,000
Fixed assets	725,000	550,000	475,000	500,000
Other noncurrent assets	0	0	0	0
Total assets	$1,500,000	$1,635,000	$1,725,000	$2,000,000
Current liabilities	$ 565,000	$ 670,000	$ 795,000	$1,000,000
Long-term liabilities	310,000	330,000	285,000	250,000
Total liabilities	875,000	1,000,000	1,080,000	1,250,000
Net worth	625,000	635,000	645,000	750,000
Total liabilities &				
net worth	$1,500,000	$1,635,000	$1,725,000	$2,000,000

6. *Current Assets to Current Liabilities* was close to the industry standard, showing that Company B had an essentially normal cushion against bad-debt losses or possible writedowns of inventory.

Based on those findings, the advisor concluded that the cash flow pressure Matt had been feeling was simply normal for a company in that line of business with sales approaching $5 million.

Matt was unconvinced. Surely business should not be a constant scramble to pay suppliers and reduce the credit line. That kind of pressure takes the fun out of doing the company's primary work. While burdened by thoughts of more bills coming due, Matt came across a notice from his trade association that a regional meeting would feature a seminar on analyzing financial statements for better business decisions. Perhaps he could find the answer to his problem there. Later

Table 25-2.　Primary and secondary ratios for Company B over four years.

	19X6	19X7	19X8	19X9
Primary (causal) ratios				
Net Profit to Net Sales				
Company	2.4%	0.3%	0.5%	3.0%
Industry standard	2.7%	1.0%	2.1%	3.2%
Net Sales to Total Assets				
Company	2.8 times	2.8 times	2.8 times	2.5 times
Industry standard	2.5 times	2.4 times	2.5 times	2.4 times
Collection Period				
of Accounts Receivable				
Company	30 days	41 days	42 days	46 days
Industry standard	42 days	44 days	43 days	44 days
Cost of Sales to Inventory				
Company	8.0 times	6.8 times	6.0 times	5.0 times
Industry standard	5.7 times	5.3 times	5.5 times	5.1 times
Net Sales to Fixed Assets				
Company	5.9 times	8.2 times	10.0 times	10.0 times
Industry standard	10.5 times	10.0 times	10.5 times	10.3 times
Net Sales to Net Worth				
Company	6.8 times	7.1 times	7.4 times	6.7 times
Industry standard	6.9 times	6.7 times	6.9 times	6.8 times
Long-Term Liabilities				
to Total Noncurrent				
Assets				
Company	0.4 times	0.6 times	0.6 times	0.5 times
Industry standard	0.5 times	0.5 times	0.5 times	0.5 times
Secondary (effect) ratios				
Net Profit to Net Worth				
Company	16.0%	2.4%	3.5%	20.0%
Industry standard	18.6%	6.7%	14.5%	21.6%
Total Liabilities				
to Net Worth				
Company	1.4 times	1.6 times	1.7 times	1.7 times
Industry standard	1.7 times	1.8 times	1.8 times	1.8 times
Current Liabilities				
to Net Worth				
Company	0.9 times	1.1 times	1.2 times	1.3 times
Industry standard	1.4 times	1.4 times	1.4 times	1.4 times
Net Sales				
to Working Capital				
Company	20.2 times	10.8 times	10.4 times	10.0 times
Industry standard	10.9 times	11.1 times	10.9 times	10.2 times
Current Assets				
to Current Liabilities				
Company	1.4 times	1.6 times	1.6 times	1.5 times
Industry standard	1.5 times	1.4 times	1.4 times	1.5 times

	19X6	19X7	19X8	19X9
Cash and Short-Term Investments plus Accounts Receivable to Current Liabilities (Quick Ratio)				
Company	0.6 times	0.8 times	0.8 times	0.7 times
Industry standard	0.7 times	0.7 times	0.7 times	0.7 times
Total Noncurrent Assets to Net Worth				
Company	1.2 times	0.9 times	0.7 times	0.7 times
Industry standard	0.7 times	0.7 times	0.7 times	0.7 times
Long-Term Liabilities to Working Capital				
Company	1.5 times	0.8 times	0.6 times	0.5 times
Industry standard	0.5 times	0.6 times	0.5 times	0.6 times
Net Profit to Total Assets				
Company	6.7%	0.9%	1.3%	7.5%
Industry standard	6.9%	2.1%	5.2%	7.7%

that month, he sat in the meeting room trying to keep pace with all kinds of financial terminology that was only vaguely familiar to him. Matt was encouraged, nevertheless, by the seminar leader, who said that the material he was distributing for later review would enable every participant to make a step-by-step analysis of his or her company's financial statement by using the cause-and-effect ratio approach. The following weekend, Matt spread out the material on his desk and started the process.

Results of Low Net Sales to Fixed Assets

He was surprised to see that the first four ratios used in the seminar were the same as those in his financial consultant's report. Maybe his advisor was right after all. The fifth ratio in the seminar material—*Net Sales to Fixed Assets*—had, however, not been included by the consultant. In fact, his advisor had told Matt that fixed assets would not be a factor in cash flow unless *Current Assets to Current Liabilities* was weakened by such acquisitions. On the other hand, the seminar material, based on the cause-and-effect system, emphasized that each of the causal ratios must be carefully considered and that any major difference between a company's causal ratio and the industry standard will have an effect on the company's competitive position. The material also pointed out that comparatively low *Net Sales to Fixed Assets* results in a reduction of working capital relative to net sales, and consequently, higher *Net Sales to Working Capital*.

> A low *Net Sales to Fixed Assets* ratio reduces working capital sufficiency (shown by an increase in *Net Sales to Working Capital*).

Matt saw immediately that Company B's *Net Sales to Fixed Assets* was extremely low in comparison with the industry standard. He was proud of his business's modern equipment and the high-tech image Company B had acquired in recent years, but he had not realized that his investment in fixed assets was so far out of line in relation to net sales. Turning quickly to *Net Sales to Working Capital*, he found that the seminar material was exactly right: Company B's ratio was nearly twice as high as the typical ratio for the comparison group. As the narrative explained, high *Net Sales to Working Capital* causes periodic cash flow difficulties. Even relatively slight delays in shipments or customer payments place a strain on the company's comparatively small amount of working capital available to support net sales.

> A low *Collection Period of Accounts Receivable* and high *Cost of Sales to Inventory* tend to increase *Current Assets to Current Liabilities* by enabling the company to generate cash more quickly and thereby reduce current liabilities. In fact, a low *Collection Period of Accounts Receivable* and high *Cost of Sales to Inventory* can cause a company with inadequate working capital to show *Current Assets to Current Liabilities* higher than the industry standard. Despite favorable *Current Assets to Current Liabilities* (which indicates a comparatively large cushion for meeting current obligations in the event of bad-debt losses or inventory writedowns), a company with inadequate working capital in relation to sales volume is subject to cash flow problems every time customer payments are temporarily slow, shipments are delayed, or sales dip briefly.

In addition, the seminar material listed high *Total Noncurrent Assets to Net Worth* and high *Long-Term Liabilities to Working Capital* as other likely results of having low *Net Sales to Fixed Assets*. Right again. Company B's *Total Noncurrent Assets to Net Worth* was higher than 1.0, indicating that long-term debt was required to provide the company with any working capital whatsoever. In turn, this caused very high *Long-Term Liabilities to Working Capital*, which shows that Company B was under comparatively great pressure to repay long-term debt by diverting current cash flow or by actually reducing the net amount of working capital. Matt had found that Company B did indeed have a cash flow problem. More importantly, he was able to identify the cause.

Return to the Industry Norm

Returning to the two remaining causal ratios, Matt found that *Net Sales to Net Worth* and *Long-Term Liabilities to Total Noncurrent Assets* were essentially in line with industry standards. He now knew that he must concentrate on reducing Company B's fixed assets in relation to net sales. A few calculations showed that depreciation of existing equipment coupled with modest sales growth would boost *Net Sales to Fixed Assets* to the industry norm within two years.

Matt thought long and hard about the relative benefit of Company B's high-tech image versus his cash flow worries. Since no radical action was needed, Matt decided that, for the time being, Company B should concentrate on developing new applications for its existing equipment. Within six months, he found that cash flow had begun to improve noticeably. In fact, by the end of the year, he awarded himself a significant cash bonus and bought a small sailboat. Reported net profit fell to a negligible amount, but net cash flow was boosted by high depreciation and low capital expenditures. Matt found that he was able to be more relaxed about customer payments and was spending far less time juggling collections and accounts payable. In addition, Company B was able to concentrate on larger jobs and more complex work because the firm could now carry increased work-in-process inventory. The basis for Company B's high-tech image was shifting from an equipment list to innovative applications.

As of 19X9, Matt has settled Company B near the middle of the industry with respect to basic financial structure. He has devised plans for achieving higher profitability in very specialized operations, but he expects to avoid daring financial moves in order to concentrate his energy on Company B's manufacturing innovations. With that in mind, Matt faithfully reviews each of the 16 key financial ratios every year and works to keep all of the causal ratios—except *Net Profit to Net Sales*, which he hopes to boost through two pending contracts—within the range of common experience in the industry.

A Single Unfavorable Ratio

An experienced analyst familiar with the cause-and-effect ratio approach would have quickly identified *Net Sales to Fixed Assets* as the only causal ratio that was unfavorable from a conservative point of view at the end of 19X6. Obviously, Company B's owner was seeking to place his business in a less financially aggressive posture through reduced debt pressure and greater freedom from working capital squeezes. Thus, the other two causal ratios that were not in line with common industry experience, the *Collection Period of Accounts Receivable* and *Cost of Sales to Inventory*, could not have been the source of problems from the owner's perspective, since both of them were already on the conservative side. In fact, the speedy collection of accounts receivable (shown by Company B's low *Collection Period of Accounts Receivable*) and the rapid turnover of inventory (demonstrated by high *Cost of Sales to Inventory*) clearly had the effect of accelerating cash flow and reducing debt. Therefore, only one ratio could have caused Company B's perceived distress: *Net Sales to Fixed Assets*.

That's exactly how quickly you can solve many formerly perplexing financial problems with cause-and-effect ratio analysis.

Chapter 26

Company C:
An Unnecessary Fall

Company C has served as our example of a business with multiple financial deficiencies, based on a comparison of 19X9 results with standards for the industry. Only a few years ago, however, Company C was regarded as a solidly profitable firm with a conservative financial structure.

When T. J. Champion died suddenly in late 19X6, his son, Peter, left his mid-level financial position in a major computer manufacturing concern to take control of Company C, where he had worked each summer from junior high through graduate school. Observing Company C's unspectacular growth over the years, Peter had long been impatient with his father's cautious, step-by-step guidance of the family business. His father, in turn, had been indifferent to financial theories and complex methodologies: "Paper shuffling at the expense of people" and "B.S. is the right degree for accounting" were two of his recurring phrases. T. J. had not asked Peter's business advice since a major disagreement five years earlier. Although T. J. had willed the company's stock to his wife with the expectation that she would work out a transfer to key employees, a series of trades and promises among the family members soon gave Peter majority ownership of Company C. Now Peter could put his ideas to work.

During the first week, he loaded his accounting software on Company C's computer and began to develop numerous, highly detailed 60-month projections of operations and cash flow. Between financial calculations, developing a new policies and procedures manual, and telephoning major clients to announce his position with the company, Peter spent virtually all of his time in the office, far removed from the shop floor. He delegated day-to-day decisions to the general manager, Frank Garcia, who had, in effect, been T. J.'s manufacturing partner. Peter did, however, take pride in imposing certain new procedures that he considered more businesslike: obtaining quotations on every material purchase over $500 and receiving written comments on all discrepancies between estimated and actual labor on every job. He began an ambitious effort to develop special software for optimum scheduling of every piece of equipment in the plant. By the end of 19X7, several key employees had left, plans for a new automated assembly process had been scrapped, and delayed shipments had become more common. Nevertheless, sales volume relative to the previous year was actually better than that of the typical company in the industry because of bids and orders in the pipeline—new work obtained during T. J.'s last days. With the hearty concurrence of his mother and his sister, the remaining minority shareholders, Peter declared a substantial dividend at the end of 19X7. Comparative results for 19X6 and 19X7 are shown in Table 26-1 and Table 26-2.

Except for noting the unexpected decline in *Net Profit to Net Sales*, Peter had no interest in basic financial measures. During his M.B.A. training in the mid-1980s, Peter was taught that traditional ratio analysis would soon give way to computerized cash flow projections through spreadsheet software. In his zest for learning these new techniques, he neglected to heed his professors' warnings that such projections are only as good as the underlying assumptions about the *Collection Period of Accounts Receivable*, *Cost of Sales to Inventory*, and *Net Sales to Fixed Assets*. Instead, he busily constructed projections that assumed

Table 26-1.   Income statement and balance sheet for Company C for four years.

	19X6	*19X7*	*19X8*	*19X9*
Income statement				
Net sales	$11,000,000	$11,500,000	$12,000,000	$12,500,000
Cost of sales	8,250,000	8,740,000	9,240,000	9,750,000
Selling & administrative				
expenses	2,130,000	2,170,000	2,190,000	2,150,000
Net profit				
before interest expense	620,000	590,000	570,000	600,000
Interest expense	180,000	240,000	370,000	450,000
Net profit before taxes	440,000	350,000	200,000	150,000
Income taxes	150,000	120,000	60,000	50,000
Net profit after taxes	$ 290,000	$ 230,000	$ 140,000	$ 100,000
Depreciation expense	$ 250,000	$ 270,000	$ 290,000	$ 300,000
Balance sheet				
Cash & short-term				
investments	$ 200,000	$ 150,000	$ 120,000	$ 100,000
Accounts receivable	1,220,000	1,420,000	1,810,000	2,090,000
Inventory	1,380,000	1,640,000	2,150,000	2,500,000
Other current assets	50,000	50,000	50,000	50,000
Current assets	2,850,000	3,260,000	4,130,000	4,740,000
Fixed assets	1,100,000	1,200,000	1,300,000	1,400,000
Other noncurrent assets	100,000	150,000	350,000	510,000
Total assets	$4,050,000	$4,610,000	$5,780,000	$6,650,000
Current liabilities	$1,900,000	$2,390,000	$3,270,000	$3,780,000
Long-term liabilities	650,000	710,000	990,000	1,330,000
Total liabilities	2,550,000	3,100,000	4,260,000	5,110,000
Net worth	1,500,000	1,510,000	1,520,000	1,540,000
Total liabilities &				
net worth	$4,050,000	$4,610,000	$5,780,000	$6,650,000

Table 26-2. Primary and secondary ratios for Company C over four years.

	19X6	19X7	19X8	19X9
Primary (causal) ratios				
Net Profit				
to Net Sales				
Company	4.0%	3.0%	1.7%	1.2%
Industry standard	.7%	1.0%	2.1%	3.2%
Net Sales				
to Total Assets				
Company	2.7 times	2.5 times	2.1 times	1.9 times
Industry standard	2.5 times	2.4 times	2.5 times	2.4 times
Collection Period				
of Accounts Receivable				
Company	40 days	45 days	55 days	61 days
Industry standard	42 days	44 days	43 days	44 days
Cost of Sales				
to Inventory				
Company	6.0 times	5.3 times	4.3 times	3.9 times
Industry standard	5.7 times	5.3 times	5.5 times	5.1 times
Net Sales				
to Fixed Assets				
Company	10.0 times	9.6 times	9.2 times	8.9 times
Industry standard	10.5 times	10.0 times	10.5 times	10.3 times
Net Sales				
to Net Worth				
Company	7.3 times	7.6 times	7.9 times	8.1 times
Industry standard	6.9 times	6.7 times	6.9 times	6.8 times
Long-Term				
Liabilities				
to Total Noncurrent				
Assets				
Company	0.5 times	0.5 times	0.6 times	0.7 times
Industry standard	0.5 times	0.5 times	0.5 times	0.5 times
Secondary (effect) ratios				
Net Profit				
to Net Worth				
Company	29.3%	23.2%	13.2%	9.7%
Industry standard	18.6%	6.7%	14.5%	21.6%
Total Liabilities				
to Net Worth				
Company	1.7 times	2.1 times	2.8 times	3.3 times
Industry standard	1.7 times	1.8 times	1.8 times	1.8 times
Current Liabilities				
to Net Worth				
Company	1.3 times	1.6 times	2.2 times	2.5 times
Industry standard	1.4 times	1.4 times	1.4 times	1.4 times

	19X6	19X7	19X8	19X9
Net Sales				
to Working Capital				
Company	11.6 times	13.2 times	14.0 times	13.0 times
Industry standard	10.9 times	11.1 times	10.9 times	10.2 times
Current Assets				
to Current Liabilities				
Company	1.5 times	1.4 times	1.3 times	1.3 times
Industry standard	1.5 times	1.4 times	1.4 times	1.5 times
Cash and Short-Term				
Investments plus				
Accounts Receivable				
to Current Liabilities				
(Quick Ratio)				
Company	0.7 times	0.7 times	0.6 times	0.6 times
Industry standard	0.7 times	0.7 times	0.7 times	0.7 times
Total Noncurrent Assets				
to Net Worth				
Company	0.8 times	0.9 times	1.1 times	1.2 times
Industry standard	0.7 times	0.7 times	0.7 times	0.7 times
Long-Term Liabilities				
to Working Capital				
Company	0.7 times	0.8 times	1.2 times	1.4 times
Industry standard	0.5 times	0.6 times	0.5 times	0.6 times
Net Profit				
to Total Assets				
Company	10.9%	7.6%	3.5%	2.3%
Industry standard	6.9%	2.4%	5.2%	7.7%

work would be completed and shipped when scheduled, all paperwork would be ready for immediate invoicing, customers would continue to pay within 15 days of net 30-day terms, and equipment would be purchased as required to meet competitive conditions. He did not feel the need to compare 19X7 financial ratios to previous results because he regarded Company C as a new organization unshackled from the stodgy and unimaginative methods of the past.

Failure to Track Financial Measures

Because Peter did not understand that cause-and-effect ratio analysis will always be a fundamental "reality check" of financial calculations—whether as input in a software package or as an independent test of past performance and future projections—he did not see the value of tracking Company C's year-to-year trends or comparing them with industry norms. If he had done so, he would have found that Company C's basic financial structure had become less favorable, from a conservative point of view, in almost every respect despite comparatively high

Net Profit to Net Sales. The 19X7 situation was certainly not alarming, but the increase in the *Collection Period of Accounts Receivable* and the decline in *Cost of Sales to Inventory*, coupled with a decline in *Net Sales to Fixed Assets*, caused *Total Liabilities to Net Worth* to rise. During the same period, *Current Assets to Current Liabilities* dropped a notch for the same reasons.

During 19X8, Peter felt increasing frustration and financial pressure as four more long-term employees retired early or joined competing companies. In reviewing Company C's 19X8 performance with his banker, Peter was advised to examine the firm's escalating *Total Liabilities to Net Worth* and declining *Current Assets to Current Liabilities*. In December 19X8, the mid-point of Company C's fiscal year, Frank Garcia suggested that Peter seek outside advice about current operations and basic financial structure. For that perceived insult, Peter ordered Frank to keep his attention focused on production and customer relations, which had, in fact, been the entire basis of the company's ability to maintain a steady flow of work during otherwise very difficult times. Within two weeks, Frank and his top supervisor had given notice.

Only after Peter had received Company C's preliminary financial statement for the year ended June 30, 19X9, did he come to grips with the extent of the concern's financial difficulties. The one and only financial ratio he regularly checked—*Net Profit to Net Sales*—had fallen for the third straight year, even though sales had again shown modest growth. Maybe someone from the outside could, after all, provide a new analytical technique that would identify the source of the profit decline. Peter was certain that Company C's cash flow pressure was the result of foul-ups by inexperienced personnel, but he was now willing to consider the possibility that some new method might offer a clue to internal improvement. Through his business school contacts, Peter was put in touch with Tom Dworak, a professor and consultant from the main campus of the state university. Emphasizing his private university M.B.A. in their first meeting, Peter recited a litany of complaints about his employees' inability to carry out his grand plans, then produced financial statements to prove his point. Tom asked Peter whether he had converted the raw data to financial ratios. Learning that he had not done so, he suggested that Peter tell him more about Company C while Tom's graduate assistant performed the calculations. Peter was visibly incredulous at the idea that a respected professor of business management would be interested in basic financial ratios. He had expected to find complex statistical models, impressive "number-crunching" routines, and fancy graphic displays.

A Picture of Overall Deficiency

A few minutes later, Tom scanned the numbers for fiscal 19X9 and then passed them across the desk to Peter. The key financial ratios showed that Company C was deficient in virtually every important area of financial management: profit margin, collection of accounts receivable, inventory turnover/throughput, fixed asset activity, and investment adequacy. The combined effect of two causal ratios—comparatively low asset utilization (low *Net Sales to Total Assets*) and relatively low investment adequacy (high *Net Sales to Net Worth*)—resulted in very high financial leverage (very high *Total Liabilities to Net Worth*), a clearly unfavorable condition. Because Company C had used long-term debt to finance a large proportion of noncurrent assets (shown by high *Long-Term Liabilities to Total Noncurrent Assets*), working capital pressure was not as great as might otherwise be expected. Nevertheless, Company C's *Current Assets to Current Liabilities* was significantly lower than the industry standard, while the business's comparatively high *Net Sales to Working Capital* indicated a relatively small amount of working capital to support sales volume. Working capital was clearly dependent on long-term debt, as shown by *Long-Term Liabilities to Working Capital*, which was much higher than the industry norm.

When Tom asked Peter, as diplomatically as possible, how he could have allowed Company C to drift so far from normal industry performance, Peter mumbled something about every company having a unique set of circumstances. Tom quickly agreed and reached into his consulting file to prove Peter's point. He showed Peter the data in Table 26-3 and Table 26-4, with all company identification removed, of course, to preserve client confidentiality. Pointing out the close similarity of the comparison company's fiscal 19X9 performance to that of Company C, Tom explained that while both organizations temporarily appeared to be almost interchangeable, they were actually following very different paths. Company C had shown a general deterioration of financial control, while the comparison company had simply outrun its financial resources in responding to demand from its customers.

Tom reinforced Peter's idea that each company is unique by explaining that he had been urging management of the other business to hold back the sales volume projected for 19X0, unless an infusion of new capital could be arranged. He stressed the fact that unusually rapid growth can impair a company's financial structure. He then suggested that Peter take time to study each element of Company C's financial structure for possible improvement. He concluded by stating that Peter should not expect his company to solve its problems through rapid growth. Instead, he advised step-by-step analysis of the key financial ratios.

Low *Net Profit to Net Sales* reduces *Net Profit to Net Worth*, a key indicator of the company's ability to increase net worth through retained earnings. Low *Net Profit to Net Worth* will, in turn, have the effect of raising *Total Liabilities to Net Worth* whenever sales volume is expanded more rapidly than net worth is increased.

A high *Collection Period of Accounts Receivable*, low *Cost of Sales to Inventory*, and low *Net Sales to Fixed Assets* all reduce *Net Sales to Total Assets*. Low *Net Sales to Total Assets* increases *Total Liabilities to Net Worth*. High *Net Sales to Net Worth*, which indicates relatively low owners' equity to support net sales, also increases *Total Liabilities to Net Worth*.

Low asset utilization reduces *Current Assets to Current Liabilities*. A high *Collection Period of Accounts Receivable* and low *Cost of Sales to Inventory*

Table 26-3. Income statement and balance sheet for Company Z for four years.

	19X7	19X8	19X9	Projected 19X0
Income statement				
Net sales	$450,000	$700,000	$1,125,000	$1,800,000
Cost of sales	351,000	543,000	875,000	1,405,000
Selling & administrative expenses	77,000	124,000	195,000	310,000
Net profit before interest expense	22,000	33,000	55,000	85,000
Interest expense	8,000	20,000	40,000	62,000
Net profit before taxes	14,000	13,000	15,000	23,000
Income taxes	5,000	5,000	5,000	8,000
Net profit after taxes	$ 9,000	$ 8,000	$ 10,000	$ 15,000
Depreciation expense	$ 23,000	$ 16,000	$ 27,000	$ 40,000
Balance sheet				
Cash & short-term investments	$ 9,000	$ 9,000	$ 10,000	$ 9,000
Accounts receivable	73,000	114,000	192,000	286,000
Inventory	82,000	133,000	221,000	320,000
Other current assets	4,000	5,000	4,000	9,000
Current assets	168,000	261,000	427,000	624,000
Fixed assets	50,000	77,000	121,000	189,000
Other noncurrent assets	18,000	27,000	17,000	46,000
Total assets	$236,000	$365,000	$565,000	$859,000
Current liabilities	$ 75,000	$172,000	$330,000	$543,000
Long-term liabilities	40,000	63,000	107,000	164,000
Total liabilities	115,000	235,000	437,000	707,000
Net worth	121,000	130,000	128,000	152,000
Total liabilities & net worth	$236,000	$365,000	$565,000	$859,000

decrease *Current Assets to Current Liabilities* by adding to current assets and current liabilities (thereby reducing the proportionate relationship between them without actually decreasing working capital). Low *Net Sales to Fixed Assets* reduces working capital by decreasing current assets and/or increasing current liabilities.

Peter asked for a photocopy of Tom's calculations, thanked him for the opportunity to meet, and left the office. He has not called again, and Company C's survival plan is not known.

New Tack for Company Z

Interestingly, Jim Jamison, the owner of Company Z, the business that Professor Dworak discussed with Peter, recently contacted Tom to say that they have scaled

Table 26-4. Primary and secondary ratios for Company Z over four years.

	19X7	*19X8*	*19X9*	*19X0*
Primary (causal) ratios				
Net Profit to Net Sales				
Company	3.1%	1.9%	1.3%	1.3%
Industry standard	1.0%	2.1%	3.2%	Unknown
Net Sales to Total Assets				
Company	1.9 times	1.9 times	2.0 times	2.1 times
Industry standard	2.4 times	2.5 times	2.4 times	Unknown
Collection Period of Accounts Receivable				
Company	59 days	59 days	62 days	58 days
Industry standard	44 days	43 days	44 days	Unknown
Cost of Sales to Inventory				
Company	4.3 times	4.1 times	4.0 times	4.4 times
Industry standard	5.3 times	5.5 times	5.1 times	Unknown
Net Sales to Fixed Assets				
Company	9.0 times	9.1 times	9.3 times	9.5 times
Industry standard	10.0 times	10.5 times	10.3 times	Unknown
Net Sales to Net Worth				
Company	3.7 times	5.4 times	8.8 times	11.8 times
Industry standard	6.7 times	6.9 times	6.8 times	Unknown
Long-Term Liabilities to Total Noncurrent Assets				
Company	0.6 times	0.6 times	0.8 times	0.7 times
Industry standard	0.5 times	0.5 times	0.5 times	Unknown
Secondary (effect) ratios				
Net Profit to Net Worth				
Company	11.6%	10.0%	11.7%	15.5%
Industry standard	6.7%	14.5%	21.6%	Unknown
Total Liabilities to Net Worth				
Company	1.0 times	1.8 times	3.4 times	4.7 times
Industry standard	1.8 times	1.8 times	1.8 times	Unknown
Current Liabilities to Net Worth				
Company	0.6 times	1.3 times	2.6 times	3.6 times
Industry standard	1.4 times	1.4 times	1.4 times	Unknown
Net Sales to Working Capital				
Company	4.8 times	7.9 times	11.6 times	22.2 times
Industry standard	11.1 times	10.9 times	10.2 times	Unknown
Current Assets to Current Liabilities				
Company	2.2 times	1.5 times	1.3 times	1.1 times
Industry standard	1.4 times	1.4 times	1.5 times	Unknown

(continued)

Table 26-4.   *Continued.*

	19X7	*19X8*	*19X9*	*19X0*
Cash and Short-Term Investments plus Accounts Receivable to Current Liabilities (Quick Ratio)				
Company	1.1 times	0.7 times	0.6 times	0.5 times
Industry standard	0.7 times	0.7 times	0.7 times	Unknown
Total Noncurrent Assets to Net Worth				
Company	0.6 times	0.8 times	1.1 times	1.5 times
Industry standard	0.7 times	0.7 times	0.7 times	Unknown
Long-Term Liabilities to Working Capital				
Company	0.4 times	0.7 times	1.1 times	2.0 times
Industry standard	0.6 times	0.5 times	0.6 times	Unknown
Net Profit to Total Assets				
Company	5.9%	3.6%	2.7%	2.7%
Industry standard	2.4%	5.2%	7.7%	Unknown

back their expansion plans. Tom is pleased that Jim has finally realized how the rapid rise of *Net Sales to Net Worth* between 19X6 and 19X9 had placed a tremendous strain on Company Z's financial structure, particularly on *Total Liabilities to Net Worth* and *Current Assets to Current Liabilities*, and that 19X0 should be a year of consolidation, not further expansion. In fact, if Company Z had actually attempted to implement its original plans for 19X0 (shown in Table 26-3 and Table 26-4), the business would almost surely have encountered extreme financial difficulty, despite its steady (although low) profit margin and its outstanding sales growth. Because Jim does not wish to consider outside investment, Company Z must rely on retained earnings to increase net worth in order to support sales expansion.

In his reply to Jim, Tom emphasized that although the company's *Net Sales to Total Assets* has actually shown a slight increase during the past two years, this ratio remains noticeably below the industry norm. All three ratios relating to the three key asset items are unfavorable in relation to the median for the company's comparison group: The *Collection Period of Accounts Receivable* is comparatively high, *Cost of Sales to Inventory* is relatively low, and *Net Sales to Fixed Assets* is comparatively low. Each of these measures indicates that the specific asset item represents a large proportion of net sales. In other words, Company Z's relatively low *Net Sales to Total Assets* is attributable to comparative inefficiencies in all three key areas of asset management. If asset utilization could be improved in any, or all, of these areas, debt pressure could be correspondingly reduced. In terms of ratios, higher *Net Sales to Total Assets* would lower Company Z's *Total Liabilities to Net Worth*, which now stands well above the industry norm. Greater asset utilization would also have the effect of boosting Company Z's relatively low *Current Assets to Current Liabilities*.

Company Z, Professor Dworak stated in his letter, faces a basic problem: Its comparatively low *Net Profit to Net Sales* does not enable the business to generate and retain earnings at a sufficiently rapid rate to support the company's sales growth. In other words, sales have been increasing at a faster pace than net worth can be boosted through retained earnings, resulting in a steady rise in *Net Sales to Net Worth*. This, in turn, has produced an ongoing increase in *Total Liabilities to Net Worth*, an unfavorable trend. Company Z's relatively low *Net Profit to Net Worth* is an indicator of the business's problem in generating retained earnings to increase net worth at a sufficient rate to support the growth in sales.

Although Company C and Company Z appear almost interchangeable based on fiscal 19X9 results, Company C clearly faces the greater challenge in surviving to see the next millennium. Company Z's management can decide to reduce sales growth and concentrate on improving the business's profit margin and its asset utilization, both of which have remained remarkably stable during a period of rapid expansion. Simply putting the brakes on sales volume and improving basic operations would keep existing financial pressures from growing more severe, and, through the effect of net profit and retained earnings, would increase Company Z's financial strength through the passage of time. Company C, on the other hand, must take decisive action to arrest unfavorable trends in virtually every area of operations and financial structure.

Clearly, the analyst should make a specific effort to detect trends when assessing a company's financial position. Careful consideration of year-to-year shifts, together with an evaluation of the company's current status in comparison with similar organizations, will reveal much about a company's future prospects.

The Significance of Trends

As you gain experience with the cause-and-effect ratio approach, you will consider the cumulative effect of small year-to-year changes in the causal ratios. Very large deviations from the norm, or major shifts from one year to the next, will readily call themselves to your attention. On the other hand, a number of seemingly minor changes in the causal ratios can, in the aggregate, produce significant improvement or deterioration in a company's financial structure. These subtle movements in financial relationships are likely to escape detection until the key ratios drift outside the range of common experience for the industry, unless the analyst directs specific attention to identifying trends.

The adverse change in six of Company C's causal ratios between 19X6 and 19X7 was somewhat difficult to discern for two major reasons:

1. Small shifts from one year to the next should not cause great concern until a continuing trend is evident.

2. Company C reported a comparatively high profit margin during 19X7 (because, as we learned earlier, a backlog of orders had the effect of masking operating inefficiencies).

By 19X9, however, a systematic trend analysis would have revealed the fact that every causal ratio had moved in an unfavorable direction, with the possible exception of the increase in *Long-Term Liabilities to Total Noncurrent Assets*, which boosted working capital as part of an effort to compensate for the changes in the other causal ratios. Certainly, Company C's gradual deterioration should serve as a reminder to pay attention to relatively subtle year-to-year differences in the causal ratios.

Company Z, the business used by Professor Dworak for direct comparison, also showed a recent unfavorable trend with respect to most of the causal ratios. There was, however, one causal ratio—*Net Sales to Net Worth*—that exhibited especially severe deterioration. Direct examination of that key financial factor demonstrated that the problem was attributable to sales growth at a greater rate than owners' equity could be boosted through retained earnings. Consequently, Company Z's management has clear choices among three alternatives: Restrict the expansion of sales volume to a level that can be supported by an increase in net worth, obtain outside investment, or face increasingly great debt pressure and potential bankruptcy.

Chapter 27

Company D: Look to the Future

As seen throughout Part III, Company D has shown the effects of attempting to counterbalance certain extreme characteristics (in this case, very low owners' equity) by means of other extreme financial factors (very high asset utilization and very high long-term debt). Now we find that Company D's uncommon financial structure is the result of a recent leveraged buyout. Because the business's fundamental position has been altered so radically by the refinancing, previous operating results and balance sheet data have little relevance to future prospects. In fact, Company D's new ownership is relying on a total reorganization, including a three-year agreement with both plant and clerical workers, to achieve a complete turnaround of a virtually bankrupt enterprise.

Until recently, Company D had been a division of a national conglomerate. The steady decline of this unit during the previous four years had been the result of an unwise acquisition of a growing business by an incompatible corporation bent on satisfying short-term expansion goals. The original company, which had gained a national reputation for quality production and personal service, had been purchased from the estate of the founder by the conglomerate as part of an ambitious plan to use the facility to produce parts for a major military contract. Because the local work force had not responded to changes in organizational procedures (which included numerous layoffs) in the manner anticipated by the merger and acquisition experts, the parent company had decided to cut its mounting losses by subcontracting the military component work and closing the plant.

For a variety of personal and business reasons, the plant manager and four of his top employees, including the controller transferred from corporate headquarters two years earlier, developed a plan to reorganize the division as an independent company and continue production of the components for the conglomerate at slightly less than ordinary market price while reestablishing the outside customer base. Because such an arrangement would provide greater continuity for the parent organization's military work, a deal was quickly consummated, with major assistance from the community's largest bank. The new management team had obtained a personal commitment from the local union leadership and the sales and administrative staff to generate maximum output of quality parts, with no increase in pay for the years 19X0 and 19X1, in exchange for the promise of no layoffs without direct consultation and approval from the workers' organization during that time. Management has recently gone a step further and has proposed a gradual redesign of both plant layout and work assignments in direct cooperation with the bargaining unit and the office employees. The first year's results reported by the reorganized company, together with management's financial projections for 19X0 and 19X1, are shown in Table 27-1 and Table 27-2.

Start of a Turnaround

Although the first 12 months of operations were burdened by numerous one-time expenses anticipated in the reorganization (as well as by a few costly mistakes),

Table 27-1.   Income statement and balance sheet for Company D over three years.

		Projected	
	19X9	*19X0*	*19X1*
Income statement			
Net sales	$50,000,000	$60,000,000	$75,000,000
Cost of sales	40,000,000	45,000,000	56,250,000
Selling & administrative expenses	8,500,000	9,350,000	11,675,000
Net profit before interest expense	1,500,000	5,650,000	7,075,000
Interest expense	550,000	850,000	1,000,000
Net profit before taxes	950,000	4,800,000	6,075,000
Income taxes	300,000	1,600,000	2,025,000
Net profit after taxes	$ 650,000	$ 3,200,000	$ 4,050,000
Depreciation expense	$ 500,000	$ 900,000	$ 1,475,000
Balance sheet			
Cash & short-term investments	$ 100,000	$ 500,000	$ 600,000
Accounts receivable	2,850,000	4,925,000	8,225,000
Inventory	4,900,000	5,700,000	7,200,000
Other current assets	550,000	300,000	300,000
Current assets	8,400,000	11,425,000	16,325,000
Fixed assets	2,450,000	4,000,000	7,000,000
Other noncurrent assets	550,000	250,000	250,000
Total assets	$11,400,000	$15,675,000	$23,575,000
Current liabilities	$ 5,400,000	$ 5,900,000	$ 6,900,000
Long-term liabilities	4,450,000	5,025,000	7,875,000
Total liabilities	9,850,000	10,925,000	14,775,000
Net worth	1,550,000	15,675,000	23,575,000
Total liabilities & net worth	$11,400,000	$15,675,000	$23,575,000

Table 27-2.   Primary and secondary ratios for Company D over three years.

		Projected	
	19X9	*19X0*	*19X1*
Primary (causal) ratios			
Net Profit to Net Sales			
Company	1.9%	8.0%	8.1%
Industry standard	3.2%	Unknown	Unknown
Net Sales to Total Assets			
Company	4.4 times	3.8 times	3.2 times
Industry standard	2.4 times	Unknown	Unknown
Collection Period *of Accounts* *Receivable*			
Company	21 days	30 days	40 days
Industry standard	44 days	Unknown	Unknown
Cost of Sales to Inventory			
Company	8.2 times	7.9 times	7.8 times
Industry standard	5.1 times	Unknown	Unknown
Net Sales to Fixed Assets			
Company	20.4 times	15.0 times	10.7 times
Industry standard	10.3 times	Unknown	Unknown
Net Sales to Net Worth			
Company	32.3 times	12.6 times	8.5 times
Industry standard	6.8 times	Unknown	Unknown
Long-Term Liabilities *to Total Noncurrent* *Assets*			
Company	1.5 times	1.2 times	1.1 times
Industry standard	0.5 times	Unknown	Unknown
Secondary (effect) ratios			
Net Profit to Net Worth			
Company	61.3%	101.1%	69.0%
Industry standard	21.6%	Unknown	Unknown
Total Liabilities *to Net Worth*			
Company	6.4 times	2.3 times	1.7 times
Industry standard	1.8 times	Unknown	Unknown
Current Liabilities *to Net Worth*			
Company	3.5 times	1.2 times	0.8 times
Industry standard	1.4 times	Unknown	Unknown
Net Sales to Working Capital			
Company	16.7 times	10.9 times	8.0 times
Industry standard	10.2 times	Unknown	Unknown

(continued)

Table 27-2. *Continued.*

| | 19X9 | Projected | |
		19X0	19X1
Current Assets			
to Current Liabilities			
Company	1.6 times	1.9 times	2.4 times
Industry standard	1.5 times	Unknown	Unknown
Cash and Short-Term			
Investments plus			
Accounts Receivable			
to Current Liabilities			
(Quick Ratio)			
Company	0.5 times	0.9 times	1.3 times
Industry standard	0.7 times	Unknown	Unknown
Total Noncurrent Assets			
to Net Worth			
Company	1.9 times	0.9 times	0.8 times
Industry standard	0.7 times	Unknown	Unknown
Long-Term Liabilities			
to Working Capital			
Company	1.5 times	0.9 times	0.8 times
Industry standard	0.6 times	Unknown	Unknown
Net Profit to Total Assets			
Company	8.3%	30.6%	25.8%
Industry standard	7.7%	Unknown	Unknown

the company showed a profit, only slightly below the 2.0% target established by management, and a distinct improvement over 19X8. Nevertheless, as the management team recently reemphasized to employee representatives, Company D must generate and retain maximum profits over the next two years in order to survive. Not only is the business obligated to repay its massive debt, but customers cannot be expected to make concessions and pay their bills within an average of 21 days for very long. An arrangement negotiated in late 19X9 with the selling corporation and supported informally by four of Company D's other top five customers called for payment in 30 days or less during 19X0, but a gradual shift to standard industry practice, remittance in approximately 45 days on net 30-day terms, is expected during the next two years. As a practical matter, the *Collection Period of Accounts Receivable* is likely to rise to 40 days by 19X1, but remain slightly lower than the current industry standard. That would cause accounts receivable to become three times larger within two years if the company achieves its projected 50% increase in net sales.

> A low *Collection Period of Accounts Receivable* increases *Net Sales to Total Assets*, which, in turn, reduces *Total Liabilities to Net Worth*. A low *Collection Period of Accounts Receivable* also increases *Current Assets to Current Liabilities*, although it does not actually boost the amount of working capital.

The extremely rapid throughput of work, as reflected in *Cost of Sales to Inventory*, is also projected to move down slightly toward the industry norm during the next two years. Although the work force is not likely to maintain the same extraordinarily energetic dedication to production through hard work alone, management anticipates that the reorganization of the plant and certain work rules, together with the modernization of equipment, will boost long-term productivity and net profit. On the other hand, management's plan calls for the production of increasingly sophisticated and complex parts and subassemblies, which will tend to increase work-in-process inventory, regardless of other productivity improvements. The net effect is projected as a small decrease in *Cost of Sales to Inventory*. In view of the planned 50% increase in sales volume, Company D will experience a major rise in the dollar amount of inventory by the end of 19X1.

High *Cost of Sales to Inventory* increases *Net Sales to Total Assets*, which, in turn, reduces *Total Liabilities to Net Worth*. High *Cost of Sales to Inventory* also increases *Current Assets to Current Liabilities*, although it does not actually boost the amount of working capital.

In addition, the old-fashioned plant must be redesigned, and the nearly obsolete equipment replaced, if the company is to survive beyond the mid-19X0s. At the present time, Company D's production success is largely attributable to a skilled work force, but technological changes now occurring in the industry will soon make modernization of physical facilities a necessity. Major capital expenditures will be required, in any case, simply to support the planned 50% increase in sales volume. Based on management's projections of new investment in plant and equipment, *Net Sales to Fixed Assets* would decline from an almost astronomical 20.4 in 19X9 to 10.7 in 19X1, similar to the 19X9 industry standard of 10.3. Future sales growth, coupled with the effects of depreciation, will allow Company D to increase its *Net Sales to Fixed Assets* somewhat during the years beyond 19X2, according to current estimates.

High *Net Sales to Fixed Assets* increases *Net Sales to Total Assets*, which, in turn, reduces *Total Liabilities to Net Worth*. High *Net Sales to Fixed Assets* also increases working capital sufficiency and raises *Current Assets to Current Liabilities*.

Need for High Return on Sales

Management's plans are entirely dependent on achieving a high *Net Profit to Net Sales* ratio in 19X0 and 19X1. Rapid growth at a low profit margin would be disastrous, because it would cause an even greater—probably crushing—debt burden. All too many business strategies are based simply on increasing sales and profit dollars. They do not consider whether owners' equity (net worth) can be expanded at a rate sufficient to support the rise in assets that accompanies sales growth. Company D's projections indicate that *Net Sales to Net Worth* will decline from 32.3 to 8.5 by 19X1, showing that net worth will be boosted at a faster rate than sales are expected to increase. This reduction in *Net Sales to Net Worth* would make a major contribution to a stronger financial structure. In fact, projections for *Total Liabilities to Net Worth* indicate the effects of the boost in net worth: Total liabilities would decline from $6.40 to $1.70 per dollar of net worth between 19X9 and 19X1.

> High *Net Sales to Net Worth*, which shows a low level of owners' equity in support of net sales, increases risk by raising *Total Liabilities to Net Worth*. At the same time, it boosts the percentage reward to owners by increasing *Net Profit to Net Worth*.

The Next Strategic Decision

Management is determined to build a strong financial structure as quickly as possible in order to maximize its options by the end of the grace period in 19X1. At that time, the company will face a critical strategic decision: to pursue continued rapid growth, but at a profit margin that is expected to drop significantly (due to wage and salary adjustments), or to stabilize operations and distribute a greater portion of income to employees and owners. But unless Company D is successful in improving its financial structure through retained earnings in the next two years, its options will be severely limited and its very survival will be in jeopardy.

The relative significance of key financial ratios is influenced by the specific business context. In some cases, background information about the company's plans and previous performance is not available, and the analyst must reach a working conclusion "by the numbers." When making any highly important financial decision, however, the analyst—whether a business owner, a management employee, an investor, or a credit grantor—needs to perform an in-depth investigation and interpret each of the financial ratios in relation to previous history and management purpose. A fundamentally unfavorable financial position becomes particularly dangerous when management appears to be unaware of the situation or indifferent to its implications, or when trend studies show that the company is moving in the opposite direction from management's stated goals. A numerically similar financial position becomes less worrisome when management has acknowledged the problem and developed specific, credible plans to strengthen the company's financial structure. A record of improvement (or deterioration) in the key ratios will do much to affect the analyst's interpretation of a company's competitive position.

One Extraordinary Deficiency

Although the basic financial structure of Company D revealed by the causal ratios is somewhat unusual, it is not difficult to understand. One extraordinarily deficient causal ratio, *Net Sales to Net Worth*, which shows extremely low investment adequacy, has required management to take heroic measures to maintain some semblance of financial balance. The *Net Sales to Total Assets* ratio and all three of the major contributory ratios (*Collection Period of Accounts Receivable*, *Cost of Sales to Inventory*, and *Net Sales to Fixed Assets*) have been managed with extreme care to reduce debt and increase working capital, thereby compensating, to some extent, for very low investment adequacy. *Long-Term Liabilities to Total Noncurrent Assets* far above the industry norm also offsets this net worth deficiency to a small extent.

Nevertheless, *Total Liabilities to Net Worth*, an important secondary measure, is much higher than the industry standard, an unfavorable net effect of the interaction of the causal ratios. *Current Liabilities to Net Worth* is also far above the group median. In addition, working capital sufficiency is relatively low, as shown by the company's comparatively high *Net Sales to Working Capital*. Similarly, *Long-Term Liabilities to Working Capital* was more than twice as high as the standard, and Company D's ratio greater than 1.0 showed that long-term borrowing was required to maintain a positive working capital position. All of these adverse financial indicators are traceable to one causal ratio: *Net Sales to Net Worth*. The case of Company D not only points out the dramatic influence that can be wielded by a single causal ratio, but it also emphasizes the particular importance of adequate owners' equity in achieving satisfactory financial balance.

At the same time, Company D's experience shows that compensating advantages can enable a business to survive under extremely difficult circumstances. By means of very high *Net Sales to Total Assets* (augmented by very high *Long-Term Liabilities to Total Noncurrent Assets*), Company D has been able to raise its *Current Assets to Current Liabilities* slightly above the industry standard. Although cash flow pressure is indicated by high *Net Sales to Working Capital*, the moderate *Current Assets to Current Liabilities* ratio demonstrates that Company D is maintaining an adequate balance between current assets and current liabilities—despite the major disadvantage of severe undercapitalization.

Chapter 28

Ratio Analysis: A Tool for Making Policy Decisions

Because cause-and-effect ratio analysis sets forth, in a logical structure, the fundamental financial condition of a company, this management tool can be particularly helpful in making major policy decisions. Alternative projections will enable management to see the effect of contemplated competitive moves on each element of the company's financial structure and to indicate the company's resulting position vis-à-vis other businesses in the industry. Obviously, application of cause-and-effect analysis will not produce clairvoyance, but sound estimates of the impact of particular actions can be derived by means of this versatile method.

Let us briefly observe the manner in which management might use ratio analysis as a tool in making specific policy decisions. Table 28-1 shows summarized figures for Companies A, B, C, and D. Once again, Company A represents superior performance, while Company B is similar to the industry norm, and Company C exhibits multiple financial deficiencies. Company D's financial control is excellent in some respects and far from industry standards in other areas. With this background, we can examine several important questions that management in each company might encounter in the near future.

Decision 1: Purchase of Adjoining Property

First, suppose that an improved property adjoining the company's plant has recently been listed for sale. Should the company purchase this property and integrate it with its existing facilities if the total cost is equal to the depreciated (book) value of its existing plant and equipment combined? The ratios in Table 28-2 help to provide the answer for each company's management.

Because of Company A's solid financial foundation, a proposal to purchase the adjoining property necessitates little soul-searching by management to reach the conclusion that well-considered expansion is supportable and possibly wise. The likely need for added facilities is illustrated by a comparatively high degree of utilization of present fixed assets. The extent of plant expansion, however, must be predicated upon the amount of sales increase that Company A can realistically expect. Company A's investment in plant and equipment would temporarily become very high through a $124,000 addition in this area, with a drop in *Net Sales to Fixed Assets* to 6.0, versus the 10.3 standard. Nevertheless, the company has sufficient working capital to support a 20% down payment and still maintain *Current Assets to Current Liabilities* and *Net Sales to Working Capital* at more conservative levels than the industry standards. Similarly, Company A's *Total Liabilities to Net Worth* would remain substantially lower than the industry norm, if the balance of the purchase price were financed on a long-term basis. The effects of depreciation and continued profitability will strengthen working capital and reduce total debt over time.

Company A's profit picture is quite good, and the business can withstand

Table 28-1. Comparison of income statement and balance sheet for four companies.

	Company A	Company B	Company C	Company D
Income statement				
Net sales	$1,500,000	$5,000,000	$12,500,000	$50,000,000
Cost of sales	1,110,000	3,775,000	9,750,000	40,000,000
Selling & administrative expenses	296,000	1,000,000	2,150,000	8,500,000
Net profit before interest expense	94,000	225,000	600,000	1,500,000
Interest expense	18,000	75,000	150,000	950,000
Net profit before taxes	76,000	150,000	150,000	950,000
Income taxes	26,000	50,000	50,000	300,000
Net profit after taxes	$ 50,000	$ 100,000	$ 100,000	$ 650,000
Depreciation expense	$ 24,000	$ 100,000	$ 300,000	$ 500,000
Balance sheet				
Cash & short-term investments	$ 52,000	$ 100,000	$ 100,000	$ 100,000
Accounts receivable	152,000	625,000	2,090,000	2,850,000
Inventory	170,000	750,000	2,500,000	4,900,000
Other current assets	24,000	25,000	50,000	550,000
Current assets	398,000	1,500,000	4,740,000	8,400,000
Fixed assets	124,000	500,000	1,400,000	2,450,000
Other noncurrent assets	14,000	0	510,000	550,000
Total assets	$536,000	$2,000,000	$6,650,000	$11,400,000
Current liabilities	$220,000	$1,000,000	$3,780,000	$ 5,400,000
Long-term liabilities	62,000	250,000	1,330,000	4,450,000
Total liabilities	282,000	1,250,000	5,110,000	9,850,000
Net worth	254,000	750,000	1,540,000	1,550,000
Total liabilities & net worth	$536,000	$2,000,000	$6,650,000	$11,400,000

Table 28-2. Primary and secondary ratios for four companies.

	Company A	Company B	Company C	Company D
Primary (causal) ratios				
Net Profit				
to Net Sales				
Company	5.1%	3.0%	1.2%	1.9%
Industry standard	3.2%	3.2%	3.2%	3.2%
Net Sales				
to Total Assets				
Company	2.8 times	2.5 times	1.9 times	4.4 times
Industry standard	2.4 times	2.4 times	2.4 times	2.4 times
Collection Period				
of Accounts				
Receivable				
Company	37 days	46 days	61 days	21 days
Industry standard	44 days	44 days	44 days	44 days
Cost of Sales				
to Inventory				
Company	6.5 times	5.0 times	3.9 times	8.2 times
Industry standard	5.1 times	5.1 times	5.1 times	5.1 times
Net Sales				
to Fixed Assets				
Company	12.1 times	10.0 times	8.9 times	20.4 times
Industry standard	10.3 times	10.3 times	10.3 times	10.3 times
Net Sales				
to Net Worth				
Company	5.9 times	6.7 times	8.1 times	32.3 times
Industry standard	6.8 times	6.8 times	6.8 times	6.8 times
Long-Term				
Liabilities				
to Total Noncurrent				
Assets				
Company	0.4 times	0.5 times	0.7 times	1.5 times
Industry standard	0.5 times	0.5 times	0.5 times	0.5 times
Secondary (effect) ratios				
Total Liabilities				
to Net Worth				
Company	1.1 times	1.7 times	3.3 times	6.4 times
Industry standard	1.8 times	1.8 times	1.8 times	1.8 times
Net Sales				
to Working Capital				
Company	8.4 times	10.0 times	13.0 times	16.7 times
Industry standard	10.2 times	10.2 times	10.2 times	10.2 times
Current Assets				
to Current				
Liabilities				
Company	1.8 times	1.5 times	1.3 times	1.6 times
Industry standard	1.5 times	1.5 times	1.5 times	1.5 times

	Company A	Company B	Company C	Company D
Total Noncurrent Assets to Net Worth				
Company	0.5 times	0.7 times	1.2 times	1.9 times
Industry standard	0.7 times	0.7 times	0.7 times	0.7 times

any temporary reduction in return during the period of construction or transition. Both receivables collection and inventory turnover are exceptionally sound and will aid in supporting a diversion of funds into fixed assets. For that matter, if Company A's sales expansion should be based in part on the assumption of somewhat more marginal credit risks, it can afford selective acceptance of certain accounts that do not measure up to its present high standards. If profit can be generated through additional sales to more marginal customers, Company A stands to gain, for its past performance in controlling accounts receivable indicates that its bad-debt losses are unlikely to become significant if management maintains a watchful eye on the marginal customers. Management of Company A can, then, undertake any expansion plans that it finds justifiable on the basis of projected sales with the assurance that the company's financial condition will easily support additional fixed assets of $124,000.

Sales Growth a Factor

Company B might well devote serious thought to acquiring the neighboring property. Company B's management must, however, review several factors before reaching a decision. Is sales volume likely to grow during the next two or three years? Will any such increase require additional physical plant capacity? Would the acquisition of the adjoining property make the company more attractive to a prospective buyer or otherwise meet definable future requirements? Because Company B enjoys no special advantage with respect to profitability or financial structure, management should have a solid reason for incurring the short-term financial pressure that a significant purchase would entail. You can see that Company B's utilization of present facilities is currently near the industry norm: *Net Sales to Fixed Assets*, at 10.0, is virtually identical to the 10.3 standard for the concern's comparison group. Further, the company's *Total Noncurrent Assets to Net Worth* is directly in line with the industry median. An additional $500,000 investment in plant capacity would push Company B much above average. The company would feel some strain, beyond doubt; but with all other factors remaining roughly equal, the burden on the company's financial structure will not be especially great. The major determinants are, then, Company B's anticipated sales growth and the sales and profit increases permitted by the proposed expansion—or, possibly, a well-defined strategic purpose not related to current operations.

What effect would Company B find on its working capital and debt structure from the combination of fixed asset expansion and future sales growth? The answer depends upon the type of financing that is available for the contemplated enlargement of the plant. If $400,000 could be secured through long-term mortgage borrowing, with the balance coming from cash and increased current liabilities, debt pressure would increase but would not become oppressive. Financial leverage, shown by *Total Liabilities to Net Worth*, would rise from 1.7 to 2.2, while *Current Assets to Current Liabilities* would slip from 1.5 to 1.4. This situation would present no problem, assuming that the other causal ratios, particularly *Net Profit to Net Sales*, remained similar to industry norms or, preferably, improved.

A plant expansion is, of course, ordinarily intended to support an increase in sales volume. This, in turn, will result in higher accounts receivable and inventory, requiring still higher debt. As long as Company B boosts sales volume gradually, the company's basic financial structure should be able to support both the real estate acquisition and higher sales levels. Naturally, achievement of superior performance in one or more causal areas—a reduction of the *Collection Period of Accounts Receivable*, a rise in *Cost of Sales to Inventory*, or an increase in *Net Profit to Net Sales*—would help to hold down debt and decrease pressure on working capital.

The timing of management's decision to expand is of paramount importance. Should management defer the addition to plant capacity until the company's financial situation becomes somewhat more solid? Probably not, if sales expansion is a likely option, although management must take care not to overload the company's financial structure with overly rapid growth in sales, inventory, and accounts receivable. By understanding the company's present financial position and by becoming aware of changes that will result from its contemplated expansionary move, the management of Company B can arrive at an informed response to the present opportunity. In the event that the company does add to existing facilities, it will, temporarily at least, fall from a balanced condition to one of imbalance. If, however, through reference to industry norms, management succeeds in restoring equilibrium, the company will then stand at a higher level of sales, profit, and financial resources, better able to meet competitive challenges.

Reorganization Required

The answer in Company C's case must be a resounding "No!"—unless management has developed a specific plan for fundamental reorganization of the business. Let us study the reasons behind this conclusion in some detail. Company C's *Net Sales to Fixed Assets* is substantially below the industry standard, and its fixed asset exposure is already too great for its net worth, resulting in very high *Total Noncurrent Assets to Net Worth*. If Company C should assume a $1,400,000 expansion program in its present overtaxed condition, the result would be a fixed asset burden that would place the company's existence in still greater jeopardy. Although an exceedingly optimistic observer may ponder possible long-range advantages in purchasing contiguous property, concern for Company C's immediate survival dictates a negative answer to the proposal.

If no other equity capital is available—and in the face of low profitability and a weak financial structure, additional investment would not be easy to attract—what would happen to working capital and debt structure should Company C attempt this expansion by means of creditor support? If the company should try to finance a 20% down payment for this acquisition from present working capital ($50,000 from its cash balance and $230,000 from even higher current liabilities), it would find its *Net Sales to Working Capital* rising even higher. At more than 16.0 (versus the industry standard of 10.2), this ratio would show greatly increased cash flow pressure. *Current Assets to Current Liabilities* would drop to 1.2, another sign of working capital imbalance. Through postponement of payment of creditors' bills, the company would invite further collection efforts, and possibly lawsuits. Financial leverage, already high, would rise to 4.2, threatening total loss of freedom in management action. Finally, Company C possesses no compensating advantages to offset the foregoing deficiencies. If, for instance, its inventory could be turned more rapidly, or its receivables were not so slow, some liquid funds would be generated to offset overexpansion of fixed assets. But the company is deficient in these areas and others, and no internal support can be found. Even given compensating advantages, Company C would have little basis for considering expansion under present circumstances.

Risk of Bankruptcy

For a business of Company D's size—$50 million in annual sales—a $2,450,000 expansion of fixed assets would not ordinarily have a significant impact on basic financial structure. Due to its strained financial position, however, Company D must approach each transaction with care. In view of the company's extraordinarily high fixed asset activity, shown by its 20.4 *Net Sales to Fixed Assets*, the need for an increase in this area would not be the least bit surprising. But would this acquisition be the right move to improve profit margin and strengthen Company D's basic financial structure through retained earnings? If not, it could push Company D to the brink of bankruptcy. A close examination of the business's financial structure shows that the purchase would exceed total owners' equity. The additional $2,450,000 in debt that would be required (since Company D's cash balance is far short of current needs, and other internal sources of funds are nonexistent) would boost *Total Liabilities to Net Worth* from 6.4 to 7.9. Such a small rise in debt relative to net sales might not ordinarily be noticed, but the jump in *Total Liabilities to Net Worth* would surely send a shiver through Company D's creditors, unless they could be assured that the new fixed assets were part of a well-considered plan to improve profitability.

Simply increasing current liabilities by $490,000 to provide a down payment would drop *Current Assets to Current Liabilities* from 1.6 to 1.4. This ratio's extreme sensitivity to such a small change in working capital could be predicted by Company D's very high *Net Sales to Working Capital*, which would rise from 16.7 to 19.9 through a $490,000 increase in current liabilities (with no corresponding increase in current assets). If the acquisition of the adjoining property happens to be entirely compatible with management's existing, well-considered plans for capital expenditures, then such a move might be justifiable—and even highly beneficial. Otherwise, however, management should pass up this opportunity, to avoid imperiling the company's existence. Future acquisition of the same property may be far more costly, but management must recognize that it is necessary for Company D to survive in order to prevail. Possible future cost is insignificant in comparison.

Companies A, B, C, and D have the same question to answer, and each management decision maker must arrive at his or her decision on the basis of an understanding of the company's relative strengths and weaknesses, which are clearly disclosed by cause-and-effect ratio analysis. As we have noted, and as we explore at length in the final chapter, accurate and complete industry statistics can make the analyst's efforts considerably less difficult and his results more exact.

Decision 2: Rapid Expansion

Let us examine another major question that has suddenly confronted the management of Companies A, B, C, and D. In this case, each of the four companies has the opportunity to obtain a major contract that would expand sales volume by 50%, as quickly as the work could be brought into the plant. Each company is also fortunate to find that a recent reorganization by one of the community's largest employers has provided an adequate supply of second-shift personnel so that all work could be performed with no addition to plant and equipment—rare good fortune indeed. The increased sales volume would lower fixed costs as a percentage of net sales, but offsetting expenses, such as shift differentials and training costs, plus certain price concessions would only permit each company to maintain its present profit margin. No increase in profit percentage is likely in the foreseeable future. Should Companies A, B, C, and D accept the new work?

Assuming that sales volume can be increased to an annualized rate 50% higher than last year's volume within three months, we can make a rough projection of the effect on the companies' financial structure by increasing current assets 50%, raising current liabilities by the same dollar amount that current assets are increased, and assuming no change in fixed assets and other noncurrent assets. Because of additional expenses that are invariably incurred to achieve such a dramatic change in operations, it would be reasonable to assume no increase in net worth at the three-month mark.

In the case of Company A, current assets, current liabilities, total assets, and total liabilities would increase by approximately $200,000. On an annualized basis, net sales would be $2,250,000. Under those assumptions, three causal ratios would change significantly: *Net Sales to Total Assets* would rise from 2.8 to 3.1, *Net Sales to Fixed Assets* would jump from 12.1 to 18.1, and *Net Sales to Net Worth* would increase from 5.9 to 8.9. When *Net Sales to Net Worth* rises faster than *Net Sales to Total Assets* (when the effects of a boost in sales volume cannot be offset by improvements in asset utilization), total debt will increase faster than net worth. For Company A, *Total Liabilities to Net Worth* would experience a steep rise from 1.1 to 1.9, but, after the projected changes, this important secondary ratio would be only slightly above the industry norm. *Current Assets to Current Liabilities* would decline rather sharply from 1.8 to 1.4; however, this key secondary ratio would be nearly in line with the comparison group median. The favorable condition of Company A's *Net Sales to Total Assets* and all three of its component ratios—the *Collection Period of Accounts Receivable, Cost of Sales to Inventory*, and *Net Sales to Fixed Assets*—would compensate for the fact that the company's *Net Sales to Net Worth* would become comparatively high (showing a relatively low level of net worth in support of sales volume) immediately after the 50% expansion of operations. Provided that the new work will allow the company to maintain or improve its present, relatively advantageous *Net Profit to Net Sales, Total Liabilities to Net Worth* could be readily reduced through retained earnings. If management is prepared to assume the headaches that will surely accompany such a radical increase in growth, Company A's financial structure will definitely support the move.

Company B, which has neither financial problems nor competitive advantages, would place considerable strain on its existing resources by undertaking a 50% increase in sales volume. Nevertheless, the business should be able to accept the offered work without resorting to outside investment or special financing. Assuming that current assets will rise at the same 50% rate anticipated for sales volume, Company B would experience an increase of $750,000 in current assets, current liabilities, total assets, and total liabilities. *Current Assets to Current Liabilities* would fall to 1.3 (versus the 1.5 industry median), and *Total Liabilities to Net Worth* would climb to 2.7 (compared with the 1.8 median), but neither of these conditions would be especially alarming. Lacking any compensating advantages in the form of favorable causal ratios, Company B would find that a rapid increase in *Net Sales to Net Worth* (from 6.7 to 10.0) would cause greater debt pressure and a greater likelihood of cash flow difficulties than Company A would experience. Nevertheless, if Company B's management has good reason to believe that adequate *Net Profit to Net Sales* can be achieved on the additional work, the contemplated sales expansion can be supported from the company's own resources. Although significant debt pressure would accompany this move, the potential reward appears to outweigh the risk.

Need to Increase Owners' Equity

Company C would, in all likelihood, need to obtain additional owners' equity or arrange special term financing in order to support a 50% sales increase. If a rise in *Total Liabilities to Net Worth* from 3.3 to 4.3 would not discourage ordinary credit grantors from providing funds for the company's expansion, then a decline in *Current Assets to Current Liabilities* from 1.3 to 1.2 would almost surely do so. Restrictions on Company C's cash lifeline would become evident almost immediately after the company contracts for the new work and begins to expand inventory, and would grow worse as accounts receivable rise. Obviously, Company C must make arrangements for new investment or term financing in advance of any such commitment, or risk total financial embarrassment. Investors and term lenders are almost certain to insist that the company find some means of improving its *Net Profit to Net Sales* before making any additional funds available. If Company C's profit margin cannot be raised to the industry standard, at a minimum, then the value of the expansion is highly questionable. Clearly, management must find satisfactory solutions to these problems before considering any significant sales expansion.

There is an alternative: Approximately 75% of Company C's anticipated increase in current assets could, in effect, be funded by successful management action to bring accounts receivable and inventory in line with common practice in the industry. If the *Collection Period of Accounts Receivable* and *Cost of Sales to Inventory* could be held to the industry norm, less than $600,000 in additional net worth or term financing would be required. If superior performance could be achieved in these two areas, no additional funds would be needed. Such improvements, however, ordinarily take months to attain, and their successful achievement at the same time that management attention is consumed with the demands of a sudden 50% increase in sales appears unlikely. As a practical matter, therefore, Company C should not accept the offer of additional work without arranging appropriate financing, if available, or additional investment, if necessary.

No matter what decision Company C's management might make with respect to the expansion, the company should initiate concerted efforts to improve the collection of accounts receivable and to accelerate inventory turnover. Until the fundamental problems evident in these two areas are corrected, the company's ability to accept new opportunities will be severely limited. If, however, the company should attempt to expand without taking action to correct its critical weaknesses in control of accounts receivable and inventory—and without making satisfactory arrangements for investment or intermediate-term financing—management may have occasion to regret this move in bankruptcy court.

Company D simply cannot afford to increase sales by 50% unless *Net Profit to Net Sales* is increased dramatically. The present level of debt is virtually unsupportable, and only the prospect of a highly favorable profit margin and a spectacular rate of reinvestment would induce investors or lenders to participate in Company D's future growth. Basically, two causal measures—low *Net Profit to Net Sales* and, most importantly, high *Net Sales to Net Worth*—have placed Company D in extreme financial distress. Consequently, the essential element in convincing creditors or investors to support any sales expansion is a believable promise of a higher profit margin. Without the backing of outside parties, Company D cannot hope to accept the new work.

Decision 3: The President's Bonus

Referring again to Companies A, B, C, and D, let us consider one more situation requiring evaluation and decision by management. In this case, the company's president would like to declare himself a bonus of $75,000 for personal reasons. Overlooking the propriety of this transaction for the moment, does the financial condition of each of these companies permit the president to give realistic consideration to such a bonus?

Because of Company A's comparatively strong financial condition—shown by a favorable rating on every secondary ratio, including high *Current Assets to Current Liabilities* and relatively low *Total Liabilities to Net Worth*—the concern, as small as it is, can accommodate the president's personal plans. Assume, for example, that Company A would fund this transaction by reducing cash by $20,000 and increasing accounts payable by $55,000. Current assets would decline to $378,000, current liabilities would rise to $275,000, total liabilities would reach $337,000, and net worth would be reduced to $179,000. *Current Assets to Current Liabilities* would become 1.4, slightly below the industry norm, while *Total Liabilities to Net Worth* would reach 1.9, only slightly above the 1.8 median for Company A's comparison group. Whether the $75,000 bonus would conflict with possible expansion plans for the company or might otherwise have a restrictive effect on the company's operations cannot be determined from the data at hand; however, based on the information we have, the president of Company A can declare the $75,000 bonus he desires without placing an undue burden on the concern's financial structure. Company A's ability to absorb a sudden $75,000 payout is attributable to its superior standing with respect to the seven causal ratios.

A Matter for Thought

Because Company B's causal ratios are similar to the industry norms, the business is facing no financial problems. At the same time, Company B enjoys no competitive advantages. Consequently, the matter of the $75,000 bonus requires somewhat more deliberation than in the case of Company A. If Company B were to reduce cash by $20,000 and increase accounts payable by $55,000 to cover the proposed bonus, current assets would stand at $1,480,000, current liabilities would be $1,055,000, total liabilities would rise to $1,305,000, and net worth would decline to $675,000. As a result, Company B's *Current Assets to Current Liabilities* would decline to 1.4, slightly below the industry standard, and the company's *Total Liabilities to Net Worth* would rise to 1.9, a level of debt slightly above the norm in relation to owners' equity. The reduction in *Current Assets to*

Current Liabilities and the increase in *Total Liabilities to Net Worth* are both attributable to a change in one causal ratio: *Net Sales to Net Worth* would rise from 6.7 to 7.4, a noticeable decline in the amount of owners' equity as a proportion of sales volume. This decrease in investment adequacy relative to sales volume would cause working capital to become less sufficient in relation to sales activity (shown by a rise in *Net Sales to Working Capital* from 10.0 to 11.8) and would thereby reduce *Current Assets to Current Liabilities*, since no compensating advantages are anticipated.

Although Company B's annual sales volume is more than three times greater than that of Company A, granting a $75,000 bonus would have much the same impact on the financial structure of these two companies. In fact, after paying out $75,000, Company A and Company B would have almost identical readings for *Current Assets to Current Liabilities* and *Total Liabilities to Net Worth* (rounded to one decimal place), due to the stronger pre-bonus financial structure of the smaller business. The analyst must bear in mind that basic financial structure may be as important as company size (whether measured by sales volume or total capitalization) in determining the impact of management actions. In addition to projecting the short-term effect of the proposed bonus, the president will, of course, also have to consider whether the $75,000 cash outflow might be incompatible with Company B's plans for future growth and improvement of the company's competitive position.

Since Company C generates annual sales $11 million greater than Company A's $1,500,000 volume, paying a $75,000 bonus would not seem to pose a major problem. Once the key financial ratios are reviewed, however, serious questions arise. Our knowledge of Company C's weak financial condition immediately suggests that the president would be well advised to forgo any bonus until the business can successfully address the numerous problems it faces. Since Company C's cash balance is comparatively small, the entire $75,000 would have to come from stretching out trade payables, a move almost certain to build tremendous creditor pressure. Consequently, current liabilities would rise to $3,855,000 (versus current assets of $4,740,000) and total liabilities would climb to $5,185,000, while net worth would slip to $1,465,000.

Current Assets to Current Liabilities would erode to 1.2, a dangerously low level, particularly in view of Company C's high *Collection Period of Accounts Receivable* and low *Cost of Sales to Inventory*. *Total Liabilities to Net Worth* would move upward to 3.5, versus the industry standard of 1.8. Both of these adverse developments are traceable to one causal ratio: *Net Sales to Net Worth* would climb from 8.1 to 8.5, well above the 6.8 industry norm. This comparatively low level of owners' equity available to support sales volume would necessarily cause high debt and tight working capital unless compensating advantages are present. An examination of the concern's other causal ratios reveals no positive offsets. Thus, the president of Company C should shelve any plans for extra compensation until his company is on more solid financial footing.

Bonuses Common in Marginal Concerns

Those who feel that the bonus under consideration in this example is highly unlikely have probably reviewed very few financial statements of marginal concerns. There are innumerable cases of generous bonuses and heavy borrowing from meager company resources on the part of their executives, even those managing businesses with deficit net worth. In such situations, creditors must share the blame with the owners, for their tolerance and unquestioning credit extension encourage and perpetuate this practice.

Because of Company D's relatively great size, a $75,000 bonus would not ordinarily have any noticeable financial impact. Consequently, the decision whether to grant such a bonus would be a personnel matter, not a significant financial management issue. In this case, however, the company shows an exceedingly small amount of owners' equity in relation to its sales volume, and even this relatively minor transaction (versus net sales of $50 million) would result in a noticeable weakening of Company D's financial structure. In fact, a rise in the causal ratio *Net Sales to Net Worth* from 32.3 to 33.9 would produce an increase in *Total Liabilities to Net Worth* from 6.4 to 6.7, pushing this key secondary measure even farther above the industry norm of 1.8. Under the circumstances, Company D's president should quickly dismiss the idea of a bonus and concentrate on the immediate task of increasing the company's chances of survival.

The projected effects of other major policy moves, including such matters as reducing or raising prices, shortening or lengthening selling terms, increasing inventory to accommodate customer requests, or acquiring a competing firm, can also be clearly understood through the application of cause-and-effect ratio analysis.

Chapter 29

Measures to Restore Financial Health

Financial imbalance and physical illness are similar in many respects, and the analyst—whether he is the owner or an officer of the business, one of its credit grantors, or an independent industry analyst—assumes the role of doctor. Although a wise individual consults his physician whenever a significant symptom appears and also schedules a regular check-up in order to be assured that his health remains good or to detect possible incipient disease, many people neglect medical attention until their illnesses are far advanced. Companies, too, often perform self-examination or seek guidance only after financial distress has reached serious proportions. The informed business principal, however, knows the value of a periodic financial review.

Symptoms of financial disease include tightening of working capital, increasing debt pressure, and distortion of any of the nine secondary ratios. The degree of deviation from normal indicates the seriousness of the situation and the speed with which curative measures must be applied. Medical journals report that certain symptoms are common to several different physical illnesses, but they note that various methods of diagnosis plus consultations with experts will, in most cases, disclose the true cause underlying the symptoms. Unless a doctor knows with reasonable certainty the identity of the disease he is treating, he must be cautious in advising medication or surgery, because each disease has its own cure and the prescription for one might complicate or increase the severity of another.

To treat a symptom without knowing its cause is as dangerous to the business patient as it is to the medical patient. To help you gain a familiarity with fundamental financial diagnosis through cause-and-effect ratio analysis, we have examined various causes of financial imbalance. But accurate diagnosis will not, by itself, bring recovery. Once the analyst has determined the cause of a company's financial difficulties, he or she must be aware of the corrective actions available in order to offer sound, specific recommendations.

Working Capital Deficiency

The analyst will often encounter a company beset by working capital problems, as determined through examination of these four symptoms:

1. Insufficient working capital to support net sales (high *Net Sales to Working Capital*)
2. Unfavorable working capital balance (low *Current Assets to Current Liabilities*)
3. Poor liquidity (low *Cash and Short-Term Investments plus Accounts Receivable to Current Liabilities*)
4. Inordinate dependence on long-term debt to maintain working capital (high *Long-Term Liabilities to Working Capital*)

How should working capital be strengthened? Can any compensating advantages be implemented quickly to improve *Current Assets to Current Liabilities* on a temporary basis while more fundamental corrective actions are being developed? The answers, of course, will depend upon the fundamental cause or causes of the working capital deficiency identified through cause-and-effect ratio analysis. Is there one broad universal cure for working capital problems, a cure that will be permanent? Some credit grantors may say, "Yes, increase net worth and add the cash to the bank account or pay some current bills." But this course of action does not necessarily produce a permanent solution. It is, instead, similar to a blood transfusion, which, unless basic corrective measures are taken, may have to be repeated again and again because it provides only temporary relief from the discomfort or impairment resulting from a serious underlying problem. Through an understanding of cause-and-effect relationships, the analyst knows that one symptom of working capital problems, a depressed *Current Ratio*, is traceable to any one, or a combination, of six deep-seated illnesses:

1. Excessive fixed assets (low *Net Sales to Fixed Assets*)
2. Operating losses (very low or negative *Net Profit to Net Sales*)
3. Undercapitalization (high *Net Sales to Net Worth*)
4. Sluggish or questionable inventory (low *Cost of Sales to Inventory*)
5. Slow or uncollectible receivables (high *Collection Period of Accounts Receivable*)
6. Financing noncurrent assets from working capital (low *Long-Term Liabilities to Total Noncurrent Assets*)

A cure for excessive fixed assets cannot apply with equal effectiveness to a case of slow accounts receivable, for the two problems are fundamentally dissimilar. Nor are operating losses likely to require the same medication as slow inventory turnover. Clearly, the analyst-doctor must prescribe his working capital cure only after he knows why working capital is in its present condition.

Heavy Debt

To illustrate another common symptom of financial imbalance, suppose that a company's financial structure is debt-heavy and that its operating freedom has been severely curtailed. Is there a panacea that will ensure the permanent financial health of this company? Someone may suggest, "Profits must be earned and retained in the business." But if the debt-to-equity relationship is high due to a rapid increase in sales volume—at a faster rate than net worth can be expanded through retained earnings—an attempt to generate even more profit through still greater sales activity may lead the company into bankruptcy. When the sales growth curve is too steep, even record-setting profits may not generate sufficient cash flow to cover obligations as they come due. Or the fundamental problem may be excessive fixed assets that are responsible for a cost structure which makes profit difficult, if not impossible, to realize. Profit is, of course, one of the ingredients in any prescription for improved financial health, but it is no universal elixir. In fact, the realization of adequate profit is itself dependent upon a certain degree of overall financial soundness. For any financial imbalance, the proper cure clearly depends on the diagnosis of the condition and treatment of the specific cause and not on a general palliative for the symptom.

We now consider a few of the fundamental causes of financial imbalance and note specific corrective measures that can be applied.

Excessive Fixed Assets

If you find that fixed assets are excessive with respect to net sales (*Net Sales to Fixed Assets* is relatively low), four primary courses of action are open to remedy this situation:

1. *Restrict further investment in fixed assets.* Not only will any increase in sales volume raise *Net Sales to Fixed Assets*, but the effect of depreciation will reduce the book value of fixed assets over time.

2. *Redesign production, selling, or office facilities to increase the sales-generating potential of existing space and equipment.* Rearrangement of existing fixed assets, particularly with the active involvement of employees, may well enable the company to produce substantially higher sales volume with no additional capital expenditures. In other cases, acquisition of a comparatively small amount of additional fixed assets (such as a material handling system, telecommunications capability, or a more flexible computing capacity) has permitted companies to vastly increase the productivity of their existing space and equipment.

3. *Sell idle machinery and parts, unused vehicles, and unnecessary equipment.* Other companies in the same or related industries may profitably use this equipment and may gladly pay cash for it. As production needs change, excess equipment—with actual cash value—is often simply shunted to one side. Many an organization has started with good used equipment bought from a competing business.

4. *Develop compensating advantages.* Such advantages include improved inventory turnover, faster collection of receivables, a relatively high level of long-term liabilities, and higher profit return, all of which would permit greater than typical investment in fixed assets.

The foregoing is not a complete list of alternatives, but it suggests that there is more than one way to deal with excessive fixed assets. A single approach is, of course, seldom sufficient; the solution to this problem generally consists of a combination of measures. Any action that accomplishes a reduction of fixed assets in relation to net sales is in the nature of a permanent cure. Certain compensating advantages (such as improved inventory turnover and more rapid collection of accounts receivable) that may be instituted for the purpose of relieving immediate debt pressure often prove to be permanent benefits. Long-term borrowing that affects neither fixed assets nor net worth directly is a temporary expedient that simply shifts the burden from current debt to future obligations, thus "buying time" for the overextended company to effect essential corrective measures. Retained earnings will gradually build net worth; depreciation charges will decrease fixed assets. Thus, unless the degree of imbalance is insurmountably high, this combination will ultimately restore equilibrium.

Abnormal Collection Period of Accounts Receivable

If the *Collection Period of Accounts Receivable* is abnormally high or abnormally low, the following moves should be considered:

1. *Selling terms can be either shortened or lengthened.* You must first consider the competitive element, for many accounts are motivated in their purchasing not only by quality of product and price, but by terms of sale and credit arrangements as well. Each company's terms, however, must be determined by individual circumstances and need not exactly parallel those of others in the same industry.

2. *Cash discount can be injected into selling terms, existing cash discount can be increased, or cash discount can be eliminated entirely, thus restricting all sales to a net basis.* The choice will depend upon the particular needs of the company under analysis. The effect of any of these discount moves will vary, of course, with the manner—whether sales-minded or apparently adversarial—in which the matter is approached and activated.

3. *Greater selectivity in accepting accounts can be imposed, or liberalization of credit policy can be instituted.* The choice, again, will depend on the nature of the particular company's problem. If the *Collection Period of Accounts Receivable* is abnormally high, greater selectivity would be appropriate.

4. *Either a more systematic collection follow-up can be established or the*

relaxing of arbitrary payment demands can be inaugurated. Again, the choice depends upon the individual collection situation.

5. *A professional credit manager can be hired, or the education and training of the employee now handling the credit function can be improved.* Both courses of action can pay dividends in stabilizing the entire credit-and-collection program.

6. *Slow receivables can be factored or discounted with a finance company or bank.* Again, a cost element enters the picture, for factoring and discounting services are not free. If increased sales can be stimulated through such a move, or if the immediate release of cash is adequate to permit the earning of purchase discounts to offset the added financing costs, then this approach may be entirely justified. But if, despite the increase in available funds, the company will still be obliged to struggle along, able to pay bills on a net basis at best, then little benefit will have been gained, and the costs will eat heavily into profit. The company contemplating such a move must also consider the suspicion (invalid though it may be) about its solvency that is sometimes created among trade creditors, a concern occasionally shared by customers. Much depends on the type of receivables financing, whether old-line factoring, discounting of individual receivables, or blanket borrowing against receivables, as well as on the recourse element and notification feature.

7. *Compensating advantages can, perhaps, be developed.* A substantial reduction of inventory, or possibly fixed assets, in relation to sales volume might free sufficient cash to permit the company to carry excess receivables until they can be brought under control.

Sluggish Inventory Turnover (or Throughput)

If *Cost of Sales to Inventory* shows sluggish movement of raw material, work-in-process, or stock on hand, the company has available many corrective actions:

1. *Review the turnover rate of the various inventory components.* Items for which demand is exceedingly low relative to existing supply should be noted. Salespeople can then place emphasis on clearing them out, possibly at discount prices. At the same time, management can curtail their reorder or manufacture. When there is no active market for certain items among active customers, alternative markets or, possibly, auctions may be the source of some cash.

2. *Analyze the inventory system to ensure that articles are not purchased in excessive quantity or in advance of need.* Overly conservative purchasing practices to assure that no item is ever in short supply can actually harm a company's competitive position through the tie-up of funds in excessive inventory. Speculative impulses to stockpile large quantities in advance of rumored or suspected price increases can put a crimp on cash flow and should be resisted. At the same time, care must be taken to maintain an adequate breadth and depth of inventory

to meet well-analyzed customer requirements. Even the most modern, sophisticated, and computerized system should be periodically reviewed by management to assess its actual effectiveness. In fact, a substandard or declining *Cost of Sales to Inventory* ratio may raise as many questions about the system itself as about management policy.

3. *Purchase merchandise on consignment.* The choice of this approach depends, of course, upon satisfactory agreements with major suppliers. Consignment purchasing makes inventory available without the necessity of remitting payment until the merchandise is actually sold or converted. Such an arrangement can provide the company with a complete line of goods, which would be impossible for the company to obtain through its own cash flow. By using the consigned stock and completing its marketing cycle, the company can use its current sales revenue to meet its obligations. Consignment agreements thus reduce inventory exposure and provide impetus to sales, while the supplier, who holds title to the consigned goods, is exposed only to the risk of loss on the accounts receivable created as the goods are withdrawn (assuming that the merchandise is insured against physical damage). A greater than average amount of paperwork is necessarily involved in this type of arrangement.

4. *Initiate field warehousing.* Field warehousing accomplishes essentially the same objectives as consignment, except that the supplier is in a more secure position because of the presumably watchful actions of the warehousing company and the issuance of a warehouse receipt. This receipt can be used for borrowing purposes by the supplier, yet the goods are in the purchaser's warehouse (under the supervision and control of the warehouse company) for immediate access, provided that the terms and conditions of the agreement are met.

5. *Obtain loans on inventory.* Sources of such financing include banks, finance companies, and factors. Although loans of this kind are generally short-term and provide no permanent solution to slow movement of inventory, they may aid the company in revamping inventory procedures, speeding turnover, and averting the need for future loans.

6. *Analyze the physical layout of the warehouse and storage areas.* Management may find that alteration of design and methods would accelerate movement of material and improve inventory turnover.

7. *Promote increased sales while holding inventory levels constant.* This fundamental approach is so obvious that it hardly needs mentioning, but it does require action in two areas, and, all too often, emphasis is placed on sales alone. An evaluation of the physical layout of the plant or retailing area (as distinct from the warehouse or storage area) may, for example, suggest opportunities for generating increased sales with no rise in inventory.

8. *Develop compensating advantages to offset slow inventory turnover.* Improving the collection of accounts receivable and raising net sales in relation to fixed assets are likely to be the most effective approaches to compensating for slow inventory turnover.

This list suggests some of the many ways that inventory problems may be attacked.

Inadequate Owners' Equity

In the event that *Net Sales to Net Worth* shows that owners' equity is inadequate to support sales volume, what choices of action are open to the company to restore financial balance? Let us consider a few of the most likely alternatives:

1. *Retain earnings*. If the company is profitable, management must consider whether net worth can be increased at a faster rate than sales volume is expanded. A reduction of owners' compensation to accomplish that goal may be indicated. In assessing the feasibility of this approach, you must determine whether reported profit is subject to drastic markdown through either inventory overvaluation or the existence of extremely doubtful receivables. Some companies find that taking advantage of profitable growth opportunities causes *Net Sales to Net Worth* to increase steadily despite the retention of all available earnings. In this situation, there is a compelling reason to attract additional capital or develop compensating advantages so that the profitable venture will not be threatened with extinction because it has overreached its financial resources.

2. *Institute (or maintain) compensating advantages*. As we have seen earlier, compensating advantages take the form of comparatively strong performance in other key areas, such as receivables collection, inventory turnover, and utilization of fixed assets.

3. *Seek outside investment*. If operations are profitable, but retained earnings are insufficient to provide adequate owners' equity to support rapidly increasing sales volume, and if the single deficient component is capital, then the interest of investors should be stimulated. When *Net Sales to Net Worth* is steadily rising, management cannot assume that larger profit dollars will be sufficient to meet the greater debt load that accompanies significant sales growth. Expansion plans may need to be curtailed, or outside investment may be required. Company owners must be alert, however, to the effects of equity dilution and the possibility of loss of management control in the process of raising needed funds.

4. *Reduce, then eliminate, losses*. If, on the other hand, *Net Sales to Net Worth* has increased because of an erosion of owners' equity through significant losses, or if expanding net sales at a faster rate than net worth can support those sales has recently resulted in a net loss, then a thorough study must be undertaken to determine the profitability of each customer. Amazingly enough, management is likely to find several significant customers who buy at unattractive price levels, require costly extra services without affording adequate compensation, make arbitrary adjustments or endless deductions from invoices based on alleged unsuitability of goods, take unearned cash discounts, require special credit terms,

are extremely slow and expensive to collect from, and represent poor credit risks with high bad-debt loss potential—customers who, in other words, are undesirable from virtually every point of view. Other accounts will represent varying degrees of profitability and potential. Selective elimination of undesirable customers can prove to be a definite gain, not only because such elimination increases profits but also because it decreases pressure on owners' equity (reduces *Net Sales to Net Worth*). As an alternative to eliminating such low-margin or unprofitable accounts, the company can charge them prices sufficient to compensate for the extraordinary services rendered. While this type of customer may bluster and threaten to take his business elsewhere, competitors are not likely to bid too aggressively for an unprofitable or disagreeable account. Through increased prices to compensate for special circumstances, a loss may be converted to a net profit.

Low Long-Term Liabilities in Proportion to Total Noncurrent Assets

This is frequently an important element, and occasionally the only causal factor, responsible for moving a company's financial structure substantially away from the industry norm. When *Long-Term Liabilities to Total Noncurrent Assets* is decidedly on the low side, and the secondary ratios indicate that the company is suffering working capital difficulties as a result, refinancing of noncurrent assets (particularly plant and equipment) should be considered. If, on the other hand, the secondary ratios indicate that the company is essentially in line with the industry standards for working capital sufficiency and working capital balance despite low *Long-Term Liabilities to Total Noncurrent Assets*, then no action is indicated.

Operating Losses

If the company's lack of balance derives from operating losses, as indicated by a negative percentage for *Net Profit to Net Sales*, you must determine whether this situation results from factors connected with any of the other causal ratios or from excessive expenses of a purely operational nature. In other words, are the losses caused by inadequate sales in relation to fixed assets, by inventory write-offs, or by bad debts? Or can they be traced through a step-by-step review of operating expense percentages? In the latter case, a detailed comparison of costs—showing each item as a proportion of net sales on a year-to-year basis and in relation to industry experience—will bring to light significant deviations. Does the operating loss reflect a long-term development? Or is it the result of unusual, nonrecurring expenses? As described more fully in Appendix B1, high expense percentages in virtually all operating areas usually suggest poor pricing practices rather than inadequate cost control (since few companies are deficient in almost every aspect of operations). If analysis of price versus cost should suggest that, indeed, price is in line with industry practice and that, nevertheless, most costs are out of line, a radical transformation of the company's methods would be required.

Once understanding of the company's financial condition has been achieved, management may utilize the services of specialists (in, say, inventory control or fixed asset utilization) as required. But recognition of the need for improvement must necessarily precede remedial measures, and cause-and-effect ratio analysis heightens management awareness by providing a precise picture of the company's financial structure. Once the nature of a specific difficulty is determined, management can design and implement the proper corrective actions by drawing upon its business experience and, on occasion, by enlisting the aid of outside consultants.

Part VI

The Versatility of Cause-and-Effect Ratio Analysis

Cause-and-effect ratio analysis can be used to make better business decisions in a wide variety of circumstances. Internal analysts—company owners, managers, and financial personnel—may have occasion to consider their company's competitive position as part of periodically reviewing financial performance, preparing the budget for the coming year, formulating a new strategy, or developing an organized response to market challenges. In all of these situations, the cause-and-effect approach can provide important insight into the company's existing strengths and weaknesses and the likely impact of alternative strategies on its basic financial structure. Outside analysts—business advisors, credit grantors, and investors—who have access to the company's financial data can obtain a similar understanding of the company's competitive position through this approach. As we see in the following examples, cause-and-effect ratio analysis is an extremely versatile decision-making tool. In Chapters 30 and 31, we study six different situations faced by company owners, while in Chapter 32 we will look at four examples of the use of the cause-and-effect approach by outside analysts.

Chapter 30

Analysis of Strategic Moves

A basic understanding of the principles of cause-and-effect ratio analysis will enable a business owner or manager to make strategic moves with greater assurance. A systematic analysis of a company's financial past and its present competitive position cannot, of course, eliminate all uncertainty about the future, but the ability to identify the key causal factors and project their effect under a variety of future conditions gives the knowledgeable analyst a major advantage in considering how to respond to situations he or she encounters. The busy owner/executive does not need to memorize every aspect of the cause-and-effect ratio approach or even be able to recall all of the 16 key ratios. Once he understands that certain ratios cause changes in the remaining ratios and knows where to find an explanation of each of the 16 important financial measures, he can perform his own basic strategic analysis. In most cases, consultation with an accountant or other financial advisor will help the businessperson to avoid possible errors in interpretation and to obtain additional ideas for further improvement. Beyond that, an understanding of the fundamentals of the cause-and-effect approach will enable him to take the first critical steps in evaluating the company's competitive position and considering management actions. The three examples in this chapter illustrate step-by-step application of ratio analysis to gain greater insight into the results that can be expected from alternative strategies.

Strong Financial Structure Aid in Fight for Survival

Over a period of 20 years, UVW Company had expanded its audio and consumer electronics business to a dozen stores in shopping malls in five contiguous counties. As the first retailer in the area to specialize in audio equipment, the company had grown to enjoy a dominant position. Consequently, Hank Kelton, the founder and president, was not especially worried when a competing business opened at an adjacent strip mall near one of his newer stores. He was certain that the market could not support two audio stores with extensive inventories, and he wondered why anyone would even try to challenge his company's position.

Within three months, however, he found that the competitor's strategy of low prices, no frills, and a large inventory of low-margin items had taken away almost half of his business at one location and seemed to be having a negative effect on a second store about 25 minutes from the first site. Even before Hank had formulated a well-considered marketing response, the competing organization, owned and operated by a young couple who had been audio and electronics buyers for a large department store chain, opened a second store at a new mall across the highway from one of UVW Company's most profitable units. Again, the competitors made immediate inroads into UVW's market share, changing a healthy profit into a loss at that location. Results for the previous fiscal year are shown in Table 30-1. The operating figures in Table 30-2 indicate the extent of the losses at that store during the most recent six months. As a first step toward a new strategic plan, Hank annualized the six-month results, as shown in Table 30-2, in order to facilitate direct comparison and to prepare for calculation of the key financial ratios in Table 30-5. He realized that he must take quick action to avoid the total annihilation of UVW Company, since the competitors' strategy was clearly aimed at direct confrontation, and they were winning.

With no financial data on his competitors, Hank could not make a formal

Table 30-1.   Income statement for last fiscal year for unit of UVW Company.

	High-margin sales	Low-margin sales	Total
Net sales	$300,000	$700,000	$1,000,000
Cost of sales	180,000	476,000	656,000
Selling & administrative expenses	104,000	202,000	306,000
Net profit before interest expense	16,000	22,000	38,000
Interest expense	5,000	5,000	10,000
Net profit before taxes	11,000	17,000	28,000
Income taxes	4,000	6,000	10,000
Net profit after taxes	$ 7,000	$ 11,000	$ 18,000

Table 30-2.   Income statement for most recent six months (annualized) for unit of UVW Company.

	High-margin sales	Low-margin sales	Total
Net sales	$300,000	$200,000	$500,000
Cost of sales	180,000	146,000	326,000
Selling & administrative expenses	104,000	100,000	204,000
Net profit before interest expense	16,000	(46,000)	(30,000)
Interest expense	5,000	1,000	6,000
Net profit before taxes	11,000	(47,000)	(36,000)
Income taxes	4,000	(14,000)	(10,000)
Net profit after taxes	$ 7,000	$ (33,000)	$ (26,000)

comparison, but he knew from his personal observation of their stores, together with a few discreet inquiries, that their occupancy costs were similar to his own, as the somewhat higher rent at their new locations was offset by less extensive leasehold improvements. Their personnel costs were apparently lower (owing to relatively inexperienced salespeople compared with his "audio consultants"), and their inventory was significantly larger in total dollars, although their selection was not as broad as that of UVW Company. Special credit terms for large purchases were about the same, and both stores honored two national credit cards. It required little analysis to determine that UVW Company needed comparatively high prices to cover its substantially greater personnel costs and still make a healthy profit. Although the rival company's inventory carrying costs in total dollars were somewhat above those incurred by UVW, Hank's competitors were obviously attempting to generate faster inventory turnover on a relatively limited selection of popular items.

No Basis for Competition

Hank observed that his company had several relative strengths: a certain degree of customer loyalty (or consumer inertia), a continuing appeal to individuals needing knowledgeable explanation or reassurance before purchasing, a more attractive display area, and a broader selection of basic equipment, as well as more high-margin extras. But no matter how he studied the situation, Hank concluded that there was no opportunity for "differentiation" or "segmentation" that would permit two competing audio stores to survive with any reasonable financial reward. He could simply fold up each store as his competitors made their challenge, withdrawing whatever portion of his net worth remained after liquidating inventory and paying hefty lease charges, or he could engage in a demolition derby of price-cutting.

Before deciding whether to fight, Hank needed more information. Did his competitors have any unusual financial resources? All of his inquiries through friends and credit channels indicated that they had simply invested their personal savings and obtained a bank loan with help from the owner of the malls in which their stores were located. Next, Hank began to assess the financial strength of his own company. To match his competitors' prices while maintaining his present service and selection, he could expect to incur substantial losses until UVW could regain at least half of its lost business, as indicated by the income statement projections in Table 30-3 for one of the two units already under competitive pressure. Those projections were based on data for the last complete fiscal year, contained in Table 30-1, and for the most recent six months of the new year, displayed in Table 30-2. In addition, Hank felt that UVW Company's former price level on certain items could never be fully reinstated. Would the financial structure of UVW Company be strong enough to carry the business through the loss period? To find the answer, Hank calculated the key financial ratios in Table 30-5 from the income statement data in Tables 30-1, 30-2, and 30-3, together with the balance sheet data in Table 30-4. He had learned about the cause-and-effect

Table 30-3.   Income statement based on next-year projections for unit of UVW Company.

	Next year projected		
	High-margin sales	Low-margin sales	Total
Net sales	$300,000	$450,000	$750,000
Cost of sales	180,000	306,000	486,000
Selling & administrative expenses	104,000	152,000	256,000
Net profit before interest expense	16,000	(8,000)	8,000
Interest expense	5,000	3,000	8,000
Net profit before taxes	11,000	(11,000)	0
Income taxes	4,000	(4,000)	0
Net profit after taxes	$ 7,000	$ (7,000)	$ 0

Table 30-4.   Balance sheet for unit of UVW Company.

	Last fiscal year	Most recent six months	Next year projected
Cash & short-term investments	$ 30,000	$ 30,000	$ 30,000
Accounts receivable	40,000	40,000	40,000
Inventory	170,000	140,000	175,000
Other current assets	10,000	10,000	10,000
Current assets	250,000	220,000	255,000
Fixed assets	70,000	70,000	70,000
Other noncurrent assets	0	0	0
Total assets	$320,000	$290,000	$325,000
Current liabilities	$170,000	$153,000	$205,000
Long-term liabilities	50,000	50,000	50,000
Total liabilities	220,000	203,000	255,000
Net worth	100,000	87,000	70,000
Total liabilities & net worth	$320,000	$290,000	$325,000

ratio approach from his son, who had recently received his M.B.A., and he followed the step-by-step instructions in an outline his son had sent him last year. Then he called his accountant for comparable ratios, which he also entered on his worksheet, as shown in Table 30-5.

Evaluation of Financial Strength

Hank had always considered UVW Company to be fairly strong financially, based on yearly conversations with his accountant and his banker, but he had never

Table 30-5.   Primary and secondary ratios for unit of UVW Company.

	Last fiscal year	Most recent six months	Next year projected
Primary (causal) ratios			
Net Profit to Net Sales			
Company	2.8%	(7.2)%	0.0%
Industry standard	3.0%	3.0%	Unknown
Net Sales to Total Assets			
Company	3.1 times	1.7 times	2.3 times
Industry standard	3.0 times	3.0 times	Unknown
Collection Period			
of Accounts Receivable			
Company	15 days	29 days	19 days
Industry standard	12 days	12 days	Unknown
Cost of Sales to Inventory			
Company	3.9 times	2.3 times	2.8 times
Industry standard	4.0 times	4.0 times	Unknown
Net Sales to Fixed Assets			
Company	14.3 times	7.1 times	10.7 times
Industry standard	20.0 times	20.0 times	Unknown
Net Sales to Net Worth			
Company	10.0 times	5.7 times	10.7 times
Industry standard	11.4 times	11.4 times	Unknown
Long-Term Liabilities			
to Total Noncurrent Assets			
Company	0.7 times	0.7 times	0.7 times
Industry standard	0.8 times	0.8 times	Unknown
Secondary (effect) ratios			
Net Profit to Net Worth			
Company	28.0%	(41.4)%	0.0%
Industry standard	30.0%	30.0%	Unknown
Total Liabilities			
to Net Worth			
Company	2.2 times	2.3 times	3.6 times
Industry standard	2.8 times	2.8 times	Unknown
Current Liabilities			
to Net Worth			
Company	1.7 times	1.8 times	2.9 times
Industry standard	2.0 times	2.0 times	Unknown
Net Sales to Working Capital			
Company	12.5 times	7.5 times	15.0 times
Industry standard	15.0 times	15.0 times	Unknown
Current Assets			
to Current Liabilities			
Company	1.5 times	1.4 times	1.2 times
Industry standard	1.4 times	1.4 times	Unknown

(continued)

Table 30-5. *Continued.*

	Last fiscal year	Most recent six months	Next year projected
Cash and Short-Term Investments plus Accounts Receivable to Current Liabilities (Quick Ratio)			
Company	0.4 times	0.5 times	0.3 times
Industry standard	0.3 times	0.3 times	Unknown
Total Noncurrent Assets to Net Worth			
Company	0.7 times	0.8 times	1.0 times
Industry standard	0.8 times	0.8 times	Unknown
Long-Term Liabilities to Working Capital			
Company	0.6 times	0.7 times	1.0 times
Industry standard	0.9 times	0.9 times	Unknown
Net Profit to Total Assets			
Company	8.8%	(12.4)%	0.0%
Industry standard	9.0%	9.0%	Unknown

evaluated the business's strengths and weaknesses in detail. As he scanned the first few causal ratios for the last full year of operation, he felt a sense of relief that his instincts had been correct. *Net Sales to Total Assets* was slightly higher than the industry norm, showing moderately favorable asset utilization, while *Net Sales to Net Worth* was somewhat on the low side, indicating a relatively high level of owners' equity versus the company's sales volume. In combination, these factors tended to reduce debt and strengthen working capital. On the other hand, both the *Collection* expectations. *Net Sales to Total Assets* had dropped dramatically. In fact, all unfavorable, but Hank knew that the asset items they measured were comparatively small components of total financial structure in this line of business. The major asset item, inventory, was under basic control, as indicated by the company's moderate on a technical basis, by a decline in *Net Sales to Net Worth.* Although owners' equity had been eroded to some extent by the net operating loss, the steep decline industry norms during the previous year.

Turning to the ratios that measure effect, Hank found that the outline he had received from his son was indeed correct. UVW Company exhibited a comparatively low *Total Liabilities to Net Worth*, showing a low level of debt in proportion to owners' equity, and *Current Assets to Current Liabilities* slightly higher than the industry norm, demonstrating moderately favorable working capital balance. The other secondary ratios were either similar to the industry norms or relatively favorable.

Next, he evaluated the figures from an interim financial statement covering the first six months of operation in the new year, again for one of the two stores under competitive pressure. Within this short span of time, several of the key ratios had undergone significant changes, none favorable, confirming Hank's expectations. *Net Sales to Total Assets* had dropped dramatically. In fact, all three of the major component measures, the *Collection Period of Accounts* possessed substantial personal resources of their own or had an unusual ability to become less favorable. *Net Profit to Net Sales* had gone from a solid positive percentage to a negative number. These factors were counterbalanced somewhat, on a technical basis, by a decline in *Net Sales to Net Worth*. Although owners' equity had been eroded to some extent by the net operating loss, the steep decline in sales volume resulted in a decrease in this causal measure. Because Hank had managed to scale back inventory somewhat in order to match stock on hand to anticipated demand, most of the secondary ratios did not appear significantly weaker. *Total Liabilities to Net Worth* was up only slightly, and the *Current Assets to Current Liabilities* was down only slightly, but both were moving in an unfavorable direction—and the negative trend would necessarily continue as long as losses were incurred.

Price Battle to Win War

Finally, Hank studied the ratios based on his projections of UVW Company's income statement and balance sheet after one year of all-out price cutting to recapture half of the company's lost sales. His figures are shown in the right-hand column of Table 30-5. Although the projected price changes would have an effect on the financial structure of the total organization, he projected the figures for a single location in order to gain a clear picture of the comparative differences between future operations and historical results. Hank's figures anticipated even lower pricing by his competitors, but he was confident that no company could last for more than one year at the price levels he projected, unless the owners possessed substantial personal resources of their own or had an unusual ability to obtain outside investment under difficult circumstances. But could UVW Company itself survive such a battle? Hank's review of the ratios suggested to him that a one-year struggle back to the break-even point would put the company under the type of debt pressure it had not experienced since his pioneering efforts to draw audio customers away from department stores and appliance stores many years before. Yet the projected ratios in Table 30-5 demonstrated that the battle would not cripple the company financially. Hank devoutly hoped, however, that the recovery would not take more than one year.

His projections showed that, at the end of next year, *Total Liabilities to Net Worth* would be 3.6, noticeably above the industry norm, but still lower than the upper quartile (the top of the range of common experience), which was more than 5.0, according to his accountant. In addition, his projections included a substantial increase in inventory to avoid any possible stock-outs that would impede UVW Company's effort to win back its former place in the market. This combination of moves would put the company in a possible cash squeeze, as indicated by the projected 1.2 *Current Assets to Current Liabilities*, but Hank's accountant assured him that a 1.1 figure was not uncommon in the industry. Hank also reviewed *Net Sales to Working Capital*, and found that the projected ratio, at 15.0, was actually identical to the industry norm, indicating that UVW Company's cash flow would not be unusually vulnerable to peaks and valleys during the year.

Hank did not relish the prospect of brutal competition, but he was prepared to fight for his company's future. After conferring with his accountant and his lawyer about all aspects of his proposed pricing change, and then discussing the new strategy with his sales force, Hank redirected UVW Company's advertising campaign to stress price as well as the company's usual themes of service, selection, and reputation. He was pleased to see how quickly his company was able to recapture a large segment of the price-shopping market. Nevertheless, for a three-month period, the rival business forced a price cut deeper than he had anticipated, and UVW Company's losses were even worse than projected, despite the relatively rapid gain in unit sales. In addition, his competitors opened two more stores just as UVW Company's recovery campaign began. Despite these unforeseen developments, his earlier analysis of the key financial ratios strengthened his resolve to continue UVW Company's battle for survival, although the competitors' moves caused Hank to worry that he might have misjudged their financial strength. He soon heard, however, from various business sources that his rivals were hopelessly overextended. Before the end of the year, "for rent" signs appeared at all of their locations.

Throughout the battle, Hank had reassessed his pricing strategy, as well as his basic financial structure. Eventually, he concluded that much of the pricing pattern that had been forced on UVW Company by its competition actually made good economic sense. By identifying items that had been priced too high, as well as costly, slow-moving components that were being subsidized by the overpriced items, Hank had developed a more rational pricing scheme. Unfortunately for his competitors, they did not gain any financial reward from making the free-market economy more efficient in their community.

An Advantage in Strategic Planning

The cause-and-effect ratio approach is useful in strategic planning. The key ratios not only help the business decision maker to judge his company's strengths and weaknesses, but they also allow him to project the business's position after making an aggressive strategic move or responding to a competitor's action. Many companies with significant deficiencies in their basic financial structure have been put in a disadvantageous, or even perilous, position by decision makers who do not understand the fundamentals of financial statement analysis. Some owners and managers are blissfully unaware that they have any significant financial problems; others have no idea how to identify the root causes or take appropriate corrective action. They may have a vague notion of their business mission or even a specific marketing plan, but they clearly have no financial strategy. There are, of course, also many companies that have been established with a substantial financial handicap from the very outset—most often owners' equity that is inadequate to support expected sales volume or fixed assets much greater than required—and are only able to rectify the situation over a considerable period of profitable operation. For these companies, financial strategy is limited to shoring up deficiencies and hoping that retained earnings will save the day.

Most successful business decision makers operate with an actual *strategic plan*—a set of specific ideas about the company's future in relation to its competition and to its own available resources, backed up by financial data. The plan does not have to be filled with lengthy paragraphs, huge statistical tables, or fancy graphics. A strategic plan may be only two columns of numbers that reflect management's understanding of the company's present condition and the changes (if any) management expects to achieve at a specific time in the future. The plan may be developed by the privileged company that dominates its market in order to allow for orderly growth and increased profit, or it may reflect an embattled company's response to a specific competitive threat, a change in the requirements of customers, or the terms of sale offered by suppliers. In any case, the company that has formulated a specific plan is almost always in a superior position to evaluate its present situation and make confident financial moves. An understanding of cause-and-effect ratio analysis is an important advantage in developing an effective strategic plan.

Ratio Projections Test Likely Effects of Competitive Moves

During the past two years, IJK Company had lost a small but important segment of its retail furniture business to two large competitors who were offering extended credit terms. Although Marjorie Anderson, the majority owner of IJK Company, had made continuing efforts to compete on the basis of personal service and a keen sense of her suburban customers' taste, the rapid expansion of the entire metropolitan area had brought her company into direct rivalry with larger stores. The competitors' appeal to customers was clearly more a matter of cash flow incentives than aesthetic offerings, but their methods were working to a worrisome extent. In response to Marjorie's request, Bob Harriman, the company's local CPA, had compiled data from several sources that showed a major difference in both competitive tactics and financial structure within the furniture retailing industry.

As Bob briefly explained, larger companies generally offer far more liberal credit terms and have a substantially greater investment in fixed assets. On the other hand, they are able to turn their inventory at a higher rate than smaller companies and earn a higher profit margin. The net result is that the larger companies typically report *Net Sales to Total Assets* decidedly lower than that of their smaller competitors, but attain *Net Profit to Total Assets* that is similar to that of IJK Company. The challenge for IJK Company is twofold:

1. Determine whether the company's net worth (owners' equity) is sufficient to support more liberal credit terms in line with those offered by its bigger rivals.
2. Estimate whether prices can be raised (or costs reduced) to offset the expenses associated with carrying higher accounts receivable—and thereby produce a higher net profit margin.

After doing considerable comparison shopping and talking with old friends, new customers, and suppliers, Marjorie made various estimates of the effect of selective price increases coupled with extended credit terms. Her best estimate would result in a 2.5% boost in total sales revenue, based on last year's sales mix. Assuming no increase in units sold during the next year, would the extended terms yield an adequate profit, and could they be supported by the company's financial structure?

To find the answers, Marjorie computed the level of accounts receivable that would result in the 45-day *Collection Period* that Bob Harriman's data had shown to be typical of IJK Company's competitors. Dividing projected annual sales of $4,100,000 by 365 yielded $11,233 average days' sales; multiplying the average days' sales by 45 resulted in a projected level of accounts receivable equal to $505,000—versus the $152,000 in receivables on the books at the end of the last fiscal year. How would this increase of $353,000 affect IJK Company's financial balance? Making the least favorable assumption, that the $353,000 jump in accounts receivable would occur with no increase in net worth through retained earnings, Marjorie simply added $353,000 to year-end accounts receivable and added a similar $353,000 to current liabilities. She assumed that the annual administrative costs and bad-debt charges would be 14% of the total amount of the additional accounts receivable and that all of the increase in current liabilities would bear interest at an annual rate of 11%. She then recalculated the key financial ratios, as shown in Table 30-7, based on the recast figures, in Table 30-6.

Marjorie was somewhat worried that IJK Company's *Total Liabilities to Net Worth* would rise to 2.1, versus the industry norms of 1.8 and 1.5 for comparatively small concerns and substantially larger companies, respectively. Bob Harriman checked his sources and found that *Total Liabilities to Net Worth* ratios of 3.5 to 4.0 were not uncommon among furniture retailers. Marjorie also inquired about the possibility of an unfavorable reaction from the bank as a result of the likely decline of *Current Assets to Current Liabilities* to 1.5. Bob replied that most industry sources showed that a 1.3 ratio was within the range of common experience in the industry and suggested that Marjorie could refer her banker to him for further details if any question should arise. Now convinced that IJK Company could match the company's larger competitors with respect to extended credit terms, Marjorie initiated an advertising campaign that emphasized the

Table 30-6.   Income statement and balance sheet for IJK Company for two years.

	Most recent year	Next year projected
Income statement		
Net sales	$4,000,000	$4,100,000
Cost of sales	2,400,000	2,400,000
Selling & administrative expenses	1,412,000	1,462,000
Net profit before interest expense	188,000	238,000
Interest expense	76,000	114,000
Net profit before taxes	112,000	124,000
Income taxes	38,000	42,000
Net profit after taxes	$ 74,000	$ 82,000
Balance sheet		
Cash & short-term investments	$ 120,000	$ 120,000
Accounts receivable	152,000	505,000
Inventory	908,000	908,000
Other current assets	60,000	60,000
Current assets	1,240,000	1,593,000
Fixed assets	180,000	180,000
Other noncurrent assets	60,000	60,000
Total assets	$1,480,000	$1,833,000
Current liabilities	$ 720,000	$1,073,000
Long-term liabilities	160,000	160,000
Total liabilities	880,000	1,233,000
Net worth	600,000	600,000
Total liabilities & net worth	$1,480,000	$1,833,000

company's new policy, together with its long-standing advantages of personal attention and a selection of furniture selected especially for upscale and middle-market buyers. During the next 12 months, IJK Company went far beyond preventing further erosion of its customer base. In fact, unit sales rose by more than 15% as a result of combining liberal credit with superior selection. Marjorie often thanked Bob for his help and reminded him of the importance of the industry data he provided in reassuring her that her business instincts were correct.

The Importance of Reviewing Key Ratios According to Size Categories

Whenever data for several size categories are available, you should check the key ratios for the entire range of industry composites in order to determine whether some or all of the important financial measures show a consistent relationship with sales volume, total assets, or any other variable relating to

Table 30-7. Primary and secondary ratios for IJK Company.

	Most recent year	Next year projected
Primary (causal) ratios		
Net Profit		
to Net Sales		
Company	2.8%	3.0%
Industry standard	2.5%	Unknown
Industry standard: Competitors	3.0%	Unknown
Net Sales		
to Total Assets		
Company	2.7 times	2.2 times
Industry standard	3.0 times	Unknown
Industry standard: Competitors	1.5 times	Unknown
Collection Period		
of Accounts Receivable		
Company	14 days	45 days
Industry standard	15 days	Unknown
Industry standard: Competitors	45 days	Unknown
Cost of Sales		
to Inventory		
Company	2.6 times	2.6 times
Industry standard	2.8 times	Unknown
Industry standard: Competitors	3.1 times	Unknown
Net Sales		
to Fixed Assets		
Company	22.2 times	22.8 times
Industry standard	40.0 times	Unknown
Industry standard: Competitors	15.0 times	Unknown
Net Sales		
to Net Worth		
Company	6.7 times	6.8 times
Industry standard	5.0 times	Unknown
Industry standard: Competitors	2.1 times	Unknown
Long-Term Liabilities		
to Total Noncurrent Assets		
Company	0.7 times	0.7 times
Industry standard	0.9 times	Unknown
Industry standard: Competitors	0.6 times	Unknown
Secondary (effect) ratios		
Net Profit		
to Net Worth		
Company	18.7%	20.7%
Industry standard	14.0%	Unknown
Industry standard: Competitors	14.0%	Unknown

	Most recent year	Next year projected
Total Liabilities		
to Net Worth		
Company	1.5 times	2.1 times
Industry standard	1.8 times	Unknown
Industry standard: Competitors	1.5 times	Unknown
Current Liabilities		
to Net Worth		
Company	1.2 times	1.8 times
Industry standard	1.3 times	Unknown
Industry standard: Competitors	1.1 times	Unknown
Net Sales		
to Working Capital		
Company	7.7 times	7.9 times
Industry standard	8.0 times	Unknown
Industry standard: Competitors	7.0 times	Unknown
Current Assets		
to Current Liabilities		
Company	1.7 times	1.5 times
Industry standard	1.8 times	Unknown
Industry standard: Competitors	1.8 times	Unknown
Cash and Short-Term Investments plus Accounts Receivable to Current Liabilities (Quick Ratio)		
Company	0.4 times	0.6 times
Industry standard	0.5 times	Unknown
Industry standard: Competitors	0.7 times	Unknown
Total Noncurrent Assets		
to Net Worth		
Company	0.4 times	0.4 times
Industry standard	0.5 times	Unknown
Industry standard: Competitors	0.7 times	Unknown
Long-Term Liabilities		
to Working Capital		
Company	0.3 times	0.3 times
Industry standard	0.5 times	Unknown
Industry standard: Competitors	0.6 times	Unknown
Net Profit		
to Total Assets		
Company	7.6%	6.7%
Industry standard	7.5%	Unknown
Industry standard: Competitors	7.5%	Unknown

company size in that line of business. If such a relationship is identified, you should consider how the company's operating pattern or financial structure may be expected to change as the business grows larger. Of equal importance, you should take into account the possibility that the financial strengths of larger companies may enable them to threaten the competitive position of the company under evaluation. In many industries, the smaller units enjoy advantages of financial flexibility and lower cost structure; but in others, the larger organizations exhibit the greatest competitive advantages, particularly with respect to capitalization and large-scale purchasing. You should be alert to such relationships in the review of each company. Today's successful small company can quickly become tomorrow's victim of direct competition by a larger organization. A careful review of the key financial ratios from one size category to the next will often reveal the problems (and opportunities) that might arise from challenges by larger or smaller rivals.

Analysis of Net Profit to Net Worth: A Change in Financial Strategy

An article in the monthly newsletter published by his national trade association suggested to Fred Richmond that his basic business strategy required reexamination. Specifically, he had learned that *Net Profit to Net Worth* was an important indicator of company performance. The article, part of a series about the cause-and-effect ratio approach, said that a business owner should not only evaluate his personal compensation in relation to the norm for owners and officers of companies of similar size, but he should also direct his efforts to achieving *Net Profit to Net Worth* at least equal to the industry norm for comparable companies. As stated in the article, all companies cannot possibly be above average, but the business owner who aims for superior performance must consider means of increasing both his personal compensation and the rate of return on his ownership stake in the business.

That made sense to Fred, so he got out his financial statement and calculated *Net Profit to Net Worth* for A&B Corporation (of which he was 90% shareholder and the only active owner) by dividing net profit before taxes by net worth. The first time he ran the numbers, he was startled to find that his ratio was only 0.1, versus the industry norm of nearly 20.0%. Then he double-checked the article and found that although this key financial measure is called a ratio, it is truly a percentage, meaning that the ratio must be multiplied by 100. He tried again, this time hitting the % key on his calculator to yield 11.8%, definitely better than before, but still significantly below the 19.0% figure cited in the article. Observing that 11.8% was about the same as the interest rate his company was paying on its line of credit, Fred suddenly became aware that his rate of return was rather low in relation to the risks of business ownership. As Fred reviewed the article again, he learned that his comparatively low ratio was, nevertheless, probably higher than the effective rate of return on his ownership interest, since the shareholders' equity in a company is likely to have actual value greater than the net worth shown on its balance sheet. A higher value might well result from either the sale of the company on the open market or the orderly liquidation of its assets (particularly if real estate or major equipment is owned by the business). In one sense, this higher potential value is only a theoretical amount for an owner who is steadfastly committed to continued operation of the company. At the same time, the opportunity to earn a return on funds that might be released through sale of the business should not be totally ignored. If the net worth of A&B Corporation as shown on the balance sheet was, in fact, lower than the value of shareholders' equity that would be realized in the free market, then Fred's real rate of return on his investment in the business would necessarily be lower than *Net Profit to Net Worth*. A larger denominator (net worth adjusted for market value) would cause the percentage to fall.

The article explained that one common reason for low *Net Profit to Net Worth* is comparatively high compensation of officers and executives. When Fred computed his personal compensation of $70,000, plus his wife's $12,000 pay as corporate secretary—a total of $82,000—as a percentage of the company's $3 million sales volume, he found that the 2.7% figure was actually lower than the 3.0% industry norm suggested in the article for companies with sales volume similar to that of A&B Corporation. Fred drew the inevitable conclusion that he was not receiving as much money, in the form of compensation plus net profit, as the typical owner in his line of wholesaling. But why? His company's reputation in the local market was unparalleled, and his conversations with friends at industry conventions and seminars had left him with the impression that the A&B Corporation was in better financial condition than most competitors. How could there be a problem? Surely A&B Corporation's accountant or banker would have pointed out poor performance in a key profit area. On rereading the article, however, Fred learned that because outside financial advisors are particularly concerned with helping their clients to avoid difficulties, they often assume that a very conservative financial structure is desirable. As a result, the article said, only by performing his own analysis may a business owner discover that he is receiving a substandard return on the investment in his company. Now that I know that, thought Fred, how do I find the source of the problem? The article in the industry newsletter suggested that association members who wanted to learn more about *Net Profit to Net Worth* would benefit from a newly published guidebook containing a straightforward explanation of cause-and-effect ratio analysis. Fred sent for a copy, especially pleased that it was available at a nominal fee.

The day that the guidebook arrived, he set aside time in the evening to calculate the key financial ratios for A&B Corporation from the company's financial statement data shown in Table 30-8. He then compared them with the industry norms displayed in a financial management report he had received from the association months earlier but had never opened. Those comparisons are

Table 30-8.   Income statement and balance sheet for A&B Corporation.

Income statement

Net sales	$3,000,000
Cost of sales	2,400,000
Selling & administrative expenses*	498,000
Net profit before interest expense	102,000
Interest expense	39,000
Net profit before taxes	63,000
Income taxes	21,000
Net profit after taxes	$ 42,000

Balance sheet

Cash & short-term investments	$ 45,000
Accounts receivable	303,000
Inventory	429,000
Other current assets	15,000
Current assets	792,000
Fixed assets	240,000
Other noncurrent assets	45,000
Total assets	$1,077,000
Current liabilities	$ 361,000
Long-term liabilities	180,000
Total liabilities	541,000
Net worth	536,000
Total liabilities & net worth	$1,077,000

*Including officers'/owners' compensation of $82,000

displayed in Table 30-9. Because Fred had made an ongoing effort to attend regional meetings of the association and had gone to almost every national convention, he felt that he had acquired a good sense of industry conditions and trends without the need for formal financial analysis. He had also talked finance with his accountant on a quarterly basis and had met at least twice a year with his banker, so he had no reason to believe that his company was deficient in any aspect of operations or financial structure. The ratio comparisons, however, suggested to Fred that he may have been overly conservative in his financial approach. In reality, he was not afraid to take prudent financial risks in order to obtain a larger reward; he had simply assumed that his basic business strategy was superior to that of his competitors in every area. After reading the background information in the industry guidebook, Fred realized that he had not paid much attention to the risk-versus-reward concept. By taking a very conservative approach, he would almost necessarily give up some reward that A&B Corporation might achieve through a more aggressive strategy.

The association manual informed Fred that *Net Profit to Net Worth* is determined by the interaction of *Net Profit to Net Sales* and *Net Sales to Net Worth,* the latter of which measures the adequacy of owners' equity in relation to

Table 30-9.   Primary and secondary ratios for A&B Corporation.

Primary (causal) ratios

Net Profit to Net Sales	
Company	2.1%
Industry standard	1.7%
Net Sales to Total Assets	
Company	2.8 times
Industry standard	3.8 times
Collection Period of Accounts Receivable	
Company	37 days
Industry standard	41 days
Cost of Sales to Inventory	
Company	5.6 times
Industry standard	10.6 times
Net Sales to Fixed Assets	
Company	12.5 times
Industry standard	27.8 times
Net Sales to Net Worth	
Company	5.6 times
Industry standard	11.4 times
Long-Term Liabilities to Total Noncurrent Assets	
Company	0.6 times
Industry standard	0.8 times

Secondary (effect) ratios

Net Profit to Net Worth	
Company	11.8%
Industry standard	19.0%
Total Liabilities to Net Worth	
Company	1.0 times
Industry standard	1.9 times
Current Liabilities to Net Worth	
Company	0.7 times
Industry standard	1.5 times
Net Sales to Working Capital	
Company	7.0 times
Industry standard	13.0 times
Current Assets to Current Liabilities	
Company	2.2 times
Industry standard	1.6 times
Cash and Short-Term Investments plus	
Accounts Receivable	
to Current Liabilities (Quick Ratio)	
Company	1.0 times
Industry standard	1.0 times
Total Noncurrent Assets to Net Worth	
Company	0.5 times
Industry standard	0.6 times

(continued)

Table 30-9.   *Continued*.

Long-Term Liabilities to Working Capital	
Company	0.4 times
Industry standard	0.5 times
Net Profit to Total Assets	
Company	5.8%
Industry standard	6.5%

sales volume. Already fully aware that A&B Corporation's *Net Profit to Net Worth* was on the low side, he now returned to Table 30-9 and checked his company's comparative standing with respect to the two causal ratios that were responsible for this result. Although *Net Profit to Net Sales* achieved by A&B Corporation was somewhat higher than the industry norm, the company's very low *Net Sales to Net Worth* was significantly below the percentage reported by the typical company in the industry comparison group. Fred wondered why *Net Sales to Net Worth* had become so low. Obviously, A&B Corporation had been retaining earnings at a faster rate than sales volume had grown. Was that really necessary?

In reading further, Fred found reference to the fact that low *Net Sales to Net Worth* has the effect of reducing *Total Liabilities to Net Worth*. A comparison of A&B Corporation's *Total Liabilities to Net Worth* of 1.0 with the 1.9 median revealed that the company was keeping its debt-to-equity relationship at an unusually low level. That, Fred realized, was attributable to his policy of limiting total liabilities to approximately the same dollar figure as owners' equity. As A&B Corporation had grown, Fred had steadily increased the company's net worth through retained earnings, even when he found it necessary to reduce his personal income temporarily to attain that goal. Although he had not been thinking in terms of ratio analysis, he had in fact been attempting to hold the company's *Total Liabilities to Net Worth* to 1.0. This conservative goal was not based on financial theory or comparative analysis; it was simply the result of Fred's instinct about the appropriate level of debt. In most small and medium-size companies, management does not set specific goals for financial leverage. Instead, cash availability and creditor pressure often determine the amount of funds disbursed to owners versus the amount of earnings retained to boost net worth. Through the ratio comparisons, Fred saw that his extremely conservative approach had definitely reduced A&B Corporation's *Net Profit to Net Worth*.

Fred wondered, however, why the company's *Net Sales to Net Worth* was so much lower than the comparison standard while *Total Liabilities to Net Worth* was only somewhat lower than the industry norm. Once again, the cause-and-effect ratio approach contained in the association manual furnished the answer. In that publication, Fred read that *Total Liabilities to Net Worth* not only is influenced by *Net Sales to Net Worth* but is also directly affected by a second causal measure, *Net Sales to Total Assets*. A&B Corporation's *Net Sales to Total*

Assets was definitely on the low side, so Fred searched for a further explanation. He learned that low *Net Sales to Total Assets* tends to increase *Total Liabilities to Net Worth,* but this effect can be offset by low *Net Sales to Net Worth.* When total assets are increased in relation to net sales (when *Net Sales to Total Assets* declines), the additional amount of assets must be covered by higher debt, an increase in net worth, or a combination of funds from both sources. Even as *Net Sales to Total Assets* declines, it is possible to hold *Total Liabilities to Net Worth* constant—by reducing *Net Sales to Net Worth.* As a result, Fred had not only lowered A&B Corporation's *Net Sales to Net Worth* to meet a conservative target for *Total Liabilities to Net Worth,* he had further reduced *Net Sales to Net Worth* to compensate for relatively low *Net Sales to Total Assets.*

Fred was not surprised that A&B Corporation's *Net Sales to Total Assets* was below that of most competitors. He credited much of the company's success to his emphasis on attractive physical facilities, even if the cost may have been relatively high, and to an inventory selection that was both broad and deep. He was proud of the fact that customers of A&B Corporation would find, in stock, virtually anything that any competitor offered from a catalog. As a result, A&B Corporation was able to maintain a premium pricing structure. Fred's review of *Cost of Sales to Inventory* and *Net Sales to Fixed Assets* showed that A&B Corporation had indeed committed an unusually large amount of funds to these two asset items, leading to relatively low *Net Sales to Total Assets.* But did this higher level of total assets boost the company's profitability? The premium price charged by A&B Corporation more than offset the company's higher inventory carrying costs and higher depreciation charges, as indicated by *Net Profit to Net Sales* somewhat on the high side. The small additional profit percentage in relation to net sales was not, however, sufficient to generate *Net Profit to Total Assets* equal to the industry norm.

Need for Two Major Changes

Fred now saw that A&B Corporation would need to make two major changes in order to bring *Net Profit to Net Worth* up to the median for comparable companies. First, the company would have to boost its net profit in relation to its total assets. This might be accomplished on the revenue side by raising prices selectively or by reducing costs, thereby increasing *Net Profit to Net Sales.* At the same time, *Net Sales to Total Assets* might be increased by improving *Cost of Sales to Inventory* or boosting *Net Sales to Fixed Assets.*

The second move that now occurred to Fred was simply to raise *Net Sales to Net Worth* by holding owners' equity constant while sales volume continued its steady upward trend. In fact, he could boost his annual personal compensation by more than $60,000 (based on last year's results) without harming A&B Corporation's basic financial structure. On the other hand, the company was already carrying interest-bearing debt because of its large asset base, even though its owners' equity was very high in relation to net sales. Until interest-bearing obligations were paid down from cash generated by higher profits or from the reduction of assets, the interest costs on any additional debt (that might be avoided by further retention of earnings) would offset personal income that could be generated on funds withdrawn from the company. Consequently, Fred elected to defer any major boost in compensation until the paydown of debt could be accomplished. He did, however, plan to confer with his accountant about the most advantageous methods of taking more money out of the company in the future.

In thinking about the possibility of holding net profit to nearly zero by boosting his personal salary and bonus or by increasing fringe benefits, Fred recognized that *Net Profit to Net Worth* is highly dependent on the compensation of owners and officers. If *Net Profit to Net Sales* falls to zero through withdrawal of funds in the form of salaries, bonuses, and benefits, *Net Profit to Net Worth* will decline to zero as well. Fred realized that in the event he would make such a move, he would need to restate *Net Profit to Net Worth* for internal analysis in order to track his company's progress. One method he found in the association manual is to calculate net profit before taxes plus owners'/officers' compensation as a percentage of net worth and to compute a similar benchmark ratio for the comparison group. Another useful approach is to "normalize" compensation by subtracting typical owners'/officers' compensation for comparable companies from the actual remuneration of the company's executives and then calculate the difference as a percentage of net worth.

Rise in Personal Income

Fred saw no reason to make rapid changes in A&B Corporation's operating pattern or its financial structure, but he did undertake a gradual effort to improve his company's *Net Profit to Net Worth*. A careful study of the relationship between A&B Corporation's unusually high inventory and fixed assets and its profitability led to selective reductions in inventory, a less aggressive program of upgrading fixed assets, and a small price increase in certain areas. Although the results were not dramatic, Fred succeeded in boosting his personal income by $30,000 per year as a result of his investigation of *Net Sales to Net Worth*.

Despite its popularity as a measure of return on shareholders' equity in publicly traded companies, *Net Profit to Net Worth* is generally considered a less valuable measure in privately held companies because it is greatly affected by owners' decisions about their own compensation. Nevertheless, *Net Profit to Net Worth* is useful in alerting company owners to the possibility that they are receiving substandard return on the funds they have invested in the company. Particularly as the owner approaches retirement age, he should consider whether a greater proportion of earnings might be withdrawn from the company and invested in a more balanced portfolio. Credit grantors are unlikely to make such a suggestion, because they prefer to see a relatively conservative financial structure, which provides them with a greater cushion against possible adverse developments. Accountants, too, often suggest conservative strategies to protect their clients from unexpected reverses, although some financial advisors now tend to place greater emphasis on aggressive money management than on basic company operations. Consequently, in many cases the company owner must initiate his own evaluation of *Net Profit to Net Worth*. Such an assessment of competitive position with respect to both personal compensation and the company's rate of return on equity can often go beyond enhancing the owner's individual financial status. It may well reveal the opportunity to improve the company's total financial strategy.

Chapter 31

Cause-and-Effect Analysis:
A Tool, Not a Dictate

Although cause-and-effect ratio analysis is extremely helpful in pointing out a company's variances from industry standards, this approach is certainly not intended to supersede management judgment. After a careful review of all key financial factors, a business owner or manager may decide to continue the company's present course of action even if it is likely to prolong an apparently unfavorable difference between the company's performance and that of its typical competitor, as described in published norms for the company's line of activity. In some cases, management may accept the calculated risk of incurring still greater financial imbalance in order to achieve certain strategic objectives, particularly if contingency plans have been developed and the company's actions have the support of creditors. In the first example in this chapter, a company owner finds that gradual, relatively minor changes in several key areas will help him achieve his objectives. The second example shows how insight from the cause-and-effect ratio approach can help management assess alternative courses of action, even if the ultimate decision is to risk moving further from the norm. In certain areas of financial management, the objectives of the owner may overrule any other interpretation of the key ratios, as shown in the third example. Although cause-and-effect ratio analysis can help business decision makers improve their understanding of the key elements that determine every company's competitive strengths and weaknesses, this management tool can only supplement, certainly not replace, the knowledge developed by business owners, their key employees, and their financial advisors.

Significant Effects From Subtle Combinations of Causal Ratios

Ted Daras was frustrated by his inability to find the cause of the E&F Corporation's working capital insufficiency. He had carefully calculated the key financial ratios shown in Table 31-2 from the company's financial statement data in Table 31-1. For comparative purposes, Ted had expanded Table 31-2 to include the industry standards displayed in the annual financial management report he had received from his national trade association. Within minutes, he had verified his

Table 31-1. Income statement and balance sheet for E&F Corporation.

Income statement

Net sales	$11,000,000
Cost of sales	8,624,000
Selling & administrative expenses	1,740,000
Net profit before interest expense	636,000
Interest expense	296,000
Net profit before taxes	340,000
Income taxes	116,000
Net profit after taxes	$ 224,000
Depreciation expense	$ 672,000

Balance sheet

Cash & short-term investments	$ 108,000
Accounts receivable	1,796,000
Inventory	1,188,000
Other current assets	32,000
Current assets	3,124,000
Fixed assets	3,092,000
Other noncurrent assets	32,000
Total assets	$6,248,000
Current liabilities	$2,344,000
Long-term liabilities	2,036,000
Total liabilities	4,380,000
Net worth	1,868,000
Total liabilities & net worth	$6,248,000

original impression that his company's working capital position was weaker than that of the typical aerospace machining company. Four secondary measures—relatively high *Net Sales to Working Capital*, low *Current Assets to Current Liabilities*, low *Cash and Short-Term Investments plus Accounts Receivable to Current Liabilities (Quick Ratio)*, and comparatively high *Long-Term Liabilities to Working Capital*—had consistently shown that Ted's concerns about working capital and cash flow were well founded. His review of the seven causal ratios, however, had not revealed any highly significant difference between his company's values and the industry norms. In re-reading the accompanying explanation of the cause-and-effect ratio approach, Ted encountered the admonition that the nine ratios that measure effect are determined by the *combined influence* of the seven causal ratios. He decided to make one more careful review of the causal ratios to see whether a certain combination of relatively small differences could have produced such major deviations in the secondary ratios that measure working capital. To aid himself in his investigation, he read the complete explanation of each ratio as he compared the figures.

Table 31-2.   Primary and secondary ratios for E&F Corporation.

Primary (causal) ratios

Net Profit to Net Sales	
Company	3.1%
Industry standard	2.9%
Net Sales to Total Assets	
Company	1.8 times
Industry standard	1.8 times
Collection Period of Accounts Receivable	
Company	60 days
Industry standard	60 days
Cost of Sales to Inventory	
Company	7.3 times
Industry standard	7.4 times
Net Sales to Fixed Assets	
Company	3.6 times
Industry standard	3.7 times
Net Sales to Net Worth	
Company	5.9 times
Industry standard	5.9 times
Long-Term Liabilities to Total Noncurrent Assets	
Company	0.7 times
Industry standard	0.8 times

Secondary (effect) ratios

Net Profit to Net Worth	
Company	18.2%
Industry standard	14.3%
Total Liabilities to Net Worth	
Company	2.3 times
Industry standard	2.2 times
Current Liabilities to Net Worth	
Company	1.3 times
Industry standard	0.9 times
Net Sales to Working Capital	
Company	14.1 times
Industry standard	8.7 times
Current Assets to Current Liabilities	
Company	1.3 times
Industry standard	1.8 times
Cash and Short-Term Investments plus	
Accounts Receivable	
to Current Liabilities (Quick Ratio)	
Company	0.8 times
Industry standard	1.0 times
Total Noncurrent Assets to Net Worth	
Company	1.7 times
Industry standard	1.7 times

Long-Term Liabilities to Working Capital	
Company	2.6 times
Industry standard	1.8 times
Net Profit to Total Assets	
Company	5.4%
Industry standard	4.7%

E&F Corporation's *Net Profit to Net Sales* was not a likely suspect for two reasons: This key ratio was slightly favorable in relation to the industry norm, and it has only an indirect, cumulative effect on a company's working capital position. *Net Sales to Total Assets* was equal to the industry standard, so it could not be the cause of insufficient working capital. In addition, this key indicator, which summarizes total asset utilization, does not directly influence a company's working capital position. The *Collection Period of Accounts Receivable* did not answer his question. Not only was this key measure in line with the industry norm, but the *Collection Period of Accounts Receivable* does not have a direct influence on a company's working capital level which would be reflected in *Net Sales to Working Capital*. The *Collection Period of Accounts Receivable* does have a major impact on *Current Assets to Current Liabilities*, which measures a company's balance between current assets and current liabilities, but an increase or decrease in accounts receivable will not change the dollar amount of working capital (the excess of current assets over current liabilities) except if there are bad debt write-offs. Ted found E&F Corporation's *Cost of Sales to Inventory* slightly lower than the norm, but this ratio also exerts no direct influence on a company's working capital level. Like the *Collection Period of Accounts Receivable*, *Cost of Sales to Inventory* is a major factor in determining *Current Assets to Current Liabilities*, but not *Net Sales to Working Capital*.

The next causal measure, *Net Sales to Fixed Assets*, finally suggested one reason for E&F Corporation's working capital weakness. Although only slightly lower than the industry benchmark, this ratio showed that E&F Corporation had committed a comparatively large amount of funds to fixed assets in relation to the company's sales volume. The fact that the industry norm of 3.7 for aerospace machining companies was substantially lower than the typical value in most industries also indicated that fixed assets wielded an unusually important influence on total financial structure. *Net Sales to Net Worth*, which has a major impact on *Net Sales to Working Capital*, was equal to the industry standard, exerting a moderating effect. Consequently, *Net Sales to Net Worth* was neither a favorable nor an unfavorable influence on E&F Corporation's working capital position. The last of the seven primary possibilities, *Long-Term Liabilities to Total Noncurrent Assets*, showed Ted another cause for the working capital problems his company had been experiencing. E&F Corporation's relatively low value for this ratio might at first appear to be a favorable indicator, since a low level of debt is ordinarily considered to be a desirable attribute. With respect to working capital, however, low *Long-Term Liabilities to Total Noncurrent Assets* exerts an unfavorable influence, causing the company to fund fixed assets and other noncurrent assets from a comparatively great increase in current liabilities or a reduction of current assets. Particularly when fixed assets are a major factor in a company's financial structure, as in the case of the aerospace machining industry, matching long-term liabilities to total noncurrent assets is an especially important principle of financial management. Because of the relative size of fixed assets, a small change in this ratio—even from 0.8 to 0.7—can cause a significant reduction in working capital.

High Net Sales to Working Capital

Ted concluded that E&F Corporation's comparatively high *Net Sales to Working Capital*, indicating a relatively small amount of working capital to support sales volume, was traceable to a combination of slightly low *Net Sales to Fixed Assets* and slightly low *Long-Term Liabilities to Total Noncurrent Assets*. To confirm his findings, he decided to work back from ratios to dollar amounts. First, he divided E&F Corporation's net sales of $11 million by the industry benchmark of 3.7 to determine the level of fixed assets his company would have had if its ratio had been in line with the median for the aerospace machining industry. He obtained a figure of $2,973,000, compared with $3,092,000 on the books of E&F Corporation at year-end. The seemingly minor difference between 3.6 and 3.7 represented $119,000 in fixed assets that required funding from a combination of liabilities and owners' equity. Next, Ted added the $2,973,000 amount of fixed assets from his previous calculation to the $32,000 of miscellaneous (other noncurrent) assets reported by E&F Corporation to obtain the total amount of noncurrent assets that the company would have had if the key financial factors had been equal to the industry norm. Then he multiplied the $3,005,000 total by the 0.8 median *Long-Term Liabilities to Total Noncurrent Assets*. The result, $2,404,000, was the amount of long-term liabilities E&F Corporation would have had if its relationship between long-term debt and noncurrent assets had been similar to that of the typical competitor. This $2,404,000 figure was $368,000 greater than the $2,036,000 in long-term debt actually held by E&F Corporation at the end of its last fiscal year. In fact, the rounded industry ratio of 0.8 could have been as high as 0.845, resulting in a calculated amount of $2,539,000 for long-term liabilities on total noncurrent assets of $3,005,000.

If the $119,000 difference in fixed assets and the $368,000 difference in long-term liabilities calculated from the industry medians had been available to reduce the company's current liabilities of $2,344,000, the resulting $1,857,000 balance of short-term debt would have greatly improved E&F Corporation's working capital ratios. With working capital growing to $1,267,000 ($3,124,000 in current assets minus the calculated $1,857,000 in current liabilities), *Net Sales to Working Capital* would have declined to 8.7, identical to the industry standard. Simultaneously, *Current Assets to Current Liabilities* would have improved to 1.7, not far below the median value. Depending on assumptions about rounding of the industry medians on which the dollar calculations were based, *Current Assets to Current Liabilities* might have climbed to 1.8 through the reduction of current liabilities by means of decreasing fixed assets and raising long-term debt.

> *Net Sales to Working Capital,* which indicates the sufficiency of a company's working capital in relation to its sales volume, is influenced by three causal measures: *Net Sales to Fixed Assets, Net Sales to Net Worth,* and *Long-Term Liabilities to Total Noncurrent Assets.* Because of this combination of influences, comparatively subtle variances from the median values for two or three of these causal ratios may result in significant shifts in *Net Sales to Working Capital* and in the other secondary ratios that are linked to this measure, particularly *Current Assets to Current Liabilities* and *Cash and Short-Term Investments plus Accounts Receivable to Current Liabilities (Quick Ratio).*

Ted could now see that a combination of relatively small differences in the causal ratios can produce significant changes in the nine ratios that measure effect. Because E&F Corporation's working capital situation was by no means desperate, Ted perceived no immediate need to consider refinancing fixed assets on a long-term basis. He did, however, resolve to keep a close watch on additional commitments to fixed assets and to seek longer payment arrangements on his machinery loans in the future.

In most cases, you will find one or more of the seven causal ratios substantially different from the industry norm. Such clear-cut variances from typical values will ordinarily explain why some or all of the nine secondary ratios are out of line with comparative standards. Occasionally, however, the secondary measures (particularly those that relate to working capital) show significant differences from the industry medians because of a subtle combination of slightly favorable or unfavorable values for the causal ratios. When the underlying reason (or reasons) for such differences is not immediately apparent from obvious variances in the causal ratios, you must make a special effort to review the specific combinations of those ratios that exert direct influence on those particular secondary measures which require further explanation.

Special Strategy for Values Beyond Normal Range

In preparing her financial plan for the coming year, Sally Sharpe faced two important questions. Can our company continue to grow this rapidly? Should we buy a new building before real estate prices take off again? In less than four years, Sally and her husband, Will, had built their suburban sporting goods and fitness equipment store into an enterprise grossing nearly $3 million annually. They had both been highly successful high school coaches, she in basketball and he in football and track, when they encountered the opportunity to purchase a long-established, old-fashioned sporting goods store in an area that was expected to grow dramatically within the next few years. They agreed with projections that major residential construction would soon follow a controversial new highway nearing completion, so they invested their savings in buying the store, more for its reputation as the only such place in town than for its inventory of fishing rods, hunters' boots, and basketballs. They immediately began promoting runners' clothes, ski apparel, mountain bikes, and other adult items, while contacting their coaching friends and advertising in the suburban weekly and local merchandiser to promote their standard lines of athletic items.

A combination of purchasing mistakes and lower-than-anticipated sales had made the first year disappointing, but several new subdivisions brought eager customers into the area late in the second year. Since then, demand had exceeded their most optimistic expectations, and they had expanded their operations into two adjoining retail spaces. The last two years had been decidedly profitable. Nevertheless, such rapid growth had placed tremendous strain on C&D Company's underlying financial resources. The bank had continued to increase the company's line of credit in rough proportion to the growth of inventory, but for the past six months suppliers had been calling about late payments with ever greater frequency.

As she had done each year, Sally converted C&D Company's financial statement data, displayed in Table 31-3, into selected percentages and ratios and then lined up her concern's results next to the industry data she had obtained through her banker. Those ratio comparisons are presented in Table 31-4. Although unaware of the value of detailed information provided by national trade associations, she had gained a general picture of C&D Company's competitive position from a page of data about sporting goods retailers taken from the *RMA Annual Statement Studies*. Scanning the information for firms with total assets between $1 million and $10 million, Sally could see immediately that C&D Company's *Total Liabilities to Net Worth*, its *Current Assets to Current Liabilities*, its *Fixed Assets to Net Worth* (a variant of *Total Noncurrent Assets to Net Worth*), its *Net Profit to Net Worth*, and its *Net Sales to Working Capital* were all significantly different from the respective industry medians. *Fixed Assets to Net Worth*, a secondary ratio contained in the RMA publication, is designed to measure the proportion of owners' equity committed to fixed assets. It performs much the same function as *Total Noncurrent Assets to Net Worth*, but does not include other noncurrent (miscellaneous) assets, which occasionally absorb a large amount of net worth that would otherwise be available for working capital. In the case of C&D Company, however, other noncurrent assets did not have a significant influence on basic financial structure.

Sally did not have the benefit of instruction in the cause-and-effect ratio approach and could not find a comparative value for *Net Sales to Net Worth* (which would have immediately pinpointed C&D Company's inadequate owners' equity in relation to sales volume). Nevertheless, by sifting through the RMA ratios, she was able to discern that net worth was low in relation to three other factors.

Table 31-3.   Income statement and balance sheet for C&D Company.

Income statement	
Net sales	$2,700,000
Cost of sales	1,822,500
Selling & administrative expenses	712,000
Net profit before interest expense	165,000
Interest expense	67,500
Net profit before taxes	97,500
Income taxes	33,000
Net profit after taxes	$ 64,500
Balance sheet	
Cash & short-term investments	$ 81,000
Accounts receivable	135,000
Inventory	783,000
Other current assets	54,000
Current assets	1,053,000
Fixed assets	108,000
Other noncurrent assets	27,000
Total assets	$1,188,000
Current liabilities	$ 868,500
Long-term liabilities	162,000
Total liabilities	1,030,500
Net worth	157,500
Total liabilities & net worth	$1,188,000

Her reading of the explanations sent along by her banker informed her that high *Total Liabilities to Net Worth* demonstrates comparatively great debt pressure. She also learned that high *Fixed Assets to Net Worth* is considered another unfavorable factor from a conservative point of view because it shows that a high proportion of owners' equity has been committed to illiquid assets, thereby reducing working capital. *Net Profit to Net Worth* represented a favorable financial relationship because it demonstrated the potential for a proportionate buildup of owners' equity from retained earnings, even though C&D Company's extremely high percentage reflected very low net worth rather than unusually high net profit. The company's low *Current Assets to Current Liabilities* and high *Net Sales to Working Capital* indicated severe debt pressure.

Effects of Expansion

Sally knew that another year of rapid expansion would push the key financial ratios even further from the industry norm. But should a projected increase of *Total Liabilities to Net Worth* from its present 6.5 value to 10.0, instead of, say, 9.0, make a significant difference in her decision to expand sales volume? She

Table 31-4. Primary and secondary ratios for C&D Company.

Primary (causal) ratios

Net Profit to Net Sales

Company	3.6%
Industry standard	2.6%
Mid-range (lower and upper quartile)	Unknown

Net Sales to Total Assets

Company	2.3 times
Industry standard	2.3 times
Mid-range	1.8 to 2.8 times

Collection Period of Accounts Receivable

Company	18 days
Industry standard	7 days
Mid-range	2 to 25 days

Cost of Sales to Inventory

Company	2.3 times
Industry standard	2.5 times
Mid-range	1.8 to 3.1 times

Net Sales to Fixed Assets

Company	25.0 times
Industry standard	22.7 times
Mid-range	9.6 to 65.2 times

Net Sales to Net Worth

Company	17.1 times
Industry standard	7.4 times*
Mid-range	Unknown

Long-Term Liabilities to Total Noncurrent Assets

Company	1.2 times
Industry standard	0.7 times*
Mid-range	Unknown

Secondary (effect) ratios

Net Profit to Net Worth

Company	61.9%
Industry standard	13.8%
Mid-range	3.1% to 34.5%

Total Liabilities to Net Worth

Company	6.5 times
Industry standard	2.2 times
Mid-range	1.4 to 3.9 times

Current Liabilities to Net Worth

Company	5.5 times
Industry standard	1.7 times*
Mid-range	Unknown

Net Sales to Working Capital

Company	14.6 times
Industry standard	8.2 times
Mid-range	5.5 to 18.9 times

Current Assets to Current Liabilities	
Company	1.2 times
Industry standard	1.6 times
Mid-range	1.2 to 2.1 times
Cash and Short-Term Investments plus	
Accounts Receivable	
to Current Liabilities (Quick Ratio)	
Company	0.2 times
Industry standard	0.2 times
Mid-range	0.1 to 0.6 times
Fixed Assets to Net Worth	
Company	0.9 times
Industry standard	0.4 times
Mid-range	0.1 to 0.9 times
Long-Term Liabilities to Working Capital	
Company	0.9 times
Industry standard	0.6 times*
Mid-range	Unknown
Net Profit to Total Assets	
Company	8.2%
Industry standard	4.8%
Mid-range	0.7% to 11.3%

*Derived.

Note: The industry standard is the RMA median for all ratios except *Net Profit to Net Sales*, which is expressed as the average in accordance with common practice in the presentation of operating statement percentages. As previously indicated, *Net Profit to Net Sales, Net Profit to Net Worth,* and *Net Profit to Total Assets* are based on net profit before taxes.

Source: Industry standards © Robert Morris Associates 1989. Reprinted with permission.

already recognized that her company was well above the upper quartile of 3.9 shown in the RMA data. How high is too high?

Sally had reasonable confidence in her banker's willingness to continue to support further expansion, but she was somewhat concerned about a few of the company's key suppliers. Could they be expected to accept even later payments as an implied condition of larger orders? And what if—in the worst case—a competing company should suddenly appear on the scene? Sally did not worry too much about that possibility, but even if a rival should make inroads into C&D Company's market, she envisioned simply scaling back inventory to meet reduced demand and using the increased cash to pay suppliers and the bank.

Sally had always recognized that one of the important factors enabling her firm to carry an unusual level of debt was financial flexibility. That observation essentially answered her second question about purchasing a new building. Even if C&D Company's financial structure could possibly support additional fixed assets, which was a doubtful proposition in view of the firm's debt-heavy condition, an ongoing obligation to meet principal payments would impair the company's ability to reduce assets and debt in the event that demand should fall. The continued rise in real estate prices in C&D Company's market area might argue eloquently for locking in a mortgage payment schedule and enjoying capital appreciation on the property, but Sally understood that she was in the sporting goods business, not real estate speculation.

The key financial ratios had been useful in focusing her attention on the issues of greatest concern, but they could not dictate management action. Knowing that her "bankers' ratios," particularly *Total Liabilities to Net Worth* and *Current Assets to Current Liabilities*, were comparatively weak, Sally had a frank discussion with her loan officer about the possibility that the bank might suddenly impose a restriction on C&D Company's credit line. After reviewing her ratio comparisons and her reasons for planning continued but more moderate growth, her banker assured her that as long as the company maintained sound control of its assets and achieved a reasonable profit margin, he would continue to expand the line of credit to help finance inventory. They both understood that some of the financial ratios would become even more unfavorable while growth continued, and they talked about the dangers inherent in that situation. To help him keep the line current and to monitor the company's progress, the banker suggested quarterly meetings throughout the year to review results for the previous three months and to evaluate C&D Company's financial structure. Even though the key financial ratios simply confirmed Sally's view of her company's financial situation and did not provide her with precise limits or strict guidelines, they enabled her to identify specific areas of concern and to communicate more effectively with her banker.

In a highly leveraged business, each major creditor assumes a role similar to that of a partner. Whether that relationship has evolved on a cooperative basis or is the result of the creditor's becoming enmeshed in escalating debt before recognizing the extent of the peril, management must make an ongoing effort to keep the company's banker and its most important suppliers informed about management plans. A series of unpleasant facts rationally presented in a timely manner is less likely to disturb a company's relationship with creditors than is a single unfavorable surprise. Understanding cause-and-effect ratio analysis will enable a company owner or manager to explain the company's situation and to offer specific plans for maintaining a mutually beneficial relationship.

Need for Cooperation From Creditors

Once management recognizes that the company's projected plan of action will cause certain key measures to move in an even more unfavorable direction from industry norms, a reevaluation of the organization's strategy is important, particularly with respect to obtaining the cooperation of major creditors. Not only do the key ratios indicate areas of concern to both management and creditors, but a value higher or lower than a specific benchmark used by bankers and suppliers may trigger serious repercussions. In most cases, a business decision maker will benefit from alerting the people involved in the credit transaction to any significant changes that may be expected to occur with respect to the company's financial indicators, rather than hoping that a computerized screening program will allow the numbers to pass certain tests without comment. Even if no specific financial formulas are used by the company's credit grantors, continued deterioration of the key financial ratios will eventually result in a limit on further funding. To maintain some semblance of control over the timing of possible changes in relationships with creditors, the company owner or manager should devote attention to understanding the language of financial management, recognizing the important financial indicators, providing timely information to bankers and key suppliers, and seeking regular confirmation of credit relationships.

Understanding Management Objectives: Road to a Different Interpretation

As Jack Shapiro, president and sole owner of the ABC Company, the largest carpet wholesaler in the area, drove downtown to meet with his financial advisor for the company's annual financial review, he looked forward to being congratulated on another fine year of profitability and smooth operations. Instead, he was doubly surprised. First, he learned that Kevin Haggerty, the consulting firm's senior partner and Jack's long-time advisor, was at home with a minor illness and that Kevin's son, Timothy, would be meeting with Jack instead. Then, only minutes into the meeting, Timothy advised Jack that he was operating inefficiently and penalizing his own return on invested capital. He even pointed out to Jack various quotations from his extensive reference library. There it was in black and white: "A low *Net Sales to Working Capital* ratio may indicate an inefficient use of working capital." "Laxity in financial management often results from too much working capital," said another source. "Excessive working capital destroys the control of turnover ratios commonly used in conducting an efficient business." As shown in Table 31-6, based on the results displayed in Table 31-5, the ABC Company's *Net Sales to Working Capital* was definitely on the low side in comparison with other wholesalers of floor coverings with total assets in the $1 million–$10 million range. Jack had not noticed any of the supposed difficulties that result from maintaining a relatively high level of working capital in relation to net sales, but he asked the young consultant to tell him more.

Timothy pointed out that relatively high *Net Profit to Net Sales*, which the ABC Company clearly enjoyed, should result in a superior *Net Profit to Net Worth*. Yet the company's *Net Profit to Net Worth* was not far above the industry norm. Timothy advised Jack to become more financially aggressive in order to gain a higher rate of return on the money he had invested, primarily through retained earnings, in his company. Jack listened politely, asked to borrow a copy of the *RMA Annual Statement Studies* from which Timothy had drawn his comparative figures, and left.

Low *Net Sales to Net Worth* (a high level of owners' equity in relation to sales volume) increases working capital (lowers *Net Sales to Working Capital*) and

Table 31-5.   Income statement and balance sheet for ABC Company.

Income statement

Net sales	$12,000,000
Cost of sales	8,700,000
Selling & administrative expenses	2,820,000
Net profit before interest expense	480,000
Interest expense	144,000
Net profit before taxes	336,000
Income taxes	120,000
Net profit after taxes	$ 216,000
Depreciation expense	$ 170,000

Balance sheet

Cash & short-term investments	$ 360,000
Accounts receivable	1,570,000
Inventory	1,705,000
Other current assets	120,000
Current assets	3,755,000
Fixed assets	600,000
Other noncurrent assets	240,500
Total assets	$4,595,000
Current liabilities	$2,340,000
Long-term liabilities	445,000
Total liabilities	2,785,000
Net worth	1,810,000
Total liabilities & net worth	$4,595,000

reduces *Total Liabilities to Net Worth*, strengthening financial structure from the viewpoint of creditors. On the other hand, it reduces *Net Profit to Net Worth*.

Jack remembered the basic elements of cause-and-effect ratio analysis he had learned the previous year at a seminar sponsored by his chamber of commerce. Within a few minutes, he had satisfied himself that the ABC Company was essentially where he wanted the business to be. ABC maintained comparatively high owners' equity in relation to net sales—comparatively low *Net Sales to Net Worth*—in order to support attractive facilities in a prime location, a somewhat liberal (but well-controlled) credit-and-collection policy, and an extensive inventory for quick delivery. This approach had led to a slightly better markup, which was combined with lower interest costs and careful management of overhead to produce favorable *Net Profit to Net Sales* and *Net Profit to Net Worth* higher than the industry norm, while maintaining comparatively low *Total Liabilities to Net Worth*. As the *RMA Annual Statement Studies* observed, "A lower ratio generally indicates greater long-term financial safety. A firm with a low debt/worth ratio usually has greater flexibility to borrow in the future." Jack reviewed the ratios in Table 31-6 with considerable satisfaction. Since sleeping

Table 31-6.   Primary and secondary ratios for ABC Company.

Primary (causal) ratios

Net Profit to Net Sales
Company	2.8%
Industry standard	1.5%

Net Sales to Total Assets
Company	2.6 times
Industry standard	3.1 times

Collection Period
  of Accounts Receivable
Company	48 days
Industry standard	41 days

Cost of Sales to Inventory
Company	5.1 times
Industry standard	5.9 times

Net Sales to Fixed Assets
Company	20.0 times
Industry standard	47.1 times

Net Sales to Net Worth
Company	6.6 times
Industry standard	10.2 times*

Long-Term Liabilities
  to Total Noncurrent Assets
Company	0.5 times
Industry standard	0.8 times*

- -

Secondary (effect) ratios

Net Profit to Net Worth
Company	18.6%
Industry standard	13.1%

Total Liabilities to Net Worth
Company	1.5 times
Industry standard	2.3 times

Current Liabilities to Net Worth
Company	1.3 times
Industry standard	1.9 times*

Net Sales to Working Capital
Company	8.5 times
Industry standard	11.5 times

Current Assets to Current Liabilities
Company	1.6 times
Industry standard	1.6 times

Cash and Short-Term
  Investments plus Accounts
  Receivable to Current Liabilities
  (Quick Ratio)
Company	0.8 times
Industry standard	0.7 times

(continued)

Table 31-6. *Continued.*

Total Noncurrent Assets to Net Worth	
Company	0.5 times
Industry standard	0.5 times*
Long-Term Liabilities to Working Capital	
Company	0.3 times
Industry standard	0.4 times*
Net Profit to Total Assets	
Company	7.3%
Industry standard	3.6%

*Derived.
Note: The industry standard is the RMA median for all ratios except *Net Profit to Net Sales,* which is expressed as the average in accordance with common practice in the presentation of operating statement percentages. As previously indicated, *Net Profit to Net Sales, Net Profit to Net Worth,* and *Net Profit to Total Assets* are based on net profit before taxes.
Source: Industry standards © Robert Morris Associates 1989. Reprinted with permission.

well was a high priority for him, Jack decided to file Timothy's suggestions for review at another time.

The analyst who is in a position to offer advice to company management should not pass judgment on the concern's financial structure until the objectives of the owners are well understood. Naturally, any danger signals should be pointed out. Likewise, any opportunities for improvement revealed by comparative analysis should be thoroughly explained to management. With respect to the balance between risk and reward, however, the analyst must often defer to the preferences of the individuals who have elected to accept that risk. Some business owners prefer to sacrifice potential earnings in order to operate with greater assurance that any unexpected adverse developments, such as the bankruptcy of a major customer or supplier, will be only an inconvenience, not a threat to the company's cash flow, its credit standing, or its very survival. Other business owners are willing to live with relatively great financial risk in order to maximize return on their investment. Ordinarily, the analyst has a greater responsibility to advise the inordinate risk taker of potential problems than to suggest that the low-risk operator might assume more debt. Presenting ideas for achieving higher *Net Profit to Net Worth* is commendable, but you must recognize that boosting return beyond a certain point may not be a high priority for the owner.

Chapter 32

Many Uses in External Analysis

Some outside analysts, including accountants and other financial advisors, use ratio analysis in cooperation with management to evaluate a company's progress and its plans. Credit grantors and prospective investors are, on the other hand, often somewhat removed from intimate knowledge of the objectives of the company's owners or managers. In fact, they may find themselves in an essentially adversarial position, requiring them to piece together a reasonable picture of the company's operations and financial position from numbers alone. In either situation, the cause-and-effect ratio approach gives the analyst a framework for placing the company's operating performance and financial structure in perspective and for identifying the cause or causes of any significant variance from industry standards. The outside analyst must frequently work with data from a single fiscal period; consequently, he or she must reach a conclusion without the benefit of trend studies. If the analysis based on one year's data is inconclusive, and if the decision is a matter of importance to the analyst, he or she should make every effort to obtain specific figures for previous periods and go beyond the simplified examples in the following pages.

Similar Secondary Ratios, but Different Causes, Point to Different Responses

When Floyd Washington first reviewed the credit requests from LMN Company and OPQ Corporation, he was inclined to be extremely cautious in both cases. But as credit manager for a large electrical appliance manufacturer, he realized that his decision could make a major difference in the future of each of the wholesalers under consideration, so he continued his usual thorough study of the financial statements he had requested. He converted the raw data for each company, shown in Table 32-1, into the key financial ratios displayed in Table 32-2. Then he inserted special industry norms, which he developed each year for his own analytical purposes, in Table 32-2, to assist him in assessing the respective strengths and weaknesses of these two companies. He observed that both LMN Company and OPQ Corporation appeared identical in terms of the three ratios so

Table 32-1. Income statement and balance sheet for LMN Company and OPQ Corporation.

	LMN Company	OPQ Corporation
Income statement		
Net sales	$50,000,000	$25,000,000
Cost of sales	38,000,000	18,500,000
Selling & administrative expenses	11,000,000	5,125,000
Net profit before interest expense	1,000,000	1,375,000
Interest expense	250,000	875,000
Net profit before taxes	750,000	500,000
Income taxes	250,000	165,000
Net profit after taxes	$ 500,000	$ 335,000
Depreciation expense	$ 250,000	$ 500,000
Balance sheet		
Cash & short-term investments	$ 1,250,000	$ 1,250,000
Accounts receivable	4,500,000	4,625,000
Inventory	5,000,000	6,000,000
Other current assets	250,000	500,000
Current assets	11,000,000	12,375,000
Fixed assets	1,250,000	2,500,000
Other noncurrent assets	250,000	125,000
Total assets	$12,500,000	$15,000,000
Current liabilities	$ 9,400,000	$10,625,000
Long-term liabilities	1,000,000	1,875,000
Total liabilities	10,400,000	12,500,000
Net worth	2,100,000	2,500,000
Total liabilities & net worth	$12,500,000	$15,000,000

closely watched by many credit grantors: _Total Liabilities to Net Worth, Current Assets to Current Liabilities_, and _Cash and Short-Term Investments plus Accounts Receivable to Current Liabilities (Quick Ratio)_. All three ratios showed significant competitive disadvantages for both companies and more than ordinary exposure for creditors. Comparatively high _Total Liabilities to Net Worth_ demonstrates that suppliers and other lenders have a relatively small margin of protection in the worst event: bankruptcy. Shrinkage of assets in liquidation might wipe out all of owners' equity and result in a loss to creditors. Comparatively low _Current Assets to Current Liabilities_ shows that the cushion between current assets and current liabilities is less than that of the typical competitor, possibly jeopardizing the company's ability to meet current obligations in the event of a significant bad-debt loss or a writedown of inventory. Similarly, low _Cash and Short-Term Investments plus Accounts Receivable to Current Liabilities (Quick Ratio)_ demonstrates that a relatively small amount of liquid assets is available to

Table 32-2. Primary and secondary ratios for LMN Company and OPQ Corporation.

	LMN Company	OPQ Corporation
Primary (causal) ratios		
Net Profit to Net Sales		
Company	1.5%	2.0%
Industry standard	2.0%	2.0%
Net Sales to Total Assets		
Company	4.0 times	1.7 times
Industry standard	3.0 times	3.0 times
Collection Period of Accounts Receivable		
Company	33 days	68 days
Industry standard	36 days	36 days
Cost of Sales to Inventory		
Company	7.6 times	3.1 times
Industry standard	6.0 times	6.0 times
Net Sales to Fixed Assets		
Company	40.0 times	10.0 times
Industry standard	25.0 times	25.0 times
Net Sales to Net Worth		
Company	23.8 times	10.0 times
Industry standard	10.0 times	10.0 times
Long-Term Liabilities		
to Total Noncurrent Assets		
Company	0.7 times	0.7 times
Industry standard	0.5 times	0.5 times
Secondary (effect) ratios		
Net Profit to Net Worth		
Company	35.7%	20.0%
Industry standard	20.0%	20.0%
Total Liabilities to Net Worth		
Company	5.0 times	5.0 times
Industry standard	2.3 times	2.3 times
Current Liabilities to Net Worth		
Company	4.5 times	4.3 times
Industry standard	1.6 times	1.6 times
Net Sales to Working Capital		
Company	29.4 times	14.3 times
Industry standard	11.0 times	11.0 times
Current Assets to Current Liabilities		
Company	1.2 times	1.2 times
Industry standard	1.5 times	1.5 times
Cash and Short-Term		
Investments plus Accounts Receivable		
to Current Liabilities (Quick Ratio)		
Company	0.6 times	0.6 times
Industry standard	0.7 times	0.7 times

(*continued*)

Table 32-2. *Continued.*

	LMN Company	OPQ Corporation
Total Noncurrent Assets to Net Worth		
Company	0.7 times	1.1 times
Industry standard	0.4 times	0.4 times
Long-Term Liabilities to Working Capital		
Company	0.6 times	1.1 times
Industry standard	0.4 times	0.4 times
Net Profit to Total Assets		
Company	6.0%	3.3%
Industry standard	6.0%	6.0%

cover current liabilities, making the prompt sale of inventory a high priority. But Floyd was not satisfied with a defensive, watchdog-of-the-treasury approach to the credit function. Because he viewed credit management as a sales tool for his company, he sought to find the causes for each company's problems so that he could make a better judgment of their prospects for success.

Despite close similarity of these two credit applicants with respect to financial leverage and working capital tightness, LMN Company and OPQ Corporation were otherwise very different businesses, each requiring a distinctive approach, as Floyd discovered when he compared the seven causal ratios with industry standards he had developed from his files. OPQ Corporation reported a moderate profit margin on net sales and demonstrated a moderate level of owners' equity in support of sales volume (*Net Sales to Net Worth* similar to the industry norm). The cause of OPQ Corporation's financial imbalance was poor asset management, summarized by very low *Net Sales to Total Assets*. In fact, all three of the major asset components—accounts receivable, inventory, and fixed assets—showed low activity levels.

LMN Company, on the other hand, reported very high *Net Sales to Total Assets*. The *Collection Period of Accounts Receivable* was low, *Cost of Sales to Inventory* was high, and *Net Sales to Fixed Assets* was also on the high side, all favorable factors from a credit grantor's viewpoint. Nevertheless, LMN Company was suffering from high financial leverage and tight working capital because the firm had a very small amount of owners' equity in relation to sales volume (very high *Net Sales to Net Worth*). In addition, LMN Company's *Net Profit to Net Sales* was on the low side. Further inquiry revealed that LMN Company had more than doubled its sales volume during the last two years, while OPQ Corporation had grown at a steadily slower pace for some time.

> Identical secondary ratios, particularly *Total Liabilities to Net Worth* and *Current Assets to Current Liabilities*, may result from various patterns of interaction among the seven causal ratios.

Separate Strategies

Armed with the critical information provided by the causal ratios, Floyd Washington was able to develop a separate strategy for each company. In the case of LMN Company, he made clear that credit was not unlimited; he would, however, work with management on a quarterly basis to increase the limit, provided that the company's basic financial structure did not become further impaired. Joining his company's sales representative in a meeting with LMN Company's president, he offered his sincere congratulations on the company's impressive growth, but he also explained, with reference to the key financial ratios, how overexpansion can lead to serious consequences. He repeated his pledge to review LMN Company's situation on a quarterly basis. Floyd's credit strategy proved to be sound. During the next three years, LMN Company accelerated its growth, straining its financial resources to the limit; but by attracting outside investors at two critical points, the company was successful in righting its financial balance. LMN Company eventually became one of Floyd's largest accounts.

OPQ Corporation proved to be a more challenging situation. At first, that firm's management had no interest in receiving advice from a supplier, and Floyd felt compelled to impose a strict credit limit. As the company's asset management gradually worsened, however, additional credit became a desperate need for OPQ Corporation, and the owner reluctantly agreed to talk with Floyd about finding a mutually acceptable means of improving their relationship. After meeting for only a few minutes, Floyd became aware that the owner had begun to lose his management perspective and was attempting to meet competitive pressures on a day-to-day basis without the benefit of comparative information relating to previous performance or industry conditions. The owner, who had personally directed OPQ Corporation's expansion of credit, inventory, and facilities since the company's inception, was obviously skeptical of Floyd's industry standards for the *Collection Period of Accounts Receivable* and *Cost of Sales to Inventory.* "We just couldn't be that far out of line," he said. "Everything we've done has been in direct response to our competitors." Nevertheless, he agreed to let Floyd exchange ideas with his credit manager about possible improvements in those areas. Later, he also followed Floyd's suggestion to perform a critical analysis of inventory turnover by product line. Within a year, OPQ Corporation's balance sheet began to show the beneficial effects of a lower *Collection Period of Accounts Receivable* and higher *Cost of Sales to Inventory.* Although OPQ Corporation continued to grow only slowly, the business gradually shifted a significantly larger proportion of its purchases to Floyd's company, a satisfying outcome for both parties.

Credit grantors who concentrate entirely on the ratios that measure effect—particularly *Total Liabilities to Net Worth, Current Assets to Current Liabilities,* and *Cash and Short-Term Investments plus Accounts Receivable to Current*

Liabilities (Quick Ratio)—will miss opportunities to refine their lending decisions and add a few marginal, but promising, accounts to their portfolio. Those who seek to understand the causes of financial imbalance are in a far better position to take selective risks and, in so doing, enable their small and mid-size business clients to grow into prominent and profitable customers.

For their part, company owners and managers should give careful consideration to any advice offered by trade creditors and bankers. In some instances, such suggestions are designed more for the advisor's benefit than for the long-term growth of the company, but many credit grantors are able to provide helpful ideas for improving operations and basic financial structure. Since a satisfactory relationship with suppliers and bankers is an important ingredient in business success, company owners and managers should make a conscientious effort to understand the basis for their advice—and to formulate an alternative plan, if appropriate, in response to those suggestions. Even if evaluation by management shows that creditors' ideas are misdirected, the attention of outside analysts to the company's well-being should not be ignored.

Proper Standards: A Way to Change a Banker's Evaluation

Ken Archer had been somewhat uneasy about his credit line for some time. A takeover of his local bank by a statewide holding company had led to the early retirement of the only two loan officers he had known since he began his machine tool distribution company 20 years ago. Other than a cute notice in the mail and an invitation to a cocktail party held last month when he was on the road, Ken had not heard from his new bank until a pleasant voice reminded him that he must submit DEF Company's financial statement for review prior to renewal of the company's line of credit. As he had done for many years, Ken mailed in his statement without comment. He fully expected the automatic renewal he had always received whenever his company required no increase in the line. Two weeks later, however, he received a second call from Wendy Moyer, the company's new loan officer, suggesting a meeting at the bank as soon as possible.

At that meeting, Ken was startled to learn that the bank's state-of-the-art computerized credit screening program had indicated a potential problem with continuing DEF Company's line at its present level. Specifically, the credit analysis department had identified the company's *Total Liabilities to Net Worth* as being equal to the 2.5 value that automatically set in motion a request for further investigation, while its *Current Assets to Current Liabilities*, at 1.3, was also in the review zone. As Wendy explained, this computer program provided only preliminary indicators of the need for more careful evaluation, but a second round of analysis by a loan review specialist had shown that DEF Company was above the industry median with respect to *Total Liabilities to Net Worth*, an unfavorable finding, and below the industry norm for *Current Assets to Current Liabilities*, another unfavorable indicator. In addition, *Net Profit to Net Sales* was lower than the industry median, showing that the company's profit margin was particularly likely to decline in the event of price competition or increases in interest rates. Under the circumstances, the bank would expect to reduce its credit line from $650,000 to $500,000.

Ken simply could not believe that the analysis was correct. He had never bothered to review most of the financial ratios he had received for years from the company's national trade association because he had only been interested in the percentages relating to gross margin, net profit, and owners' compensation, but he was certain that he was managing DEF Company in a responsible, conservative manner. Although he was inclined to tell Wendy how insulted he felt to be evaluated by a computer program that ignored his 20 years of experience, he realized that he had a limited number of alternatives and decided to do some basic research first. He asked his banker to send him a copy of the comparative industry standards at once so that he could begin to see what the problem might be. She promised quick action and offered to help in any way she could.

The next day, Ken received a summary of the composite profile for industrial equipment and machinery wholesalers of similar size (total assets between $1 million and $10 million) included in the *RMA Annual Statement Studies*. Late that evening, he began his analysis by converting DEF Company's dollar figures, as shown in Table 32-3, to the key financial ratios displayed in the industry report

Table 32-3. Income statement and balance sheet for DEF Company.

Income statement

Net sales	$7,500,000
Cost of sales	6,550,000
Selling & administrative expenses	785,000
Net profit before interest expense	165,000
Interest expense	37,500
Net profit before taxes	127,500
Income taxes	44,500
Net profit after taxes	$ 83,000
Depreciation expense	$ 25,000

Balance sheet

Cash & short-term investments	$ 75,000
Accounts receivable	1,050,000
Inventory	150,000
Other current assets	37,500
Current assets	1,312,500
Fixed assets	150,000
Other noncurrent assets	37,500
Total assets	$1,500,000
Current liabilities	$ 975,000
Long-term liabilities	100,000
Total liabilities	1,075,000
Net worth	425,000
Total liabilities & net worth	$1,500,000

published by his national trade association. Then he made a direct comparison of his company's ratios with those shown in the RMA publication and those in the industry report. The results are displayed in Table 32-4. Ken quickly discovered that the RMA standards were largely determined by wholesalers that stocked large quantities of inventory and required substantially greater fixed assets to do so. Many machine tool distributors, however, have minimal inventory and fixed assets: Consequently, they can support a higher level of debt in relation to net worth and can operate with a smaller cushion between current assets and current liabilities because their assets are highly liquid, consisting, in fact, almost entirely of cash and accounts receivable. Relative to the performance of other machine tool distributors, DEF Company's results were adequate to good in all three areas of primary concern to the bank. *Total Liabilities to Net Worth* was low (a favorable factor), *Current Assets to Current Liabilities* was equal to the norm, and *Net Profit to Net Sales* was definitely on the high side (another favorable factor). Ken's comparison with companies in precisely the same line of sales activity did, however, show that the DEF Company's *Net Sales to Total Assets* was somewhat lower than the norm. Nevertheless, the company's relatively high investment adequacy (shown by comparatively low *Net Sales to Net Worth*) reduced *Total*

Table 32-4. Primary and secondary ratios for DEF Company.

Primary (causal) ratios

Net Profit to Net Sales	
Company	*1.7%*
Industry standard: RMA	*2.5%*
Industry standard: AMTDA	*0.4%*
Net Sales to Total Assets	
Company	*5.0 times*
Industry standard: RMA	*2.5 times*
Industry standard: AMTDA	*5.9 times*
Collection Period	
of Accounts Receivable	
Company	*51 days*
Industry standard: RMA	*46 days*
Industry standard: AMTDA	*41 days*
Cost of Sales to Inventory	
Company	*43.7 times*
Industry standard: RMA	*5.2 times*
Industry standard: AMTDA	*94.4 times*
Net Sales to Fixed Assets	
Company	*50.0 times*
Industry standard: RMA	*23.7 times*
Industry standard: AMTDA	*145.2 times*
Net Sales to Net Worth	
Company	*17.6 times*
Industry standard: RMA	*8.3 times**
Industry standard: AMTDA	*29.8 times*

Long-Term Liabilities
  to Total Noncurrent Assets

Company	0.5 times
Industry standard: RMA	0.6 times*
Industry standard: AMTDA	0.2 times

Secondary (effect) ratios

Net Profit to Net Worth

Company	30.0%
Industry standard: RMA	15.6%
Industry standard: AMTDA	6.3%

Total Liabilities to Net Worth

Company	2.5 times
Industry standard: RMA	2.3 times
Industry standard: AMTDA	2.9 times

Current Liabilities to Net Worth

Company	2.3 times
Industry standard: RMA	1.8 times*
Industry standard: AMTDA	2.8 times

Net Sales to Working Capital

Company	22.2 times
Industry standard: RMA	11.7 times
Industry standard: AMTDA	27.8 times

Current Assets to Current Liabilities

Company	1.3 times
Industry standard: RMA	1.4 times
Industry standard: AMTDA	1.3 times

Cash and Short-Term
  Investments plus Accounts
  Receivable
  to Current Liabilities (Quick Ratio)

Company	1.2 times
Industry standard: RMA	0.7 times
Industry standard: AMTDA	1.2 times

Total Noncurrent Assets to Net Worth

Company	0.4 times
Industry standard: RMA	0.6 times*
Industry standard: AMTDA	0.3 times

Long-Term Liabilities to Working Capital

Company	0.3 times
Industry standard: RMA	0.6 times*
Industry standard: AMTDA	0.1 times

Net Profit to Total Assets

Company	8.5%
Industry standard: RMA	4.5%
Industry standard: AMTDA	2.2%

---

*Derived.

Note: The industry standards are medians for all ratios except *Net Profit to Net Sales*, which is expressed as the average in accordance with common practice in the presentation of operating statement percentages. As previously indicated, *Net Profit to Net Sales*, *Net Profit to Net Worth*, and *Net Profit to Total Assets* are based on net profit before taxes.

Source: RMA data © 1989 Robert Morris Associates. Reprinted with permission. AMTDA data © 1989 American Machine Tool Distributors' Association.

Liabilities to Net Worth and raised *Current Assets to Current Liabilities* in relation to the standards for competing companies.

To make certain of his interpretation of the data, Ken called the industry consultant who had prepared the financial management report for his trade association. The consultant congratulated Ken on his diligent and systematic application of the cause-and-effect guidelines contained in the industry report and agreed to confirm his findings to the bank officer, if necessary. The next step proved to be easy. When Wendy Moyer saw Ken's comparisons, accompanied by a copy of the industry report, she quickly forwarded the necessary paperwork to continue the credit line at $650,000.

As emphasized throughout this book, accurate measurement of a company's competitive position depends upon the availability of data from businesses of similar size, in the same line of business activity, from the same (or nearly the same) fiscal period. You must seek the most directly applicable industry statistics—and must be prepared to revise your evaluation as more appropriate data come to your attention.

Mixed Signals: A Guessing Game for Outside Analysts

Hal Lundberg knew from experience that financial statement analysis provides valuable information for making better business decisions but does not always furnish a clear-cut answer to every question. As vice president of finance and the credit authority in his family's equipment leasing company, Hal had found that many of his most difficult judgments involved business owners who were highly successful operators but left their companies in a weak financial position through excessive withdrawals. He was faced with just such a situation in the case of RST Enterprises, the fastest-growing hairstyling company on the local scene. Its innovative concepts and elegant service were accompanied by premium fees. The owner, known as Mister Phillip to his clientele, appeared to be an astute businessman who supported a grand lifestyle with the income from his small, but lucrative, company, founded only three years earlier. On the other hand, as Hal discovered, Mister Phillip's policy of retaining virtually no earnings in the company had made the survival of the business vulnerable to even slight changes in competitive conditions. With no financial stake to defend, the owner's opportunities for management planning had given way to short-term maneuvers based on guesswork and whim. Consequently, lending decisions relating to RST Enterprises had been reduced to speculation regarding the competence and character of the borrower.

In response to a recent request to finance $50,000 of new equipment for RST, Hal had insisted upon receiving the company's latest financial statement. At first, Mister Phillip had refused, but he eventually provided the information displayed in Table 32-5. A quick glance at the dollar figures told Hal that he would find little

Table 32-5. Income statement and balance sheet for RST Enterprises.

Income statement	
Net sales	$750,000
Operating expenses*	725,000
Net profit before interest expense	25,000
Interest expense	15,000
Net profit before taxes	10,000
Income taxes	4,000
Net profit after taxes	$ 6,000
Balance sheet	
Cash & short-term investments	$ 10,000
Accounts receivable	0
Inventory (hair care products)	15,000
Other current assets	10,000
Current assets	35,000
Fixed assets	85,000
Other noncurrent assets	25,000
Total assets	$145,000
Current liabilities	$ 50,000
Long-term liabilities	80,000
Total liabilities	130,000
Net worth	15,000
Total liabilities & net worth	$145,000

Including officers'/owners' compensation of $145,000.

comfort in the financial ratios, which he nevertheless calculated to obtain a more complete picture of the company's position. He listed the ratios of greatest interest next to data from the *RMA Annual Statement Studies* for hairstylists with total assets less than $1 million, as shown in Table 32-6. Hal could see that RST Enterprises was making efficient use of its fixed assets, indicated by comparatively high *Net Sales to Fixed Assets*. Although Mister Phillip spared no expense on furnishings and equipment, the company's total sales volume and asset utilization were boosted by virtue of its nearly exorbitant pricing structure. The considerable spread between net sales and ordinary operating costs enabled Mister Phillip to grant himself outstanding compensation, while the net profit of RST Enterprises was very small indeed. Because retained earnings were substandard in relation to the company's sales activity, *Total Liabilities to Net Worth* was far above the norm, even in this highly leveraged line of business. Hal had reached the conclusion that retained earnings were inadequate by studying the two causal ratios that influence *Total Liabilities to Net Worth—Net Sales to Total Assets* and *Net Sales to Net Worth*. RST Enterprises reported very high *Net Sales to Total Assets*, indicating comparatively efficient utilization of the company's business resources (primarily because of high *Net Sales to Fixed Assets* noted

Table 32-6.   Primary and secondary ratios for RST Enterprises.

Primary (causal) ratios

Net Profit to Net Sales
    Company   1.3%
    Industry standard   5.1%
Net Sales to Total Assets
    Company   5.2 times
    Industry standard   3.7 times
Collection Period of Accounts Receivable
    Company   0 days
    Industry standard   0 days
Cost of Sales to Inventory
    Company   N/A
    Industry standard   N/A
Net Sales to Fixed Assets
    Company   8.8 times
    Industry standard   7.9 times
Net Sales to Net Worth
    Company   50.0 times
    Industry standard   23.3 times*
Long-Term Liabilities to Total Noncurrent Assets
    Company   0.7 times
    Industry standard   0.4 times*

- -

Secondary (effect) ratios

Net Profit to Net Worth
    Company   66.7%
    Industry standard   45.0%
Total Liabilities to Net Worth
    Company   8.7 times
    Industry standard   5.3 times
Current Liabilities to Net Worth
    Company   3.3 times
    Industry standard   3.0 times*
Net Sales to Working Capital
    Company   xx times†
    Industry standard   xx times†
Current Assets to Current Liabilities
    Company   0.7 times
    Industry standard   0.9 times
Cash and Short-Term
  Investments plus Accounts Receivable
  to Current Liabilities (Quick Ratio)
    Company   0.2 times
    Industry standard   0.6 times
Total Noncurrent Assets to Net Worth
    Company   7.3 times
    Industry standard   3.7 times*

Long-Term Liabilities to Working Capital	
Company	*xx times†*
Industry standard	*† times*
Net Profit to Total Assets	
Company	6.9%
Industry standard	9.1%

*Derived.

†Deficit working capital.

Note: The industry standard is the RMA median for all ratios except *Net Profit to Net Sales,* which is expressed as the average in accordance with common practice in the presentation of operating statement percentages. As previously indicated, *Net Profit to Net Sales, Net Profit to Net Worth,* and *Net Profit to Total Assets* are based on net profit before taxes.

Source: Industry standards © 1989 Robert Morris Associates. Reprinted with permission.

earlier), which tends to reduce financial leverage. Miscellaneous (other noncurrent) assets, representing Mister Phillip's investments in an affiliated business intended to manufacture hair care products, were on the high side, tending to reduce asset utilization. Nevertheless, RST Enterprises reported *Net Sales to Total Assets* of 5.2 versus the industry norm of 3.7.

High Debt the Result of Owner's Compensation

Asset utilization clearly was not the cause of the problem. Instead, the high level of debt in relation to owners' equity was largely traceable to the company's high *Net Sales to Net Worth.* The company's low level of net worth in support of sales volume was the direct result of the policy of paying out almost all available funds to the owner. From Hal's perspective, the ratio comparisons told two stories: one of successful operations and another of poor management of the company's basic financial structure, or possibly a purposeful strategy of minimizing financial commitment to the business.

High *Net Sales to Net Worth,* which shows a comparatively small amount of owners' equity in relation to sales volume, is a major cause of high *Total Liabilities to Net Worth.* Inadequate net worth in support of net sales may be the result of rapid sales growth, operating losses, or insufficient retained earnings because of overly generous compensation of owners.

Hal felt obligated to discuss his concerns with Mister Phillip. At a meeting in the small but opulent office of RST Enterprises, Hal explained that, as a credit grantor, he was worried about the possibility that some temporary cash flow problem would jeopardize the entire business organization. He also made every effort to convey his belief that Mister Phillip himself would benefit from considering certain actions that might help to maintain the company's success—and the owner's superior personal income—over the long term. Mister Phillip ended the discussion abruptly, before Hal could make the specific suggestions that he considered mutually advantageous. Hal was disappointed at the outcome because he had a strong feeling that he had lost the opportunity to obtain a profitable, growing account for his own small company. Within two years, however, after experiencing irreversible financial difficulties with RST Enterprises, Mister Phillip was creating a new sensation in another part of the country.

The outside analyst faces greater uncertainty than does the company owner or manager in interpreting the future impact of the information provided by the key financial ratios. Although the cause-and-effect ratio approach enables every knowledgeable analyst to identify a company's competitive strengths and weaknesses as of the period for which financial information is available, only management can decide what actions will be taken in response to those facts. As a result, the outside analyst is often faced with mixed signals, most frequently the trade-off between operating strengths and underlying financial weaknesses. No matter how screamingly obvious the financial indicators may be, the analyst representing a creditor or potential investor cannot be certain that management will take prudent action. If the outside analyst guesses wrong, he or she either may fail to gain considerable potential profit from a new account (or investment) or may suffer a significant outright loss.

Several different management traits may cause a company to exhibit strong sales growth, substantial owners' compensation, and even a high profit margin on sales while reporting deficiencies in many of the basic financial ratios. As a practical matter, the company owner or manager who is capable of promoting rapid growth for his company and developing an outstanding income for himself does not necessarily understand why a sound financial structure is required for long-term business survival and success, or how to achieve the proper financial balance for his company. Lack of knowledge may lead to financial disaster. Many business decision makers believe that higher sales will cure all financial ills. They may be familiar with the basic principles of financial management, but choose to ignore them in their headlong pursuit of greater sales volume. On the other hand, some individuals simply make every effort to hold their personal financial exposure to the lowest possible level. They are often able to entice unwary creditors into virtually unlimited financing through their outward signs of affluence, frequently acquired with the creditors' own funds. Case-by-case research, an inquisitive attitude, and an occasional unpleasant experience will refine the analyst's ability to identify the business principal who is likely to take direct, positive action on information about his company's financial weaknesses and, at the same time, avoid the chronic wishful thinker, the financial incompetent, and the conniver.

Ratios Helpful in Analyzing Business Start-Up Alternatives

The idea of operating his own business had long appealed to Ron Adams. With his background in computer operations, supervision, and personnel work, he was confident that he could create an organization to fill either of two growing needs in his community: a temporary help service oriented to office and computer functions, or a data preparation and processing company intended primarily to meet customers' peak requirements, serve as a back-up in emergencies, and conduct special projects. Ron's discussions with friends in local industry, utility companies, financial service organizations, and market research concerns had indicated to him that demand was strong in both areas.

But what about the financial aspects? Ron had only a little more than $30,000 to invest in a new venture. Obviously, the data processing service would require a greater outlay for equipment than would the temporary help company, but he assumed that it would generate comparatively greater revenue. The biggest problem in the temporary help organization was likely to be a build-up of accounts receivable while cash was needed to pay employees. Some financing would presumably be available from one of the banks, but how much? And what amount would he really need? In actual business operation, what level of sales could he support with his $30,000 investment? A bit perplexed about the whole process, Ron called George Bartow, a consultant friend, for a little free advice. In their meeting that evening, George cautioned Ron to conduct a thorough investigation—including a study of national and regional growth trends, plus an analysis of information about local demand and competition, profitability patterns, technological changes, legal liability, and franchising possibilities, among other issues—before investing in any line of business. He strongly recommended contacting the appropriate national trade associations and mentioned that Ron could identify them in a directory available at the public library. To give Ron a preliminary understanding of the financial issues, George pulled a copy of the *RMA Annual Statement Studies* from his desk drawer and offered to show him how to extract the important numbers from the report.

Ron expressed eagerness to gain this information, but before beginning to review the numbers, George offered another caution. He urged Ron to consider the difficulty of managing cash flow, both that of the company and that of his household, during the first year in business. Obtaining a roster of steady clients at the initiation of operations is extremely difficult, and finding suitable employees for either the temporary help service or the data processing operation, just when those employees might be needed, would be an equal, if not greater, challenge. Holding on to top workers, particularly if demand oscillates between slack time and overtime, is still another problem. How long Ron's household could operate with no contribution of income from the business is another issue that George advanced for careful consideration. Finally, George began to instruct Ron about using financial ratios to compare alternative business opportunities.

Stressing that the information in the *RMA Annual Statement Studies* is calculated from financial statements of established firms, George jotted down two columns of selected financial ratios, one for temporary help services (termed "help supply services" in the RMA book) and one for computer processing and data preparation services, each column representing companies with total assets of less than $1 million. His notes are shown in Table 32-7. Referring to those ratios, George then began to develop Table 32-8. His first step was to establish $1,000 as the benchmark amount of net sales at the top of each column. Next, he referred to *Net Profit to Net Sales*, which is based on pre-tax profit in the RMA report, for each of the two lines of business. Multiplying $1,000 by .052 (the decimal fraction for the 5.2% reported by temporary help services) and .028 (the decimal fraction for the 2.8% shown by data processing services), respectively, George derived the amount of net profit before taxes per $1,000 of net sales for these companies (which, he noted, had average sales in excess of $1 million). The $52 average for temporary help services looked relatively attractive versus the $28 average for data processing services. Then he performed similar calculations based on *Officers' Compensation to Net Sales*, an operating ratio displayed in the *RMA Annual Statement Studies*. Like other operating ratios, it is computed by dividing the operating expense item (in this case, officers' compensation) by net sales and is expressed as a percentage. By this standard, the data processing service looked more promising at $89 per $1,000, compared with $32 per $1,000 for the average temporary help service.

George noted, however, that percentages for officers' compensation were much less reliable than those for net profit because of several factors, including the legal form of organization (proprietorships and partnerships, which pay no identifiable compensation to owners, versus corporations, which designate a specific amount for such payments) and the failure of many financial statements

Table 32-7. Selected financial ratios for two companies.

	Temporary help service	Data processing service
Net Profit to Net Sales	5.2%	2.8%
Officers' Compensation to Net Sales	3.2%	8.9%
Net Sales to Total Assets	7.0 times	3.0 times
Collection Period of Accounts Receivable	34 days	45 days
Net Sales to Fixed Assets	64.1 times	13.9 times
Total Liabilities to Net Worth	1.2 times	1.5 times
Net Profit to Net Worth	39.2%	11.1%

Note: The industry standard is the RMA median for all ratios except *Net Profit to Net Sales*, which is expressed as the average in accordance with common practice in the presentation of operating statement percentages. As previously indicated, *Net Profit to Net Sales and Net Profit to Net Worth* are based on net profit before taxes.
Source: © 1989 Robert Morris Associates. Reprinted with permission.

Table 32-8. Dollar projections for each $1,000 of net sales generated by two alternative business opportunities.

	Temporary help service	*Data processing service*
Dollar amounts per $1,000 of net sales		
Net sales	$1,000	$1,000
Net profit before taxes	52	28
Officers' compensation	32	89
Net profit before taxes plus officers' compensation	84	117
Accounts receivable	$ 93	$ 123
Fixed assets	16	72
Total assets	143	333
Total liabilities	78	200
Net worth	65	133
Projections based on available investment		
Net sales	$500,000	$250,000
Net profit before taxes	26,000	7,000
Officers' compensation	16,000	22,250
Net profit before taxes plus officers' compensation	42,000	29,250
Accounts receivable	$ 46,500	$ 30,750
Fixed assets	8,000	18,000
Total assets	71,500	83,250
Total liabilities	39,000	50,000
Net worth	32,500	33,250

to distinguish the remuneration of officers from that of other management or office employees. He also advised Ron to withhold judgment about actual earnings, since the figures he had presented were simply related to each $1,000 of net sales. Clearly, an equally important issue was the amount of sales volume that could be supported by Ron's proposed investment in each line of business.

To begin to address that issue, George divided the benchmark $1,000 of net sales by *Net Sales to Total Assets* for each of the two service lines. That calculation indicated that the typical temporary help service required only $143 in total assets to generate $1,000 in net sales, but that a data processing service typically had $333 tied up in assets for every $1,000 of sales volume. A comparison of *Total Liabilities to Net Worth* shows that a small data processing service (with a median ratio of 1.5, representing $1.50 in total liabilities for each $1.00 of owners' equity) is likely to finance a higher proportion of its total assets than is a small temporary help service (which reports a median ratio of only 1.2). To convert *Total Liabilities to Net Worth* to a dollar amount of net worth per $1,000 of net sales, George divided the total asset figure of $143 for temporary help services by the sum of the 1.2 ratio plus 1.0, a total of 2.2. This calculation—dividing $143 by 2.2 (the 1.2 ratio plus 1.0)—showed that the typical temporary help service had $65 in owners' equity to support each $1,000 of sales volume. The same routine—dividing $333 of total assets by 2.5 (the 1.5 *Financial Leverage Ratio* plus 1.0)—for data processing services indicated that Ron would need $133 of net worth per $1,000 in net sales to equal the median relationship in that line of business.

Puzzled by that calculation, Ron asked George why he had added 1.0 to the *Total Liabilities to Net Worth* ratio in deriving his figures. George pointed out that *Total Liabilities to Net Worth* describes total liabilities as a proportion of net worth. For temporary help services, the ratio value of 1.2, which represents the total liabilities on the balance sheet, is compared with an implied 1.0 of net worth. Total assets are composed of total liabilities, at 1.2, plus net worth, at 1.0, for a total of 2.2. George reminded Ron that they had already determined that temporary help firms typically employ total assets of $143 for each $1,000 of net sales. If that $143 is made up of total liabilities of 1.2 and net worth of 1.0, then dividing $143 by the sum, 2.2, will yield the amount of net worth (in this case, $65). With respect to data processing services, the proportionate amount of total liabilities is 1.5, again related to 1.0 of net worth. Total assets of $333 divided by 2.5—the combined amount of total liabilities, 1.5, and net worth, always 1.0 in this calculation—yields $133, the typical amount of net worth per $1,000 of net sales in a data processing service organization.

Differences in Required Net Worth

These results showed that, in very general terms, a temporary help service in the smallest RMA asset category required approximately half as much owners' equity to support sales volume as did a data processing service. George derived the estimated total liabilities for each line by subtracting calculated net worth from calculated total assets. He then showed Ron that the earlier calculations were correct by dividing the derived total liabilities by the derived net worth. For temporary help services, total liabilities of $78,000 divided by net worth of $65,000 produced *Total Liabilities to Net Worth* of 1.2. In the case of data processing services, total liabilities of $200,000 divided by net worth of $133,000 yielded a ratio of 1.5, the RMA median.

For additional background, George estimated the accounts receivable that would be required in each line of business by dividing $1,000 by 365 days to obtain $2.74 average daily sales and then multiplying $2.74 by the *Collection Period of Accounts Receivable* (yielding $93 per $1,000 of net sales for the typical small temporary help service and $123 for the typical small data processing service). In addition, he calculated the book value of fixed assets per $1,000 of sales volume by dividing that $1,000 benchmark figure by *Net Sales to Fixed Assets* for each line of business. The results: $16 in fixed assets for a temporary help company and $72 for a data processing concern.

George asked Ron to assess the significance of these calculations. After scanning the numbers carefully, Ron pointed out that the net worth required for each $1,000 of net sales was $65 for the typical temporary help service versus $133 for the typical data processing service, again assuming that the businesses are in the below $1 million asset category. In other words, for each dollar he might invest, Ron was likely to generate twice as much sales volume from a temporary help service as from a data processing company. George agreed. He then suggested that Ron multiply the $65 of net worth shown for temporary help service in the model by $1,000 in order to translate the per $1,000 ratios into real-world dollar figures. The result, $65,000, was roughly twice the amount Ron had available for investment. Since that is the case, all of the numbers could be related to Ron's potential investment by multiplying each item by 1,000 and then dividing by 2, or, more efficiently, by multiplying each item by 500. The result of these calculations is shown in the lower section of Table 32-8. Assuming $32,500 of owners' equity (obtained by multiplying $65 by 500), Ron could expect to support annual sales of $500,000 while maintaining a financial structure in line with that of the typical small temporary help company.

Turning to the estimated net worth figure of $133 for data processing services in the upper portion of Table 32-8, Ron observed that when that amount was multiplied by 1,000, the net result ($133,000) was roughly four times the dollar figure he was prepared to invest. He realized that by multiplying the figures shown above by 1,000 and then dividing each product by 4 (or, more simply, by multiplying each item by 250), he could obtain a rough approximation of the typical financial structure of a data processing company with net worth of $33,250, an amount close to his proposed investment. Compared in this way, the figures indicated that Ron might be able to earn a somewhat higher level of officers' compensation plus net profit before taxes, in relation to the amount of money he had available to invest, in a temporary help service than in a data processing company.

A comparison of *Net Profit to Net Worth* in Table 32-7 tended to confirm that observation. Ron realized, however, that *Net Profit to Net Sales*, an important component of *Net Profit to Net Worth*, was higher for temporary help services than for data processing companies, while the reverse was true for *Officers' Compensation to Net Sales*. With that knowledge, he carefully checked the sum of net profit plus officers' compensation in relation to net worth, as shown in Table 32-8. He found that those comparisons showed a relatively favorable relationship between net profit plus officers' compensation versus net worth for temporary help services. In relation to his proposed investment, Ron would be likely to carry lower accounts receivable and lower fixed assets in a temporary help company than in a data processing service, resulting in higher *Net Sales to*

Total Assets, which contributes to a higher *Return on Equity Ratio (Net Profit to Net Worth)*.

George reemphasized that the comparisons he had developed were only intended to help Ron consider some of the important issues in choosing between two lines of business activity. Further inquiry with the appropriate trade association might well reveal certain characteristics of start-up companies in each business line that would give a different impression of the opportunities and the dangers involved. As an additional consideration, available franchise arrangements might reduce (or possibly increase) financial risk in relation to potential reward. George and Ron agreed, however, that the exercise had not only provided many ideas for further evaluation but had also served as a valuable introduction to a few of the key financial ratios that Ron will find important in business management.

By converting the key financial ratios to dollar equivalents in relation to a specified base (such as net sales of $1,000), you can often develop a better sense of the typical financial structure of firms within a particular industry classification. When a specific dollar reference value (for example, a certain amount of money available to invest or a definite sales target set by management) is known, a data conversion similar to that described in this section may be helpful. Evaluating projected operating performance and basic financial structure in estimated dollar amounts based on the key financial ratios in that line of business will enable management to gain a better understanding of the actual dollar demands that might be placed on the business through competitive pressures. No single number can possibly represent the individual situation of every company within a specific line of business, but the median value for each of the key financial ratios will provide an indication of typical performance as shaped by the interactive decisions of competitors, customers, and creditors.

Part VII

Comparative Statistics: A Basis for Better Business Decisions

The analysis of a company's competitive position is greatly facilitated by ratios that represent typical performance of concerns in the same line of business. Some industries are characterized by major investment in fixed assets, while other business lines have minimal facilities that are almost always rented. The levels of accounts receivable and inventory also vary widely in relation to sales volume from one line of business to another. For example, while a *Cost of Sales to Inventory* ratio of 6.0 is the mark of an aggressive merchandiser among jewelry wholesalers, it would be a danger signal in the wholesaling of perishable items such as fresh fruits and vegetables. Identifying the basic characteristics of the company's line of business is highly valuable to the analyst, but he or she gains even greater assurance of comparability from industry statistics that categorize the companies in the sample by important company characteristics. Data that distinguish between large and small companies, between those in one region of the country and those facing different economic or seasonal conditions, and between those specializing in different product lines (such as band instruments versus keyboard instruments, or big-ticket industrial machinery versus smaller equipment) within the same general industry classification are especially valuable.

Once he has found the most useful source of data, the analyst must be particularly alert to matching the ratios for the company under evaluation with industry statistics for the same fiscal period. In many lines of business activity, the key financial ratios change significantly within one to three years, rendering the comparison of a company's 19X9 results with composite data for 19X6 both meaningless and dangerous. In addition, seasonal factors and the influence of economic cycles in certain industries require the analyst to investigate whether the fiscal year of the company under study coincides with the financial statement date of the majority of companies in the industry database. A company that closes its books six months before its typical competitor may report its condition at the peak of demand, when strain on its financial structure is greatest, although the industry statistics may show composite financial structure at the point when accounts receivable and inventory are at their annual low (and, consequently, debt is also at its lowest point). These issues, together with a discussion of important sources of comparative statistics, are considered in detail in the following chapters.

Chapter 33

The Importance of Benchmark Ratios

In evaluating a company's competitive position, you must make certain that the ratios used for comparative purposes are directly applicable to the company under scrutiny. The four most critical factors to be considered are (1) line of business activity, (2) size (in terms of sales volume, total assets, or other measure relevant to the industry) of the companies in the comparison group, (3) number of companies in the industry sample, and (4) timeliness of the data.

Differences From One Line of Business to Another

The importance of measuring the ratios of a particular business enterprise against averages and medians taken from the financial reports of companies in its specific line of activity cannot be overemphasized. To understand the wide disparity between the norms reported for different industries, observe the *Collection Period of Accounts Receivable* (in days) for selected manufacturers for the year 1988, as shown in Table 33-1. Consider, also, *Cost of Sales to Inventory* for wholesaling causal ratios are, of course, reflected in the secondary ratios. The wide range of *Sales* for selected service activities in the same table. Such variations in the causal ratios are, of course, reflected in the secondary ratios. The wide range of values in the secondary ratios in Table 33-2 indicates, once again, how important the selection of comparable data can be in arriving at meaningful conclusions about the relative financial position of an individual company.

For properly detailed evaluation of an organization's competitive strengths and weaknesses, you should seek industry statistics that have been subdivided with respect to important operating characteristics. The metal cutting equipment manufactured by machine tool builders is, for example, not only different in function from metal forming equipment produced by companies in the same industry, but subject to differences in demand and profitability as well. Although most distributors of machine tools maintain little, if any, inventory, others stock parts and supplies as well as commodity equipment. Each segment of this wholesaling/distribution line has its own specific financial structure. The computer manufacturing industry encompasses semiconductors, other components, the

Table 33-1.　Selected median industry ratios for various business lines.

Manufacturers		Wholesalers	
Collection Period of Accounts		*Cost of Sales*	
Receivable		*to Inventory*	
Logging	8 days	Fresh fruits &	
Meat packing	16	vegetables	54.5 times
Petroleum refining	27	Petroleum &	
Bottled & canned soft		petroleum	
drinks & carbonated		products (except	
waters	28	bulk stations &	
Canvas & related		terminals)	27.8
products	34	Cotton	13.0
Wood household		Confectionery	9.8
furniture (except		Farm supplies	7.7
upholstered)	46	Electrical appliances,	
Men's & boys' work		television & radio	
clothing	57	sets	5.5
Surgical, medical &		Office equipment	4.1
dental instruments &		Motor vehicle	
supplies	59	supplies & new	
Electronic computers	62	parts	3.5
Typesetting	64	Toys, hobby goods &	
		supplies	3.4
		Jewelry	3.1

Retailers		Services	
Net Sales		*Net Profit Before Taxes*	
to Fixed Assets		*to Net Sales**	
Automobiles: New &		Legal services	18.9%
used	64.7 times	Accounting, auditing, &	
Computers &		bookkeeping	16.0
software	47.4	Citrus fruit growers	11.5
Floor coverings	35.2	Racing, including track	
Drugs	35.0	operations	7.9
Dry goods & general		Telephone	
merchandise	21.3	communications	7.3
Lumber & other		Management consulting	
building material	20.2	services	5.8
Optical goods	11.8	Detective, guard, &	
Restaurants	5.6	armored car services	1.7
Liquefied petroleum		Marinas	1.2
gas	5.0	Cable & other pay TV	0.3
Vending machine		TV stations	(1.8)
operators,			
merchandise	4.9		

Net Profit to Net Sales is consistently expressed on a pre-tax basis in this book. Thus, *Net Profit to Net Sales* is interchangeable with *Net Profit Before Taxes to Net Sales,* the ratio title used in the *RMA Annual Statement Studies.*
Note: Industry medians are displayed for companies of all sizes combined. The *RMA Annual Statement Studies* also contain four asset size categories.
Source: © 1989 Robert Morris Associates. Reprinted with permission.

Table 33-2.   Selected secondary ratios for industry groups.

	Median industry ratios		
	Current Assets to Current Liabilities	Total Liabilities to Net Worth	Net Profit to Net Worth
Manufacturing			
Household audio & video equipment	1.9 times	1.4 times	32.6%
Periodicals: publishing & printing	1.1	3.7	19.4
Poultry slaughtering	1.4	1.6	4.1
Telephone & telegraph apparatus	2.6	0.9	9.2
Wholesaling			
Computers, peripherals, equipment & software	1.4 times	3.4 times	32.3%
Cotton	2.3	0.6	7.0
Fish & seafoods	1.3	3.1	19.0
Footwear	1.8	1.4	19.2
Retailing			
Bakeries	1.0 times	3.0 times	25.0%
Fast food restaurants	0.5	6.7	37.4
Furriers	1.6	3.2	9.9
Hobby, toy & game shops	2.1	1.6	23.6
Infants' clothing stores	1.8	1.3	19.4
Services			
AM & FM radio stations	1.3 times	19.7 times	21.4%
Accounting, auditing & bookkeeping	2.2	0.9	50.9
Hairstylists	0.9	4.0	40.7
Membership sports & recreation clubs	1.2	0.8	2.6

Note: Industry medians are displayed for companies of all sizes combined. The *RMA Annual Statement Studies* also contain four asset size categories. As previously indicated, *Net Profit to Net Worth* is based on net profit before taxes.
Source: © 1989 Robert Morris Associates. Reprinted with permission.

computers themselves, and peripheral devices. Office supply companies may be primarily oriented to business deliveries from a catalog, or they may serve a large downtown walk-in trade. Some may have a substantial book department. In turn, one bookstore may sell only books while others may offer a wide range of other items, from greeting cards to popular posters; still others may emphasize rare prints and expensive autographs. Bookstores affiliated with colleges and universities have a different cost structure from those serving the general public; even among college stores, there is a range of activities from sales of textbooks to offerings of trade books, best-sellers, office supplies, computers, college items, and general merchandise.

Many industry trade associations separate their survey responses in accordance with the specific characteristics of participating companies. Whenever the importance of the decision warrants the best available information, you should make every effort to obtain data from the appropriate industry group. Although many trade associations provide their financial results exclusively to their members, they are frequently willing to release limited information to outside parties. If you have a clear understanding of the cause-and-effect method of evaluating financial statements—and therefore know just what you need—you can often obtain the figures you require through a brief telephone call to association headquarters. In other cases, an individual member of the trade group may agree to provide a few key numbers.

Importance of Company Size

Company size is an important influence on financial structure in many lines of business. In one contract metalworking industry, for example, *Cost of Sales to Inventory* showed the following pattern in 1988:

Net sales	Cost of Sales to Inventory
Less than $1,250,000	13.4 times
$1,250,000 to $1,999,999	11.8
$2,000,000 to $2,999,999	8.8
$3,000,000 to $5,999,999	6.6
$6,000,000 or more	6.4

Source: © National Tooling & Machining Association.

Similarly, distributors of machine tools reported *Net Profit to Net Worth* for 1988 that was closely related to sales volume:

Net sales	Net Profit to Net Worth
Less than $3,750,000	1.9%
$3,750,000 to $7,499,999	6.2
$7,500,000 to $14,999,999	14.1
$15,000,000 or more	17.8

Source: © American Machine Tool Distributors' Association.

Certain operating results are also strongly impacted by company size, as demonstrated in Table 33-3. The three operating ratios displayed there, *Direct Material to Net Sales*, *Direct Labor to Net Sales*, and *Officers'/Owners' Compensation to Net Sales*, are calculated by dividing each of the expense items by net sales. Like other operating ratios, they are expressed as percentages. Although direct material (cost of purchases and subcontracting services used in the manu-

Table 33-3. Selected operating ratios in the contract metalworking industry.

Net Sales	Direct Material to Net Sales	Direct Labor to Net Sales	Officers'/ Owners' Compensation to Net Sales
Less than $1,250,000	19.4%	23.9%	7.0%
$1,250,000 to $1,999,999	19.6	23.6	6.8
$2,000,000 to $2,999,999	22.1	22.0	6.6
$3,000,000 to $5,999,999	24.7	22.2	5.1
$6,000,000 or more	29.3	18.8	3.5

Source: © 1989 National Tooling & Machining Association.

facture of a product) and direct labor (cost of labor to make a physical change in the product or contribute to the manufacturing process, as in machine setup) are terms specifically applicable to the manufacturing sector, certain costs on all lines of business activity are influenced by company size.

Industry trade associations enjoy an important advantage in tailoring sales volume categories (or other size groupings) to the particular characteristics of their members. In fact, some trade groups have different sales volume categories for each of their various industry segments. Multi-industry reports, such as the *RMA Annual Statement Studies*, maintain a consistent size-related classification scheme for all lines of business, often resulting in the assignment of most companies in a particular industry to only one size category. Not surprisingly, a very large proportion of manufacturing and wholesaling companies in the *RMA Annual Statement Studies* for 1988 fall within the $1 million–$10 million total assets category, while the vast majority of retailing and service companies are found within the group for total assets less than $1 million. Fewer than 20 lines of business activity reported any significant number of enterprises in the $10 million–$50 million total assets range.

Number of Companies in Comparison Group

The number of companies in the industry database and the number of companies in any subcategory are important considerations. As responses are broken down into more closely related companies, such as full-line music stores versus those specializing in keyboard instruments or sales to bands and orchestras, the number of companies in a single group is necessarily reduced. In most cases, the narrower classification is particularly valuable, but it is important to review ratios from the entire range of sales categories—or at least the adjoining (higher and lower) size groups—if the most appropriate single comparison group contains a small number of companies.

Year-to-Year Differences Within the Same Line of Business

Although the next point may seem obvious, it deserves emphasis: You must make certain to relate the ratios of an individual company to industry norms of the same, or nearest available, year. In evaluating a company's financial statement for December 31, 19X9, you cannot hope for accuracy if you compare that concern's ratios against those of its industry for 19X5. The American economy is hardly static: The dollar amount of the gross national product changes from year to year; the unemployment rate is subject to movement; housing starts do not remain constant. The operations, the profit attainment, and the financial structure of companies within each industry likewise undergo alteration with time. These constant changes render the chronological matching of industry standards and individual company ratios a necessity. Certain lines of business, moreover, are subject to rather severe fluctuations from one year to the next as a result of weather conditions, government policy, or labor agreements.

Unfortunately, some sources of financial ratios provide data that are as much as four years old when they are published—fully three years behind the information furnished by national trade associations and statistics published in the *RMA Annual Statement Studies*. The stale nature of the statistics in some other multi-industry reports is essentially concealed, with no financial statement dates shown in any tables and the actual fiscal period mentioned only in a single sentence buried in otherwise unremarkable text. Consequently, you must take care to identify the period covered by the data and be alert to the serious problems that can result from using out-of-date information.

To observe the perils of analyzing a company's competitive position from stale data, let us assume that in November 1986 an analyst had been engaged to evaluate the operating performance and financial condition of a petroleum refiner. If the analyst had decided to rely on a report published in 1986 and based primarily on 1981 data, he would have found that *Net Sales to Total Assets* for the petroleum refining industry during that year was 1.6. If the company's ratio for its most recent fiscal year (1985 in this example) had been 1.2, the analyst might reasonably have concluded that the company under scrutiny was an inefficient operator, a poor manager of business assets. In reality, the industry-wide *Net Sales to Total Assets* for the year 1985 was only 0.8 (as ultimately revealed in the 1989 multi-industry report). If information for 1985 had been available to the analyst as he was making his evaluation, that is, if he had been using trade association statistics or the *RMA Annual Statement Studies* instead of a report that was actually four years out of date when it was published in 1986, he would have concluded that the company in question was actually a superior performer with respect to generating sales in relation to total assets.

Petroleum refining may appear to be an extreme exception in view of the major changes in crude oil prices during the 1980s, but a review of the report with the four-year publication lag showed that significant shifts in key financial ratios also occurred between 1981 and 1985 among manufacturers of numerous other products, including meat products, grain mill products, bakery products, sugar and confectionery products, alcoholic beverages, bottled soft drinks and flavorings, tobacco, weaving and textile finishing, men's and boys' clothing, lumber, millwork, drugs, concrete, ferrous and nonferrous metals, cutlery, screw machine products, ordnance, special industry machinery, ships and boats, optical and medical goods—and even soap, cleaners, and toilet goods.

Among other lines of industry that reported important changes in at least one key financial ratio between 1981 and 1985 were local and interurban passenger transit, pipelines, telephone and communication services, and radio and television broadcasting—in addition to wholesalers of machinery, sporting goods, toys, metals and minerals, electrical goods, paper and paper products, apparel, and chemicals. Most retailers showed comparatively stable results during this period, in part because broad multi-industry sources of data lump all retail establishments into a small number of categories, sometimes combining such diverse industries as garden supplies and mobile home dealers.

Key financial ratios in the *RMA Annual Statement Studies*, likewise, exhibited important changes in many industries between 1981 and 1985. Table 33-4 displays a few prominent examples. A comparison of ratios based on 1985 financial statements versus those derived from 1989 data revealed differences that were similar in magnitude to those of four years earlier for numerous lines of business. The amount and direction of change of each ratio, however, varied from industry to industry between the two four-year spans. On the other hand, some business categories remained essentially stable during the entire period, 1981 to 1989.

Table 33-4. Two median secondary ratios for selected industry groups.

	Current Assets to Current Liabilities		Total Liabilities to Net Worth	
	1981	1985	1981	1985
Manufacturers				
Ball & roller bearings	1.7 times	2.2 times	1.1 times	1.5 times
Caskets & burial supplies	2.0	1.7	1.3	1.9
Frozen fruits, fruit juices & vegetables	1.4	1.1	1.8	4.1
Hosiery: Women's full-fashioned & seamless	1.5	2.1	2.2	1.5
Metal cans	2.2	1.5	0.9	1.4
Metal doors, sash, frames, molding & trim	2.1	1.6	1.1	1.7
Metal office furniture	1.9	1.5	1.4	1.8
Pulp, paper & paperboard	1.6	2.1	1.6	1.1
Sawmills & planing mills	1.7	1.3	1.3	1.7
Tanning, curing & finishing	1.4	1.7	1.2	1.9

(continued)

Table 33-4. *Continued.*

	Current Assets to Current Liabilities		Total Liabilities to Net Worth	
	1981	*1985*	*1981*	*1985*
Wholesalers				
Air conditioning, heating & refrigeration equipment & supplies	1.7 times	1.5 times	1.5 times	2.2 times
Building materials	1.7	1.5	1.3	2.0
Footwear	1.7	2.0	1.5	0.9
Hardware & paints	1.9	1.6	1.5	1.9
Laundry & dry cleaning equipment & supplies	1.8	1.5	1.0	2.0
Poultry & poultry products	1.4	1.3	2.8	2.2
Retailers				
Boats	1.5 times	1.3 times	2.4 times	3.2 times
Household appliances	1.4	1.4	2.3	2.8
Infants' clothing	1.5	2.0	1.7	1.7
Liquefied petroleum gas	1.3	1.6	1.7	1.4
Luggage & gifts	1.8	1.7	1.4	1.8
Musical instruments & supplies	1.7	1.5	1.9	2.5
Used merchandise	1.7	2.3	1.2	1.1
Services				
AM & FM radio stations	1.3 times	1.3 times	2.8 times	6.2 times
Disinfecting & exterminating services	1.5	1.3	2.3	1.5
Funeral service & crematories	1.5	1.7	1.9	1.6
Janitorial services	1.6	1.4	1.1	1.7
Laundries & dry cleaners	1.2	1.1	1.3	1.8
Linen supply	1.5	1.4	1.4	2.1
Outdoor advertising	1.3	1.1	2.2	3.4
Travel agencies	1.3	1.1	2.2	3.1

Note: Industry medians are displayed for companies of all sizes combined. The *RMA Annual Statement Studies* also contain four asset size categories.
Source: © 1982, 1986 Robert Morris Associates. Reprinted with permission.

Chapter 34

Seasonal Factors and Cyclical Influences

In evaluating a company in a seasonal or cyclical line of business, the analyst may reach extremely misleading conclusions if he or she compares the key financial ratios for a fiscal period ended five or six months before or after the fiscal closing date used by the majority of companies in the industry database. Whenever the *Collection Period of Accounts Receivable* or *Cost of Sales to Inventory* is significantly different from industry norms, the analyst should consider seasonal factors and the influence of economic cycles.

Seasonal Factors

Some enterprises, such as candy manufacturers, jewelry wholesalers, hobby shops, and amusement parks (particularly outdoor parks in the northern United States) are subject to marked seasonal influence. In most cases, these changes reflect peak demand, as with swimwear, woolen goods, and accounting services. Canners of fruits and vegetables, however, must contend with a different type of seasonal pressure; they are obliged to put up their pack at harvest time but meet a comparatively steady demand throughout the year.

Many companies have successfully countered such seasonal irregularities through diversification, adding new lines to their product mixes to fill otherwise slack periods. Power mower manufacturers, for instance, have popularized the snowblower, which has yielded them more uniform income patterns. Bicycle retailers have added ski equipment and fitness machines to their line in an effort to stabilize sales. Other businesses have resorted to varying types of off-season discounts to encourage year-round buying of highly seasonal products. For an item in which consumer interest runs only from spring through late summer, a manufacturer might offer wholesalers and retailers a 9% special discount for October purchase and payment, 7% for November, 5% for December, 3% for January, and 1% for February in an effort to move the product and receive prompt payment. Manufacturers of candy boxes must make provision for special seasons—such as Valentine's Day, Easter, Mother's Day, and Christmas—and supplement their regular product lines accordingly. Since these concerns must anticipate the need for heart-shaped boxes long before February 14, and because set-up boxes require extra warehousing and storage space, these manufacturers may try to relieve themselves of this burden and the attendant expense by offering their customers dating arrangements: the privilege of paying for the boxes in January or February if shipment can be made in October. Toy manufacturers also rely heavily on extended datings as a means of reducing storage requirements, leveling off their own production loads, and ensuring that the shelves and counters of the retail stores are loaded to meet buyers' demands when the Christmas season arrives.

Effect of Seasonal Variation

The pattern in many industries shows gradual seasonal variations, which are generally predictable. Barring extremely unusual weather, a brewer can count on a reasonably consistent pattern for his beer sales, month by month, year in and year out, with the heaviest concentration during hot weather. On the other hand, companies in many industries encounter very modest fluctuations, or none at all, throughout the year. Razor-blade sales are relatively stable, as are the sales of detergents. Retailers of uniforms experience more level demand than do bridal shops.

What does the seasonal influence mean to the analyst? Consider the answer through a brief examination of Company O, whose sales take the pattern shown in Table 34-1. If the company closes its books on April 30, inventory at that time might well be as much as $800,000 or $900,000 in anticipation of peak sales during May and June. Basing the company's *Cost of Sales to Inventory* on the $800,000 amount, the analyst would conclude that inventory turned only some 1.8 times per year, whereas he has found that the industry norm is 10.0 times annually. If

Table 34-1. Average monthly sales for Company O.

January	$ 100,000
February	120,000
March	200,000
April	350,000
May	510,000
June	370,000
July	160,000
August	125,000
September	100,000
October	70,000
November	70,000
December	80,000
Total	$2,255,000
Average monthly sales	$ 187,900

he failed to take the seasonal influence into consideration, he would have apparent reason to label Company O an astonishingly poor merchandiser with extremely dangerous inventory exposure. At May 31, receivables for Company O could very well be $700,000 or more on net 30-day terms. With annual sales of $2,255,000 (assumed to be entirely on credit), the company's credit sales per day would be $6,178. Applying this figure to $700,000 in accounts receivable, the analyst would arrive at a *Collection Period of Accounts Receivable* of more than 113 days. Finding the industry median to be 20 days, the analyst who overlooked the seasonal factor could, logically enough, say, "The company's receivables are in terrible shape, and the books must be loaded with bad debts." Had Company O instead brought its auditors in for a November 30 closing, the analyst might have found:

Accounts receivable	$100,000
Inventory	150,000

These figures related to sales would show:

Cost of Sales to Inventory	9.7 times
Collection Period of Accounts Receivable	16 days

Conclusions based upon study of April or May statements would be diametrically opposed to those derived from looking at November figures.

In a seasonal industry, a company that exhibits very low *Cost of Sales to Inventory* (showing a high level of inventory) and a low or moderate *Collection Period of Accounts Receivable* (showing low to moderate accounts receivable) is likely to be approaching its peak demand. A company with high or moderate *Cost of Sales to Inventory* (demonstrating low or moderate inventory on hand) and a high *Collection Period of Accounts Receivable* may have closed its books a month or two beyond its busiest sales period. Any such differences from typical industry practice should, of course, be carefully investigated by the analyst. An attempt to rely on clever deductions regarding possible seasonal influences instead of making a direct inquiry can be as dangerous as ignoring this factor altogether.

To facilitate compilation and comparison of financial data—and to level out their own income stream—members of the accounting profession continue to advocate the adoption of natural or fiscal year closings that coincide with the end of a company's peak season in place of the arbitrary calendar year closing at December 31. By so doing, seasonal businesses show their most liquid condition, and the profit or loss at that date is more indicative of their true attainments for the year than are figures taken in the midst of their most active periods. Moreover, with stock and production demands at a minimum, physical count is expedited. Receivables and payables are, likewise, more easily verified when they are at or near the low point for the year. In the case of Company O, either a November 30 closing or a calendar year end would be advisable.

Cyclical Influences

Many industries are subject to sharp changes in demand—and profit—that are attributable to national, regional, or local economic cycles, rather than specifically seasonal influences. Companies that supply components to automakers may, for example, suffer severe loss of revenue when The Big Three cut back operations, particularly if the suppliers' product is expected to last for the life of the car itself. On the other hand, certain makers of automobile components such as belts and hoses, which generally wear out before the total vehicle expires, may enjoy more stable demand through sales in the replacement market. Manufacturers of tooling, molds, and special machines for the automakers also have a variable demand pattern, but one that differs from that of parts producers. Because economic cycles do not begin and end on specific calendar dates, the resultant distortions in financial statement figures and in the key ratios cannot be mitigated by conforming to an industry-specific fiscal closing date.

A single fiscal year-end or a single quarter of the year in which all companies in a cyclical industry close their books would, however, reduce comparative differences due to timing. Suppose, for example, that the majority of participating companies in the industry financial report close their books during the last quarter of the year, when a business boom is beginning to wind down, and that one company in the same industry ends its fiscal year on the following July 31, when work is scarce. Ironically, the company with the July 31 closing may look unusually good in certain respects. Both accounts receivable and inventory (primarily work-in-process) will be comparatively low for that company in relation to its net sales for the entire year, so the *Collection Period of Accounts Receivable* will be low and *Cost of Sales to Inventory* will be high, both favorable indicators. In reality, the company with the July 31 closing may have demonstrated less efficient management during much of the year, but a change in the economic cycle, a change that may have a negative impact on the entire industry during the foreseeable future, will make that company look good because of the difference in fiscal years. You must be alert to the possibility that an unusual *Collection Period of Accounts Receivable* or a *Cost of Sales to Inventory* ratio significantly different from the industry norm may be attributable to the closing date in a cyclical industry.

Another situation that may lead to temporary distortion in a company's financial ratios occurs in manufacturing industries that produce a small number of items, such as special machines or yachts, during one year. Depending upon the relationship between unpredictable demand, the concern's production cycle, and its fiscal closing, a company reporting most sales on a completed contract basis may show extremely high inventory and astoundingly low accounts receivable, or vice versa, on its financial statement. Here again, the analyst must investigate the company's particular circumstances before making rash judgments about the *Collection Period of Accounts Receivable* and *Cost of Sales to Inventory*.

Impact of Changes in Accounts Receivable and Inventory on the Secondary Ratios

Rapid changes in the dollar amount of accounts receivable and inventory—as reflected in the *Collection Period of Accounts Receivable* and *Cost of Sales to Inventory*—have an impact on many of the secondary measures. The seasonal changes shown for Company O in Tables 34-2 and 34-3 are, in most respects, similar to those that would be found in a company subject to rapid fluctuations in demand from economic conditions, rather than strictly seasonal factors. As of the end of April, Company O's peak inventory level and its seasonal build-up of accounts receivable had caused *Total Liabilities to Net Worth* to climb to 3.2 times, showing $3.20 in debt for every $1.00 of owners' equity, versus a 1.0 figure for the median company in the industry. Since the majority of companies in the industry close their books at or near the time of lowest sales activity, the median

Table 34-2. Seasonal changes reflected in the income statement and balance sheet for Company O.

	April	May	November
Income statement			
Net sales	$2,255,000	$2,255,000	$2,255,000
Cost of sales	1,450,000	1,450,000	1,450,000
Selling & administrative expenses	660,000	660,000	660,000
Net profit before interest expense	145,000	145,000	145,000
Interest expense	35,000	35,000	35,000
Net profit before taxes	110,000	110,000	110,000
Income taxes	40,000	40,000	40,000
Net profit after taxes	$ 70,000	$ 70,000	$ 70,000
Depreciation expense	$ 40,000	$ 40,000	$ 40,000
Balance sheet			
Cash & short-term investments	$ 5,000	$ 10,000	$170,000
Accounts receivable	450,000	700,000	100,000
Inventory	800,000	450,000	150,000
Other current assets	10,000	10,000	20,000
Current assets	1,265,000	1,170,000	440,000
Fixed assets	165,000	165,000	165,000
Other noncurrent assets	25,000	25,000	25,000
Total assets	$1,455,000	$1,360,000	$630,000
Current liabilities	$ 990,000	$ 880,000	$120,000
Long-term liabilities	115,000	115,000	115,000
Total liabilities	1,105,000	995,000	235,000
Net worth	350,000	365,000	395,000
Total liabilities & net worth	$1,455,000	$1,360,000	$630,000

Note: Month-to-month sales, expenses, and profit are assumed to be identical to previous year.

Table 34-3. Primary and secondary ratios for Company O.

	April	May	November
Primary (causal) ratios			
Net Profit			
to Net Sales			
Company	4.9%	4.9%	4.9%
Industry standard	4.7%	4.7%	4.7%
Net Sales			
to Total Assets			
Company	1.5 times	1.7 times	3.6 times
Industry standard	3.5 times	3.5 times	3.5 times
Collection Period			
of Accounts Receivable			
Company	73 days	113 days	16 days
Industry standard	20 days	20 days	20 days
Cost of Sales			
to Inventory			
Company	1.8 times	3.2 times	9.7 times
Industry standard	10.0 times	10.0 times	10.0 times
Net Sales			
to Fixed Assets			
Company	13.7 times	13.7 times	13.7 times
Industry standard	12.5 times	12.5 times	12.5 times
Net Sales			
to Net Worth			
Company	6.4 times	6.2 times	5.7 times
Industry standard	7.0 times	7.0 times	7.0 times
Long-Term Liabilities			
to Total Noncurrent			
Assets			
Company	0.6 times	0.6 times	0.6 times
Industry standard	0.5 times	0.5 times	0.5 times
Secondary (effect) ratios			
Net Profit			
to Net Worth			
Company	31.4%	30.1%	27.8%
Industry standard	32.9%	32.9%	32.9%
Total Liabilities			
to Net Worth			
Company	3.2 times	2.7 times	0.6 times
Industry standard	1.0 times	1.0 times	1.0 times
Current Liabilities			
to Net Worth			
Company	2.8 times	2.4 times	0.3 times
Industry standard	0.7 times	0.7 times	0.7 times
Net Sales			
to Working Capital			
Company	8.2 times	7.8 times	7.0 times
Industry standard	10.2 times	10.2 times	10.2 times

Current Assets			
to Current Liabilities			
Company	1.3 times	1.3 times	3.7 times
Industry standard	2.0 times	2.0 times	2.0 times
Cash and Short-Term			
Investments plus			
Accounts Receivable			
to Current Liabilities			
(Quick Ratio)			
Company	0.5 times	0.8 times	2.3 times
Industry standard	1.2 times	1.2 times	1.2 times
Total Noncurrent Assets			
to Net Worth			
Company	0.5 times	0.5 times	0.5 times
Industry standard	0.6 times	0.6 times	0.6 times
Long-Term Liabilities			
to Working Capital			
Company	0.4 times	0.4 times	0.4 times
Industry standard	0.5 times	0.5 times	0.5 times
Net Profit			
to Total Assets			
Company	7.6%	8.1%	17.5%
Industry standard	16.5%	16.5%	16.5%

value depicts virtually the lowest debt level during the year. By comparison, when Company O's financial structure is observed at the time of peak activity, it appears dangerously strained. Placing the company's 1.3 *Current Assets to Current Liabilities* at the end of April next to the 2.0 industry standard indicates that Company O has a very low margin of safety for meeting current obligations in the event of a writedown of current assets. The extremely low *Cash and Short-Term Investments plus Accounts Receivable to Current Liabilities (Quick Ratio)*, 0.5 compared with the 1.2 industry norm, tends to confirm that judgment and demonstrates that the company is unusually dependent on selling existing inventory in order to pay its bills. The picture of Company O is a representation of the company at that time, but it should not be interpreted as evidence of a chronically poor working capital position. In fact, Company O's comparatively low *Net Sales to Working Capital* (which remains relatively constant throughout the year) shows that the spread between current assets and current liabilities was comparatively large in relation to net sales. This is a positive factor that indicates that cash flow is not especially likely to be impaired from an unexpected (temporary) delay in receiving payment from customers.

On the other hand, Company O's poor *Net Profit to Total Assets* as of April 30 implies that the concern's assets are badly managed, at least in terms of the profit they generate. Just as the seasonal increase in accounts receivable and inventory caused *Total Liabilities to Net Worth* to reach a temporarily unfavorable level, this rise in assets also accounted for Company O's comparatively poor performance as measured by *Current Assets to Current Liabilities, Cash and*

Short-Term Investments plus Accounts Receivable to Current Liabilities (Quick Ratio), and *Net Profit to Total Assets* at the end of April. Although the company had sufficient working capital in proportion to sales volume, the relationship between current assets and current liabilities had become unbalanced by the expansion of accounts receivable and inventory, on the one hand, and short-term debt, on the other. When both current assets and current liabilities rise by the same dollar amount, *Current Assets to Current Liabilities* declines; and when the bulk of such an increase in current assets is attributable to inventory, the *Quick Ratio* will also decline. The higher level of total assets will necessarily affect *Net Profit to Total Assets* by increasing the denominator while the numerator (net sales for the entire year) may remain essentially constant. Consequently, a fiscal year closing at the time of peak activity will cause *Net Profit to Total Assets* to fall to its lowest level.

The ratios calculated from financial data for the year ended May 31 do not offer a much more favorable assessment of Company O's current financial structure when compared with the industry standards. The *Quick Ratio* was somewhat stronger, showing that a portion of inventory had been converted to accounts receivable. In addition, *Total Liabilities to Net Worth* was somewhat lower, reflecting a small reduction of debt by means of cash receipts, together with an increase in net worth from recent profitable sales. Nevertheless, in relation to the industry norms, Company O's financial structure continues to give cause for concern. But let us look at the company's comparative position at the end of November. Now *Total Liabilities to Net Worth, Current Assets to Current Liabilities,* the *Quick Ratio,* and *Net Profit to Total Assets* have all shown dramatic improvement. In fact, each of these measures is superior to the respective industry standard. Further elaboration on the importance of the seasonal factor should not be required.

Effect of Changes in Sales Volume

Ironically, changes in the two causal ratios that reflect slackening demand in a cyclical industry, a warning sign to management, will produce apparently favorable effects in the secondary ratios that are so closely watched by banks and other credit grantors. Specifically, a lower *Collection Period of Accounts Receivable* and higher *Cost of Sales to Inventory* that actually result from reduced sales volume in recent months will produce higher *Current Assets to Current Liabilities* and lower *Total Liabilities to Net Worth*, indicating a stronger basic financial structure. From a creditor's standpoint, a lower level of debt provides a greater margin of safety, even if this comfortable situation results from a decline in the company's sales and profit to nearly zero. On the other side of the lender's coin, the greatest risk, as described by *Current Assets to Current Liabilities* and *Total Liabilities to Net Worth*, occurs when sales are booming. Sales growth necessarily results in higher accounts receivable unless credit terms are changed or customers unaccountably begin to pay their invoices more rapidly. A backlog of orders (or management's perception of future demand) will cause inventory to swell, possibly to record levels. These increases in assets, of course, cause liabilities to rise; the credit line may be used to its fullest even while accounts payable grow to peak levels. Consequently, *Current Assets to Current Liabilities* will suffer a noticeable decline. A rise in current assets from, say, $200,000 to $400,000, resulting in an increase in current liabilities from $100,000 to $300,000, will cause *Current Assets to Current Liabilities* to fall from 2.0 to 1.3. A concurrent rise in total assets from $200,000 to $400,000, compared with net worth (owners' equity) of $100,000, will propel *Total Liabilities to Net Worth* from 2.0 to 4.0. In reality, retention of earnings (from the presumably greater net profit that will be generated by higher net sales) may boost net worth and current assets to some extent, but the secondary ratios would not ordinarily reflect any significant change in the short run from this source. As a practical matter, a rapid increase in net sales, whether as a result of cyclical forces or carefully crafted company strategy, will cause the secondary ratios to show an apparently unfavorable trend unless net profit is extraordinarily high.

In many manufacturing industries, the inventory cycle from raw material to work-in-process to finished goods is similar to the cash cycle (from cash to inventory to accounts receivable and back to cash). Much has been written about inventory reduction through just-in-time delivery, improved shop floor scheduling, and automated material handling, but uneven inventory flow continues to occur for many reasons, including misjudgment of customer demand. The year-to-year comparison of Company O's inventory position as of May 31, displayed in Table 34-4, suggests that the company's production and sales cycle has changed significantly during the past 12 months. Although *Cost of Sales to Inventory* has remained constant at 3.2 times, the composition of inventory has undergone a radical shift. Specifically, finished goods represent more than 50% of total inventory at the end of Year 2, having climbed from 13 days to 63 days (based on cost of sales). This build-up suggests that production is outrunning the company's ability to find buyers. In addition, raw material and work-in-process have been cut to half of Year 1 levels, an indication that management has become aware of slackening demand. Clearly, these changes in inventory require additional investigation, particularly by investors and other analysts who may be concerned with near-term earnings.

The special-purpose ratios, *Work-in-Process to Raw Material* and *Finished Goods to Work-in-Process*, in Table 34-4 help to illustrate the shift in inventory between Year 1 and Year 2. Although special-purpose ratios of this kind are useful in many analytical situations, they should be carefully distinguished from the 16 key financial ratios that describe a company's fundamental financial structure. An almost infinite number of mathematical relationships can be calculated from the operating statement and the balance sheet, particularly with the aid of a computer. Restraint is advisable, however, since a proliferation of ratios would

Table 34-4.   Year-to-year comparison of inventory position for Company O.

	Year 1	Year 2
Net sales	$2,225,000	$2,225,000
Cost of sales	1,450,000	1,450,000
Inventory		
Raw material	150,000	75,000
Work-in-process	250,000	125,000
Finished goods	50,000	250,000
Total	$ 450,000	$ 450,000
Days' Cost of Sales		
Raw Material	38 days	19 days
Work-in-Process	63 days	31 days
Finished Goods	13 days	63 days
Total	114 days	113 days
Work-in-Process		
to Raw Material	1.7 times	1.7 times
Finished Goods		
to Work-in-Process	0.2 times	2.0 times

Note: *Work-in-Process to Raw Material* and *Finished Goods to Work-in-Process* are special-purpose ratios that illustrate the parallel between changes in the inventory cycle of manufacturers and changes in the cash cycle off companies in all lines of business.

divert attention from the basic principle of cause and effect illustrated by the key financial measures.

Throughout this chapter, we have seen that the analyst must take particular care to identify seasonal factors, as well as the impact of economic cycles in the company's industry and the effect of the company's specific order and delivery pattern, on ratios calculated from year-end figures. Table 34-5 contains a summary of the conditions that may signal the need for further study.

Table 34-5.　Company subject to seasonal influence or cyclical change in demand.

Cash and short-term investments	Accounts receivable	Inventory	Most likely situation
High	High[1]	High[2]	Poor asset management; possible overcapitalization
High	High[1]	Moderate or low[3]	End of profitable cycle or peak sales period; possible overcapitalization and poor control of cash and accounts receivable and inventory
High	Moderate or low[4]	Moderate or low[3]	Low point of economic cycle or seasonal pattern; possible overcapitalization
Moderate or low	High[1]	High[2]	Peak of economic cycle or seasonal pattern; possible poor management of accounts receivable and inventory
Moderate or low	High[1]	Moderate or low[3]	Poor management of accounts receivable; possible brief period of unusual sales activity
Moderate or low	Moderate or low[4]	High[2]	Start of profitable cycle or peak sales period (and possible overcapitalization); possible poor inventory control
Moderate or low	Moderate or low[4]	Moderate or low[3]	Adequate to excellent control of accounts receivable and inventory; also fiscal year similar to industry comparison group

[1]High *Collection Period of Accounts Receivable.*
[2]Low *Cost of Sales to Inventory.*
[3]High to moderate *Cost of Sales to Inventory.*
[4]Low to moderate *Collection Period of Accounts Receivable.*

Chapter 35

Sources of Comparative Statistics

As you are now well aware, timely, representative information about a company's specific line of business activity is a vital element in evaluating that business's competitive position. How else can management possibly know where the enterprise stands in relation to the company's rivals, challengers who will necessarily have an important influence on the company's prospects for survival, growth, and financial success? Indeed, few companies enjoy such a dominant market position, such a clear-cut and uncontested niche, or such an advantageous location or reputation that they have no serious competitors. Industry data may not capture the precise characteristics of any one company's specific challengers, but accurate facts and figures about companies of similar size engaged in the same business activity will provide management with an excellent opportunity to consider how financial performance might be improved. Relating the key ratios for similar businesses to the company's results is extremely helpful in focusing management attention.

Industry standards are certainly not representative of ideal performance, and they should not ordinarily be established as company goals. Most companies will be superior to typical industry results in some respects and will show comparative deficiencies in other areas of financial performance. Wise management will strive to do still better in the future, regardless of current advantages or difficulties. Nevertheless, some business decision makers seek to stay within the middle ground of industry activity in virtually all financial areas, with the exception of attempting to boost profit margin on net sales, in order to stay out of financial difficulty and concentrate on the company's primary skills in meeting customer requirements, whether in design, production, sales, or service. By using financial statement analysis as a tool to avoid serious problems (rather than attempting to maximize monetary return through high-risk strategies), these business owners and managers are able to reduce their "fire fighting" efforts and devote more of their time to improving operations. With this approach, many of them eventually generate superior profit by directing their management attention to the basic business factors they understand well—and that are appreciated by their customers. The techniques of financial management can enable such business decision makers to build a more profitable and more stable enterprise for long-term success, not simply play transitory money games. To measure financial progress, comparative data are essential.

Detailed Industry Data From National Trade Associations

For comparative standards to serve their intended purpose, they must truly reflect operating performance and financial structure in the industry they purport to represent, and they must be made available in a timely manner. Of course, no single column of numbers can possibly encompass the entire range of characteristics within any line of business activity. To provide meaningful comparisons for decision makers, data must be separated by those factors of importance to companies in that specific industry, as we saw in Chapter 33. Ordinarily, national trade associations are best able to compile and distribute financial statistics that are tailored to the particular needs of companies in their industry. With the aid of computer software, they can easily design their own highly specific surveys and produce their own unique reports that include expense percentages, key ratios, and comparative categories developed exclusively for their line of business. By means of such software, association personnel can now acquire the capability to conduct annual surveys without outside assistance, although a financial consultant familiar with appropriate statistical methods can be helpful in data analysis. Many associations prefer to engage outside consultants or accounting firms to receive the data and prepare the industry report in order to emphasize confidentiality and independent evaluation.

Although the power and flexibility of today's computer software can yield great benefits in customizing the data contained in industry reports, the analyst must direct his or her primary attention to the key financial ratios and the cause-and-effect approach. No cascade of industry-specific ratios can substitute for the analytical value of the 16 fundamental measures of financial cause and effect. In fact, a proliferation of ratios may tend to obscure the basic principles that are essential to the meaningful interpretation of financial statements.

A few industry reports now provide their readers with a straightforward, step-by-step explanation of cause-and-effect ratio analysis and specific ways to apply this technique in making better business decisions. The sponsors of these reports recognize that most business owners and managers can make far better use of industry data if they are given basic guidance about financial ratios and their value in revealing a company's comparative strengths and weaknesses. Unfortunately, all too many reports published by national trade associations and private organizations offer nothing more than a list of ratio definitions. The experienced analyst will find such a presentation satisfactory, provided that the report contains the key financial ratios, since he has already become familiar with the cause-and-effect approach and therefore knows how to identify the reasons for any financial weaknesses he may detect. The typical business owner or manager, however, would benefit greatly from a summary of the principles of cause-and-effect ratio analysis as an introductory lesson or as a review of the ideas he may have learned through this book or an industry seminar. Improving financial performance is an ongoing process of education and reeducation. Because most businesspeople do not have the opportunity (or the desire) to deal with the analytical side of financial management on a daily basis, the annual industry report should include the essentials of cause-and-effect ratio analysis for ready reference and immediate application.

Individualized Management Reports

A small number of pioneering national associations have also begun to provide their members with individualized financial management reports. Based on the principles of cause-and-effect ratio analysis, these individualized reports explain each company's specific strengths and weaknesses in comparison with the operating performance and financial structure of similar companies in the industry. In approximately 20 pages of text that accompanies the statistical comparisons, each report describes how the key causal factors of that particular concern influence the company's important secondary ratios. These reports also contain detailed expense comparisons, including special cost ratios applicable to the industry, as well as summary observations and suggestions for management consideration. Depending on the importance of the analyst's assignment, he should investigate the possibility that the company has access to such individualized financial management reports. Many companies in national associations that offer reports of this kind share them with their accountant and their banker. Even when a company's report points out the existence of operating weaknesses or deficiencies in financial structure, it also serves to focus management attention on the specific areas where action should be taken. Most credit grantors already have a perception of any serious shortcomings in a company's financial makeup, but they gain a positive impression of future prospects when management demonstrates awareness of the cause (or causes), provided, of course, that a plan of action has been developed to correct the problems identified.

Some associations also offer individual financial counseling for the businessperson who desires an independent verification of his or her own findings or who wishes to gain a more complete, particularized analysis of a company's performance through direct, confidential discussion. By drawing upon the wealth of detailed data previously gathered for the association report, an industry analyst is able to furnish any member company with an extensive evaluation of its specific strengths and weaknesses in comparison with other concerns having characteristics of particular interest to the company owner or manager. The flexibility of today's computer software enables the consultant (either a knowledgeable staff member or a professional financial analyst) to develop special composite profiles based on any item in the database, including number of employees, market area, age of business, net sales per square foot of retail space, or one of the key financial ratios. Means of achieving particular company goals, methods of improving performance in possible problem areas, and ways of maximizing superior competitive features can be thoroughly explored in discussions between company management and the industry analyst.

The financial counselor or analyst might be a full-time member of the association staff responsible for directing the industry survey and preparing the written reports, or he or she might be an independent consultant providing counseling for the association on a contract or per-engagement basis. Individual financial counseling can be furnished to interested members of the association at a cost far less than the fee they pay annually to their accountants for the preparation of their financial statements. Seminars featuring the application of the association survey to practical business problems, as well as a session in the convention program devoted to analytical comment, are conducted by several national associations to aid members in enhancing financial skills. Accountants, bankers, and credit managers should encourage such association activities, not only for the purpose of developing more reliable statistics that they can use in their own professional work, but also to promote the strengthening of business enterprises throughout the country by means of improved financial management.

Advantages of Industry Programs

Some business owners and managers who hesitate to participate in industry programs may feel that the preparation and dissemination of reliable ratios and cost data will work solely to the advantage of the weaker, marginal companies. It is true that the struggling company will benefit immensely from acquiring relevant, reliable, detailed figures that management may use to determine the business's present position and develop plans for advancement. It is equally true, however, that even the most progressive company in an industry has room for betterment and can profit from confirming its existing advantages and from recognizing potential improvements through more complete knowledge of industry conditions. The owners and managers of dynamic, forward-looking companies are often more eager to obtain comparative data and benefit from independent financial advice than are those of the weaker organizations in the field, and that is one reason for their greater success. At the same time, the less efficient operator, given an adequate education in the essentials of financial analysis through the cause-and-effect approach, can move forward and add to his industry's stability and progress. Providing information to marginal companies is actually beneficial to most competitors, since it is the company which operates in ignorance, cutting prices and offering overly generous credit terms with no analysis or planning, that so often hurts industry conditions. Moreover, companies in many industries compete with organizations in other lines of business, and the industry that provides its members with timely, useful information will advance more rapidly than one whose constituent companies are less well informed. National financial statistics will not provide direct clues to meeting foreign competition, but a well-organized industry report will direct attention to the key financial factors that must be effectively managed to meet any competitive challenges, domestic or foreign.

Computer-Based Systems of Financial Analysis

Computer-based "expert systems" are now being developed to make financial analysis readily available and understandable to virtually all business owners and managers. The early financial applications of this branch of computer science have been in the area of credit-scoring models designed to assist lenders in determining debt service potential and specifying loan covenants. Within the next few years, however, these computer tools are expected to become generally available to business decision makers to assist them in evaluating their competitive position and in projecting the financial impact of alternative actions. Company owners and managers will undoubtedly gain even more from such developments than will credit grantors, investors, and other outside analysts.

Cause-and-effect ratio analysis can be particularly valuable in such computer-based systems because it provides a logical framework for relating a company's important financial factors. Lacking the cause-and-effect approach, some of the existing financial models contain bizarre rules and suggestions. One advises strengthening *Current Assets to Current Liabilities* by simply increasing current assets. In purely mathematical terms, an increase in current assets while holding current liabilities constant would indeed raise *Current Assets to Current Liabilities*. But as a practical matter, an increase in current assets is ordinarily accompanied by a similar expansion of current liabilities, resulting in a lower *Current Ratio*. It is true that over an extended period an otherwise stable company could use retained earnings to enlarge current assets without increasing current liabilities, but such a model is unrealistic for most companies in today's dynamic business environment. The remaining alternative approaches to improving *Current Assets to Current Liabilities*—increasing current assets by either reducing fixed assets, taking on additional long-term liabilities, or seeking outside investment (while holding current liabilities constant)—are all low-probability occurrences in the real world. For most companies, the appropriate short-term approach to strengthening *Current Assets to Current Liabilities* is to reduce current assets by improving credit and collections, boosting inventory turnover, and then using the cash generated from these moves to lower current liabilities. As this example suggests, an understanding of cause-and-effect ratio analysis is a key element in the development of useful, practical computer-based systems for business owners and managers. In addition, these systems will depend on reliable and timely industry information in order to place the company's operating performance and financial structure in the proper competitive context.

Multi-Industry Studies: Potentially Valuable Sources of Data

As suggested throughout this book, industry reports prepared under the sponsorship of national trade associations usually contain the most comprehensive, detailed, and useful standards for evaluating a company's competitive position. The owner or manager of a company that has elected not to join the industry association, or an outside analyst seeking comparative information, may, however, not have access to such reports. Bank credit officers and commercial credit managers have a special need for financial data covering a wide range of industries, but collecting hundreds of reports from diverse sources would be impractical. To meet both the specialized needs of credit grantors and the more general requirements of company owners, management employees, credit grantors, accountants, investors, financial consultants, and business brokers, a number of multi-industry reports are published.

Among the most prominent of these multi-industry publications is the *RMA Annual Statement Studies*, prepared for nearly 70 years by Robert Morris Associates, the national association of bank loan and credit officers. Edited by Susan M. Kelsay, assistant director of RMA's credit division, this publication is "made possible through the voluntary cooperation of RMA's member banks, and is a product of the commercial banking community. Therefore, it is designed primarily for commercial bankers. However, because of its broad application, the *Statement Studies* has become an indispensable tool for businessmen, financial executives and others who must make sound lending and business decisions."

The 1989 edition included data compiled from nearly 93,000 financial statements in 151 manufacturing industries, 56 wholesaling lines, 57 types of retailing activity, and 75 service classifications, as well as 21 contracting lines and 9 miscellaneous categories (for example, bituminous coal mining and vegetable farming). With the exception of manufacturing industries, almost all business lines are displayed at a single four-digit Standard Industrial Classification (SIC) level, such as wholesalers of stationery and office supplies, retail hardware stores, and refuse systems. Numerous manufacturing lines (for example, electronic components and accessories) include several different product categories. Composite figures for all responding companies in each line of business are displayed in the *RMA Annual Statement Studies*, together with data from four size categories based on total assets: 0–$1 million, $1 million–$10 million, $10 million–$50 million, and $50 million–$100 million. Not surprisingly, the majority of companies in a specific line are often concentrated in the 0–$1 million or $1 million–$10 million groups. In addition to data for the most recent complete fiscal year (ending between June 30, 1988, and March 31, 1989, in the 1989 RMA edition), financial figures for the previous four years are also included. Each page in the *Annual Statement Studies* displays average percentages for gross profit, operating expenses, operating profit, all other expenses (net), and profit before taxes, as well as medians and mid-ranges for 14 important financial ratios and two additional operating factors: depreciation and officers' compensation as a percentage of net sales.

Although the *RMA Annual Statement Studies* omit two causal measures, *Net Sales to Net Worth* and *Long-Term Liabilities to Total Noncurrent Assets*, these ratios can be derived from the data provided. Similarly, the two missing effect ratios, *Current Liabilities to Net Worth* and *Long-Term Liabilities to Working Capital*, can be reconstructed, and *Total Noncurrent Assets to Net Worth* can be computed from available information. Deriving norms for these ratios from the published data may result in certain distortions, but the differences are likely to be small (except possibly in the case of *Long-Term Liabilities to Total Noncurrent Assets*). The RMA method of computing *Net Profit to Net Worth*, which omits companies with negative tangible net worth, may result in a small bias of the median toward relatively profitable businesses (since companies incurring net losses are more likely to report deficit net worth). In addition, RMA's use of the average for *Net Profit to Net Sales* and the median for *Net Profit to Total Assets* and *Net Profit to Net Worth* can, during periods of near break-even operation in certain industries, cause one measure to be negative while the others are positive. Nevertheless, a company's comparative performance can, in most cases, be readily determined.

Data on Companies in More Than One Industry

Because of clarity of presentation, the large database, the number of business lines covered, the affordable price, and the fact that the *RMA Annual Statement Studies* are widely used by bank officers and other credit grantors, this source is particularly valuable to the analyst who has occasion to assess the performance of companies in more than one industry. Nevertheless:

> RMA recommends that *Statement Studies* data be regarded only as general guidelines and not as absolute industry norms. There are several reasons why the data may not be fully representative of a given industry:
>
> 1. The financial statements used in the *Statement Studies* are not selected by any random or statistically reliable method. RMA member banks voluntarily submit the raw data they have available each year, with these being the only constraints: (a) The fiscal year-ends of the companies reported may not be from April 1 through June 29, and (b) their total assets must be less than $100 million.
>
> 2. Many companies have varied product lines; however, the *Statement Studies* categorize them by their primary product Standard Industrial Classification (SIC) number only.
>
> 3. Some of our industry samples are rather small in relation to the total number of companies in a given industry. A relatively small sample can increase the chances that some of our composites do not fully represent an industry.

4. There is the chance that an extreme statement can be present in a sample, causing a disproportionate influence on the industry composite. This is particularly true in a relatively small sample.

5. Companies within the same industry may differ in their method of operations which in turn can directly influence their financial statements. Since they are included in our sample, too, these statements can significantly affect our composite calculations.

6. Other considerations that can result in variations among different companies engaged in the same general line of business are different labor markets; geographical location; different accounting methods; quality of products handled; sources and methods of financing; and terms of sale.

For these reasons, RMA does not recommend the *Statement Studies* figures be considered as absolute norms for a given industry. Rather, the figures should be used only as general guidelines and in addition to the other methods of financial analysis. RMA makes no claim as to the representativeness of the figures printed in this book.

Dun & Bradstreet, best known as the largest credit reporting service in the country, issues an annual publication, *Industry Norms and Key Business Ratios*, for many lines of activity. This report is largely based on the concepts of Roy A. Foulke, Sr., a former Dun & Bradstreet executive and a notable pioneer in the application of ratio analysis to the evaluation of privately held firms. While the key financial ratios published in 1990 have remained essentially unchanged in analytical content since Roy Foulke's important work 40 years earlier, the Dun & Bradstreet (D&B) database now cncompasses some 800 lines of business. Twelve of the sixteen ratios that are vital to an understanding of the cause-and-effect method have been labeled "key" by Dun & Bradstreet. The D&B selection of ratios suggests a creditor's perspective, since eight of the nine ratios that measure effect are included, but only four of the seven causal ratios of particular interest to management are displayed. The presentation of *Net Sales to Total Assets* as Total Assets to Sales (and in percentage form) somewhat hinders its interpretation, but the analyst can convert this important measure to the causal ratio *Net Sales to Total Assets* by dividing the value 100 by the published percentage. Once that has been accomplished, *Net Sales to Net Worth* can be derived by dividing *Net Sales to Total Assets* by the sum of *Total Liabilities to Net Worth* (as a ratio, not in D&B's percentage form) plus 1. *Net Sales to Fixed Assets* and *Long-Term Liabilities to Total Noncurrent Assets* can be constructed from common-size balance sheet information contained in the *Industry Norms and Key Business Ratios*, but the derived values may not entirely correspond with the medians for the other published ratios.

Database of 1 Million Companies

The strongest feature of the Dun & Bradstreet database, which can also be directly accessed by computer (either on line or by diskette) under agreement with D&B, is its scope—more than 1 million relatively current company records. On the other hand, although "all the financial statements entered into D&B's financial statements go through a series of quality checks and only actual statements are used (that is, estimated, pro forma and duplicate statements are eliminated)," the sample is self-selected. In submitting their data voluntarily to Dun & Bradstreet, business owners and managers are not required to provide the same attestations of accuracy (which carry the potential for legal penalties in the event of fraudulent misrepresentation) that accompany most applications for bank loans. It is possible, therefore, that the information provided by some companies tends to be optimistic in nature. Wholesalers of sporting goods, for example, reported median *Current Assets to Current Liabilities* of 2.7 in D&B's *Industry Norms and Key Business Ratios*, versus 1.6 in the *RMA Annual Statement Studies*. While the RMA figures indicated a median *Total Liabilities to Net Worth* of 2.0, the D&B data showed a much more favorable median of 0.7 (displayed as 74.0% in their format). Similarly, the companies in the D&B database reported earning 4.4%—*after* income taxes—on net sales, but the financial statements of applicants for bank credit in the RMA database showed that those companies earned only 2.7% *before* income taxes. Companies that do not require bank loans and have no other reason to provide their financial statement to banking institutions might be found in the Dun & Bradstreet statistics, but would be excluded from the Robert Morris Associates database. Nevertheless, the wholly voluntary financial statements in the D&B *Key Industry Norms and Business Ratios* tend to show stronger operating performance and financial structure than reported by other sources of industry standards. Particularly because of the large number of industry groupings and individual companies in the Dun & Bradstreet database, the analyst should consider the value of that source in his evaluations.

Timely Census Information Available

The Bureau of the Census, U.S. Department of Commerce, prepares a *Quarterly Financial Report for Manufacturing, Mining, and Trade Corporations* in printed form and on PC diskettes. According to the Bureau of the Census,

> "The *Quarterly Financial Report* program publishes up-to-date aggregate statistics on the financial results and position of U.S. corporations. Based upon an extensive sample survey, the *Quarterly Financial Report (QFR)* presents estimated statements of income and retained earnings, balance sheets, and related financial and operating ratios for all manufacturing corporations and large mining and trade corporations. The statistical data are classified by industry and by asset size. Pertinent data are

provided, when possible, on material distortions in comparability owing to changes in accounting conventions or user needs.

The main purpose of the *QFR* is to provide timely, accurate data on business financial conditions for use by Government and private sector organizations and individuals. Among its users, the Commerce Department regularly employs *QFR* data as an important component in determining corporate profits for GNP and National Income estimates; the Federal Reserve Board uses the *QFR* to assess industrial debt structure, liquidity, and profitability; the Treasury Department estimates corporate tax liability through use of *QFR* data; the Council of Economic Advisors and Congressional Committees utilize key indicators derived from *QFR* data as they design economic policies and draft legislation; the Federal Trade Commission (FTC) utilizes the series as a basic reference point in analyzing the financial performance of American industries; and banking institutions and financial analysts draw upon the series in making investment evaluations.

The census information is very timely, being released within 75 days after the end of the first, second, and third calendar quarters and 95 days after the close of the fourth quarter. On the other hand, the categories displayed in the *QFR* are very broad, and the composite figures are dominated by large corporations. Most of the twenty-two manufacturing lines are compiled at the two-digit SIC level (for example, fabricated metal products), while wholesaling is divided into only two lines (durable goods and nondurable goods) and retailing is separated into three large categories: general merchandise, food, and all others. Service lines of business are not included. Manufacturing industries are divided into two size categories: total assets less than $25 million and total assets $25 million and over. Wholesale and retail industries are restricted to companies with assets of $50 million or more.

Only five ratios, all secondary measures, are included in the *QFR*. Nevertheless, aggregate dollar figures in the report permit the calculation of all sixteen key financial ratios on a dollar-weighted basis. Although the *QFR* statistics are not directly applicable to the operations and financial structure of most U.S. companies, they are useful to investors in publicly traded companies and can be helpful to owners and managers of privately held companies in tracking comparative industry trends.

Information on Small Companies

Information about relatively small companies is contained in *Financial Studies of Small Business*, published by Financial Research Associates. Begun in the late 1970s, this publication presents composite financial data covering companies with total assets less than $1 million. Companies of this size, which are contained in a single classification in the *RMA Annual Statement Studies*, are separated into four groups—total assets $10,000 to $100,000, $100,000 to $250,000, $250,000 to $500,000, and $500,000 to $1 million—by the *Financial Studies of Small Business*. A supplementary section displays the composite data in four sales volume categories: $10,000 to $250,000, $250,000 to $500,000, $500,000 to $1 million, and $1 million and over. In addition, the report contains financial statistics about the companies in each line of business that reported pre-tax profit on net sales within the upper 25% of participants in their group. Composite information about companies with fiscal years ending between May 1988 and April 1989 was included in the 1989 edition available in the third quarter of that year. More than 1,000 certified public accounting firms submit a sample (approximately 15%) of the financial statements in their current files for compilation in the *Financial Studies of Small Business*.

Most of the roughly 60 lines of business (which vary, depending on the number of statements submitted by cooperating accountants) include data representing between 50 and 100 companies nationally, substantially smaller samples than those displayed in the *RMA Annual Statement Studies* or the D&B *Key Financial Ratios* in most categories. The companies in the *Financial Studies of Small Business* sample are, however, drawn from a much narrower sales volume range. Some of the industry lines, such as retail apparel, are rather broad; but most lines of business are comparable to the four-digit SIC categories used in the *RMA Annual Statement Studies*. A total of 5 manufacturing industries, 3 wholesaling lines, 18 retailing classifications, 22 service and professional categories, and 5 contracting lines are found in the 1989 edition of the *Financial Studies of Small Business*. Five of the seven causal ratios and six of the nine secondary ratios are displayed in this publication. Because of the nature of the statistical methods used, an attempt to derive the missing causal measures—*Net Sales to Fixed Assets* and *Long-Term Liabilities to Total Noncurrent Assets*—would introduce large errors in many cases. An effort to calculate industry norms for *Net Sales to Working Capital*, *Total Noncurrent Assets to Net Worth*, and *Long-Term Liabilities to Working Capital*, which were omitted from the *Financial Studies of Small Business*, would also result in potentially significant distortions.

The *Financial Studies*, including current information and five-year historical data, are also distributed on PC diskettes. Lacking the perspective of cause-and-effect analysis, the ratio displays provided by this data service are somewhat redundant and incomplete at the same time. Nevertheless, the analyst seeking information about comparatively small companies should investigate this source.

An *Almanac of Business and Industrial Ratios* has been published by Prentice-Hall for several years under the direction of Leo Troy, Ph.D. The statistics, compiled from aggregate data supplied by the Internal Revenue Service, cover more than 3 million business units (including 131,000 eating and drinking places, 60,000 insurance agents, 128,000 firms classified as "other real estate," 127,000 offices of physicians, and 261,000 "business services except advertising" within approximately 200 "lines of activity"), but the information is not made available to the public until three years after the close of business for the enterprises included in the study. Only two of the seven causal ratios and six of the nine ratios that measure effect are included in the *Almanac*. This publication may be a useful research tool for analysts interested in tracing certain historical trends, but it should be used with caution in making current business decisions.

Private Multi-Industry Databases

Banks, leasing companies, and other credit grantors that are primarily concerned with comparative performance within a certain geographic region can now construct their own customized industry-by-industry databases through the same computer software developed for national trade associations. Because a regional bank or leasing company ordinarily has numerous borrowers within the same industry (or closely related lines of business), existing information about those companies can easily be compiled into a standard comparison group that will provide benchmark data for evaluating any member of that category. This special comparison group may not be statistically valid in the strictest sense, but the data will allow the analyst to gain a useful perspective on such pertinent questions as, Why did this company's *Net Profit to Net Sales* decline while its *Total Liabilities to Net Worth* increased in relation to the results reported by similar companies in this region during the last year? Investors can also use such software to analyze the strengths and weaknesses of publicly traded companies in relation to their peers in the same line of business activity or those having a similar conglomerate profile. For example, changes in *Cost of Sales to Inventory* and *Net Sales to Fixed Assets* may say much about a company's quality of earnings and its prospects for market appreciation.

Statistical Validity

As noted earlier, each edition of the *RMA Annual Statement Studies* contains a lengthy cautionary statement about the validity of group data, owing to the manner in which the sample is selected. Although information compiled by national trade associations is not subject to all of the influences described by Robert Morris Associates, membership surveys involve their own statistical difficulties. No industry sample compiled by a trade group can, for instance, be clearly labeled as statistically valid since respondents are self-selected. Owners and managers may choose to withhold their data for any number of reasons: fear of disclosure of confidential information, lack of detailed or timely financial data in the industry report, poor performance (resulting in embarrassment by management or a belief that the unusual results would distort the industry database), difficulty in converting the company's chart of accounts to the format of the industry questionnaire, or shortage of staff time (or the owner's time) to complete the survey form when requested.

Our own extensive analyses indicate that industry statistics are overrepresented by the larger and more profitable companies in most industries. In actual practice, the representativeness of industry surveys designed for small and medium-size companies cannot be accurately estimated by accepted statistical methods because the universe of companies in specific lines of business is not well defined with respect to the characteristics that determine operating performance and financial structure. In other words, there is no satisfactory profile of all companies in most lines of business to use as a standard for comparing the validity of the sample contained in the industry survey.

What, then, is the analytical value of industry financial data? Statisticians have not undertaken any definitive studies of this issue, but our experience has demonstrated that many of the currently published industry surveys yield statistics that exhibit reasonable data distributions, follow patterns consistent with external indicators of financial performance, and consistently distinguish companies in one line of business from those in other lines. Such data are clearly useful in identifying those characteristics of a specific company that differ significantly from typical industry benchmarks.

As a practical matter, comparative statistics are most often used to distinguish unusually strong or weak elements in a company's financial makeup. They are not intended to be precise standards for the fine-tuning of a company's operations or its financial structure. These arguments in favor of industry statistics should not dissuade you from an attitude of healthy skepticism. You should scrutinize every source of industry data before using it as the basis for evaluating a company's comparative strengths and weaknesses. Some industry statistics are decidedly superior to others in timeliness, comprehensiveness, detail, methodology, and analysis.

Conclusion

The vast majority of small and moderate-size companies hope to grow in time. They aspire to even greater financial freedom and stability. To achieve this goal, business owners and managers must be able to evaluate their company's progress, identify immediate problems, recognize competitive strengths and weaknesses, and plan future moves with greater understanding of the probable outcome. Evaluation and planning clearly require knowledge: By acquiring greater knowledge, and the confidence that follows, the business decision maker can greatly improve his or her ability to guide the company to success.

Cause-and-effect ratio analysis—which provides insight into the elements of financial balance, the opportunities and the dangers that accompany bold or extraordinary business moves, and the means to restore and maintain company stability—serves as a foundation for sound financial management. To gain the greatest value from this analytical system, however, the decision maker also needs reliable, detailed data about the company's specific line of business activity, as we have seen throughout this book. Fortunately, steady improvements are being made in the provision of industrywide financial information.

Some day, perhaps in the not too distant future, every company owner and manager—and every credit grantor and investor—will have the opportunity to apply cause-and-effect ratio analysis with maximum effectiveness through access to meaningful data in every line of manufacturing, wholesaling, retailing, and service activity.

APPENDIX A

Financial Structure and Performance Measurement: Related Ratios and Concepts

The seven primary ratios and nine secondary ratios reveal the fundamental financial strengths and weaknesses of any company. They cannot, however, cover every aspect of financial management. Other specialized ratios—all linked to the seven causal ratios—are highly useful in providing further insight into a company's financial structure and operating performance, particularly when a specific condition has been identified through examination of the sixteen key financial ratios. The most important of these ancillary ratios are described and illustrated in this Appendix.

With increased experience, you will encounter certain concepts that are directly related to cause-and-effect ratio analysis but offer a different perspective for considering the key financial ratios. Occasionally the terminology used in describing certain concepts that were developed for evaluating publicly traded companies is applied in a different manner from that appropriate to the analysis of financial statements of privately held companies. In the following pages, we explore the most important of the related concepts, examine the differences in terminology, and review the calculation and meaning of statistics displayed in industry reports.

Appendix A1

Working Capital Vulnerability

Working capital, the amount by which current assets exceed current liabilities, is dependent on the actual value of accounts receivable and inventory. If either of these components of current assets represents a large proportion of working capital, a significant decline on the value of that asset item through bad-debt losses or inventory writedowns will result in substantial working capital shrinkage. As accounts receivable and inventory grow in relation to working capital, a company's liquidity becomes increasingly vulnerable to any such losses in value. For that reason, two special ratios, *Inventory to Working Capital* and *Accounts Receivable to Working Capital,* are used to test that vulnerability. These measures are especially sensitive to significant, sometimes dangerous, shifts in the components of a company's liquidity. Therefore, you may wish to compute these ancillary ratios for any company that has shown working capital weakness: low *Current Assets to Current Liabilities* or high *Net Sales to Working Capital.* Likewise, the two tests of working capital vulnerability are particularly useful in further analysis of any business that has evidenced questionable management of either of the two major current asset items, as indicated by a high *Collection Period of Accounts Receivable* or low *Cost of Sales to Inventory.*

Both *Accounts Receivable to Working Capital* and *Inventory to Working Capital* are calculated by the same basic method. The first step is to determine working capital by subtracting current liabilities from current assets. Next, the relevant asset item—accounts receivable or inventory—is divided by working capital. With current assets of $300,000 and current liabilities of $200,000, Company B reported working capital of $100,000 ($300,000 minus $200,000). Thus, that company's *Accounts Receivable to Working Capital* was 1.3 (accounts receivable of $125,000 divided by working capital of $100,000, with the result rounded from the actual 1.25 value), and its *Inventory to Working Capital* was 1.5 ($150,000 divided by $100,000), as shown in Table A1-1.

The combination of a rapid rise in inventory and only modest growth in working capital, or an inventory build-up and an actual working capital decline, will cause a rise in *Inventory to Working Capital.* This may be an important warning sign, particularly for a manufacturing, wholesaling, or retailing concern within an industry that is strongly affected by season, style, year-to-year model changes, or outright fad. Operating difficulties are frequently disguised by means of inflated inventory values. The coincidence of these occurrences is flagged by

Table A1-1. *Accounts Receivable to Working Capital* and *Inventory to Working Capital* for four companies.

	Company A	Company B	Company C	Company D
Net sales	$1,500,000	$5,000,000	$12,500,000	$50,000,000
Cost of sales	1,110,000	3,775,000	9,750,000	40,000,000
Accounts receivable	152,000	625,000	2,090,000	2,850,000
Inventory	170,000	750,000	2,500,000	4,900,000
Current assets	398,000	1,500,000	4,740,000	8,400,000
Current liabilities	220,000	1,000,000	3,780,000	5,400,000
Accounts Receivable to Working Capital				
Company	0.9 times	1.3 times	2.2 times	1.0 times
Industry standard	Unknown	Unknown	Unknown	Unknown
Inventory to Working Capital				
Company	1.0 times	1.5 times	2.6 times	1.6 times
Industry standard	Unknown	Unknown	Unknown	Unknown
Causal factors				
Collection Period of Accounts Receivable				
Company	37 days	46 days	61 days	21 days
Industry standard	44 days	44 days	44 days	44 days
Cost of Sales to Inventory				
Company	6.5 times	5.0 times	3.9 times	8.2 times
Industry standard	5.1 times	5.1 times	5.1 times	5.1 times
Net Sales to Working Capital				
Company	8.4 times	10.0 times	13.0 times	16.7 times
Industry standard	10.2 times	10.2 times	10.2 times	10.2 times

an increase in *Inventory to Working Capital*. Company C's comparatively high ratio would warrant further investigation into both operating results and basic financial structure.

Similarly, a jump in accounts receivable at a faster rate than working capital is expanded, or an increase in accounts receivable coupled with a decrease in working capital, indicates a change in the company's operations, which will be reflected in higher *Accounts Receivable to Working Capital*. Profit reduction (even outright operating losses) attributable to bad debts is often accompanied by further accumulation of questionable receivables as part of an ongoing effort to promote higher sales through even more liberal credit terms. A rise in *Accounts Receivable to Working Capital* will focus attention on such practices.

Of course, not all increases in *Accounts Receivable to Working Capital* or *Inventory to Working Capital* indicate such potentially dangerous developments that could threaten the company's basic financial structure. Nevertheless, even companies with a stable relationship between accounts receivable, inventory, and working capital can experience significant current asset losses and a resultant decline in liquidity. Book figures for inventory are subject to major reduction in value from many influences. Style change, obsolescence, physical deterioration, and customer preference for other types of material are among those conditions that may account for a drastic slash in the dollar figure assigned to inventory on a company's ledgers. Undetected pilferage and theft, often of inadequately insured or even totally uninsured goods, has caused many a shock to management when the losses were ultimately discovered through physical inventory counts. Even today, a surprising number of auditor's reports on small or medium-size companies qualify the inventory figure as simply taken from clients' books, without physical count and without verification of material prices. Consequently, a review of *Inventory to Working Capital* is suggested for any company that shows a relatively low *Cost of Sales to Inventory*.

Accounts receivable are also subject to unexpected reduction in value through bad-debt losses, many of which are attributable to inadequate credit-and-collection procedures. Smaller companies typically do not subscribe to credit reporting services, such as Dun & Bradstreet, or specialized industry credit publications. Nor do most small companies belong to the National Association of Credit Management, from which their officers could derive the benefit of mingling with those who extend credit, attending group meetings with persons in their own industries whose problems may closely parallel theirs, or going to classes presenting the rudiments and advanced techniques of good credit and financial management. Nor do they subscribe to credit-interchange services through which they would gain at least some knowledge of their customers' payment practices. In the majority of cases, the small company hires no employee with training in credit management or collection techniques, specialties that require considerable professional education and experience. Because of the large number of companies that operate with inadequate informational tools and without trained credit experts on their staffs, it is not surprising that even in periods of unprecedented prosperity, receivables of many small and medium-size businesses rise to highly dangerous proportions relative to sales, relative to working capital, relative to invested capital, and relative to profit. Whenever a company shows a comparatively high *Collection Period of Accounts Receivable*, calculation of *Accounts Receivable to Working Capital* is an important step in analyzing the extent to which working capital is vulnerable to possible bad-debt charges.

Comparison With Industry Standards

To gain perspective on the ratios that indicate working capital vulnerability, it is useful to compare the company's condition with industry standards. Most industry studies, unfortunately, do not include these ratios. Nevertheless, the company's relative position can be determined from the causal ratios that, in turn, influence *Accounts Receivable to Working Capital* and *Inventory to Working Capital*. In some cases, accounts receivable or inventory are very high in relation to working capital because of poor control of either or both of those key assets. Other companies find that their working capital is particularly vulnerable to a decline in accounts receivable or inventory (or both) because working capital is insufficient to support existing sales volume.

The relevant data for Companies A, B, C, and D are displayed in Table A1-1. Company A, in its usual conservative position, reports comparatively low values for both *Accounts Receivable to Working Capital* and *Inventory to Working Capital*. The key current asset items, accounts receivable and inventory, are under comparatively tight control, as indicated by the relatively low *Collection Period of Accounts Receivable* and relatively high *Cost of Sales to Inventory*. In addition, Company A's working capital sufficiency is a comparatively high proportion of net sales, as shown by relatively low *Net Sales to Working Capital*.

We have seen that Company A's two ratios that measure working capital vulnerability are on the low side in relation to Companies B, C, and D. But how does Company A stand in relation to the rest of the industry? Despite the fact that industry standards are seldom published for these ratios, we can make a reasonable estimate from the other key measures. It is important to recognize that industry medians do not maintain an entirely consistent relationship with one another in the same way that averages do; therefore, deriving unpublished ratios from published figures in industry reports is not always a satisfactory approach. In most cases, however, standards computed from other published ratios are useful for general comparison. To illustrate the process, we will derive industry standards for *Accounts Receivable to Working Capital* and *Inventory to Working Capital*. The easiest method is to set industry net sales equal to $1,000. To estimate industry working capital for this exercise, divide $1,000 in net sales by 10.2, the industry standard for *Net Sales to Working Capital*. The result is $98. Next, estimate industry accounts receivable as follows: Divide $1,000 in net sales by 365 to determine average daily net sales of $2.74; then multiply $2.74 by 44 days, the industry median for the *Collection Period of Accounts Receivable*. The result is $121. With estimated industry accounts receivable of $121 and estimated industry working capital of $98, we can derive an industry standard for *Accounts Receivable to Working Capital* of 1.2 times.

To derive *Inventory to Working Capital*, we need information about the cost of sales percentage. We learned earlier that cost of sales for the typical company in the industry was approximately 79% of net sales. Therefore, we multiply $1,000 in estimated net sales by 0.79, having converted 79% to a decimal fraction (by dividing 79 by 100). The resulting $790 is then divided by 5.1, the industry standard for *Cost of Sales to Inventory*. This operation yields estimated inventory of $155. Since we have already estimated working capital to be $98, the industry standard for *Inventory to Working Capital* is calculated as 1.6 (155 divided by 98).

In relation to the derived industry standards, Company A is again found to be conservatively managed, with low working capital vulnerability. Company B is, once again, near the middle of the four companies and in line with the industry standards. Because the three ratios that influence *Accounts Receivable to Working Capital* and *Inventory to Working Capital* are similar to the industry standards, the two measures of working capital are, as expected, also similar.

Company C's high level of accounts receivable (shown by a high *Collection Period of Accounts Receivable*) and high level of inventory (revealed by low *Cost of Sales to Inventory*) tended to increase working capital vulnerability, an unfavorable condition from a conservative perspective. In addition, the amount of working capital available to support sales volume was comparatively low (indicated by relatively high *Net Sales to Working Capital*). As a result, a decline in value of either accounts receivable or inventory would have a relatively strong negative effect on Company C's working capital position. *Accounts Receivable to Working Capital* was 2.2 for Company C versus an estimated 1.2 for the industry standard, while *Inventory to Working Capital* was 2.6 versus the derived standard of 1.6.

Company D's working capital is no more vulnerable to bad-debt losses and inventory writedowns than that of the typical concern in the industry, despite very low working capital sufficiency in relation to net sales (very high *Net Sales to Working Capital*). Extremely tight control of accounts receivable and inventory are holding these key asset items to a normal (for this industry) proportion of working capital. In fact, Company D's *Accounts Receivable to Working Capital* is somewhat on the low side. Such stringent asset management, designed to compensate for the company's extremely low capitalization, may result in restrictions in some operating areas, but it has done much to strengthen basic financial structure, particularly in reducing working capital vulnerability.

In many lines of business, both accounts receivable and inventory are greater than working capital for the typical company. In other words, *Accounts Receivable to Working Capital* and *Inventory to Working Capital* exceed 1.0 for the majority of companies in those industry classifications. Whenever that condition is found, a 20% drop in accounts receivable or inventory through bad-debt losses or writedowns of inventory will result in a decline in working capital greater than 20%. In fact, for a company with *Accounts Receivable to Working Capital* of 2.0, a bad-debt write-off equal to 20% of accounts receivable will cause working capital to fall by 40%. A ratio of 5.0, not at all uncommon, would see working capital wiped out completely in the event of the same 20% reduction in accounts receivable. When working capital is highly vulnerable to changes in accounts receivable and inventory, a loss that might otherwise be absorbed as an unfortunate occurrence can become a threat to the existence of the business.

Summary: Accounts Receivable to Working Capital

Purpose   Measures the dependence of a company's working capital—the excess of current assets over current liabilities—on the stated value of its accounts receivable.

Calculation	Subtract current liabilities from current assets to obtain working capital, then divide accounts receivable by working capital.
Example	Your company's current assets were $300,000, your current liabilities were $200,000, and your accounts receivable were $125,000 at year-end. What was your *Accounts Receivable to Working Capital*?
	Solution: Working capital = 300,000 − 200,000 = 100,000; then 125,000 ÷ 100,000 = 1.3
Financial impact	A *low* ratio is a *favorable* condition from a conservative perspective: It shows a comparatively large spread between current assets and current liabilities in relation to accounts receivable, thus a low vulnerability of working capital to a reduction of accounts receivable through bad debts.
Operational impact	A *low* ratio tends to reduce the probability of bill-paying difficulty from bad debts.
Definition	Working capital equals current assets minus current liabilities.
Critical value	When current liabilities are greater than current assets, working capital will be in a deficit position and a meaningful ratio cannot be calculated. In such a case, treat *Accounts Receivable to Working Capital* as a very large number for comparative purposes. Deficit working capital is a serious condition which warrants close management attention.
Range of common experience	Insufficient industry data.

Summary: Inventory to Working Capital

Purpose	Measures the dependence of a company's working capital—the excess of current assets over current liabilities—on the stated value of its inventory.
Calculation	Subtract current liabilities from current assets to obtain working capital, then divide inventory by working capital.
Example	Your company's current assets were $300,000, your current liabilities were $200,000, and your inventory was $150,000 at year-end. What was your *Inventory to Working Capital*?

	Solution: Working capital = 300,000 − 200,000 = 100,000; then 150,000 ÷ 100,000 = 1.5
Financial impact	A *low* ratio is a *favorable* condition from a conservative perspective: It shows a comparatively large spread between current assets and current liabilities in relation to inventory, thus a low vulnerability of working capital to a writedown of inventory.
Operational impact	A *low* ratio tends to reduce the probability of bill-paying difficulty from inventory losses due to obsolescence, price changes, damage, pilferage, or other causes.
Definition	Working capital equals current assets minus current liabilities.
Critical value	When current liabilities are greater than current assets, working capital will be in a deficit position, and a meaningful ratio cannot be calculated. In such a case, treat *Inventory to Working Capital* as a very large number for comparative purposes. Deficit working capital is a serious condition that warrants close management attention.
Range of common experience	Insufficient industry data.

Appendix A2

Coverage of Interest and Long-Term Liabilities

Maintaining an adequate margin of safety for meeting bank obligations is an important element in business survival and success. The *Interest Coverage Ratio* (*Net Profit Before Taxes plus Interest Expense to Interest Expense*) and the *Debt Coverage Ratio* (*Net Profit After Taxes plus Depreciation to Current Maturities of Long-Term Debt*) indicate the extent to which a company faces potential difficulty in meeting interest and principal payments, especially in the event of a decline in profit. Although these coverage ratios are of particular interest to commercial loan officers and credit analysts, they should also be understood by company owners and managers.

Interest Coverage Ratio

The *Interest Coverage Ratio* measures a company's ability to cover its interest payments from pre-tax net profit. It is also known as the *EBIT* (*Earnings Before Interest and Taxes*) *to Interest Ratio*. By showing funds generated by operations plus nonoperating transactions as a proportion of interest expense for the year, the *Interest Coverage Ratio* indicates a company's margin of safety to meet interest payments. This measure recognizes the possibility that net profit may decline or interest rates may rise. As the *Interest Coverage Ratio* increases, a company becomes less likely to experience problems in meeting interest payments if either, or both, of these possibilities should become a reality. The *Interest Coverage Ratio* is calculated on net profit *before* taxes because interest payments are tax deductible.

The value for this ratio is found by summing net profit before taxes and interest expense and then dividing this total by interest expense. For Company B, net profit before taxes was $150,000 and interest expense was $75,000. Dividing the sum—$225,000—by interest expense of $75,000 produced a ratio of 3.0.

As a practical matter, management will almost always find some way to pay interest when due in order to avoid a default on its line of credit or long-term loan, even when the *Interest Coverage Ratio* falls below 1.0. Although a pre-tax net loss means, by definition, that earnings before interest and taxes are insufficient to pay interest expense, a company will meet its interest obligations by reducing current assets, increasing current liabilities, or diverting funds that otherwise might have been used to replace fixed assets. The availability of depreciation (a noncash charge) to pay current obligations is described in connection with the *Debt Coverage Ratio* later in this section.

Zero interest expense results in an infinitely high value, a ratio that cannot be computed by conventional means. Producing the highest possible rating for this ratio (assuming a pre-tax net profit), a zero interest condition can simply be treated as an arbitrarily high number, such as 999.9, for comparative purposes.

Interaction of Two Elements

The *Interest Coverage Ratio* reflects the interaction of both elements: pre-tax net profit and interest expense. It will decline as a result of either a reduction in net profit or a rise in interest expense. In most industries, net profit is more volatile than interest rates. Consequently, the profit factor is ordinarily responsible for any major changes in a company's *Interest Coverage Ratio*. During the late 1970s, however, the influence of interest rates became painfully apparent to many companies, especially those with heavy debt burdens or low profit margins. The amount by which the *Interest Coverage Ratio* exceeds 1.0 is the proportion by which interest rates can rise and still be covered by earnings before interest and taxes, all other factors remaining equal.

Turning to Table A2-1, we find that Company C would be unable to cover its interest payments from earnings before interest and taxes if the interest rate charged by its bank rose by a significant amount. To determine the rate that a company could pay on the interest-bearing debt it owed for the past year and still achieve a net profit, simply multiply the applicable interest rate for that year by the *Interest Coverage Ratio*. For Company C, profit would disappear completely if interest rates were increased by a factor greater than 1.3, for example, from an annual rate of 10.0% to 13.5% per year. Company A's highly conservative financial condition, on the other hand, could absorb an interest rate increase equal to 5.2 times the present rate—from, say, 10% to more than 50%. Companies B and D were generally in line with the industry standard. Company B could meet interest payments from earnings before interest and taxes even if interest rates were to rise to three times their current level, while Company D would suffer a small loss at that rate of interest.

Company A achieves its high *Interest Coverage Ratio* by virtue of high pre-tax net profit and low interest expense in relation to its sales volume. *Interest Expense to Net Sales*, a commonly published operating ratio, is displayed in Table A2-1 for the purpose of illustrating the components of the *Interest Coverage Ratio*. Dividing interest expense by net sales yields *Interest Expense to Net Sales*, which is ordinarily expressed in percentage form. A combination of high asset utilization (high *Net Sales to Total Assets*) and high investment adequacy (low

Table A2-1. *Interest Coverage Ratio* **for four companies.**

	Company A	Company B	Company C	Company D
Net sales	$1,500,000	$5,000,000	$12,500,000	$50,000,000
Net profit before taxes	76,000	150,000	150,000	950,000
Interest expense	18,000	75,000	450,000	550,000
Total assets	536,000	2,000,000	6,650,000	11,400,000
Total liabilities	282,000	1,250,000	5,110,000	9,850,000
Net worth	254,000	750,000	1,540,000	1,550,000
Interest Coverage Ratio				
(Net Profit Before Taxes				
plus Interest Expense				
to Interest Expense)				
Company	5.2 times	3.0 times	1.3 times	2.7 times
Industry standard	2.8 times	2.8 times	2.8 times	2.8 times
Causal factors				
Net Profit to Net Sales				
Company	5.1%	3.0%	1.2%	1.9%
Industry standard	3.2%	3.2%	3.2%	3.2%
Interest Expense				
to Net Sales				
Company	1.2%	1.5%	3.6%	1.1%
Industry standard	1.8%	1.8%	1.8%	1.8%
Net Sales				
to Total Assets				
Company	2.8 times	2.5 times	1.9 times	4.4 times
Industry standard	2.4 times	2.4 times	2.4 times	2.4 times
Net Sales				
to Net Worth				
Company	5.9 times	6.7 times	8.1 times	32.3 times
Industry standard	6.8 times	6.8 times	6.8 times	6.8 times
Total Liabilities				
to Net Worth				
Company	1.1 times	1.7 times	3.3 times	6.4 times
Industry standard	1.8 times	1.8 times	1.8 times	1.8 times

Net Sales to Net Worth) enabled Company A to hold interest expense to a comparatively low level. Company B is near the industry standard with respect to both net profit and interest expense as a percentage of net sales. Not surprisingly, Company B's *Interest Coverage Ratio* is also in line with the typical value in the industry comparison group. Company B maintained asset utilization and investment adequacy close to the industry norm, resulting in moderate interest expense.

Company C's low *Interest Coverage Ratio* is attributable to both low pre-tax net profit and high interest expense. This is a worrisome combination for lenders, since a company with a low pre-tax profit margin is especially vulnerable to price cutting by competitors, which may result from their efforts to bolster sagging sales volume or may arise from attempts to increase market share in a growing industry. Company C's ability to meet interest payments from earnings before interest and taxes is threatened by the relatively great likelihood of operating losses, as well as by the ever-present possibility of significant rises in interest rates. This prospect is particularly unappealing to creditors, in view of Company C's high *Total Liabilities to Net Worth*, which indicates a comparatively low margin of protection against ultimate loss in the event of liquidation. The company's high percentage of interest expense in relation to net sales is traceable to a combination of low asset utilization (low *Net Sales to Total Assets*) and low investment adequacy (high *Net Sales to Net Worth*).

Company D also indicates comparatively low pre-tax *Net Profit to Net Sales*, but this business's *Interest Coverage Ratio* is very close to the industry standard because interest expense has been held to a relatively low percentage of net sales. This low interest expense figure may seem surprising in light of what we have already learned about Company D, particularly the concern's very high *Total Liabilities to Net Worth*. Further examination of Company D's financial structure, however, will remind us that the concern also has extremely high asset utilization. Its very efficient use of total assets in generating net sales is indicated by unusually high *Net Sales to Total Assets*. Although Company D's net worth was comparatively low in relation to net sales, which resulted in high *Total Liabilities to Net Worth*, the company needed a comparatively small amount of total liabilities to support its relatively low level of total assets. As a consequence, Company D incurred comparatively little interest expense as a percentage of net sales and enjoyed a moderate *Interest Coverage Ratio*.

As we have seen, interest expense and the *Interest Coverage Ratio* are influenced by investment adequacy (*Net Sales to Net Worth*) and asset utilization (*Net Sales to Total Assets*). In addition, interest expense is determined by the proportion of interest-bearing debt to total liabilities and the interest rate on interest-bearing debt.

Debt Coverage Ratio

The *Debt Coverage Ratio* indicates a company's ability to meet its principal repayments of long-term debt as they come due. By comparing the funds generated during the past year versus the amount of long-term debt that must be repaid within the next 12 months, this ratio indicates how well the company is able to retire long-term obligations through after-tax cash flow without reducing working capital. It is important to recognize, however, that net cash flow (net profit plus depreciation) can be absorbed by increases in accounts receivable and inventory or by other asset expansion during the year. Thus, net cash flow will not necessarily be available to pay current maturities of long-term debt. Sound asset management and adequate net cash flow are both necessary to assure proper debt service.

Calculation of this ratio involves summing net profit after taxes and depreciation expense for the previous year to determine net cash flow and then dividing this amount by the current maturities of long-term debt at the end of the last fiscal year. In the case of Company B, net profit after taxes was $100,000, equal to the amount of depreciation. When the sum—$200,000—was divided by the $75,000 shown for current maturities of long-term debt on the balance sheet at year-end, the *Debt Coverage Ratio* was found to be 2.7.

Long-term debt is ordinarily incurred to finance the acquisition of fixed assets, which are, in turn, intended to generate profit. Depreciation charges (which do not require cash outlays) and the net profit produced by the company's operations—making use of the additional fixed assets—are expected to provide sufficient net cash flow to retire long-term debt. The *Debt Coverage Ratio* measures a company's performance in that regard. Debt coverage is calculated on net profit *after* taxes because principal repayment is not tax-deductible. Depreciation expense is a noncash charge, an accounting entry to allow for the decline in value of fixed assets due to wear and obsolescence; therefore, depreciation is added back to after-tax net profit in determining net cash flow. In other words, the amount shown as depreciation expense is actually available to repay debt—unless cash is absorbed by other balance sheet items, such as increased accounts receivable, a higher inventory level, or additional plant and equipment. Net profit after taxes plus depreciation expense is also called *cash throw-off* by bankers.

Interaction of Three Elements

The *Debt Coverage Ratio* summarizes the interaction of three financial elements: after-tax net profit, depreciation, and current maturities of long-term debt. An increase in either of the two components of net cash flow—net profit or depreciation—or a reduction in currently scheduled payments on long-term debt would cause the *Debt Coverage Ratio* to rise. In most companies, depreciation and current principal payments on long-term debt are closely linked and relatively stable. After-tax net profit is ordinarily the variable factor that is most likely to cause significant changes in the *Debt Coverage Ratio*. Nevertheless, this ratio is the best indicator of the effectiveness with which management has obtained long-term financing based on a repayment schedule in line with depreciation allowed for the underlying assets.

When the *Debt Coverage Ratio* falls below 1.0, or even becomes a negative value, as a result of an after-tax loss, company management will make every effort to meet current payments on loan principal. The severe difficulties that would result from a default on scheduled remittances to the bank or leasing company ordinarily prompt a reduction of inventory, more rapid collection of accounts receivable, or delays in paying suppliers to avoid missing a principal payment. Nevertheless, when the company's ability to continue operations would be jeopardized by further asset reductions or deferral of accounts payable, a rescheduling of debt becomes inevitable. To avoid or at least anticipate such an eventuality, bankers pay particularly close attention to the *Debt Coverage Ratio*.

If a company has no long-term debt (or no current maturities of such debt), the *Debt Coverage Ratio* will be an undefined value, representing the highest possible rating but one that may give your computer a serious problem. For comparative purposes, an arbitrarily high value, such as 999.9, will be sufficient.

In Table A2-2, we see how our old friends, Companies A, B, C, and D, compare with respect to the *Debt Coverage Ratio*. Company A, as usual, has a conservative financial structure. The organization's low depreciation percentage tends to reduce debt coverage, but current maturities of long-term debt represent an unusually small proportion of net sales. Ultimately, a comparatively high percentage of after-tax profit to net sales results in a high *Debt Coverage Ratio* for Company A. The company's low depreciation expense and low percentage of current maturities of long-term debt in relation to net sales are both attributable to comparatively high *Net Sales to Fixed Assets*. To illustrate the components of the *Debt Coverage Ratio*, Table A2-2 includes three special-purpose ratios: *Net Profit After Taxes to Net Sales*, *Depreciation to Net Sales*, and *Current Maturities of Long-Term Debt to Net Sales*. The first two measures, *Net Profit After Taxes to Net Sales* and *Depreciation to Net Sales*, relate the two elements of net cash flow (net profit and depreciation) to sales volume. (Throughout the remainder of this book, *Net Profit to Net Sales* is calculated on a pre-tax basis.) Like other operating ratios, they are expressed in percentage form. The third component of the *Debt Coverage Ratio*, current maturities of long-term debt, is also related to the level of sales, represented in Table A2-2 by a special-purpose ratio, *Current Maturities of Long-Term Debt to Net Sales*. This ratio, which is displayed as a percentage, relates the amount of debt to be repaid (a claim against net cash flow) during the next 12 months to net sales for the previous year.

Company B remains true to form: Causal factors in line with the industry standards produce a *Debt Coverage Ratio* similar to the comparison group median. In Company B's case, both of the causal ratios that have a strong influence on depreciation and current maturities of long-term debt, *Net Sales to Fixed Assets* and *Long-Term Liabilities to Total Noncurrent Assets*, are similar to the industry norms. Company C reports depreciation somewhat on the high side and current maturities of long-term debt very high in proportion to net sales. When a very low after-tax profit percentage is factored in, Company C's *Debt Coverage Ratio* is much lower than the industry norm. The comparatively high depreciation expense is traceable to low *Net Sales to Fixed Assets*. Company C's high level of current maturities of long-term debt in relation to net sales was influenced by both low *Net Sales to Fixed Assets* and high *Long-Term Liabilities to Total Noncurrent Assets*.

Company D also shows relatively low *Debt Coverage Ratio*, but the com-

Table A2-2. *Debt Coverage Ratio* **for four companies.**

	Company A	Company B	Company C	Company D
Net sales	$1,500,000	$5,000,000	$12,500,000	$50,000,000
Net profit after taxes	50,000	100,000	100,000	650,000
Depreciation	24,000	100,000	300,000	500,000
Fixed assets	124,000	500,000	1,400,000	2,450,000
Miscellaneous (other noncurrent) assets	14,000	0	510,000	550,000
Current maturities of long-term debt	18,000	75,000	390,000	650,000
Long-term liabilities	62,000	250,000	1,330,000	4,450,000
Debt Coverage Ratio (Net Profit After Taxes plus Depreciation to Current Maturities of Long-Term Debt)				
Company	4.1 times	2.7 times	1.0 times	1.8 times
Industry standard	2.5 times	2.5 times	2.5 times	2.5 times
Causal factors				
Net Profit After Taxes to Net Sales				
Company	3.3%	2.0%	0.8%	1.3%
Industry standard	2.1%	2.1%	2.1%	2.1%
Depreciation to Net Sales				
Company	1.6%	2.0%	2.4%	1.0%
Industry standard	1.9%	1.9%	1.9%	1.9%
Current Maturities of Long-Term Debt to Net Sales				
Company	1.2%	1.5%	3.1%	1.3%
Industry standard	Unknown	Unknown	Unknown	Unknown
Net Sales to Fixed Assets				
Company	12.1 times	10.0 times	8.9 times	20.4 times
Industry standard	10.3 times	10.3 times	10.3 times	10.3 times
Long-Term Liabilities to Total Noncurrent Assets				
Company	0.4 times	0.5 times	0.7 times	1.5 times
Industry standard	0.5 times	0.5 times	0.5 times	0.5 times

pany's pattern of debt coverage is actually very different. After-tax profit for
Company D was comparatively weak (although better than Company C's percent-
age), and depreciation was very low in relation to sales volume. Nevertheless,
Company D achieved a *Debt Coverage Ratio* only somewhat lower than the group

norm by holding current maturities of long-term debt to a comparatively low level of net sales. Group data for *Current Maturities of Long-Term Debt to Net Sales* are seldom published, but Company D reports a value below that of Company B, which has consistently shown a moderate financial structure. Company D's very high *Net Sales to Fixed Assets* has caused depreciation to represent a relatively small proportion of net sales. Even though Company D reports extraordinarily high *Long-Term Liabilities to Total Noncurrent Assets*, the company's extremely high utilization of fixed assets held total non-current assets to a very low level in relation to net sales. As a result, long-term liabilities (and current maturities of those liabilities) represented a comparatively small proportion of net sales. From these comparisons, we can see that the *Debt Coverage Ratio* is influenced both by net cash flow (after-tax net profit plus depreciation) and by the amount of long-term liabilities and the rate at which they come due for payment. Long-term debt is influenced by investment adequacy (*Net Sales to Net Worth*), fixed asset activity (*Net Sales to Fixed Assets*), and the amount of other noncurrent assets (such as investments in affiliated companies).

More Comprehensive Coverage Measures

Although interest expense and current maturities of long-term debt are often closely related, some companies show much higher coverage in one area than in the other. A difference in the relative position of the *Interest Coverage Ratio* versus the *Debt Coverage Ratio* may be attributable to the company's basic financial leverage, its balance between current liabilities and long-term financing, its use of interest-bearing debt versus trade payables, the maturity schedule of long-term debt versus the depreciation schedule, interest rates, and numerous other factors. To determine whether a company will have enough cash available to meet both elements of debt service—interest expense and principal repayment—various calculations have been proposed for use in credit analysis.

Unfortunately, there is no entirely accurate formula possible because interest expense is tax deductible and principal payments are not. In most calculations of this kind, principal payments are simply increased by the company's income tax rate (to account for the amount of income taxes attributable to the after-tax net profit presumably required to meet those payments). This approach ignores several important facts. Some companies can cover all current maturities of long-term debt through depreciation alone, while others must rely on after-tax profits to pay some portion of long-term debt as it comes due. In addition, some companies will have much higher net profit than principal payments; in this case, income taxes (which obviously must be paid before funds can be applied to current maturities) will be understated, and coverage will be overstated.

At this point, you may recognize that paying rent or making remittances to the leasing company can be every bit as important to a company's continued operation as interest and principal payments to the bank. To cover that situation, additional formulas have been devised. But what about other fixed costs for utilities, insurance, property taxes, or key personnel? Even more comprehensive formulas have been developed to relate (1) all revenue net of variable costs to (2) fixed costs, interest expense, and current maturities of long-term debt. Through this more comprehensive approach, such formulas include operating leverage (fixed costs in relation to variable costs) as well as financial leverage (debt in relation to equity). Some of these formulas are expressed as coverage (revenue divided by obligations), and others are stated in terms of potential revenue decline (1.0 minus the ratio of obligations to revenue).

One of the more widely publicized formulas is illustrated in Table A2-3. Especially in the case of a company that has been experiencing cash flow difficulties or is contemplating major new financing, you may find certain coverage formulas valuable in assessing the company's likelihood of encountering a cash crisis. It is important to note, however, that a company may not be faced with a default on interest or principal, even when the sum of total cash available after paying variable expenses plus noncash charges is not sufficient to meet interest, principal payments, and fixed operating costs. In reality, such a failure to meet those critical obligations (cash insolvency) will occur only if assets cannot be reduced to provide the needed funds. Although, as noted in Table A2-3, the comprehensive coverage formulas are not precisely correct, you may encounter them in dealing with major banks and other lenders that make use of extensive computer-generated calculations.

Table A2-3.   Coverage formula for four companies.

	Company A	Company B	Company C	Company D
Net sales	$1,500,000	$5,000,000	$12,500,000	$50,000,000
Variable operating costs	1,102,000	3,750,000	9,560,000	38,000,000
Fixed operating costs	304,000	1,025,000	2,340,000	10,500,000
Total operating costs	1,406,000	4,775,000	11,900,000	48,500,000
Net operating profit	94,000	225,000	600,000	1,500,000
Interest expense	18,000	75,000	450,000	550,000
Net profit before taxes	76,000	150,000	150,000	950,000
Income taxes	26,000	50,000	50,000	300,000
Net profit after taxes	$ 50,000	$ 100,000	$ 100,000	$ 650,000
Depreciation	$ 24,000	$ 100,000	$ 300,000	$ 500,000
Current maturities of long-term debt	18,000	75,000	390,000	650,000

Formula:

Percentage Decline in Total Revenue Possible While Maintaining Ability to Cover Interest Expense, Current Maturities of Long-Term Debt, and Fixed Operating Costs (Critical Revenue Decline Percentage)

$$\left[1 - \left(\cfrac{\cfrac{\text{Fixed}}{\text{Costs}} - \text{Depreciation} + \cfrac{\text{Interest}}{\text{Expense}} + \cfrac{\text{Current Maturities}}{(1 - \text{Marginal Tax Rate})}}{\text{Net Sales} \times \text{Contribution Margin*}} \right) \right] \times 100$$

Company A: $\left[1 - \left(\cfrac{304{,}000 - 24{,}000 + 18{,}000 + \left(\cfrac{18{,}000}{1.00 - 0.40} \right)}{1{,}500{,}000 \times 0.265} \right) \right] \times 100 = 17.5\%$

Company B: $\left[1 - \left(\cfrac{1{,}025{,}000 - 100{,}000 + 75{,}000 + \left(\cfrac{75{,}000}{1.00 - 0.40} \right)}{5{,}000{,}000 \times 0.250} \right) \right] \times 100 = 10.0\%$

Company C: $\left[1 - \left(\cfrac{2{,}340{,}000 - 300{,}000 + 450{,}000 + \left(\cfrac{390{,}000}{1.00 - 0.40} \right)}{12{,}500{,}000 \times 0.235} \right) \right] \times 100 = \dagger$

Company D: $\left[1 - \left(\cfrac{10{,}500{,}000 - 500{,}000 + 550{,}000 + \left(\cfrac{650{,}000}{1.00 - 0.40} \right)}{50{,}000{,}000 \times 0.240} \right) \right] \times 100 = 3.0\%$

*Contribution Margin $= 1 - \dfrac{\text{Variable Operating Costs}}{\text{Net Sales}}$

For further details, see Appendix B2, "Break-Even Analysis."

†This formula, used by some banking institutions to evaluate debt service, indicates that Company C is currently unable to cover fixed operating costs plus interest and principal payments although the firm actually has very thin positive coverage. The error is attributable to the assumption in the formula that current maturities of long-term debt must be covered entirely from after-tax profit, when, as a practical matter, the cash to meet principal payments is provided by depreciation as well as after-tax earnings. Consequently, the amount of calculated income tax liability, $260,000, attributable to the presumed after-tax profit required for coverage of current maturities is significantly higher than the actual amount, $50,000, paid by Company C.

Note: The net sales amount is not necessarily equal to cash revenue; however, because this formula is ordinarily generated from financial statement data, net sales is used as the input.

Summary: Interest Coverage Ratio (Net Profit Before Taxes plus Interest Expense to Interest Expense)

Popular names   *Interest Coverage Ratio*; *EBIT (Earnings Before Interest and Taxes) to Interest Ratio*

Purpose   Measures a company's margin of safety in covering interest expense from pre-interest and pre-tax earnings.

Calculation   Add net profit before taxes and interest expense, then divide the sum by interest expense.

Example   Your company's net profit before taxes was $30,000, and your interest expense was $15,000, during your last fiscal year. What was your *Interest Coverage Ratio*?

	Solution: 30,000 + 15,000 = 45,000; then 45,000 ÷ 15,000 = 3.0
Financial impact	A *high* ratio is a *favorable* condition from a conservative perspective: It indicates a comparatively great margin of safety for payment of interest expense from profitable business operations.
Operational impact	A *high* ratio tends to reduce the risk of failing to meet interest payments as they come due, increases operating freedom, and lowers the probability of disadvantageous changes in credit terms.
Critical values	A ratio *less* than 1.0 shows a pre-tax net loss after interest expense. A *negative* ratio shows a net loss before interest expense. In such cases, interest payments are met by diverting cash available from depreciation (a noncash charge), reducing total assets, or increasing current liabilities.
Range of common experience	2.3 times to 3.3 times.

Summary: Debt Coverage Ratio (Net Profit After Taxes plus Depreciation to Current Maturities of Long-Term Debt)

Popular names	*Debt Coverage Ratio*; *Net Cash Flow Sufficiency Ratio*
Purpose	Measures a company's margin of safety in covering the portion of long-term debt due within 12 months from net cash flow (after-tax net profit plus depreciation).
Calculation	Add net profit after taxes and depreciation, then divide the sum by current maturities of long-term debt.
Example	Your company's net profit after taxes was $20,000 and your depreciation was $20,000 during the year; your current maturities of long-term debt were $15,000 at year-end. What was your *Debt Coverage Ratio*?
	Solution: 20,000 + 20,000 = 40,000; then 40,000 ÷ 15,000 = 2.7
Financial impact	A *high* ratio is a *favorable* condition from a conservative perspective: It indicates a comparatively great margin of safety for repayment of debt principal from net cash flow.
Operational impact	A *high* ratio tends to reduce the risk of failing to meet principal payments on long-term debt and thereby increases operating freedom.

Critical values

A ratio *less* than 1.0 shows that net cash flow for the past year was insufficient to cover principal payments on long-term debt scheduled for the next 12 months. A *negative* ratio shows a net loss before depreciation expense, indicating that cash outflow was greater than cash inflow. In such a case, current maturities of long-term debt are met by reducing total assets, increasing other current liabilities, or refinancing debt on a long-term basis.

Range of common experience

2.0 times to 3.1 times.

Appendix A3

The Influence of Financial Leverage on Return on Equity

In the analysis of most closely held companies, financial leverage is appropriately defined as a company's mix of *non-interest-bearing liabilities* (such as trade credit and accrued expenses) plus *interest-bearing debt* (including mortgages and bank credit lines) in relation to its *net worth* (owners' equity). The use of other people's money is intended to enable owners to boost their return on invested capital. That objective is achieved when pre-tax *Net Profit to Net Worth* is higher than pre-tax *Net Profit plus Interest Expense to Total Assets* (a variant of *Net Profit to Total Assets*).

To evaluate this influence of financial leverage, interest expense is added back to pre-tax net profit, and the sum is divided by total assets to obtain pre-tax *Net Profit plus Interest Expense to Total Assets*. This ratio is expressed in percentage form. The resulting measure indicates the amount of profit earned relative to total assets *before* considering the amount (or cost) of borrowed funds. In effect, this ratio shows the percentage return that the owners would receive on their investment if the company had no liabilities whatsoever. On the other hand, the pre-tax *Net Profit to Net Worth* is calculated *after* deducting interest expense because, as a practical matter, interest must be paid before owners can obtain a return on their investment. If the owners earn a higher percentage on their investment after paying interest on borrowed funds than they would have received without using other people's money, then the strategy has been successful in terms of financial return to the owners. In other words, when pre-tax return on equity *after* interest expense is higher than pre-tax return on assets *before* deducting interest expense, a company is using its financial leverage (summarized by *Total Liabilities to Net Worth*) to increase profit for owners. The company's risk of financial difficulty or restrictions on management freedom as a result of such borrowing has, however, not been considered in this relationship.

Comparing a company's pre-tax *Net Profit to Net Worth* (after interest expense) with its pre-tax *Net Profit plus Interest Expense to Total Assets* shows whether the business's basic operating pattern and financial structure—particularly its debt-to-worth relationship and management's ability to strike a proper balance between trade credit and interest-bearing debt—have made a positive contribution to the percentage of pre-tax profit earned on each dollar of owners' equity (net worth). By using funds from outside sources (whether in the form of trade credit or borrowed money) to support sales volume, a company may boost its *Net Profit to Net Worth* above the percentage that would have been achieved by employing only the investment by owners (their original investment plus retained earnings). On the other hand, incurring a large amount of interest-bearing debt in proportion to owners' equity can, under the wrong circumstances, produce the opposite result: a lower *Net Profit to Net Worth*, and even outright losses, from burdensome interest payments, particularly in the event of a sudden rise in interest rates. If the company's debt is fixed in nature (as in the case of borrowing for a plant expansion, equipment modernization, or a leveraged buyout), a decline in sales volume from reduced customer demand or increased price competition can turn a leverage advantage into an interest-cost handicap that drags down operating profit, diminishes *Net Profit to Net Worth,* and perhaps threatens the company's very existence through major losses.

Even when debt is more flexible, such as a line of credit which is used only for sales peaks, great reliance on borrowed funds can put a company in a difficult position if interest rates rise sharply. In this situation, management must choose between allowing high interest costs to penalize *Net Profit to Net Worth* or reducing sales, thereby losing both market share and the advantage of spreading fixed costs over higher sales volume. Break-even analysis (as described in Appendix B2) would be helpful in making the best choice between these two undesirable alternatives, but the important point is that a less leveraged company would not face that trade-off. During periods of lower interest rates, however, the more highly leveraged company may enjoy an advantage with respect to *Net Profit to Net Worth*—assuming that a reasonable *Net Profit to Net Sales* can be maintained in the industry during times of lower demand. There is a saying in financial analysis: On the one hand there's the other hand. Trade-offs are inherent in financial strategy; when conditions change, the desirability of one position versus another is rapidly reversed. For that reason, the middle-of-the-road position is frequently most favorable for small and medium-size companies—those companies that have little control over competitive prices and are unable to obtain advantageous interest rates.

Table A3-1 shows that all four of our familiar companies, A, B, C, and D, have made positive use of outside funds to increase *Net Profit to Net Worth*. In the case of Company C, the relationship between pre-tax *Net Profit to Net Worth* and pre-tax *Net Profit plus Interest Expense to Total Assets* is only marginally favorable because of comparatively high interest expense. As we found earlier, Company C's interest burden is traceable to poor asset utilization (low *Net Sales to Total Assets*) combined with relatively low investment adequacy (high *Net Sales to Net Worth*). On the other hand, Company D's shareholders have profited greatly (at least in the short run) from the use of outside funds to boost *Net Profit to Net Worth* far above *Net Profit plus Interest Expense to Total Assets.* Although

Table A3-1.   Financial leverage and return on equity.

	Company A	Company B	Company C	Company D
Net sales	$1,500,000	$5,000,000	$12,500,000	$50,000,000
Net profit	76,000	150,000	150,000	950,000
Total assets	536,000	2,000,000	6,650,000	11,400,000
Net worth	254,000	750,000	1,540,000	1,550,000
Interest expense	18,000	75,000	450,000	550,000
Net Profit to Net Worth				
Company	29.9%	20.0%	9.7%	61.3%
Industry standard	21.6%	21.6%	21.6%	21.6%
Net Profit plus Interest				
Expense to Total Assets				
Company	17.5%	11.3%	9.0%	13.2%
Industry standard	12.0%	12.0%	12.0%	12.0%
Total Liabilities				
to Net Worth				
Company	1.1 times	1.7 times	3.3 times	6.4 times
Industry standard	1.8 times	1.8 times	1.8 times	1.8 times
Net Sales to Total Assets				
Company	2.8 times	2.5 times	1.9 times	4.4 times
Industry standard	2.4 times	2.4 times	2.4 times	2.4 times
Net Sales to Net Worth				
Company	5.9 times	6.7 times	8.1 times	32.3 times
Industry standard	6.8 times	6.8 times	6.8 times	6.8 times

Note: The profit ratios, *Net Profit to Net Worth* and *Net Profit plus Interest Expense to Total Assets,* are calculated on a pre-tax basis. For reasons explained in Chapter 3, net profit before income taxes is ordinarily the most useful benchmark for analyzing the operating performance of privately held companies. Consequently, pre-tax net profit percentages are displayed throughout this book, except as specifically noted in special applications, such as debt coverage, net cash flow, or sustainable growth. *Net Profit plus Interest Expense to Total Assets* is a variant of the secondary ratio *Net Profit to Total Assets.*

both Company C and Company D show very high *Total Liabilities to Net Worth*, Company D actually has a low level of interest-bearing debt in relation to net sales because of very high *Net Sales to Total Assets*. Consequently, Company D is able to obtain maximum benefit from financial leverage with respect to *Net Profit to Net Worth*. At the same time, Company D's extremely high *Total Liabilities to Net Worth* (due to very low investment adequacy, shown by very high *Net Sales to Net Worth*) makes the future of the business vulnerable to the decisions of creditors.

As we learned in our study of the key secondary measures in Part III, *Total Liabilities to Net Worth* indicates the extent to which a company has used outside funds (both trade credit and interest-bearing debt) in an attempt to increase its *Net Profit to Net Worth*. A relatively high ratio shows a comparatively great reliance on money from other sources versus owners' investment (net worth). As this ratio is increased, the risk of creditor pressure or potential failure to cover obligations tends to rise.

This book emphasizes the comparative position of a company with respect to the key financial factors. The starting point for obtaining a relatively favorable *Net Profit to Net Worth* while maintaining a moderate or favorable debt-to-equity structure (reflected in *Total Liabilities to Net Worth*) is a favorable pre-tax *Net Profit plus Interest Expense to Total Assets*.

Effect of Owners' Compensation

It is important to recognize that officers'/owners' compensation has a major impact on pre-tax net profit. In fact, when officers'/owners' compensation is taken into account, the relationship between pre-tax *Net Profit to Net Worth* and pre-tax *Net Profit plus Interest Expense to Total Assets* can change dramatically. In extreme cases, an increase in officers'/owners' compensation can cause a pre-tax net loss (after deducting interest expense), leading to the possibly erroneous conclusion that the company's financial strategy is highly unfavorable. To evaluate a company's situation with respect to the influence of *Total Liabilities to Net Worth* on *Net Profit to Net Worth*, it is useful to increase pre-tax net profit by the amount of officers'/owners' compensation and then compute *Net Profit plus Interest Expense to Total Assets* and *Net Profit to Net Worth* (after deducting interest expense). Following this adjustment, the achievement of *Net Profit to Net Worth* higher than *Net Profit plus Interest Expense to Total Assets* shows a positive result with respect to increasing the percentage of profit generated on owners' investment through the use of outside funds.

Some financial publications suggest that interest-bearing funds should not be used to support company operations when the interest rate charged by lenders exceeds the company's pre-tax *Net Profit plus Interest Expense to Total Assets*. Before reaching that conclusion, however, other factors must be taken into account. Additional trade credit or other non-interest-bearing funds may be obtained as a result of incurring additional interest-bearing debt. For example, accounts payable may be increased to support a larger amount of inventory at the same time that bank borrowing is used to carry a higher level of accounts receivable. In that case, the effective cost of borrowed funds is the amount of interest paid on the new interest-bearing debt divided by the total amount of new liabilities: both interest-bearing funds and "free" money.

Companies often incur interest-bearing debt for long-term purposes, such as modernization or expansion designed to improve market share or to reduce expense percentages over a period of several years, rather than to achieve an immediate rise in *Net Profit to Net Worth*. A narrowly focused, short-term analysis of the relationship between pre-tax *Net Profit to Net Worth* and *Net Profit plus Interest Expense to Total Assets* might discourage investment in an otherwise profitable long-term strategy. In strategic planning, management must consider all major elements of financial structure, including asset utilization, investment adequacy, and working capital sufficiency, as well as the competitive environment in which the company operates. Analysis of the relationship between

Net Profit to Net Worth and *Net Profit plus Interest Expense to Total Assets* requires judgment, not simplistic calculations of a single formula. Nevertheless, the comparisons described above are helpful to management in considering whether profit as a proportion of net worth can be safely increased by changing the company's operating pattern and its basic financial structure.

We have, of course, been analyzing *Net Profit to Net Worth* by means of accounting procedures, relating profit after depreciation to the amount of net worth shown on the balance sheet. In most cases, restating net worth to reflect the market value of fixed assets would result in a larger denominator (net worth) and, consequently, a lower percentage return. The actual market value of a 100% ownership share of the company might also substantially exceed the book value of owners' equity. Such differences between net worth as shown on the books and actual market value should be borne in mind when comparing a company's *Net Profit to Net Worth* based on accounting data with alternative investment opportunities.

Effect of Financial Leverage and Interest Rates

An illustration of the effect of financial leverage and interest rates on *Net Profit plus Interest Expense to Total Assets* and *Net Profit to Net Worth* is given in Table A3-2 and Table A3-3, which show selected financial data and key financial ratios for Company P. Within the three-year period from the end of Year 1 through the end of Year 4, a combination of strong demand and price inflation caused many companies in the industry to experience rapid growth in sales volume—approximately 25% per year. At the same time, the annual interest rates to small borrowers jumped from 10% to 20%. Although we can hope that such situations

Table A3-2. Selected financial data for Company P over four years.

	Year 1	Year 2	Year 3	Year 4
Net sales	$10,000,000	$12,500,000	$16,000,000	$20,000,000
Net profit before interest expense	450,000	600,000	800,000	1,000,000
Interest expense	150,000	200,000	400,000	700,000
Net profit before taxes	300,000	400,000	400,000	300,000
Total assets	4,000,000	5,000,000	6,400,000	8,000,000
Interest-bearing debt	1,500,000	2,000,000	2,650,000	3,500,000
Total liabilities	2,500,000	3,250,000	4,400,000	5,800,000
Net worth	1,500,000	1,750,000	2,000,000	2,200,000

Table A3-3. Key financial ratios for Company P over four years.

	Year 1	Year 2	Year 3	Year 4
Primary (causal) ratios				
Net Profit				
to Net Sales	3.0%	3.2%	2.5%	1.5%
Net Sales				
to Total Assets	2.5 times	2.5 times	2.5 times	2.5 times
Net Sales				
to Net Worth	6.7 times	7.1 times	8.0 times	9.1 times
Secondary (effect) ratios				
Net Profit plus Interest Expense				
to Total Assets	11.3%	12.0%	12.5%	12.5%
Net Profit				
to Net Worth	20.0%	22.9%	20.0%	13.6%
Total Liabilities				
to Net Worth	1.7 times	1.9 times	2.2 times	2.6 times

Note: The profit ratios, *Net Profit to Net Sales, Net Profit plus Interest Expense to Total Assets,* and *Net Profit to Net Worth,* are calculated on a pre-tax basis. For reasons explained in Chapter 3, net profit before income taxes is ordinarily the most useful benchmark for analyzing the operating performance of privately held companies. Consequently, pre-tax net profit percentages are displayed throughout this book, except as specifically noted in special applications, such as debt coverage, net cash flow, or sustainable growth. *Net Profit plus Interest Expense to Total Assets* is a variant of the secondary ratio *Net Profit to Total Assets.*

will remain rare, businesspeople who rode the economic roller coaster of the late 1970s and early 1980s will recognize the example as an accurate representation of that period.

Company P, which ended Year 1 in a moderately profitable and moderately leveraged position, had reason to enjoy the surge of business in Year 2, particularly since interest rates remained stable at 10%. As shown in Table A3-3, both pre-tax *Net Profit plus Interest Expense to Total Assets* and pre-tax *Net Profit to Net Worth* moved upward, due to a small rise in *Net Profit to Net Sales.* The substantial positive spread between *Net Profit to Net Worth* and *Net Profit plus Interest Expense to Total Assets* demonstrates that financial leverage was helping shareholders to receive a higher rate of return on their invested capital. In Year 3, a jump in interest rates from 10% to 15% caused a small decline in *Net Profit to Net Worth* despite a rise in *Total Liabilities to Net Worth.* Pre-tax *Net Profit plus Interest Expense to Total Assets* had increased during Year 3, but the effect of higher interest rates pushed down pre-tax *Net Profit to Net Worth* to Year 1 levels.

A further climb in interest rates to 20% in Year 4 caused a substantial plunge in *Net Profit to Net Worth* despite—or actually because of—a continued rise in *Total Liabilities to Net Worth.* Company P's basic operating efficiency in relation to total assets remained strong; in fact, *Net Profit plus Interest Expense to Total Assets* held at a solid 12.5%. Nevertheless, extremely high interest rates caused shareholders of Company P to earn only 13.6% on the book value of owners' equity while money market funds and other passive investments were at far higher yields. On balance, however, the shareholders of Company P did receive a small boost from financial leverage. Because of the mix of non-interest-bearing liabilities in the company's financial structure, pre-tax *Net Profit to Net Worth* was still slightly higher than pre-tax *Net Profit plus Interest Expense to Total Assets*.

Financial data and key ratios for Company Q, a more highly leveraged business, are displayed in Tables A3-4 and A3-5. Company Q's basic strategy had been one of steady investment in modern facilities and carrying a large work-in-process inventory as a result of relatively complex production. Reflecting that strategy, the company's *Net Sales to Total Assets* was comparatively low. Combined with investment adequacy on the low side in relation to sales volume (high *Net Sales to Net Worth*), low *Net Sales to Total Assets* resulted in high *Total Liabilities to Net Worth* at the end of Year 1. Although Company Q's pre-tax *Net Profit plus Interest Expense to Total Assets* was very close to that of Company P, Company Q's higher *Total Liabilities to Net Worth* produced a superior pre-tax *Net Profit to Net Worth*: 24.0% versus 20.0%. During Year 2, with rapid sales growth and stable interest rates, Company Q attained even higher *Net Profit to Net Worth*, thanks to a combination of higher *Net Profit plus Interest Expense to Total Assets* and higher *Total Liabilities to Net Worth*.

In Year 3, however, the increase in interest rates drove Company Q's pre-tax *Net Profit to Net Worth* down below Year 1 results and below Company P's percentage. Both companies reported identical pre-tax *Net Profit plus Interest Expense to Total Assets* ratios, but at a 15% rate of interest, Company Q's high proportion of interest-bearing debt acted as a drag on *Net Profit to Net Worth*. Nevertheless, with a mixture of non-interest-bearing liabilities in its total financial structure, Company Q showed a positive spread between pre-tax *Net Profit to Net Worth* and pre-tax *Net Profit plus Interest Expense to Total Assets*, again providing a higher return to owners from the use of outside funds. Year 4, on the

Table A3-4.   Selected financial data for Company Q over four years.

	Year 1	Year 2	Year 3	Year 4
Net sales	$10,000,000	$12,500,000	$16,000,000	$20,000,000
Net profit				
before interest				
expense	600,000	780,000	1,050,000	1,310,000
Interest expense	300,000	380,000	750,000	1,300,000
Net profit before taxes	300,000	400,000	300,000	10,000
Total assets	5,250,000	6,550,000	8,400,000	10,500,000
Interest-bearing debt	3,000,000	3,800,000	5,000,000	6,500,000
Total liabilities	4,000,000	5,050,000	6,700,000	8,800,000
Net worth	1,250,000	1,500,000	1,700,000	1,700,000

Table A3-5.   Key financial ratios for Company Q over four years.

	Year 1	Year 2	Year 3	Year 4
Primary (causal) ratios				
Net Profit				
to Net Sales	3.0%	3.2%	1.9%	0.1%
Net Sales				
to Total Assets	1.9 times	1.9 times	1.9 times	1.9 times
Net Sales				
to Net Worth	8.0 times	8.3 times	9.4 times	11.8 times
Secondary (effect) ratios				
Net Profit plus Interest Expense				
to Total Assets	11.4%	11.9%	12.5%	12.5%
Net Profit				
to Net Worth	24.0%	26.7%	17.6%	0.6%
Total Liabilities				
to Net Worth	3.2 times	3.4 times	3.9 times	5.2 times

Note: The profit ratios, *Net Profit to Net Sales, Net Profit plus Interest Expense to Total Assets,* and *Net Profit to Net Worth,* are calculated on a pre-tax basis. For reasons explained in Chapter 3, net profit before income taxes is ordinarily the most useful benchmark for analyzing the operating performance of privately held companies. Consequently, pre-tax net profit percentages are displayed throughout this book, except as specifically noted in special applications, such as debt coverage, net cash flow, or sustainable growth. *Net Profit plus Interest Expense to Total Assets* is a variant of the secondary ratio *Net Profit to Total Assets.*

other hand, illustrates the danger of a highly leveraged situation. The rise in interest rates to 20%, coupled with a further increase of Company Q's comparatively high *Total Liabilities to Net Worth,* caused interest costs to depress *Net Profit to Net Sales* to nearly zero. Consequently, Company Q's *Net Profit to Net Worth* was barely positive, even with *Net Profit plus Interest Expense to Total Assets* standing at the highest point in the company's history. Company Q was actually fortunate to maintain a solid net profit before interest expense by virtue of comparatively low operating costs as a percentage of net sales. A company with a similar financial structure and lower earnings before interest and taxes would have been plunged into a net loss condition by the rise in interest rates.

Higher Asset Utilization as an Option

Improving asset utilization, thereby increasing *Net Sales to Total Assets,* offers management the option of lowering *Total Liabilities to Net Worth* and reducing interest costs or increasing *Net Sales to Net Worth* as a strategy for boosting *Net Profit to Net Worth.*

Table A3-6 illustrates two alternative strategies, with respect to *Total Liabilities to Net Worth,* for a company with superior *Net Sales to Total Assets.* Company ABC holds its *Interest Expense to Net Sales* (a commonly published operating ratio calculated by dividing interest expense by net sales) to the industry

Table A3-6. *Total Liabilities to Net Worth:* **Two alternative strategies.**

	Typical company	Company ABC	Company XYZ
Net sales	$1,000,000	$1,000,000	$1,000,000
Net profit	40,000	40,000	46,000
Total assets	500,000	400,000	400,000
Total liabilities	300,000	300,000	240,000
Net worth	200,000	100,000	160,000
Non-interest-bearing debt	$ 120,000	$ 120,000	$ 120,000
Interest-bearing debt	180,000	180,000	120,000
Interest expense	18,000	18,000	12,000
Total Liabilities to Net Worth			
Company	1.5 times	3.0 times	1.5 times
Industry standard	1.5 times	1.5 times	1.5 times
Net Sales to Total Assets			
Company	2.0 times	2.5 times	2.5 times
Industry standard	2.0 times	2.0 times	2.0 times
Interest Expense to Net Sales			
Company	1.8%	1.8%	1.2%
Industry standard	1.8%	1.8%	1.8%
Net Profit to Net Worth			
Company	20.0%	40.0%	28.8%
Industry standard	20.0%	20.0%	20.0%

norm, despite *Total Liabilities to Net Worth* twice as high as the industry standard. This somewhat surprising finding is traceable to the company's relatively high *Net Sales to Total Assets.* For small and mid-size businesses that do not command the attention of the financial press, interest rates generally fall within a very narrow range regardless of a company's *Total Liabilities to Net Worth* (which might be expected to affect the interest rate because it indicates the degree of creditor exposure to potential writedowns of assets).

Company XYZ has chosen to use the comparative advantage of its relatively high *Net Sales to Total Assets* to reduce both total liabilities and net worth by maintaining *Total Liabilities to Net Worth* in line with typical industry practice. As a result, Company XYZ's *Interest Expense to Net Sales* is well below the industry norm. Company XYZ's interest-bearing debt is substantially less than that of Company ABC, because the level of non-interest-bearing liabilities is the same for both businesses while Company XYZ's total liabilities are lower than those of Company ABC. Nevertheless, Company XYZ's strategy of using superior asset utilization to hold net worth to a very low level in relation to net sales produced an outstanding *Net Profit to Net Worth.*

It is important to note, however, that Company ABC's *Total Liabilities to Net Worth* is unusually high and that the company must maintain its comparatively high *Net Sales to Total Assets* in order to avoid bill-paying difficulty. Company

XYZ's *Net Profit to Net Worth* was higher than the norm, but management did not take full advantage of its outstanding asset utilization, which was equal to that of Company ABC. A company that is able to maintain *Net Sales to Total Assets* well above the industry standard can ordinarily allow the *Total Liabilities to Net Worth* ratio to exceed the norm to some degree in order to boost *Net Profit to Net Worth*.

Factors Affecting Financial Leverage and Return on Equity

We have seen throughout this book that financial leverage (measured by *Total Liabilities to Net Worth*) of most privately held businesses is not primarily the result of attempts to optimize capital structure or attain a specific financial goal. Far more often, *Total Liabilities to Net Worth* simply reflects the interaction of underlying causal factors: asset utilization (*Net Sales to Total Assets*) and investment adequacy (*Net Sales to Net Worth*), influenced by profitability (*Net Profit to Net Sales*).

Nevertheless, the current emphasis on financial leverage in management publications suggests that the relationship between *Total Liabilities to Net Worth* and *Net Profit to Net Worth* should be evaluated from that perspective. To do so, we can review selected financial ratios for Companies A, B, C, and D in Table A3-7, which presents two viewpoints of *Net Profit to Net Worth*. The causal factors, *Net Profit to Net Sales* and *Net Sales to Net Worth*, whose influence we examined in Chapter 12, are redisplayed in Table A3-7 as they appeared in Table 12-1. In addition, Table A3-7 includes an alternative view of causality with respect to *Net Profit to Net Worth*. This perspective assumes that financial leverage (*Total Liabilities to Net Worth*) is managed by company decision makers to such an extent that it can be considered a causal influence on *Net Profit to Net Worth*. For this analysis, *Net Profit to Total Assets*, a secondary ratio that interacts with *Total Liabilities to Net Worth* to produce *Net Profit to Net Worth*, is also displayed. The standard *Return on Assets Ratio*, *Net Profit to Total Assets*, is used in this analysis of *Net Profit to Net Worth*, which is based on the Du Pont formula (described in detail in Appendix A4). As we know from our review of Chapter 20, *Net Profit to Total Assets* is calculated on pre-tax net profit *after* interest expense has been subtracted. Because the causal ratio *Net Sales to Total Assets* is a primary determinant of both *Total Liabilities to Net Worth* and *Net Profit to Total Assets*, this key factor is included, as well.

In Table A3-7, we find that Company A has gained its advantageous *Net Profit to Net Worth* from superior *Net Profit to Total Assets*, which more than offsets the effect of the company's relatively low *Total Liabilities to Net Worth*. As we have learned, low *Total Liabilities to Net Worth*—indicating low debt pressure in relation to the capital of the owners—is regarded as a favorable factor from a conservative point of view, but tends to hold down *Net Profit to Net Worth*. Company A's relatively high *Net Profit to Total Assets* was traceable to

Table A3-7.   Two perspectives on *Net Profit to Net Worth*.

	Company A	Company B	Company C	Company D
Net sales	$1,500,000	$5,000,000	$12,500,000	$50,000,000
Net profit	76,000	150,000	150,000	950,000
Total assets	536,000	2,000,000	6,650,000	11,400,000
Net worth	254,000	750,000	1,540,000	1,550,000
Net Profit to Net Worth				
Company	29.9%	20.0%	9.7%	61.3%
Industry standard	21.6%	21.6%	21.6%	21.6%
Causal factors				
Net Profit to Net Sales				
Company	5.1%	3.0%	1.2%	1.9%
Industry standard	3.2%	3.2%	3.2%	3.2%
Net Sales to Net Worth				
Company	5.9 times	6.7 times	8.1 times	32.3 times
Industry standard	6.8 times	6.8 times	6.8 times	6.8 times
Causal factors: Another *viewpoint*				
Total Liabilities *to Net Worth*				
Company	1.1 times	1.7 times	3.3 times	6.4 times
Industry standard	1.8 times	1.8 times	1.8 times	1.8 times
Net Profit to Total Assets				
Company	14.2%	7.5%	2.3%	8.3%
Industry standard	7.7%	7.7%	7.7%	7.7%
Net Sales to Total Assets				
Company	2.8 times	2.5 times	1.9 times	4.4 times
Industry standard	2.4 times	2.4 times	2.4 times	2.4 times

Note: The secondary ratio *Net Profit to Total Assets* (described in Chapter 20) is used in this analysis of *Net Profit to Net Worth*. It is important to distinguish this ratio, which is calculated on pre-tax net profit *after* interest expense has been subtracted, from pre-tax *Net Profit plus Interest Expense to Total Assets* displayed in the previous tables in this Appendix.

two favorable factors: comparatively high *Net Profit to Net Sales* and *Net Sales to Total Assets* above the industry norm. *Net Profit to Total Assets*, a secondary ratio, is fully described in Chapter 20.

True to form, Company B shows moderate *Net Profit to Net Worth* as a direct result of moderate *Net Profit to Total Assets* (due to moderate *Net Profit to Net Sales* and moderate *Net Sales to Total Assets*) and moderate *Total Liabilities to Net Worth*.

Company C's comparatively low *Net Profit to Net Worth* is traceable to its very low *Net Profit to Total Assets*. *Total Liabilities to Net Worth* is substantially higher than the industry norm, indicating relatively great debt pressure (and consequent strain on management), but this financial leverage is not sufficient to produce a *Net Profit to Net Worth* equal to the group norm. Relatively low *Net Profit to Total Assets* (attributable to comparatively low *Net Profit to Net Sales* and *Net Sales to Total Assets* on the low side) has the effect of depressing *Net Profit to Net Worth*.

Company D's extremely high *Net Profit to Net Worth* reflects both *Net Profit to Total Assets* somewhat above the group norm and very high financial leverage, that is, very high *Total Liabilities to Net Worth*. To obtain *Net Profit to Net Worth* from these two ratios, multiply *Net Profit to Total Assets* by the sum of *Total Liabilities to Net Worth* plus 1.0. For example, Company D's *Total Liabilities to Net Worth*, at 6.4, plus 1.0 equals 7.4; 8.3% times 7.4 equals 61.3% (after allowance for differences due to rounding). Company D's proportionate relationship between net worth and total assets was 1.0 to 7.4 (6.4 in total liabilities and 1.0 in net worth). Thus, *Net Profit to Total Assets* of 8.3% is multiplied by 7.4 (*Total Liabilities to Net Worth* of 6.4 plus 1.0 for the net worth portion of total assets) to yield *Net Profit to Net Worth* of 61.3%.

Summary: Net Profit plus Interest Expense to Total Assets

Popular name	*Pre-Interest Return on Assets*
Purpose	Measures a company's ability to produce profit on assets employed, before considering the effect of interest expense, which is traceable to *investment adequacy* and *financial leverage*, as well as *asset utilization*.
Calculation	Add pre-tax net profit and interest expense, then divide the sum by total assets; multiply result by 100, converting ratio to a percentage.
Example	Your company's pre-tax net profit was $30,000 and your interest expense was $20,000 for the year; your total assets were $400,000 at year-end. What was your *Net Profit plus Interest Expense to Total Assets?*
	Solution: pre-tax net profit plus interest expense = 30,000 + 20,000 = 50,000; then 50,000 ÷ 400,000 = .125; then .125 × 100 = 12.5%
Financial impact	A *high* ratio is a *favorable* result: It indicates a comparatively high rate of return, before interest expense, on assets employed and tends to increase *return on equity*.
Operational impact	A *high* ratio tends to reduce interest cost over time.
Definition	Net profit *before taxes* plus interest expense is used as the basis for measuring comparative profitability (versus *Net Profit to Net Worth*, previous performance, or external standards).
Special reminder	Net profit plus interest expense is expressed as a percentage, not as a simple ratio, relative to total assets.

Critical value   A negative percentage shows that combined operating
                          activities and asset management resulted in a net loss
                          before subtracting interest expense. In such a case, *Net
                          Profit to Net Worth* for the period will necessarily be
                          negative.

Range of common   Insufficient industry data.
experience

Appendix A4

Return on Investment: The Du Pont Formula

A method of considering the ratio relationship between operating profit, asset utilization, and financial leverage was popularized by the Du Pont organization (E. I. Du Pont de Nemours and Company) approximately 40 years ago, and variations have proliferated since that time. In its simplest form, the "Du Pont formula" is stated as: *Net Profit to Net Sales* multiplied by *Net Sales to Total Assets* multiplied by *Total Assets to Net Worth* equals *Net Profit to Net Worth*. This formula says, in effect, that *Net Profit to Net Worth* can be increased by raising return on sales, asset utilization, and/or financial leverage. *Total Assets to Net Worth*, used to represent financial leverage in the Du Pont formula, is simply a variation of *Total Liabilities to Net Worth*, but this alternative measure makes the formula easier to calculate. *Total Assets to Net Worth* can be quickly derived by adding 1.0 to *Total Liabilities to Net Worth*; a debt-to-equity ratio of 1.7 converts to an assets-to-equity ratio of 2.7. In the case of Company B, shown in Table A4-1, *Net Profit to Net Sales* of 3.0% times *Net Sales to Total Assets* of 2.5 multiplied by *Total Assets to Net Worth* of 2.7 (the sum of *Total Liabilities to Net Worth* of 1.7 plus 1.0) yields *Net Profit to Net Worth* of 20.3%. This percentage is not identical to the actual 20.0% value for Company B's *Net Profit to Net Worth*, owing to rounding. If *Total Liabilities to Net Worth* had been expressed to one more decimal place (1.67 instead of 1.7), the rounded percentage for *Net Profit to Net Worth* would have been 20.0%.

For the purpose of comparing divisional performance, the Du Pont Company recommended using gross assets (total assets with fixed assets stated at original cost instead of depreciated value) on the theory that the original investment in fixed assets should be recovered through depreciation. Regardless of the merit of this debatable premise, almost all present applications of the Du Pont formula use net (book) value of total assets and the net value of owners' equity in its computation.

A Drawback

One major drawback of the Du Pont formula is its assumption that financial leverage is purposefully directed by company management. While large corpora-

Table A4-1. The Du Pont formula and key financial ratios for four companies.

	Company A	Company B	Company C	Company D
Net sales	$1,500,000	$5,000,000	$12,500,000	$50,000,000
Net profit before taxes	76,000	150,000	150,000	950,000
Total assets	536,000	2,000,000	6,650,000	11,400,000
Total liabilities	282,000	1,250,000	5,110,000	9,850,000
Net worth	254,000	750,000	1,540,000	1,550,000

Causal ratios

	Company A	Company B	Company C	Company D
Net Profit to Net Sales	5.1%	3.0%	1.2%	1.9%
Net Sales to Total Assets	2.8 times	2.5 times	1.9 times	4.4 times
Net Sales to Net Worth	5.9 times	6.7 times	8.1 times	32.3 times

Secondary (effect) ratios

	Company A	Company B	Company C	Company D
Total Liabilities to Net Worth	1.1 times	1.7 times	3.3 times	6.4 times
Net Profit to Net Worth	29.9%	20.0%	9.7%	61.3%

Formula:

$$\frac{\text{Net Profit}}{\text{Net Sales}} \times \frac{\text{Net Sales}}{\text{Total Assets}} \times \frac{\text{Total Liabilities}}{\text{Net Worth}} + 1 = \frac{\text{Net Profit}}{\text{Net Worth}}$$

Calculation:

Company A	$5.1 \times 2.8 \times (1.1 + 1) = 30.0\%$
Company B	$3.0 \times 2.5 \times (1.7 + 1) = 20.3\%$
Company C	$1.2 \times 1.9 \times (3.3 + 1) = 9.8\%$
Company D	$1.9 \times 4.4 \times (6.4 + 1) = 61.9\%$
Industry standard	$3.2 \times 2.4 \times (1.8 + 1) = 21.5\%$

Alternative formula 1:

$$\frac{\text{Net Profit}}{\text{Net Sales}} \times \frac{\text{Net Sales}}{\text{Total Assets}} \times \frac{\text{Net Sales}}{\text{Net Worth}} \div \frac{\text{Net Sales}}{\text{Total Assets}} = \frac{\text{Net Profit}}{\text{Net Worth}}$$

Calculation:

Company A	$5.1 \times 2.8 \times (5.9 \div 2.8) = 29.9\%$
Company B	$3.0 \times 2.5 \times (6.7 \div 2.5) = 20.1\%$
Company C	$1.2 \times 1.9 \times (8.1 \div 1.9) = 9.7\%$
Company D	$1.9 \times 4.4 \times (32.3 \div 4.4) = 61.3\%$
Industry standard	$3.2 \times 2.4 \times (6.8 \div 2.4) = 21.6\%$

Alternative formula 2:

$$\frac{\text{Net Profit}}{\text{Net Sales}} \times \frac{\text{Net Sales}}{\text{Net Worth}} = \frac{\text{Net Profit}}{\text{Net Worth}}$$

Note: Slight apparent errors occur as a result of rounding.
Note: Although Formula 2 is obviously the most simplified, it fails to emphasize that three factors—profit margin, asset utilization, and investment adequacy—all interact to produce *Net Profit to Net Worth*. On the other hand, it focuses attention on the role of *Net Sales to Net Worth*, a primary factor in basic financial management.

tions may, in fact, manage financial leverage with some precision, most small and medium-size companies find that their financial leverage is largely dictated by the combination of asset management, investment adequacy, and profitability. With the exception of a limited number of publicly traded corporations, management rarely makes a conscious attempt to fine-tune *Total Liabilities to Net Worth* in order to increase return on equity. In fact, only companies with ready access to capital markets are able to optimize their capital structure when other financial factors, such as interest rates, change. Instead, management of smaller companies ordinarily takes a more passive view of financial leverage. *Total Liabilities to Net Worth* is ordinarily regarded as an effect, not a cause. If, for example, a business owner or manager finds that financial leverage had increased during the year, he will seek the cause: sales growth (at a rate faster than the increase in net worth), declining asset utilization, or operating losses. In fact, as we have seen in our earlier study of *Total Liabilities to Net Worth*, this secondary measure is directly attributable to the interaction of *Net Sales to Total Assets* and *Net Sales to Net Worth*.

To illustrate the Du Pont formula, Table A4-1 displays the dollar figures and the key financial ratios for Companies A, B, C, and D, together with the actual calculation of the equation for each company. Net profit before taxes is used as the primary profitability factor because, when financially feasible, most small and medium-size companies distribute a portion of return on equity as compensation to owners and officers and rarely declare significant dividends. The focus of management attention in closely held companies is ordinarily pre-tax profit, rather than after-tax return. The Du Pont formula makes clear the fact that Company A derives its comparatively high *Net Profit to Net Worth* from relatively high *Net Profit to Net Sales* multiplied by relatively high *Net Sales to Total Assets*, which together more than offset the effect of comparatively low *Total Liabilities to Net Worth*. Company B generates a moderate *Net Profit to Net Worth* because its profit margin, asset utilization, and financial leverage are all similar to the industry standard. Company C has incurred the risk of comparatively high *Total Liabilities to Net Worth*, but the potential reward—a high *Net Profit to Net Worth*—has eluded this concern because of its very low *Net Profit to Net Sales* and its relatively low *Net Sales to Total Assets*.

Company D has achieved an extremely high *Net Profit to Net Worth* despite a substandard profit margin on net sales. The company's very high *Net Sales to Total Assets* makes a major contribution to Company D's favorable pre-tax net profit in relation to the book value of shareholders' investment. The primary factor, however, is unusually high *Total Liabilities to Net Worth*, indicating that the business incurred a high degree of risk in attaining the outstanding return on equity. The first alternative formula in Table A4-1 shows that Company D's extremely high *Net Profit to Net Worth* can be largely traced to its *Net Sales to Net Worth*, which is nearly five times higher than the industry norm. Very low investment adequacy (a low proportion of owners' equity to support net sales) has converted a rather weak *Return on Sales Ratio* into an impressive, but risky, *Return on Equity Ratio*.

Tool to Measure Investment Adequacy

The Du Pont formula is a useful tool for emphasizing the relationship between profit margin, asset utilization, and financial leverage. Nevertheless, you should also direct attention to *Net Sales to Net Worth* when considering actions to improve *Net Profit to Net Worth*. A good understanding of a company's relative investment adequacy is especially important in strategic planning, since a low level of net worth in relation to sales volume can severely limit management moves, particularly with respect to fixed asset expansion and rapid sales growth. A business owner or manager who ignores *Net Sales to Net Worth* while attempting to boost *Net Profit to Net Worth* may inadvertently find his company at a severe competitive disadvantage. For example, a concern that has succeeded in offsetting the unfavorable effect of a poor *Net Profit to Net Sales* with *Net Sales to Total Assets* 50% higher than the industry standard and *Total Liabilities to Net Worth* also 50% above the industry norm may be surprised to discover that its *Net Sales to Net Worth* is nearly twice as high as the industry median. Such a weakness in owners' equity relative to sales volume requires adept management.

As long as the company can maintain its superior asset utilization and satisfactory relations with its creditors, serious problems may be forestalled. Nevertheless, a company that consistently earns a substandard return on its sales dollars is vulnerable to price-cutting tactics by competitors, which could quickly turn a marginal profit into a loss. Even with extraordinary asset management and enormous financial leverage, a net loss on sales translates into a negative *Net Profit to Net Worth*. The dynamic nature of business competition and economic conditions, local, regional, national, and international, suggests that rival firms with higher profit margins and stronger capitalization are likely to pose recurring threats to companies with weak earnings or inadequate owners' equity.

An additional problem that may arise from using either *Net Profit to Total Assets* or *Net Profit to Net Worth* as the primary or exclusive measure of management performance is the temptation to boost return by curtailing investment in fixed assets. Not only does such a strategy tend to reduce depreciation expense and thereby increase net profit in the short run, but it also avoids the increase in total assets that would be caused by acquisition of new (undepreciated) fixed assets. In fact, depreciation of existing fixed assets will continually contribute to the reduction of total assets in the absence of capital expenditures. Consequently, short-term profit may be higher at the same time that the asset base is reduced, thereby raising *Net Profit to Total Assets* and *Net Profit to Net Worth*, at least temporarily. Few companies, however, can remain competitive over a period of years without modernizing their facilities. Eventually, a company that has intentionally or inadvertently restricted its capital expenditures to a comparatively low level will face the prospect of making a major commitment of funds to fixed assets or risk extinction.

Appendix A5

Approaches to Performance Measurement of Management Employees: Return on Assets Employed

When measuring the financial effectiveness of an individual manager's control of a segment of the company's resources, standards for evaluating the competitive position and relative progress of the entire organization may not be directly applicable. In the case of a branch manager, plant superintendent, or divisional executive, a significant portion of the income, expenses, assets, and sources of funding for which he or she has apparent responsibility may, in reality, be controlled at the top corporate level. Even the general manager of a relatively small family-owned enterprise may not have actual decision-making power over such basic dollars-and-cents issues as customer deposits or progress payments, stretching out accounts payable to reduce bank debt, or accumulating cash and investments. Nor is the manager likely to be truly responsible for the company's underlying capital structure: its owners' equity, long-term debt, and credit line, all of which have a major impact on interest costs.

To make interdivisional comparisons more equitable, some large corporations evaluate the performance of divisional, plant, and branch managers on *Net Operating Profit to Assets Employed*. While there are several variations of this ratio, most begin by subtracting all nonoperating income (such as interest income) from net profit and adding back nonoperating expenses (including interest expense). Then, total assets are reduced by the amount of cash and short-term investments plus miscellaneous (other noncurrent) assets. The adjusted net profit (operating profit) is divided by adjusted total assets (assets employed) to obtain *Net Operating Profit to Assets Employed*. This approach measures the operating profit of the business unit against the specific assets employed in generating that profit.

A closely related measure, *Net Operating Profit to Net Assets Employed*, goes one step further. Not only are nonoperating assets (cash, short-term investments, and miscellaneous assets) subtracted from total assets in order to match operating profit with operating assets, but non-interest-bearing liabilities are also deducted. This approach reflects the premise that management is responsible only for operating assets (total assets minus cash, short-term investments, and miscellaneous assets). In addition, *Net Operating Profit to Net Assets Employed* recognizes that trade payables, accruals, progress payments, and customer deposits can be used to support those operating assets, thereby reducing the need for more permanent capital investment (owners' equity plus long-term liabilities and short-term bank financing). By emphasizing return on capital investment, this measure evaluates management performance from a shareholder's perspective. For *Net Operating Profit to Net Assets Employed* to serve as an equitable standard of resource management, the manager being evaluated must have authority to determine the amount and mix of non-interest-bearing debt.

Using operating assets net of non-interest-bearing liabilities as the basis of measurement encourages managers to obtain customer deposits and progress payments wherever they have such discretion and to take maximum advantage of trade credit. By reducing the denominator (net assets employed) through an increase of interest-free funds, a manager can boost his *Net Operating Profit to Net Assets Employed* with no rise in net profit dollars. Using *Net Profit to Total Assets* (based on pre-tax net profit) to evaluate management performance might, on the other hand, actually discourage obtaining customer payments and investing the proceeds on a short-term basis. Whenever the rate of return that could be earned on those investments is less than the company's present *Net Profit to Total Assets*, these additional assets would have a depressing effect on that ratio. Even though funds could be brought into the company at no cost and then invested for a net gain to shareholders, lower *Net Profit to Total Assets* would result from that move if the company is already generating higher *Net Profit to Total Assets* than current yields on short-term investments. Both *Net Operating Profit to Assets Employed* and *Net Operating Profit to Net Assets Employed* eliminate this distortion and thereby tend to encourage the use of interest-free money.

An Interdivisional Evaluation System

This approach to evaluating management performance is, however, not entirely objective, since the ability to build up cash and short-term investments through customer deposits and progress payments is, to a large degree, a function of industry conditions, not strictly management skill. In fact, progress payments and other customer advances may lead to lax asset management. Consequently, an interdivisional evaluation system should involve both *Net Operating Profit to Assets Employed* (before subtracting non-interest-bearing liabilities) and *Net Operating Profit to Net Assets Employed* (after netting out interest-free money). Whenever the composition or total amount of assets is known to change markedly from year to year or shows a tendency to fluctuate during the year, you should be wary of ratios based on year-end figures and use quarterly or even monthly averages of total assets, assets employed, and net assets employed for your ratio calculations. Internal evaluation of performance for the entire year should be based on representative dollar amounts for the complete period.

A company with a net operating profit of $275,000 and interest plus other nonoperating expenses (net of other nonoperating income) of $75,000 for the year would report a net profit before taxes of $200,000. If that company's total assets at the end of the year were $2 million, and its cash and short-term investments were $100,000, its assets employed would be $1,900,000. *Net Profit to Total Assets* would be 10.0% ($200,000 divided by $2 million, converted to a percentage), while *Net Operating Profit to Assets Employed* would be 14.5% ($275,000 divided by $1,900,000, expressed as a percentage). To obtain net assets employed, the amount of non-interest-bearing liabilities is subtracted from assets employed. If the company in this example had accounts payable of $325,000 and accrued expenses of $100,000 at year-end, net assets employed would be $1,475,000 (after subtracting non-interest-bearing liabilities of $425,000 from assets employed of $1,900,000). *Net Operating Profit to Net Assets Employed* would then be 18.6%, found by dividing $275,000 by $1,475,000 and expressing the result as a percentage.

A brief comparison of Divisions L, M, and N is shown in Table A5-1. Like most companies and divisions in the industry, Division L obtains no progress payments or other forms of advances from customers. In addition, Division L is similar to the industry norm with respect to *Net Profit to Total Assets* and has no unusual proportion of cash and short-term investments or miscellaneous (other non-operating) assets. Consequently, the company's *Net Operating Profit to Assets Employed* and its *Net Operating Profit to Net Assets Employed* are directly in line with the industry standard.

Both Division M and Division N have been able to develop customer relationships in their respective market areas that permit them to obtain deposits and progress payments. Division M has invested these advances on a short-term basis, producing an additional $20,000 pre-tax net profit, but *Net Profit to Total Assets* shows Division M falling behind Division L. To avoid such anomalous results, the parent corporation controlling Divisions L, M, and N has adopted *Net Operating Profit to Net Assets Employed* as the primary measure of divisional performance. By this standard, Division M is the clear leader at 24.5%, with Divisions L and N trailing. The management of Division N appears to be as efficient as that of Division L in generating net operating profit in relation to the opportunities available.

Unfortunately, *Net Operating Profit to Net Assets Employed* does not reveal that Division N's management has used $250,000 in customer advances to increase accounts receivable and inventory without any gain in net profit from these actions. By referring to *Net Operating Profit to Assets Employed* (before subtracting customer advances and other non-interest-bearing debt), the top corporate decision makers would see that Division N was comparatively deficient in the amount of net operating profit earned in relation to the assets actually used

Table A5-1. Return on assets employed for three divisions.

	Division L	Division M	Division N
Net sales	$5,000,000	$5,000,000	$5,000,000
Net operating profit	275,000	300,000	275,000
Net profit before taxes	200,000	220,000	200,000
Total assets	$2,000,000	$2,250,000	$2,250,000
Less: cash and			
short-term investments	100,000	350,000	100,000
Less: miscellaneous (other			
noncurrent) assets	0	0	0
Assets employed	1,900,000	1,900,000	2,150,000
Less: accounts payable	325,000	325,000	325,000
Less: accrued expenses	100,000	100,000	100,000
Less: due to customers			
(deposits and			
progress payments)	0	250,000	250,000
Net assets employed	$1,475,000	$1,225,000	$1,475,000
Net Profit			
to Total Assets			
Company	10.0%	9.8%	8.9%
Industry standard	10.2%	10.2%	10.2%
Net Operating Profit			
to Assets Employed			
Company	14.5%	15.8%	12.8%
Industry standard	14.6%	14.6%	14.6%
Net Operating Profit			
to Net Assets Employed			
Company	18.6%	24.5%	18.6%
Industry standard	18.8%	18.8%	18.8%

to generate that profit. An analysis of both *Net Operating Profit to Assets Employed* and *Net Operating Profit to Net Assets Employed* shows that Division M was the most efficient in employing operating assets to generate operating profit; Division L was next in line, with Division N finishing third. After customer advances were subtracted, Division M clearly produced the highest return on net assets employed, noticeably above the industry norm. Although Division N generated a substandard operating profit on operating assets, the availability of customer advances (which were used to support an expansion of accounts receivable and inventory) enabled that division to achieve a moderate return on net assets employed and pull even with Division L in this regard. If Division L could obtain any significant amount of advances from customers, management's rating based on *Net Operating Profit to Net Assets Employed* would be improved.

Net assets employed is certainly one appropriate basis for measuring management efficiency in interdivisional comparisons, but it cannot tell the entire story. As we have seen, the parent company should consider including *Net Operating Profit to Assets Employed* (before subtracting non-interest-bearing liabilities) in its evaluation scheme in order to encourage greater asset utilization. An evaluation of management performance relative to assets employed would have called attention to the fact that Division N had received no apparent gain from its higher level of non-interest-bearing debt. On a long-term basis, a high level of profit in relation to assets and capital investment is clearly a favorable characteristic. Nevertheless, overemphasis of immediate financial goals may encourage line officers and managers to boost the short-term profit-to-assets relationship at the expense of long-term competitiveness by simply deferring capital expenditures.

The percentages calculated for return on assets employed and return on net assets employed are somewhat artificial numbers designed for internal comparisons of managerial performance. They should not be used as investment standards. For that purpose, actual cash flow—which takes into account depreciation, capital expenditures, long-term financing, and changes in the components of working capital—is a better denominator than the amount of net operating profit determined by accounting conventions. Cash flow projections and analyses of actual results with respect to cash flow shift the emphasis for near-term measurement of managerial performance (and of economic conditions that may be beyond the control of management) to an evaluation of the company's strategic position and management's ability to increase shareholder value.

Appendix A6

The Importance of Sustainable Growth

In the search for more profit dollars through sales growth, many business owners and managers fail to consider how such growth can be supported by the company's financial structure without incurring a burdensome level of debt. Even when profit—in both dollars and percentages—is at record levels, a company may suddenly discover that it has increased debt at a far faster pace. Like an army advancing more rapidly than it can be supplied, an expanding company can find itself in serious difficulty as a result of its success. In fact, numerous companies have arrived in bankruptcy court after a period of unprecedented growth in sales and net profit.

Sustainable growth, in its simplest form, is the rate of increase in sales volume that can be achieved while holding a company's *Total Liabilities to Net Worth* to its present level, assuming current rates of profitability and asset utilization, and also assuming that the company plans to increase net worth through retained earnings, not by obtaining new investment. More sophisticated models of sustainable growth seek to determine the rate of increase in net sales that will permit *Total Liabilities to Net Worth* to be held to a targeted level (without regard to the present proportion) while also meeting specified goals for *Net Profit to Net Sales* and *Net Sales to Total Assets*.

If a company maintains essentially the same profit margin and asset utilization from one year to the next, the ability to increase sales volume while holding financial leverage constant is determined by the proportion of retained earnings to net worth. In most privately held businesses, *Retained Earnings to Net Worth* is close or identical to *Net Profit After Taxes to Net Worth*, since dividends from after-tax net profit are ordinarily minimal or nonexistent. Although these two measures are rarely included in industry reports, they can be easily calculated for internal analysis. *Retained Earnings to Net Worth* indicates the percentage increase in net sales that can be achieved, assuming the same *Net Profit to Net Sales* and the same *Net Sales to Total Assets*, while holding *Total Liabilities to Net Worth* constant. It is important to note that *Retained Earnings to Net Worth* is based on earnings retained (added to net worth) during the previous year only. This definition of retained earnings should not be confused with the *accumulated* retained earnings (for all previous fiscal periods combined) shown on the balance sheet.

To calculate *Retained Earnings to Net Worth*, simply divide retained earnings (the amount of after-tax profit added to net worth after payments of any dividends or other distribution of capital) by net worth. This ratio is often expressed in percentage form, by multiplying the result by 100 or pressing the % key on a calculator. For any company that does not pay formal dividends to shareholders or otherwise distribute after-tax profit, *Net Profit After Taxes to Net Worth* is an equally good approximation of sustainable growth. This ratio is computed by dividing net profit after taxes by net worth and then multiplying by 100 or pressing the % key on a calculator. For Company B, retained earnings of $100,000 divided by net worth of $750,000 yields *Retained Earnings to Net Worth* of 0.133 or 13.3%. Because Company B paid no dividends and carried all after-tax net profit into net worth, *Net Profit After Taxes to Net Worth* is identical. Dividing after-tax net profit of $100,000 by net worth of $750,000 again yields 0.133 or 13.3%.

A look at Company B's dollar data and key financial ratios in Table A6-1 will show that in the simplified model of sustainable growth—anticipating no change in basic financial relationships and no dividends—*Net Profit After Taxes to Net*

Table A6-1. Sustainable growth: Selected financial data and key financial ratios for Company B.

	Year 1	Year 2	Year 3	Year 4
Net sales	$5,000,000	$5,770,000	$6,660,000	$7,685,000
Net profit before taxes	150,000	173,000	200,000	230,500
Income taxes	50,000	57,500	67,000	77,000
Net profit after taxes	100,000	115,500	133,000	153,500
Dividends	0	0	0	0
Retained earnings	100,000	115,500	133,000	153,500
Total assets	$2,000,000	$2,308,000	$2,664,000	$3,074,000
Total liabilities	1,250,000	1,442,500	1,665,500	1,922,000
Net worth	750,000	865,500	998,500	1,152,000
Net Profit *After Taxes* *to Net Worth*	13.3%	13.3%	13.3%	13.3%
Net Profit *After Taxes* *to Net Sales*	2.0%	2.0%	2.0%	2.0%
Net Sales *to Total Assets*	2.5 times	2.5 times	2.5 times	2.5 times
Total Liabilities *to Net Worth*	1.7 times	1.7 times	1.7 times	1.7 times
Increase in net sales at the rate that holds *Total Liabilities* *to Net Worth* constant	15.4%	15.4%	15.4%	15.4%

Worth is a good approximation of the rate at which sales can be permitted to grow while maintaining the same *Total Liabilities to Net Worth*. In this case, *Net Profit After Taxes to Net Worth*, at 13.3%, is reasonably close to the 15.4% calculated through the sustainable growth formula described below. Computing *Net Profit After Taxes to Net Worth* for Year 1 and then using that percentage as an indication of the sustainable growth rate in the future does, however, somewhat understate the actual sustainable growth rate. The discrepancy occurs because the *Net Profit After Taxes to Net Worth* calculations were made at a single point in time, the end of the fiscal year. A more accurate estimation of the sustainable growth rate can be derived from the formula in Table A6-2.

A More Accurate Calculation

If you wish to go beyond the rough approximation of sustainable growth provided by *Net Profit After Taxes to Net Worth* and calculate a more accurate rate, the first step is to calculate three ratios: *Net Profit After Taxes to Net Sales*, *Net Sales to Total Assets*, and *Total Liabilities to Net Worth*. The calculation is displayed in Table A6-2, but the following explanation may be helpful: With after-tax profit of $100,000 and net sales of $5 million, Company B shows *Net Profit After Taxes to Net Sales* of .020. For the sustainable growth equation, this ratio,

Table A6-2.   A formula to determine sustainable growth for Company B.

A simplified formula:

$$\frac{P(L+1)}{(1 \div A) - [P(L+1)]}$$

P = *Net Profit After Taxes to Net Sales* (as decimal fraction); assumes that no dividends are paid; thus, retained earnings are equal to net profit after taxes
L = *Total Liabilities to Net Worth*
A = *Net Sales to Total Assets*

For Company B, the formula is calculated on Year 1 results:

$$\frac{.020(1.67+1)}{(1 \div 2.50) - [.020(1.67+1)]} =$$

$$\frac{.020(2.67)}{.4000 - [.020(2.67)]} =$$

$$\frac{.0534}{.4000 - .0534} = \frac{.0534}{.3466} = .1541$$

Expressed as a percentage, this ratio shows that Company B can increase net sales at an annual rate of 15.4% and maintain its *Total Liabilities to Net Worth* at 1.67 as long as *Net Profit After Taxes to Net Sales* remains at 2.0% and *Net Sales to Total Assets* continues to be 2.50.

which is ordinarily displayed as a percentage, should be used in the form of a decimal fraction. Because *Net Profit After Taxes to Net Sales* is such a sensitive factor in determining sustainable growth, carrying it to three decimal places is recommended. Dividing Company B's net sales of $5 million by total assets of $2 million yields *Net Sales to Total Assets* of 2.50. In this case, carrying the calculation to two decimal places instead of the usual one decimal place will provide greater accuracy. When total liabilities of $1.25 million are divided by net worth of $750,000, *Total Liabilities to Net Worth* is found to be 1.67. Using two decimal places for this ratio is recommended. Now you are ready to work with the equation.

Net Profit After Taxes to Net Sales is multiplied by the sum of *Total Liabilities to Net Worth* plus 1. For every dollar increase in net worth through retained earnings (the same as after-tax profit if no dividends are paid), the company is expected to borrow funds in the same proportion as its present *Total Liabilities to Net Worth*. Adding 1 to this ratio takes into account both liabilities (reflected in the ratio value) and net worth (a value of 1 relative to the ratio value). Each $1.00 in after-tax profit that Company B adds to net worth will permit an increase of $1.67 in total liabilities. Consequently, after-tax net profit of .020 is multiplied by 2.67—1.67 representing new debt and 1 representing the profit that will be added to net worth. Carrying out this operation, you obtain .0534, the increase in total assets from debt and equity.

Next, the value 1 is divided by *Net Sales to Total Assets* to determine ending total assets. This calculation, which shows the amount of total assets needed to generate each dollar of sales, yields .4000 for Company B (1 divided by 2.50). In other words, a $1.00 increase in net sales will require an additional $0.40 in total assets if the company maintains its *Net Sales to Total Assets* at 2.50. At this point, the increase in assets calculated earlier, .0534, is subtracted from ending assets of .4000 to obtain beginning assets of .3466. Finally, the .0534 increase in assets is divided by beginning assets of .3466 to determine the expected increase as a proportion of beginning assets. The net result—.1541—translates into a 15.4% rate of sustainable growth for Company B. An annual increase in net sales faster than 15.4% would cause a rise in *Total Liabilities to Net Worth* above Company B's present 1.67 ratio, unless *Net Profit After Taxes to Net Sales* can be increased above 2.0% or *Net Sales to Total Assets* can be boosted above 2.50.

Since one or more of the proportions that determine sustainable growth—*Net Profit to Net Sales*, *Net Sales to Total Assets*, and *Total Liabilities to Net Worth*—can be expected to change during the next year, advanced models of sustainable growth allow the various ratios to be set by management. Then the rate of sales growth that will meet the desired conditions can be calculated, ordinarily with the assistance of a computer. Depending on the ratio values determined by management, *negative growth*—an actual reduction of net sales—may be needed to satisfy the specified conditions.

Need to Boost Net Worth

The primary value of the sustainable growth concept is its emphasis on the need to boost net worth when sales volume is increased, in order to keep total liabilities from becoming too burdensome in relation to owners' equity (net worth). There is no ideal relationship between total liabilities and net worth, but the industry standard is a good point of reference, since it reflects the cumulative, interactive result of countless decisions by management, lenders, suppliers, customers, and competitors. Whenever a company's *Total Liabilities to Net Worth* is significantly different from the industry norm, it raises a question about management strategy. A business approach that differs greatly from the industry norm is not necessarily disadvantageous, but management should fully understand the reasons for the difference. Similarly, any significant change in the company's proportion of total liabilities versus net worth should be carefully considered by management. Using the sustainable growth formula in basic strategic planning will alert business owners and managers to the likelihood of any shifts in that relationship as a result of anticipated sales expansion. This management tool will also suggest changes in financial structure that will be required to maintain the liabilities-to-equity balance in its present form. On the other hand, calculation of sustainable growth may indicate the desirability of making a substantial alteration in the company's financial leverage in response to projections of sales volume, profit margin, and asset management.

On a day-to-day basis, the ability to support sales growth depends on cash flow. The balance between depreciation and current maturities of long-term debt, the timing of capital expenditures and the availability of long-term financing, and the nature of changes in the components of working capital (particularly accounts receivable and inventory) will all have a bearing on the sustainability of projected growth. Nevertheless, the sustainable growth concept warrants management consideration because almost all lenders pay close attention to *Total Liabilities to Net Worth* and may include in their loan agreements a covenant that the company's ratio will not exceed a specified value without prior approval.

Appendix A7

Z-Score: Prediction of Business Failure

Numerous studies of business failure have been made by applying financial ratio tests on a postmortem basis. From these studies, certain ratios have been identified as having predictive ability 2 to 3 years in advance of actual bankruptcy. The most well-known model of bankruptcy prediction is the so-called *Z-score*, which incorporates five ratios into a single number. In this numerical test, developed by Dr. Edward Altman some 30 years ago, each of the five ratios is weighted in accordance with its contribution to discriminating a potential business failure from a financially healthy enterprise. The sum of these five weighted ratios is a company's *Z-score*.

Earlier studies of bankruptcy had identified other financial ratios as possessing equal or greater predictive ability when considered as single, independent measures. The *Z-score* includes the five ratios that, in combination, were best able to separate companies that actually went bankrupt from those that survived and prospered. In actual business practice, a single occurrence—for example, the bankruptcy of a major customer that owes a substantial amount of money—can jeopardize a company's existence. An unfavorable event of that kind coupled with a preexisting financial weakness, such as comparatively low investment adequacy (high *Net Sales to Net Worth*), would make the situation even more serious.

Because the *Z-score* is based on analysis of publicly traded corporations, it is designed to identify the more gradual deterioration that typifies the failure of large companies. One of the five *Z-score* ratios, *Market Value of Shareholders' Equity to Total Liabilities*, is extremely difficult to determine for most small, privately held companies. The book value of owners' equity (net worth) is often substituted for market value. This is not entirely satisfactory, however, since the market value of a company in financial difficulty may be higher or lower than book value, presumably representing the wisdom of the market in assessing poor profitability or other operating factors, as well as market value of assets and financial leverage. By definition, relating total liabilities to net worth at book value shows only financial leverage, not investors' evaluation of ownership interest.

Of the five ratios that comprise the *Z-score*, only one—*Net Sales to Total Assets*—is commonly published in industry studies. As a result, comparative data are severely limited. Because of the methodology upon which it is based, the *Z-score* is expressed as a range of safety that is the same for all manufacturing companies regardless of product or process. Manufacturing concerns that show a *Z-score* of 2.675 or above are considered financially sound, based on Professor Altman's research, while those with a *Z-score* below 1.81 are regarded as prime candidates for bankruptcy.

Limitations

Relying on a single number to judge the soundness of a business may be a tidy approach, but it has the effect of concealing the specific financial factors that require management attention. In that respect, the *Z-score* is similar to learning from the doctor that your physical exam has produced a rating of 2.74, down from 3.03 the year before, but definitely above the 1.81 figure that signals impending death. If you had just received such information, you would probably be anxious for additional details. Despite its limitations as an explanatory aid, the *Z-score* is frequently included in computer-based credit analysis systems used by banks to screen loan applicants. Consequently, business owners and managers should become familiar with their company's *Z-score* and with any comparative figures that may be available for their industry.

Let us first walk through the calculation of the *Z-score* and then examine how each component relates to the likelihood of bankruptcy. To become familiar with the mechanics of the *Z-score*, refer to the data for Company B in Table A7-1. The first of the five ratios in the *Z-score* is *Working Capital to Total Assets*, a special-purpose financial measure seldom seen in industry studies. You can calculate *Working Capital to Total Assets* for Company B in two steps: Subtract current liabilities of $1 million from current assets of $1.5 million to obtain working capital of $500,000, and then divide that amount by total assets of $2 million to obtain 0.25. Carrying the ratios to two decimal places in developing the *Z-score* is recommended. To give *Working Capital to Total Assets* its proper weight in the *Z-score* formula, it must be multiplied by 1.2, yielding a weighted value of 0.30. Once all five weighted ratios have been calculated, they are summed to produce the *Z-score*.

The second ratio in the *Z-score* equation, *Accumulated Retained Earnings to Total Assets*, is also a relatively rare ratio. Because retained earnings accumulated over the years constitute virtually all of net worth in the majority of privately held companies, *Net Worth to Total Assets* may ordinarily be substituted for *Accumulated Retained Earnings to Total Assets* in computing the *Z-score*. With net worth of $750,000 and total assets of $2 million, Company B's ratio is 0.38. The *Z-score* formula calls for weighting this factor by 1.4, resulting in 0.53. The third ratio, *Net Profit Before Taxes plus Interest Expense to Total Assets*, can be readily calculated for Company B from the data in Table A7-1. Adding pre-tax net profit of $150,000 to interest expense of $75,000 and dividing the $225,000 sum by total

Table A7-1. The *Z-score* for four companies.

	Company A	Company B	Company C	Company D
Net sales	$1,500,000	$5,000,000	$12,500,000	$50,000,000
Net profit before taxes	76,000	150,000	150,000	950,000
Interest expense	18,000	75,000	450,000	550,000
Current assets	398,000	1,500,000	4,740,000	8,400,000
Total assets	536,000	2,000,000	6,650,000	11,400,000
Current liabilities	220,000	1,000,000	3,780,000	5,400,000
Total liabilities	282,000	1,250,000	5,110,000	9,850,000
Net worth	254,000	750,000	1,540,000	1,550,000
Working Capital				
to Total Assets				
Company unweighted	0.33	0.25	0.14	0.26
Company weighted				
by 1.2	0.40	0.30	0.17	0.31
Net Worth				
to Total Assets				
Company unweighted	0.47	0.38	0.23	0.14
Company weighted				
by 1.4	0.66	0.53	0.32	0.20
Net Profit Before Taxes				
plus Interest Expense				
to Total Assets				
Company unweighted	0.18	0.11	0.09	0.13
Company weighted				
by 3.3	0.59	0.36	0.30	0.43
Net Worth				
to Total Liabilities				
Company unweighted	0.90	0.60	0.30	0.16
Company weighted				
by 0.6	0.54	0.36	0.18	0.10
Net Sales				
to Total Assets				
Company unweighted	2.80	2.50	1.88	4.39
Company weighted				
by 1.0	2.80	2.50	1.88	4.39
Z-score				
Company	4.99*	4.05*	2.85*	5.43*
Industry standard	3.92	3.92	3.92	3.92

*Sum of the five *weighted* ratios above

assets of $2 million produces a ratio of 0.11. Although profitability ratios are ordinarily displayed as percentages, *Net Profit Before Taxes plus Interest Expense to Total Assets* should be expressed as a decimal fraction in the *Z-score* formula. The calculated value, which is ordinarily small in comparison with the other ratios in the formula, is given a weight of 3.3. For Company B, the weighted ratio is 0.36.

The fourth ratio, *Market Value of Shareholders' Equity to Total Liabilities*, is unknown for most privately held companies, since their stock has no ready market. Substituting *Net Worth to Total Liabilities* for this ratio does not capture the presumed wisdom of the open market in identifying the value of shareholders' equity, but there are no clearly superior alternatives. With net worth of $750,000 and total liabilities of Company B's *Net Worth to Total Liabilities* is 0.60. This ratio has a relatively low 0.6 weight in the *Z-score* formula. Multiplying 0.60 by the 0.6 factor yields a weighted ratio of 0.36. The final ratio, *Net Sales to Total Assets*, is, of course, the causal measure that summarizes the combined influence of all asset utilization ratios. For Company B, net sales of $5 million divided by total assets of $2 million produces a ratio of 2.50. Since the *Z-score* weighting factor for *Net Sales to Total Assets* is 1.0, the weighted ratio remains 2.50.

To obtain the *Z-score* for Company B, you can now simply sum the weighted ratios: 0.30, 0.53, 0.36, 0.36, and 2.50. The result, 4.05, is well above the 2.675 value that has been found to separate financially sound manufacturing companies from those that require further investigation. Company B's score indicates that the business faces little likelihood of bankruptcy, since research has identified 1.81 as the imminent danger value.

Further study of the five ratios included in the *Z-score* formula helps to show how each one affects a company's potential for bankruptcy.

1. *Working Capital to Total Assets.* This ratio, which is a somewhat artificial construct, results from the interaction of two important ratios described earlier: *Net Sales to Total Assets* (Chapter 4) and *Net Sales to Working Capital* (Chapter 15). *Working Capital to Total Assets* can be derived for use in the *Z-score* calculation by dividing *Net Sales to Total Assets* by *Net Sales to Working Capital*.

2. *Accumulated Retained Earnings to Total Assets.* For most privately held companies, this ratio is essentially a variation of *Total Liabilities to Net Worth*, because accumulated retained earnings ordinarily represent almost all of owners' equity. *Net Worth to Total Assets* (a substitute for *Accumulated Retained Earnings to Total Assets*) can be derived by dividing the value 1 by the sum of *Total Liabilities to Net Worth* plus 1. Formula: $1 \div (Total\ Liabilities\ to\ Net\ Worth + 1)$.

3. *Net Profit Before Taxes plus Interest Expense to Total Assets.* This ratio, not commonly found in industry studies, was described in Appendix A3, "The Influence of Financial Leverage on Return on Equity." It indicates the rate of return on total assets before taking into account interest expense, which is influenced by investment adequacy as well as asset management.

4. *Market Value of Shareholders' Equity to Total Liabilities.* Because this ratio can be computed only for publicly traded companies, no comparable industry statistics are available. The market value of shareholders' equity often exceeds book value, but the reverse may be true for a publicly traded company in financial difficulty. This ratio reflects the collective valuation by investors in the open market with respect to assessment of the company's future earnings poten-

tial and the likely volatility of those earnings, taking into account the company's fundamental financial structure. For analyzing privately held companies, the book value of owners' equity (net worth) is commonly substituted for market value. Book value, however, is not as sensitive to earnings changes and is clearly not future oriented. Nevertheless, market value of a privately held company is seldom known. If book value is used as a substitute for market value, *Net Worth to Total Liabilities* can be derived by dividing the value 1 by *Total Liabilities to Net Worth*.

5. *Net Sales to Total Assets.* This ratio is a primary measure described in Chapter 4. For most companies, *Net Sales to Total Assets* is the foremost factor in the *Z-score*, typically representing 40% to 60% of total value, even though it is given a weight of only 1.0. In addition, *Net Sales to Total Assets* is a key component of *Working Capital to Total Assets*, another of the five *Z-score* factors.

Total Liabilities to Net Worth is a highly important underlying factor in determining the *Z-score*, since it is an algebraic component of both *Net Worth to Total Assets* (the closest substitute for *Accumulated Retained Earnings to Total Assets*) and *Net Worth to Total Liabilities* (the closest substitute for *Market Value of Shareholders' Equity to Total Liabilities*). Net profit plays a comparatively small direct role in the total *Z-score*, although it is almost surely a major determinant of the *Market Value of Shareholders' Equity to Total Liabilities* for publicly traded companies (the source of data from which the *Z-score* was originally derived).

Other Ratios

As mentioned above, other studies of bankruptcy have identified numerous additional ratios that help to distinguish between ongoing enterprises and ultimately bankrupt companies in advance of the unfortunate event: *Net Profit Before Taxes to Net Worth*, *Net Profit Before Taxes to Net Sales*, *Net Profit Before Taxes plus Interest Expense to Interest Expense*, *Current Assets to Current Liabilities*, *Cash and Short-Term Investments plus Accounts Receivable to Current Liabilities*, *Net Profit After Taxes plus Depreciation to Total Liabilities*, and *Net Profit After Taxes plus Depreciation to Current Liabilities*. Research also indicates that asset size, the total value of shareholders' equity, and earnings stability are related to the likelihood of avoiding bankruptcy.

Comparative Analysis With Derived Industry Standards

Table A7-1 shows that the *Z-scores* of Companies A, B, and C correspond well with expectations, based on our earlier study of their financial characteristics. Company A, with the most conservative financial structure, reports the highest

Z-score among the three businesses. Company B, near the middle of the road with respect to all key financial factors, shows a *Z-score* between those of Companies A and C—and very close to the industry standard. Because of its comparatively low profit, relatively low asset utilization, and substandard investment adequacy, Company C's *Z-score* falls below the others, but remains somewhat above the 2.675 line that suggests the possibility of bankruptcy in the foreseeable future.

Company D achieves a surprisingly high *Z-score* considering its relatively low profitability, very low investment adequacy, and comparatively high financial leverage. The strength of Company D's *Z-score* is directly attributable to the company's unusually high asset utilization, reflected in *Net Sales to Total Assets*. In fact, Company D's total for the other four *Z-score* factors is actually lower than that shown by Company C. Thus, we see that the *Z-score* is strongly influenced by asset utilization, to such a great extent that Company D could remain in the "safe" category simply by maintaining *Net Sales to Total Assets* of 2.7 or greater, provided that the business was able to avoid an outright loss before meeting interest payments. On the other hand, a company in an asset-heavy industry (such as a distillery or a manufacturer of electronic equipment) must be solidly profitable, reasonably liquid, and well capitalized in order to achieve an adequate *Z-score*.

Appendix A8

Application of Ratio Analysis in Business Valuation

The dollar amounts presented in a company's financial statement do not represent the actual market value of its assets. More importantly, they rarely present an accurate picture of the ownership value of the business. Financial statements certainly provide the best information available for comparative analysis of operating results and financial structure, but the dollar figures presented in accordance with generally accepted accounting principles are not intended to show the actual amount an investor would pay to own the company or the net proceeds that might be realized by selling the assets individually.

The orderly disposal of fixed assets, for example, may generate far more—and in some cases far less—cash than the depreciated value of those assets on the company's books. Original cost may be a better estimate of their actual market value, depending on the specific industry in which a company operates and the rate of inflation in recent years. In many industries, however, the gross (undepreciated) amount of fixed assets is a highly unreliable indicator of the amount the plant and equipment would command if sold.

Similarly, inventory may have a substantially greater value than its cost to produce. On the other hand, it may ultimately prove to be unsalable at any price. Accounts receivable do not rise in value, but a significant portion of this asset item may be uncollectible. The book value of miscellaneous assets often differs greatly from market value, particularly with respect to licenses, franchises, patents, royalties, and investments in affiliated companies. As a result, the stated value of total assets is rarely equal to market value.

Nevertheless, for companies in the same industry, the relative value of assets on their respective financial statements is likely to be in line with the relative market value of those assets. In other words, if Company C's book value of total assets is substantially higher than the book value reported by Company A, the market value of Company C's assets will generally be greater than the market value of assets owned by Company A. For purposes of business valuation, however, general rules are entirely insufficient; a specific valuation of the company is required.

Disparity Between Market Value and Net Worth

The value of an ownership interest in a company is ordinarily determined by the projected financial return on that investment from ongoing operations, rather than liquidation of assets. Future earnings are usually the focus of investor attention, since the opportunity to receive dividends (or other sources of personal income, in the case of small companies) and eventual capital gains will depend on profitable operations. Since earnings frequently play a much greater role than assets in determining investor preference, the market value of a company is often far different from its net worth (owners' equity) on the balance sheet. Companies with strong prospects for sales and profit growth may be sold for many times their book value. On the other hand, the owners of many small businesses have been offered significantly less than book value for their equity interest because of a history of poor company earnings or because the success of the business is closely tied to the activities or reputation of the current owner. The lack of correspondence between net worth shown on the balance sheet and actual market value of the ownership interest means that *Net Profit to Net Worth* is not a good indicator of actual return on investment and is not ordinarily useful in business valuation.

Limitations of Net Profit to Net Worth

In addition, *Net Profit to Net Worth* does not take into consideration the amount of debt the company may be using to bolster its profit on owners' equity. Under the right conditions (as discussed in Appendix A3), incurring a high level of liabilities—interest-bearing debt as well as trade credit—in relation to net worth can boost *Net Profit to Net Worth*. Because high *Total Liabilities to Net Worth* ordinarily introduces comparatively great risk, this measure should be carefully considered when evaluating a company's *Net Profit to Net Worth*. Interest rates on corporate bonds and other debt instruments of publicly traded companies will rise when investors perceive that risk attributable to liabilities has become more significant. Similarly, the price of the company's stock will decline under those conditions (all other factors being equal), owing to investors' demand for a higher rate of return in view of the increased risk. On the other hand, risk associated with financial leverage in privately held companies is not necessarily reflected in interest rates charged on bank loans, and no other price adjustment mechanism applies to the operation of closely held companies. Consequently, risk is not properly reflected in *Net Profit to Net Worth*, again suggesting that this ratio is not a good indicator of market value.

There is a third reason why *Net Profit to Net Worth* is rarely appropriate in business valuation: Net profit is subject to major adjustments for discretionary expenses, such as officers'/owners' compensation, fringe benefits, rent (when the property is controlled by the business owners), and travel and entertainment.

Owners' compensation and return on investment are, in effect, intermingled in most small businesses. Adjustments to discretionary expenses, which can have a highly significant impact on the "bottom line," are commonly made in order to identify the portion of funds from operations that represents return on investment versus "normal" compensation and fringes. Industry figures are useful in determining typical operating expense patterns for companies of similar size.

In business valuation, net profit is ordinarily calculated before interest and income taxes, particularly when the prospective purchaser is expected to be active in the company. Since some portion of return on equity may, in actuality, be withdrawn in the form of officers' compensation, the corporate income tax is often not applicable to the same extent that it is in the analysis of a publicly traded company that provides its reward to shareholders as dividends (after tax) and capital gains (strongly affected by earnings reports based on after-tax profit). In valuing a privately held company, net profit is computed before subtracting interest expense and income taxes for a second reason: The company will almost surely have a different capital structure under the new ownership. A highly simplified example of adjustments that may be made to net profit and net worth in the initial stages of business valuation is displayed in Table A8-1. This first step in conforming accounting data to market reality reveals significant differences between *Net Profit to Net Worth* computed from book figures and the same measure calculated after preliminary adjustments.

We have seen in previous chapters that *Net Profit to Net Worth* serves many useful purposes, particularly as a measure of management's success in balancing sales growth, asset management, and financial leverage. At the same time, you must recognize that this ratio is rarely applicable in business valuation.

Table A8-1.   Preliminary adjustments to determine business valuation for four companies.

	Company A	Company B	Company C	Company D
Net profit before taxes	$ 76,000	$ 150,000	$ 150,000	$ 950,000
Adjustment to officers'/ owners' compensation[1]	+40,000	0	−100,000	−250,000
Adjustment to officers'/ owners' travel & entertainment[2]	+20,000	0	+50,000	0
Adjustment to rent/lease buildings[3]	+10,000	0	0	0
Adjustment to rent/lease equipment[3]	+10,000	0	0	0
Adjusted net profit before taxes	$156,000	$ 150,000	$ 100,000	$ 700,000
Net worth	$254,000	$ 750,000	$1,540,000	$1,550,000
Adjustment to fixed assets[4]	+62,000	+300,000	+640,000	+2,450,000
Adjusted net worth	$316,000	$1,050,000	$2,180,000	$4,000,000
Net Profit to Net Worth	29.9%	20.0%	9.7%	61.3%
Adjusted Net Profit to Adjusted Net Worth	49.4%	14.3%	4.6%	17.5%

[1]Profit is increased for companies that pay compensation higher than the norm for similar responsibilities, and decreased for companies that pay compensation lower than the norm.

[2]Profit is increased for companies that incur unusually large travel and entertainment expenses on behalf of owners and officers.

[3]Profit is increased for companies that pay higher than market rent and lease expenses for business facilities to real estate partnerships or similar companies controlled by owners and officers or their family members (on the assumption that future charges would be adjusted to market conditions or that the company would relocate to market-rate facilities).

[4]Net worth is increased for companies that report book (depreciated) value of fixed assets lower than estimated market value.

Note: Adjusted Net Profit to Adjusted Net Worth is a more realistic indication of the rate of return on shareholders' equity, but only represents a rough first approximation. This abbreviated table is simply intended as an illustration of the difference in accounting measures of return after a few preliminary adjustments relevant to business valuation.

Appendix A9

Investors' Perspective: Cash Flow in Relation to Invested Capital

Individuals and institutions that regularly invest their money in business enterprises use somewhat different measures of performance than those that are ordinarily applied to evaluation of the fundamental financial health of a privately held company. Because most professional investors are involved in the ongoing trading of one investment opportunity for another, they usually compare their cash return (in the form of dividends and capital gains) with their cash outlay. They are less concerned about reported earnings in relation to net worth or to total capitalization, as shown in the financial statement, than about the estimated present value of the future cash stream from their investment. Interestingly, however, many publications for investors emphasize ratios based on accounting data—particularly *Net Profit to Net Worth* or the *Return on Investment Ratio (Net Profit Before Taxes plus Interest Expense to Long-Term Liabilities plus Net Worth)*—in the analysis of specific stocks.

Analysts of investor behavior and stock prices, most notably Alfred Rappaport of Northwestern University and the Alcar Group, make a strong case that the net cash flow approach should also be adopted by company management and financial analysts in evaluating a company's ability to create shareholder value. They point out numerous deficiencies in using *Net Profit to Net Worth* or the *Return on Investment Ratio* to value the stock of publicly traded companies: Net profit is strongly influenced by depreciation; accounting depreciation may have no direct correspondence with *economic* (actual effective) depreciation; the variability of earnings (which affects risk to investors) is ignored; and financial leverage (a source of risk to the entire company) is also ignored. They also remind us that current company policy may be leading to the need for major capital expenditures in the near term, and that book earnings are not equivalent to cash flow (due to possible increases in accounts receivable and inventory that absorb cash before it can be used for capital expenditures, debt repayment, or dividends). In addition, book value of net worth may have very little relationship with the market value of owners' equity based on the liquidation value of total assets, and even less connection with the price of the company's shares on the open market.

These critics of *Net Profit to Net Worth* and the *Return on Investment Ratio,* as applied to investment analysis, maintain that the essence of creating shareholder value is generating net cash flow that represents a higher percentage of actual cash investment, over the long term, than the company's cost of capital (weighted for debt and equity).

Useful for Any Size Company

For most small companies, this may at first seem like a highly academic approach to financial management, but it is actually a useful concept for a business of any size. By focusing on the connection between cash flow and market value, this method of financial evaluation directs management attention to critical issues that may be ignored in traditional accounting-based analysis. Is profitability artificially high due to low depreciation of relatively old assets? Will major capital investment be needed soon? If so, where will the funds come from, how will the investment affect financial balance, and what will be the impact on future profitability? Is *Net Profit to Net Worth* overstated by comparing net profit with the book value (rather than market value) of net worth?

Table A9-1 illustrates a few of the factors to be considered when comparing rates of return. The items displayed relate only to the alternative numerators: net profit before taxes, net cash flow as determined by accounting conventions, and

Table A9-1.   Several factors for comparing rate of return.

		After officers'/ owners' compensation	Before officers'/ owners' compensation
Net sales		$5,000,000	$5,000,000
Net profit before taxes		250,000	450,000
Plus: Depreciation	+ $250,000		
Net cash flow (accounting method)		500,000	700,000
Less: Increase in accounts receivable[1]	− 25,000		
Less: Increase in inventory[2]	− 50,000		
Less: Capital expenditures[3]	− 300,000		
Plus: Increase in accounts payable	+ 25,000		
Cash flow (actual)		$ 150,000	$ 350,000

[1]Resulting from increase in *Collection Period of Accounts Receivable* from 46 days to 48 days
[2]Resulting from decrease in *Cost of Sales to Inventory* from 5.0 to 4.7
[3]Resulting in decrease of *Net Sales to Fixed Assets* from 10.0 to 9.1 owing to modernization for future growth

actual cash flow. In privately held businesses, net profit is ordinarily calculated on a pre-tax basis because the owners' investment of time and effort (which is, in reality, at least as important as money to a small enterprise) will ordinarily be withdrawn as direct compensation and fringe benefits instead of dividends. For that reason, analyzing net profit and cash flow before officers'/owners' compensation is often very informative, particularly in trend studies, since net profit can be altered from year to year through changes in executive salaries and bonuses. In addition to the alternative numerators, there are several possible denominators: net worth at book value, net worth after adjusting fixed assets for market value, and the estimated market value of a 100% ownership share. By this point, it should be evident that the professional investors' viewpoint is significantly different from that of the accountant, the banker, and other credit grantors, and that the appropriate measures of performance differ accordingly. Although a detailed examination of strategies for creating shareholder value is beyond the scope of this book, the basic approach should be studied by business owners and managers, particularly those who aspire to building an investment-grade enterprise or who hope to "go public" at some time in the future.

Appendix A10

Investment Terminology: Caution Advised

You need to be alert to the fact that certain important financial terms are defined differently in the investment community than in the management, banking, and credit transactions of small and medium-size companies. *Capitalization*, *investment*, *leverage*, and *working capital*, in particular, should be carefully examined whenever these terms are found in investment publications.

Capitalization

In most discussions of closely held companies (and throughout this book), *capitalization* is treated as the equivalent to net worth: proprietor's capital, partners' capital, or shareholders' equity. By this definition, an undercapitalized company is one that has high *Net Sales to Net Worth*, indicating a low level of owners' equity to support sales volume, or that is characterized by a high *Financial Leverage Ratio* (*Total Liabilities to Net Worth*). In traditional investment terminology, however, capitalization refers to all *permanent* funds on the right-hand side of the balance sheet: net worth plus long-term liabilities. By this definition, capitalization equals total assets minus current liabilities. Two computational issues are involved in this view of capitalization. The first relates to current maturities of long-term debt, which fall within current liabilities but are attributable to *permanent* debt (although, of course, due within one year of the statement date). The second issue arises from the increasingly common corporate practice of borrowing continually on a short-term basis. From the investor's point of view, capitalization might be better defined as interest-bearing debt plus shareholders' equity.

Investment theory, as applied to publicly traded corporations, assumes that the company under analysis has ready access to both long-term financing (through issuing corporate bonds) and the equity market (through issuing additional stock). In fact, the capitalization of publicly traded corporations was originally defined as *securities issued*. Those funds not provided by trade debt and accruals were assumed to come entirely from equity or partially from long-term debt and partially from investors, depending on management preference. A critical man-

348

agement responsibility in a publicly traded company is, in fact, to optimize the company's capital structure, to find the right balance between the cost of debt and the cost of equity. The optimum balance shifts with changes in interest rates, in the rate of return from the stock market, and in the company's specific characteristics (earnings, cash flow, capital expenditures, asset management, and financial leverage). Corporate decision makers may, under some circumstances, prefer to use only equity and no debt for all of the company's long-term funding; in this case, capitalization is equal to net worth.

Importance of Owners' Equity

The financial structure of privately held companies and small publicly traded concerns depends upon a different set of circumstances from that enjoyed by the largest corporations. Except for relatively rare leveraged buy-outs and venture capital start-ups, most small companies have only one source of permanent funds: owners' equity. For the vast majority of business enterprises, long-term debt does not come from issuing corporate bonds in the public market as a result of cost-of-capital calculations. It is, instead, borrowed from commercial lenders who expect to be paid back according to a certain schedule. Such long-term debt cannot be considered permanent capital. Not only is it usually tied to specific real estate, equipment, and vehicles, thereby restricting alternative borrowing arrangements, but there is no reasonable assurance of refinancing at the end of the loan period. Consequently, owners' equity is the only actual component of capital structure in the vast majority of small companies. Most industry reports prepared for privately held companies, therefore, treat capitalization and net worth as interchangeable.

Investment

For publicly traded corporations, the term *investment* is often used to cover the same permanent funding items as the investors' definition of capitalization: net worth plus long-term liabilities. In today's increasingly complex financial arena, however, short-term interest-bearing debt may be substituted for longer-term financing. Instead of obtaining a higher level of permanent financing to cover peak borrowing needs (and then holding cash and short-term investments during times of reduced requirements for funds), management may elect to restrict the amount of long-term financing and borrow on a short-term basis to meet periodic needs. These two strategies, however, may result in a significantly different relationship between long-term debt and equity, as well as a substantial alteration of *Return on Investment* (*Net Profit plus Interest Expense to Long-Term Liabilities plus Net Worth*).

To help you avoid confusion regarding the numerous possible definitions of investment, all financial measures in this book are clearly labeled as *Net Profit to*

Total Assets or *Net Profit to Net Worth*. Some publications consider *Net Profit to Total Assets* interchangeable with return on investment, while certain others refer to *Net Profit to Net Worth* as return on investment. From an investor's standpoint, the best definition of return on investment is net cash flow (net profit after taxes plus depreciation) to market value of shareholders' equity plus interest-bearing debt. It should be clear that financial analysts—whether owners, managers, credit grantors, accountants, industry consultants, business brokers, valuation experts, or investment specialists—must take particular care in checking the definition of any item or ratio using the term *investment*.

Financial Leverage

In the investment community, *financial leverage* is often used to describe the relationship between long-term debt and shareholders' equity, or between long-term debt plus preferred stock to common equity, within a company's capital structure. In this book and in most financial publications addressed primarily to the analysis of closely held companies, financial leverage is regarded as the relationship between all liabilities (current and long-term, interest-bearing, and interest-free), on the one hand, and owners' equity, on the other. This relationship is expressed as *Total Liabilities to Net Worth*. Few small and medium-size companies manage financial leverage in the manner of publicly traded corporations, many of which continually seek the most advantageous mix of non-interest-bearing liabilities, short-term borrowing, long-term debt, and shareholders' equity in relation to alternative yields and investors' expectations. For the closely held company, *Total Liabilities to Net Worth* results from the interaction of profit margin, asset management, investment adequacy, and the matching of long-term liabilities to noncurrent assets. Whenever using a new source of financial data, you should carefully review all definitions to avoid reaching erroneous conclusions.

Net Working Capital

In most investment publications, the term *net working capital* is interchangeable with the definition of working capital used in this book: current assets minus current liabilities. The word *net* has apparently been added to stress that working capital is the net difference between current assets and current liabilities (particularly since some financial commentators tend to confuse current assets with working capital).

At the same time, other financial publications have used the term *net working capital* to mean the amount of working capital that remains after paying both current liabilities and long-term debt: in other words, current assets minus both current liabilities and long-term liabilities. Companies with positive net working capital under this definition are considered by investment analysts to be in a particularly liquid condition, although experience has shown that certain presumably liquid assets (accounts receivable and inventory) cannot necessarily be converted to cash as expected.

By definition, a company with *Total Noncurrent Assets to Net Worth* of less than 1.0 will have positive *net* working capital (as well as positive working capital in the usual meaning of the term). This condition of liquidity is, of course, strongly influenced by a company's specific line of business. In certain industries, most companies have a relatively small financial commitment in fixed assets versus funds tied up in current assets, either because fixed assets play a comparatively insignificant role in total business activity or because a large investment in plant and equipment is overshadowed by an even larger amount of accounts receivable and inventory on the books. Such firms typically report positive net working capital (in the sense of current assets minus both current liabilities and long-term liabilities).

Investors who are particularly oriented to fundamental asset value often seek to identify companies with net working capital (defined as current assets minus all liabilities, both current and long-term) greater than the market value of equity. Called *net net* investments, such situations afford the opportunity to buy an ownership share in a company for less than the corresponding net value of the firm's current assets after all liabilities have been subtracted. The stock of a company in a positive *net net* position must, of course, be selling for less than its book value (net worth) per share. In addition, the company must also have a large amount of current assets in proportion to total assets and will ordinarily show relatively low financial leverage (low total debt versus net worth) as well.

The concept of net working capital (versus working capital, as ordinarily defined) is not especially useful in evaluating the financial structure of most small and medium-size companies, but you should be familiar with this term. It is important to note that, in order to avoid possible confusion, the definitions used in any new source of financial data should be carefully read and well understood before being applied in comparative analysis.

Appendix B

Operating Analysis and Profit Planning: Related Ratios and Concepts

Cause-and-effect ratio analysis provides a framework for measuring a company's fundamental financial structure, which limits or expands its operating capabilities in relation to its competition. The cause-and-effect approach also enables you to make systematic judgments about a company's ability to generate profit in relation to sales, assets, and owners' equity. Although this method of financial analysis was not specifically designed for evaluating the operating statement, the same logical principles of comparing one item with another and seeking causal relationships can be applied to the evaluation of a company's income, expense, and profit patterns. Application of the ratio technique to company operations is described in this special supplement.

Appendix B1

Income Statement Analysis

The cause-and-effect approach to the analysis of the key financial ratios can also be applied to the income statement, commonly called the profit-and-loss statement, the operating statement, and the income and expense statement.

Line of Business Critical

Unlike the key financial ratios, however, the causal relationships reflected in the income statement vary tremendously from one line of business activity to another. Some manufacturing industries are labor intensive, while others depend primarily on machinery and equipment. Some wholesalers carry massive inventories; others sell on a drop-ship basis. Some retailing lines are based on rapid turnover and a thin margin of profit on sales; others are characterized by low turnover, seasonal demand, and high profit margin. Service businesses that require major investment in facilities and equipment have completely different operating relationships from those that offer strictly personal or professional services. Some companies are primarily or exclusively sales organizations, while others have virtually no sales budget at all. The nearly universal applicability of the key financial ratios does not extend to income statement relationships. Consequently, the cause-and-effect approach can be described in only somewhat general terms with regard to expense patterns. Management must determine the specific factors and relationships that result in operating advantages within the company's particular line of business.

Items as Percentages

The first step in preparing the income statement for analysis is the conversion of each expense and profit (or loss) item to a percentage or ratio of a single base, such as net sales. Expressing all items as percentages permits more meaningful year-to-year comparisons and also facilitates evaluation of a company's operating expense pattern in relation to industry standards. Although net sales is the most commonly used base for generating operating percentages, other measures, such as percentages of gross margin and dollars per employee, are also useful for understanding trends and competitive position.

Comparing year-to-year expense and profit performance in raw dollars can be helpful in emphasizing the extent and impact of shifts in operating patterns, but dollar figures have limited value in the detection of causal relationships. If sales have increased by $300,000 and office compensation has risen by $15,000 during the same period, is that a favorable trend? Pre-tax profit was up by $12,000. Does that seem like good news? The answers obviously depend on the company's line of activity, as well as its sales volume and previous profit performance.

Table B1-1 shows how these dollar changes would affect Companies A and C. For Company A, the rapid sales increase would result in a slight decline in *Net Profit to Net Sales*. Nevertheless, we learned earlier that Company A's profit percentage is well above the industry norm, so a strategy based on selective price reductions to achieve a major boost in sales may be advantageous. Company C's *Net Profit to Net Sales* would definitely benefit from a move to boost profit by $12,000 on a $300,000 sales increase. Nevertheless, in view of Company C's comparatively high financial leverage (analyzed in Chapter 26), management must weigh carefully the availability of financing and the consequent risks involved in a significant sales expansion.

Office compensation would show opposite trends for Companies A and C. Because this item represents a comparatively low percentage of net sales for Company A, a $15,000 climb in office salaries and wages on a sales increase of $300,000 would cause a slight percentage rise in proportion to net sales. Company C, on the other hand, would achieve a substantial reduction in its office compensation percentage through the same dollar changes. Clearly, relating costs to an appropriate operating

Table B1-1.   The effect of change in net sales and salaries on return on sales for two companies.

	Year 1	Year 2	Change
Company A			
Net sales	$750,000	$1,050,000	+$300,000
Office salaries	33,700	48,700	+15,000
Net profit	38,000	50,000	+12,000
Office Salaries to Net Sales	4.5%	4.6%	+0.1%
Net Profit to Net Sales	5.1%	4.8%	−0.3%
Company C			
Net sales	$1,250,000	$1,550,000	+$300,000
Office salaries	100,000	115,000	+15,000
Net profit	15,000	27,000	+12,000
Office Salaries to Net Sales	8.0%	7.4%	−0.6%
Net Profit to Net Sales	1.2%	1.7%	+0.5%

factor, ordinarily net sales, is a critical first step in understanding the income statement. Industry standards for expense percentages are most frequently published as averages, since they are all related to a single factor that provides a consistent and stable basis for comparison. In addition, the average has the added benefit of being familiar to most businesspeople. A few detailed trade association reports also display the median and the range of common experience for each expense item of significance to companies in that line of activity. These statistics are explained in detail in Appendix C.

Comparisons With Industry Figures

In some cases, variances between a company's expense percentage and the average for its comparison group may be traceable to accounting classifications, rather than to actual operating differences. It is difficult, if not impossible, to be sure. But no major disparity should be ignored. If there is reason to believe that classification procedures have caused the variance from the norm, why is the company tracking costs in an unusual manner? Does the difference in classification benefit the company in some way? If so, why do most other companies in the industry not assign their costs accordingly? If variances in operating percentages appear to reflect an unusual operating pattern for the company, you must determine whether that deviation from the average represents an advantage to be increased or a disadvantage to be corrected. An item-by-item review of the company's cost structure is likely to indicate certain competitive advantages and also suggest other areas where improvements may be made. A wise owner or manager will move quickly to correct any clear deficiencies that may be discovered through comparisons with industry figures, but he will also make every effort to strengthen any competitive advantages he may find.

A below-average percentage for a specific expense item is not necessarily favorable. Too little money expended in certain areas, such as selling and administrative expenses, can actually prevent a company from realizing its full profit potential. Whether high or low, each expense percentage must be judged on its own merits. The calculation and comparison of operating percentages is only intended to emphasize those items that should be closely considered. Some relatively high expense percentages, reflecting such management strategies as above-average compensation of personnel, more expensive facilities, or a major sales campaign, may be necessary to meet specific competitive conditions and may yield superior overall profit. Only by considering each percentage difference, however, can you make an informed judgment concerning expense trends, comparative performance, and the potential for cost reduction and profit improvement.

Industry averages are only management tools; they can never be substituted for business judgment. No one can afford to ignore the experience of competitors as reflected in industry statistics, but the successful manager will not allow the averages to override his or her well-considered decisions. At the same time, the confident manager will seek out comparative data to raise constructive questions about the proper course of action and find new ideas for improving operations.

Focus on Decisions Under Management Control

In addition to net sales, several other key factors can be used as the common denominator for calculating operating percentages and ratios. Many wholesaling industries display expense and profit items as percentages of gross margin (gross profit). This approach is intended to focus on the operating decisions under management control—purchasing, pricing, and resource/cost management—by removing cost of sales from the calculations. It also emphasizes the need to relate sales representatives' commissions, the single largest expense item for many wholesaler/distributors, to gross margin rather than sales volume. Comparing operating expenses and profit with gross margin can, in addition, help some companies to answer the question, Since we have increased our gross margin as a percentage of net sales, but our net profit percentage has not kept pace, what expenses have grown faster than gross margin? All such expenses will be indicated by a year-to-year increase in those items when expressed as a percentage of gross margin. For an analysis of this kind, using gross margin as the common denominator can be very useful, but this approach can also send somewhat misleading signals.

Calculating costs and profit as percentages of gross margin implies that prices are essentially rigid (or closely controlled by competition) and that exceptional profit is primarily the result of squeezing down costs, rather than a reflection of effective selling and pricing. This approach is, generally speaking, appropriate to lines of business that obtain a large percentage of their work on a bid basis and add value to their product by means of largely mechanical and interchangeable operations. Many distributors, however, add significant value to the products they sell through more intangible contributions—outstanding design, systems work, inventory management, or related services—enabling them to increase their prices and achieve a superior net profit.

To illustrate this point, let's look at a before-and-after example in Table B1-2. Company E has decided to emphasize a high-quality image, backed up by excellent service, and to initiate gradual price increases totaling 9.5% of net sales. We will assume that the price hikes, in this case, can be absorbed by Company E's clients with relative ease. The company has been earning a 24.0% gross margin on each sales dollar, and management has recently become aware that the industry median—the gross margin earned by Company E's typical competitor—is 33.5%. As astonishing as such ignorance of industry conditions may seem, this example is a composite of several real-life cases. As a result of the business's marketing and service changes, Company E's income statement shows a significant shift in Year 2. Gross margin has been boosted to 28.3% of net sales, and

Table B1-2. Operating figures stated as percentages of net sales and gross margin for Company E.

	Year 1	Year 2	Change
Net sales	$6,000,000	$6,570,000	+ $570,000
Purchases and other cost of sales	4,560,000	4,710,000	+ 150,000
Gross margin	1,440,000	1,860,000	+ 420,000
Total selling expenses	690,000	930,000	+ 240,000
Total administrative expenses	630,000	780,000	+ 150,000
Net profit before taxes	$ 120,000	$ 150,000	+ 30,000
As Percentages of Net Sales:			
Net Sales	100.0%	100.0%	0.0%
Purchases and Other Cost of Sales	76.0	71.7	− 4.3
Gross Margin	24.0	28.3	+ 4.3
Total Selling Expenses	11.5	14.1	+ 2.6
Total Administrative Expenses	10.5	11.9	+ 1.4
Net Profit Before Taxes	2.0	2.3	+ 0.3
As Percentages of Gross Margin:			
Gross Margin	100.0%	100.0%	0.0%
Total Selling Expenses	47.9	50.0	+ 2.1
Total Administrative Expenses	43.8	41.9	− 1.9
Net Profit Before Taxes	8.3	8.1	− 0.2

management feels that the company's image has improved through additional design capability (which accounts for the increase in cost of sales), greater sales coverage, and improvements in customer service. Consequently, Company E's president believes that additional price increases—coupled with expanded design, sales, and service capabilities—would be entirely feasible until gross margin reaches at least the 33.5% industry median. How can management be sure that this strategy has actually begun to benefit the company? On a dollar basis, the results have been somewhat positive with respect to net profit, and office morale has greatly improved. But should Company E continue to add internal costs while pushing for a higher gross margin?

An outside analyst's evaluation of the company's performance will be determined by the measure selected. Looking again at Table B1-2, we see that the percentages based on gross margin suggest that the company is performing less efficiently, although its dollar profit has been increased. On the other hand, both gross margin and net profit have increased relative to sales, and we have already noted the rise in net profit dollars. Consequently, the percentages based on net sales appear to be the most accurate reflection of the company's progress. Since each approach has its own advantages, management should make a careful study of all cost items in relation to both net sales and gross margin in order to assure that the advantage gained from the increase in gross margin dollars is not squandered on unnecessary displays of new-found prosperity.

Dangers of Using Percentages of Gross Margin

A further illustration of the possibility of reaching misleading conclusions by relying on operating figures stated as percentages of gross margin is provided by Company F (also known as Joe's Rock-Bottom Sales Corporation), a newly formed distributorship working out of a goat shed on the edge of town. The principal (Joe) has decided to saturate his market area with as many sales reps as he can convince to join him. Their sales backgrounds in disco lessons, fad diets, and escort services are ideally suited to the company's marketing plan. After the first year of operation, the figures for Company F are not especially gratifying to Joe, but he is pleased to find from industry figures that his business actually outperformed the norm. But how could that be, especially in view of a disappointing net profit totaling $15,000? Company F's results are shown in Table B1-3.

By virtue of the company's minimal overhead, Company F has succeeded in making a small net profit, despite a dismally low gross margin. The profit earned by Joe's new enterprise is decidedly below that earned by a typical competitor of similar size when the bottom line is related to net sales, but Company F appears to have a bright future if the analyst relies on percentages of gross margin. Company F has generated far less money in actual dollars—and in relation to sales volume—than has its typical competitor, but the company appears more profitable as a percentage of gross margin simply because it is operating on such a thin spread. Joe's relatively narrow net profit margin on each sales dollar makes the company extremely vulnerable to price competition from cut-rate operators who do not even have an office for their sales reps, but this important fact is concealed by using gross margin as the basis for comparison. In fact, the gross margin percentages make Company F appear to be a sound model to follow.

Table B1-3. Operating figures stated as percentages of net sales and gross margin for Company F.

	Dollars	*Percentage of net sales*	*Industry standard*
Net sales	$1,600,000	100.0%	100.0%
Purchases and other cost of sales	1,414,000	88.4	66.5
Gross margin	186,000	11.6	33.5
Total selling expenses	120,000	7.5	16.5
Total administrative expenses	51,000	3.2	14.5
Net profit before taxes	$ 15,000	0.9	2.5

	Dollars	*Percentage of gross margin*	*Industry standard*
Gross margin	$186,000	100.0%	100.0%
Total selling expenses	120,000	64.5	49.3
Total administrative expenses	51,000	27.4	41.8
Net profit before taxes	$ 15,000	8.1	7.5

To achieve a *Net Profit to Net Worth* equal to the group norm, Company F would have to conduct nearly three times as much sales volume on each dollar of net worth as does its typical competitor. As a result, the company's debt would be far higher than the industry standard in relation to net worth, unless the company could manage its assets with extraordinary efficiency. These facts are obvious from the cause-and-effect relationship we have analyzed in earlier chapters: *Net Profit to Net Worth* is equal to *Net Profit to Net Sales* multiplied by *Net Sales to Net Worth*. Yet looking at Company F's operating expenses and net profit as percentages of gross margin conceals the relationship between *Net Profit to Net Sales* (the traditional "bottom line") and *Net Profit to Net Worth*.

Any of the generally accepted financial ratios could be recast in relation to gross margin, but the results would be equally uninformative, in most cases. Suppose, for example, that we attempt to substitute *Gross Margin to Net Worth* for *Net Sales to Net Worth* in order to evaluate the sufficiency of owners' equity available to support business activity (expressed, in this case, as gross margin instead of net sales). The calculation of *Gross Margin to Net Worth* is simple enough: Divide gross margin by net worth. The result, however, may send a misleading signal. For Company F, gross margin of $93,000 divided by net worth of $75,000 yields 1.2, a value substantially below the industry standard, as shown in Table B1-4. This finding, attributable to the very low gross margin achieved by Company F, suggests that the company is very well capitalized. Company F's comparatively high *Net Sales to Net Worth*, on the other hand, indicates an undercapitalized situation. This conclusion is clearly supported by the fact that Company F's financial leverage (represented by *Total Liabilities to Net Worth*) is

Table B1-4. Effect of substituting gross margin for net sales in key ratios of Company F.

Net sales	$1,600,000
Gross margin	186,000
Total assets	530,000
Total liabilities	380,000
Net worth	150,000
Gross Margin to Net Worth	
Company	1.2 times
Industry standard	2.0 times
Net Sales to Net Worth	
Company	10.7 times
Industry standard	5.9 times
Net Sales to Total Assets	
Company	3.0 times
Industry standard	2.5 times
Total Liabilities to Net Worth	
Company	2.5 times
Industry standard	1.4 times

substantially above the industry norm. In short, comparisons of ratios based on gross margin may present a distorted picture of a company's financial strengths and weaknesses. To avoid serious errors in interpretation, you must thoroughly understand the purposes and limitations of such comparisons.

Dangers of Using Percentages of Net Labor Sales

A similar approach to analyzing operating performance, often found in manufacturing industries, is the presentation of expense and profit items as percentages of *net labor sales* (or *net net sales*): net sales minus direct material and subcontracted services, adjusted for changes in inventory. Within many industries, direct material expense varies widely as a percentage of net sales. Some companies work almost exclusively on customer-supplied material, while others purchase castings, subassemblies, and value-added components for the items they manufacture and sell. Many large manufacturers and smaller design firms produce only a few critical parts and assemble the remainder of the end product. Some companies use precious metals or other unusually costly material, often subject to wide swings in price, as part of their process. As a result, expense and profit comparisons can be greatly distorted by differences in direct material.

To eliminate much of the influence of direct material, some industry studies display expense items and net profit as percentages of net labor sales. Presentation of operating figures in relation to net labor sales is intended to focus on the efficiency of production, selling, and administration by eliminating direct material from the denominator for operating percentages, but this approach is again subject to misinterpretation unless percentages of net sales are also used in the analysis. In addition to the types of distortion described in connection with percentages of gross margin, net labor sales percentages are affected by mark-up on direct material. A company whose production process involves a relatively high level of direct material as a proportion of net sales will, therefore, tend to show a relatively high net profit as a percentage of net labor sales.

To see why, suppose that a company begins to perform work on very expensive material which it purchases. Management should provide for a mark-up on the cost of direct material to cover related expenses—physical handling, scrap losses, office expense for ordering and tracking, price fluctuations, and all other costs related to this material—plus an additional percentage for profit. Assuming that the mark-up percentage holds the company's *Net Profit to Net Sales* at the original level, the extra profit on direct material will be added to the existing profit on operations (based on a normal level of direct material). The additional dollar amount of profit earned on the expensive direct material will result in a higher net profit as a percentage of net labor sales, even though net profit as a proportion of net sales is unchanged.

The relationship between net profit and net labor sales can be expressed in ratio form. The first step is to adjust direct material and subcontracted services for any changes in inventory (if this adjustment has not already been made through the company's cost accounting system). Next, this amount is subtracted from net sales to yield net labor sales. Then net profit before taxes is divided by net labor sales. The result, *Net Profit to Net Labor Sales*, is ordinarily expressed as a percentage.

The effect of mark-up on direct material is illustrated in Table B1-5. In this example, Company G has begun to employ a method of manufacturing that uses its existing equipment and personnel to produce parts in an exotic, and very expensive, material. The company's competitors have recently made the same move because of pressure from customers, who have evidenced no objection to bearing increased expenses directly related to the change in material. Company G's customers have, however, indicated that they expect costs, and prices, to remain the same in other respects. Thus, the mark-up on direct materials has the net effect of leaving *Net Profit to Net Sales* at 3.0% in Year 2. At the same time, *Net Profit to Net Labor Sales* has risen to 5.1% from 3.8%. Company G has been made more profitable in terms of total dollars by the changeover to the highly costly material, but it would be a mistake to conclude that the company is necessarily operated in a more efficient manner. In this case, *Net Profit to Net Sales* provides a more accurate picture of the change in Company G's situation than does *Net Profit to Net Labor Sales*. On the other hand, the company's year-to-year expense percentages are less distorted by using net labor sales, rather than net sales, as the common denominator.

This example suggests the benefit of calculating expense and profit items as percentages of net sales and then employing additional tests, such as percentages of net labor sales, appropriate to the company's specific characteristics and industry conditions. Not only does *Net Profit to Net Sales* tie directly with the other key financial ratios, but banks and other credit grantors ordinarily analyze

Table B1-5. The effect of markup on direct material for Company G.

	Year 1	Year 2
Net sales*	$4,000,000	$5,840,000
Direct material		
(adjusted for change in inventory)	800,000	2,400,000
Net labor sales	3,200,000	3,440,000
Other manufacturing expenses	2,220,000	2,353,200
Selling & administrative expenses	860,000	911,600
Net profit before taxes	$ 120,000	$ 175,200
Net Profit		
to Net Sales	3.0%	3.0%
Net Profit		
to Net Labor Sales	3.8%	5.1%

*Including markup on direct material: Year 1, $120,000; Year 2, $360,000.

expenses and profit in relation to net sales. Consequently, business owners and managers will benefit from understanding operating statement items as percentages of net sales even if other denominators have proved to be more valuable in certain industry situations.

Nonfinancial Factors

Analyzing the income statement in relation to nonfinancial factors often helps to place a company's expense pattern in perspective. Calculations of costs and profit per employee, per direct labor employee, per salesperson, per direct labor hour, per square foot, per transaction, per customer, per day, or per hour open for business can yield interesting insights into cost reduction, resource allocation, and profit maximization. In most cases, these special ratios are used strictly for internal purposes in detecting a company's year-to-year trends or analyzing expense patterns by quarter, month, or day of the week. Few trade associations now provide detailed figures for comparison. As more and more data are recorded on computers, however, the likelihood increases that industry databases will be created to provide interfirm comparisons of expense and profit patterns in relation to virtually any factor of importance in that line of business.

To highlight otherwise subtle shifts in cost patterns, you may wish to compute expense items as percentages of subtotals within the operating statement. Individual manufacturing costs can be expressed as percentages of cost of sales (more appropriately *cost of goods sold* or *total factory cost of shipments* in product and process industries). Similarly, individual selling and marketing expenses stand out when compared with the subtotal for that area of business activity. Each general and administrative expense item, likewise, becomes more prominent when displayed as a percentage of total general and administrative costs.

At the next level of detail, individual expense items should be compared with other cost factors that have a direct functional interrelationship or that may indicate changes in company strategy. For example, comparing direct material with each of the other manufacturing costs will dramatize a shift from in-house production to outside purchases and subcontracting. Special ratios such as *Indirect Labor to Direct Labor* and *Supervision to Direct Labor plus Indirect Labor* illustrate changes in product/process mix, personnel policies, or labor efficiency. Comparing depreciation and leasing expenses (plus utilities, property taxes, and interest expense in some cases) with total manufacturing labor will reveal trends in capital intensity, modernization, and automation. Selling and marketing expenses should be related to the company's gross margin and to net profit when analyzing the effectiveness of such outlays. A comparison of advertising expenses versus sales commissions may raise questions about external sales support. Similarly, a back-up ratio of sales support and clerical costs to sales reps' compensation may provide management with ideas for controlling selling expenses and improving resource allocation.

Use of Nonfinancial Data

Ratios can also be computed from entirely nonfinancial data. A back-up ratio of telemarketing specialists, customer service personnel, and clerical workers per outside sales rep can reveal trends, intentional or not, that affect employee performance and profitability. Information about invoices per employee, items per invoice, and average days from shipment to actual billing can help management to direct operations more effectively.

Unfortunately, few companies have made an effort to organize and analyze the data, financial and nonfinancial, that they have on hand—data that would help them to gain greater control of their operations. Some companies analyze profit on a customer-by-customer basis, but many fail to allocate overhead costs to each account even though they know that certain (often marginally profitable) customers require a disproportionate amount of sales and administrative time. A surprisingly small number of companies with computerized record-keeping systems attempt to determine whether their proportion of successful bids or productive sales calls is related to the size of the order, the sales volume of the customer, or the total annual dollar value of orders placed by that customer. They might well improve their selling efficiency and their net profit by relating their company's "hit rate" to the manner of obtaining orders—for example, wide-open bidding versus negotiations with a small number of preferred vendors versus sole source, or cold call versus walk-in versus referral. The organizational level of customer contact (plant manager or department head versus a purchasing agent), the level of communication with the customer (during bidding, design, and/or production), and the specific individuals involved in the transaction within a customer company may all fit a definite pattern that can be revealed by relatively simple data organization and analysis. If quotations involving a certain purchasing agent have a significantly lower probability of turning into profitable orders, management should be aware of that fact.

Retail customers also tend to exhibit definable patterns. A company's long-term profitability depends on identifying the personal characteristics of its customers and aligning its selling strategy and operations accordingly. Customer characteristics include the obvious demographic factors (such as age, sex, income, and education), as well as habits and preferences (including distance traveled for shopping, importance of nearby parking, response to newspaper or radio advertising, and preferred business hours). The company's reaction to those characteristics is reflected in its advertising (both content and media), breadth of selection (goods and/or services), quality, customer support (formerly called "service"), pricing, brand emphasis, specials (such as loss leaders or periodic discount sales), business hours, location, parking (or proximity), and decor. Because a community's demographic profile changes, and customer preferences within each category also change, management must be alert and responsive.

Every successful retailer is personally aware of the important variables that affect his company's sales, expenses, and profit. Few business decision makers, however, have actually begun using today's affordable microcomputer technology to obtain and analyze the solid facts that might provide an important competitive edge in developing a superior business strategy. By relating information about the characteristics of present and potential customers to operating costs and asset structure, management can direct the business toward an optimum sales/cost/ profit relationship. When an expense percentage is higher than the industry norm and the company's customers are found to have little interest in the feature or service provided, an opportunity for cost reduction is indicated. On the other hand, an expense percentage lower than the comparative standard, coupled with evidence that customers have a positive interest in that area, indicates the need for immediate management attention. A combination of more effective marketing and selling, greater outlays in certain areas of particular interest or concern to customers, selective cost reduction in nonsensitive areas, and clearly targeted pricing will help to improve the bottom line of any company.

In addition to making a positive impact on profitability, income improvements that result in lower expense percentages can also strengthen cash flow and fundamental financial structure. Comparatively high office costs, for example, may indicate processing inefficiencies which, if corrected, could lead to lower accounts receivable (through faster billing and deposits), lower inventory (through more prompt and accurate ordering), and better utilization of fixed assets (through reduced need for warehousing and even office space). All of these favorable changes would be reflected in the key financial ratios. Although the cause-and-effect ratio approach is primarily concerned with identifying a company's fundamental financial strengths and weaknesses, the basic logical principles of ratio analysis can be profitably applied in a wide variety of highly specific operating situations.

Appendix B2

Break-Even Analysis

Break-even analysis—also known as analysis of contribution to overhead and profit—is a basic management tool particularly useful to companies that have the option of acquiring capital equipment (fixed assets) as a means of reducing variable expenses. Personnel, material, subcontracting, and other cost elements that tend to vary with business activity may be decreased as a percentage of net sales through automation, computerization, or more efficient facilities. But how will the realignment of costs affect the company's profit picture as sales rise or fall from their present level? Break-even analysis is designed to answer that question. This analytical tool can also provide useful strategic insights for managing companies that face the decision of substituting highly specialized technical personnel (who become essentially fixed costs because of the substantial recruitment and training commitment) for more readily available individuals (who represent variable costs because their number might be reduced in the event of a business downturn). As expenses shift from variable to fixed, or vice versa, the equation that determines business survival and profitable growth is also changed.

Role of Fixed Costs

The basic concept underlying break-even analysis is simple: As a company makes increasing commitments to meet *fixed costs* (in the form of depreciation, interest, or payroll for highly skilled employees), it needs to make a reduction in variable costs, or increase its level of net sales. Otherwise, net profit will drop. A major investment in equipment, computer software, or high-tech personnel may enable a company to lower other labor, material, or subcontracting expenses, but it will raise the level of fixed costs, costs that must be met regardless of sales volume.

That is the key issue: Fixed costs come due month after month, whether or not the company meets its sales projections. Whereas variable costs are incurred gradually as sales increase, and can be reduced when sales decline, fixed costs represent an ongoing commitment. One major fixed cost, depreciation, is not actually a cash expense, but it ordinarily parallels the repayment schedule for loans incurred to purchase fixed assets. In any case, depreciation expense reduces net profit. Immediately following a major acquisition of fixed assets, a company often experiences a decline in profit, or even a few months of outright losses, owing to the larger amount of fixed costs. These costs will tend to depress profit until sales rise to a higher level (and thereby spread fixed costs over a larger sales base) or until the full reduction in variable costs can be achieved. The ability to support higher fixed costs over the long run depends on either of two conditions:

1. More stable, and usually greater, sales volume, which permits the orderly substitution of fixed costs for variable costs, resulting in a net profit gain
2. A higher profit in good economic times plus the financial structure to absorb reduced profit or outright losses during the down cycle

An understanding of break-even analysis will enable management to assess the financial risk involved in the acquisition of equipment and computer software or the hiring and training of specialized employees for sales expansion or cost reduction. At the same time, it is important to recognize that there is a significant (although difficult to quantify) risk in failing to respond to customer demands for increased technological capability or to keep pace with the growing capabilities of competitors.

Need to Distinguish Fixed and Variable Costs

Break-even analysis involves only a few simple calculations. The critical factor is not the arithmetic; it is management's ability to separate costs (with reasonable accuracy) into fixed and variable components—and to maintain sufficient control of costs and pricing so that actual expenses will bear a predictable relationship to sales activity.

Five factors are involved in the break-even equation:

NS = Net sales (in dollars)
VC = Variable costs (in dollars)
FC = Fixed costs (in dollars)
CM = Contribution Margin (as ratio)
BE = Break-even point (in dollars)

The difference between net sales and the total amount of variable costs is known as *contribution to overhead and profit* (COP). If COP is greater than fixed costs, the company will earn a profit. If not, the business will incur a loss. The break-even point is the level of net sales at which the contribution to overhead and profit is exactly equal to fixed costs. Above the break-even point, every additional dollar of COP goes directly to net profit.

The break-even point can be found in three simple steps. First, determine the *Contribution Margin*:

$$1.\ CM = \frac{NS - VC}{NS}$$

Contribution Margin (CM) represents the proportion of each dollar of net sales available to meet fixed expenses. This ratio is an important element in basic strategic planning, as well as a key factor in break-even analysis. The calculation of Contribution Margin may be based on historical records or future projections. If major changes in cost structure are anticipated, future projections should be made. The exact dollar amounts of *net sales* (NS) and *variable costs* (VC) are not usually critical, since the proportion will ordinarily remain essentially the same through a fairly broad sales range. Proportionate change is the characteristic that makes certain costs variable. To find the Contribution Margin for a company that reports net sales of $1 million and variable costs of $750,000, you must first subtract variable costs of $750,000 from net sales of $1 million to obtain $250,000, which represents the contribution to overhead and profit from those sales. Then simply divide the contribution amount, $250,000, by net sales, $1 million, for the result of 0.250. For break-even analysis, this ratio should be carried to three decimal places.

$$2. \text{ BE} = \text{FC} \div \text{CM}$$

Finding the *break-even point* (BE) depends on knowing *fixed costs* (FC) and relating this dollar amount to the Contribution Margin. Specifically, dividing fixed costs by the Contribution Margin will reveal the break-even point. If the company with a Contribution Margin of 0.250 has fixed costs of $200,000, the break-even point is $800,000 ($200,000 divided by 0.250). As the Contribution Margin rises, the break-even point falls, assuming that fixed costs remain the same. A company with fixed costs of $200,000 and a Contribution Margin of 0.400 would, for example, have a break-even point of only $500,000.

Once fixed costs and the Contribution Margin have been identified, the first two calculations can be combined into a single formula:

$$3. \text{ BE} = \text{FC} \div \frac{(\text{NS} - \text{VC})}{\text{NS}}$$

This is a more concise expression, but the steps involved in its calculation are essentially the same as those we have just completed.

Fixed Costs

Some costs are clearly fixed: They do not decline with a decrease in sales activity. Other costs, such as personnel expenses, are often regarded as entirely variable because they increase as sales activity grows. In reality, many of these expenses are variable when sales expand, but become essentially fixed costs during a business downturn. They often do not decline as sales activity decreases because management may decide to retain employees for many reasons: the cost of training, unemployment compensation rates, difficulty in finding replacements during a business upturn, and personal factors, among other considerations. To the extent that management can distinguish essentially fixed personnel costs from those that are truly variable, break-even analysis can be successfully applied to distributorships, retailing companies, and service concerns, as well as manufacturers and capital-intensive wholesalers.

Variable Costs

Variable costs increase and decrease in general proportion to sales activity. The ability to maintain a consistent relationship between variable costs and net sales requires knowledge of actual costs, control of those costs, and adequate pricing policies. Semi-variable costs involve both fixed charges and a variable component. They increase and decrease as sales rise and fall, but their rate of change is lower than that of net sales because they have a fixed element. Telephone service is typically a semi-variable cost: The basic fee is normally a fixed amount, but long distance and other activity charges generally vary with sales volume.

To become more familiar with break-even analysis, we can consider the issue facing Company J in Table B2-1. With net sales now standing at $14 million, Company J is planning to purchase $3.5 million of new equipment to meet customer requests for additional capabilities. The opportunity to increase sales by 25% within the next year appears entirely realistic. After the proposed acquisition of equipment, variable costs (particularly direct labor and subcontracting) are expected to rise more slowly than sales volume. But what will happen to Company J's cost structure and profit if the new sales opportunities do not materialize and variable costs remain the same? On the other hand, is there a possibility of reducing variable costs to offset the entire increase in fixed costs? The key factors that would determine net profit under those alternative outcomes are displayed in Table B2-1.

A first review of these extreme possibilities reveals substantial differences in net profit at the same level of net sales. A $784,000 increase in fixed costs (depreciation and interest expense) with no reduction in variable costs would produce a loss of $84,000 if sales volume remains at $14 million. In this case, the new acquisition and the associated fixed costs would push Company J's break-even point above present sales volume, as shown in the second column. If variable costs could be reduced to offset the entire rise in fixed costs, pre-tax net profit would remain unchanged at Company J's current level of sales. The break-even point, however, would increase from $11.2 million to $11,712,414 because of the higher level of fixed costs, as displayed in the third column. Consequently, profit would be more vulnerable to a possible decline in sales volume. Realistically, some reduction in variable costs might be achieved with no appreciable change in sales volume. Even though management intends to maintain its present work force and achieve higher profit through sales growth, some economies (possibly including a reduction of personnel) would become necessary to maintain a profit if sales cannot be increased. In that case, Company J would show a sharply reduced profit at the $14 million sales level and would incur a loss if sales volume dropped below $13,032,726, as indicated in the fourth column.

Now look at the projections for a 25% increase in sales volume, as illustrated in Table B2-2. Once again, Company J's management begins with the conservative estimate that there will be no reduction of variable costs on existing sales volume. For additional work using the new equipment, however, it is anticipated that variable costs can be cut by 10%: from $75,000 to $67,500 per $100,000 of sales. Consequently, the Contribution Margin on the additional sales would rise to 0.325 ([$100,000 − $67,500] ÷ $100,000). At annual sales of $17,500,000, the planned expansion would yield a profit of $1,053,500. In other words, a 25% increase in sales volume would boost net profit by more than 50%, provided that the reduction in variable costs can be achieved on the new work. On the other hand, the acquisition of additional equipment would require Company J to maintain sales above $13,524,528—assuming a production mix that includes 20% new work at the new Contribution Margin—in order to generate any profit at all. As noted in Table B2-1, adding the new equipment but achieving no change in the Contribution Margin (no reduction in variable costs) would require net sales of $14,336,000 to break even.

Another way of considering such an expansion is to determine the additional sales volume required to cover the new fixed costs and maintain net profit at the pre-acquisition amount. Dividing the new fixed costs of $784,000 by the Contribution Margin projected for additional sales—0.325—yields $2,412,308, the

Table B2-1. Break-even point: Effect of a proposed acquisition for Company J.

		Acquisition: alternative results		
	No acquisition	*No reduction of variable costs*	*Reduction of variable costs offsets new fixed costs*	*Some reduction of variable costs likely even if no sales growth*
Net sales	$14,000,000	$14,000,000	$14,000,000	$14,000,000
Fixed costs	2,800,000	3,584,000	3,584,000	3,584,000
Variable costs	10,500,000	10,500,000	9,716,000	10,150,000
Net profit before taxes	700,000	(84,000)	700,000	266,000
Contribution to fixed costs and profit	3,500,000	3,500,000	4,284,000	3,850,000
Contribution Margin	0.250x	0.250x	0.306x	0.275x
Break-even point (FC ÷ CM)	$11,200,000	$14,336,000	$11,712,414	$13,032,726

Table B2-2.   Break-even point: Effects of 25% increase in sales volume.

	No acquisition	Additional sales with reduced variable costs	Total sales after acquisition
Net sales	$14,000,000	$3,500,000	$17,500,000
Fixed costs	2,800,000	784,000	3,584,000
Variable costs	10,500,000	2,362,500	12,862,500
Net profit before taxes	700,000	353,500	1,053,500
Contribution to fixed costs and profit	3,500,000	1,137,500	4,637,500
Contribution Margin	0.250x	0.325x	0.265x
Break-even point (FC ÷ CM)	$11,200,000*	$2,412,308*	$13,524,528*

*The sum of the break-even point based on existing work plus the break-even point based on the new work after acquisition of new equipment does not equal the new break-even point (which assumes that all net sales in the future will consist of 20% new sales at the new margin and 80% old sales at the old margin). When one set of relationships between fixed costs, Contribution Margin, and break-even point is blended with a second set of relationships, the resulting break-even point will not be a simple sum of the two previous amounts. The new break-even point reflects both the relative proportion of fixed assets and the relative proportion of Contribution Margin, and also incorporates the assumed relative proportion of net sales.

amount of new sales needed at the new Contribution Margin. With this information, management can make a better judgment regarding the risks of the proposed acquisition.

Costs in Relation to Sales Volume

At various times during a company's growth, certain costs increase at a more rapid rate than sales volume. In some cases, an acceleration in costs relative to net sales indicates inadequate cost control; frequently, however, the cause is cost substitution. Purchasing high value-added material (such as castings or finished components) or subcontracting certain work as a substitute for direct labor is a common practice as a manufacturing company grows larger and accepts a greater variety of work. Indirect labor tends to increase faster than sales as work becomes more complex. Sales reps' compensation and outside sales commissions tend to rise more rapidly than sales as the owner/manager begins to rely on others to generate new work opportunities. If cost substitution leads to lower aggregate variable costs in relation to net sales, such a move will increase the Contribution Margin. As a result, the break-even point will be lowered, and the net profit percentage will increase at an accelerating rate above the break-even point. If, however, cost substitution results in higher variable costs and a lower Contribution Margin, it will raise the break-even point. Nevertheless, such a strategy may enable the company to produce higher net sales without the need to invest in specialized (more costly) personnel or additional equipment. As a result, the company's existing fixed costs may be spread over greater sales volume so as to generate an increase in net profit. A break-even chart will demonstrate whether a projected increase in sales volume would actually be sufficient to boost total net profit dollars—and possibly the *Net Profit to Net Sales* percentage.

Effect of High Fixed Costs

Substituting fixed costs for variable costs poses a particular danger for a company with a comparatively low profit margin (low *Net Profit to Net Sales*) or high financial leverage (high *Total Liabilities to Net Worth*). If sales decline or if interest rates rise, the company with high operational leverage (high fixed costs) and high financial leverage can find itself in a serious profit squeeze. As fixed costs rise, maintaining an adequate level of net sales becomes a matter of increasingly high priority, both to avoid losses and to maximize profit. In fact, when fixed costs represent a relatively large proportion of total costs, a company can improve its net profit margin even while variable costs are rising at a faster rate than sales. Therefore, a company with a high proportion of fixed costs is likcly to benefit from selective increases in variable costs (such as sales commissions or overtime premium) in order to spread fixed costs over higher sales volume.

A single break-even calculation is useful only within a certain sales volume range and time period. A company may need to increase fixed costs at certain points in its growth cycle or may need to alter its cost structure in response to competitive challenges. As a company grows, it may find good reasons for substituting certain variable costs, such as direct material and subcontracting, for other variable expenses, such as direct labor. Consequently, the Contribution Margin may rise or fall while fixed costs remain essentially constant. If a major change in sales volume is anticipated, or if break-even is being projected for more than three years in the future, several calculations should be performed, based on cost assumptions appropriate to changing conditions. As noted before, some costs, such as supervision, tend to increase as sales volume rises but remain fixed with a decline in sales activity. When, as a practical matter, management would be willing to absorb a temporary loss in order to retain certain personnel or other critical resources, the associated costs should be considered fixed for downside projections and variable for growth scenarios. Consequently, a company's fixed costs, Contribution Margin, and break-even point may differ significantly depending on whether the analysis is to anticipate the financial effects of a reduction in sales volume or to project the results of sales growth.

If a decrease in sales volume is anticipated, a company with relatively high variable costs and low fixed costs ordinarily enjoys a competitive advantage over a company with comparatively high fixed costs and low variable costs, assuming the same *Net Profit to Net Sales*. It is possible, however, that in times of rapid inflation coupled with declining demand, the advantage would be offset by a rapid escalation of variable costs. When significant sales growth is projected, the company that has substituted fixed costs for variable costs may have a competitive advantage, particularly during an inflationary period, but the extent of that advantage will be limited by the range of sales volume that can be supported by the existing fixed cost structure. At some point in the company's growth, additional facilities will be required. Fixed costs will then act like variable costs, increasing with sales volume, although in larger increments. On the other hand, unless special arrangements are made (such as subleasing), fixed costs will remain unchanged, even if sales volume falls dramatically.

Calculation of Profit-Achievement Point

Identifying the break-even point is, of course, only the first step in the cost analysis, since management is interested in profit attainment, not simply survival. Using the same basic break-even techniques, a *profit-achievement point* can be calculated. Profit may be targeted as a specific dollar amount, regardless of sales volume. This approach, in effect, treats net profit as a fixed cost for the purpose of calculating the profit-achievement point, which is the level of net sales sufficient to produce the projected profit. The dollar amount of desired profit is added to the dollar amount of fixed costs; the sum is divided by Contribution Margin to determine the profit-achievement point.

In most companies, however, management specifies its profit goal as a percentage of net sales. Profit is then treated as a variable cost in calculating the profit-achievement point. The percentage of profit established as the company's goal is first divided by 100 to obtain a decimal fraction; this fraction is subtracted from the Contribution Margin; then the dollar amount of fixed costs is divided by the Adjusted Contribution Margin (the difference between the original Contribution Margin and the company's profit goal). Maintaining a satisfactory profit percentage on net sales makes a company less vulnerable to price competition and cost increases. To focus management attention on profit margin, not simply profit dollars, projecting profit as a percentage of net sales is ordinarily the preferable approach.

To illustrate the second (profit percentage) approach to setting a profit-achievement point, let us suppose that management of the company in our previous example is developing financial projections for the next year. The company currently shows net sales of $14 million, a Contribution Margin of 0.250, and fixed costs of $2.8 million. Management desires to obtain a pre-tax net profit equal to 7.5% of sales volume and wants to determine the profit-achievement point. Converting 7.5% to a decimal fraction produces a ratio of .075. This fraction is now subtracted from the Contribution Margin of .250, yielding an Adjusted Contribution Margin (or profit-achievement margin) of .175. Dividing fixed costs of $2.8 million by the Adjusted Contribution Margin of .175 shows that the company's profit-achievement point is $16 million. Above that level of sales, the business will earn a pre-tax profit percentage greater than 7.5%. Conversely, if the unadjusted Contribution Margin remains at 0.250, and the company's sales volume is less than $16 million, pre-tax profit will sink below the 7.5% *Net Profit to Net Sales* sought by management.

Owners' Compensation as a Separate Expense

Because compensation granted to company owners and officers is ordinarily determined by the executives themselves and is often based on profit achievement, analyzing this expense item apart from other costs is a useful approach. Officers'/owners' compensation should ordinarily be treated as a two-part expense, with both a fixed cost component (base salary) and a variable cost component (bonus). Some companies establish a base salary for owners and officers and, in addition, set a combined goal for bonus plus profit as a percentage of net sales. Many small businesses make no formal distinction between base salary and bonus. For planning purposes, however, it is useful to identify the equivalent of base salary that should be considered a fixed cost. The extra compensation that is earned as a result of superior company performance can be classified as a variable cost in determining the break-even point and the profit-achievement point.

Net Sales in Relation to the Break-Even Point

Knowing how today's net sales volume relates to the break-even point is useful information for management. *Net Sales to Break-Even Point* is ordinarily calculated as a percentage: Divide net sales by the break-even point and multiply the result by 100 (or press the % key on a calculator). The percentage above break-even (or the increase required to reach break-even) may be found by subtracting 100 from *Net Sales to Break-Even Point*. For a company with net sales of $1 million and a calculated break-even point of $800,000, *Net Sales to Break-Even Point* is 125%: $1 million divided by $800,000 equals 1.25, which converts to 125%.

Net Sales to Break-Even Point is seldom presented in industry studies, largely because of the time required to identify (and allocate where necessary) fixed costs versus variable costs in order to find the break-even point. Nevertheless, a reasonable approximation of *Net Sales to Break-Even Point* can be calculated from the detailed operating percentages published by many trade associations. In most lines of business, certain expense items—such as supervision, building rent/lease, equipment rent/lease, depreciation, and insurance expense—can be considered fixed costs if a decline in sales volume is anticipated. Other costs—hourly personnel, direct materials or cost of goods for resale, sales commissions, and consumable supplies—tend to rise and fall in general proportion to net sales. Still others—including officers'/owners' compensation, employee benefits, telephone, and utilities—have elements of both variable cost and fixed cost. Classification and allocation of variable costs versus fixed costs will not be precise, particularly in recasting industry figures, but the analyst can derive broad comparative standards that will be helpful in detecting major competitive differences.

Once fixed and variable costs have been identified, *Net Sales to Break-Even Point* is calculated from industry operating percentages in a series of simple steps: Sum the percentages for fixed cost items; divide by 100 and multiply the result by average net sales to obtain average fixed costs; then sum the percentages for variable cost items and divide this sum by 100 and subtract the result from 1.0 to obtain average Contribution Margin. Next, divide the result in Step 1 by the result in Step 2 to find the break-even point. After that, you can easily calculate *Net Sales to Break-Even Point* by dividing net sales by the break-even point and multiplying by 100 to express the result as a percentage.

If, for example, the sum of the fixed cost percentages for a specific industry group was 20.0 and the average dollar amount of net sales was $2 million, the first calculation would yield average fixed costs of $400,000: 20.0 divided by 100 equals .200; .200 multiplied by $2 million equals $400,000. If the sum of variable cost items was 75.0, dividing this value by 100 would produce a ratio of 0.75; subtracting this result from 1.0 would show an average Contribution Margin of 0.25. Dividing average fixed costs of $400,000 by average Contribution Margin of 0.25 reveals an average break-even point of $1.6 million. When average net sales of $2 million are divided by the average break-even point of $1.6 million, *Net Sales to Break-Even Point* is found to be 125% (1.25 × 100).

A Warning

A company with *Net Sales to Break-Even Point* significantly lower than the derived industry standard is more likely to suffer a net loss in the event of a general downturn in sales or severe price competition within the industry. A low ratio is, however, only a warning flag, a sign of vulnerability, not a definitive predictor of the company's ability to meet competition or protect its market niche. The extent to which a company's profit will fall, while still remaining positive, is also influenced by its *Net Profit to Net Sales*.

The Company Compared With Industry Standards

In assessing the company's competitive position, management should consider how the relative proportions of fixed and variable costs compare with industry standards. A company with relatively high fixed costs and comparatively low variable costs enjoys a competitive advantage during sales expansions, while a business with low fixed costs and high total costs of a variable nature can, in some cases, actually benefit from a sales slowdown. In less than robust economic conditions, the low fixed cost/high variable cost company may experience a profit reduction, but the likelihood of maintaining a positive profit position is comparatively high. Unfortunately, any increase in market share gained during a recession is frequently lost during a rapid upturn, when the company's relatively high variable costs and delivery limitations often cause customers to seek other sources.

If both fixed costs and variable costs represent a comparatively high percentage of net sales, the company has a definite problem. Higher variable costs mean that the company has a smaller proportion of each sales dollar to cover fixed costs and generate a net profit, reflected in a lower Contribution Margin. With higher fixed costs to cover, the chances of achieving a comparatively high net profit are reduced to zero. If a management decision maker discovers such a relationship in his or her company, there are only two alternatives: Accept a net profit percentage below the industry norm, or make a significant change in the mix of fixed and variable costs.

This discussion of break-even analysis is based on the assumption that the company's pricing will remain constant or that prices will rise in general proportion to any increase in variable costs. If, however, prices are boosted at a faster rate than variable costs are increased—or if prices are cut to meet competitive pressure or to generate more unit sales—the Contribution Margin will change and the break-even point will be altered. A different product mix may also produce a higher or lower Contribution Margin. An increase in the Contribution Margin will lower the break-even point, since fixed costs will be divided by a larger factor. Most commentaries on break-even analysis in financial publications fail to note that the rules they state (for example, that net profit becomes more sensitive to changes in net sales as *Net Sales to Break-Even Point* declines) depend on the assumption that Contribution Margin is constant. A shift in a company's unit price relative to variable costs or a difference in product mix will often render such general statements inaccurate. Although the analyst must be alert to the somewhat artificial assumptions on which the break-even concept is based, this working tool directs attention to the critical characteristics, fixed and variable, of a company's cost structure.

Appendix B3

Cash Flow Analysis

Cash flow analysis has become an increasingly important tool for determining a company's ability to meet its future operating requirements while servicing its actual or contemplated debt. In this area of financial management and bank relations, cause-and-effect ratio analysis can be especially useful. Unfortunately, many business owners and managers assume that the various tools of financial management are mutually exclusive, that one method is old-fashioned and another is very modern. The fact is that cash flow analysis and ratio analysis are closely linked.

Debt Service

The term *debt service* does not necessarily mean actual repayment, since the growth plans of many companies call for an increase in the dollar amount, and possibly the proportion, of debt during the foreseeable future (usually a forecast period of three to five years). A revolving line of credit, either secured or unsecured short-term borrowing, is designed to support a temporary build-up of inventory and accounts receivable due to a seasonal factor or occasional surges in sales activity. Such short-term credit is ordinarily based on the ability to *clean up* or *rest* the line: that is, reduce the balance to zero, for a period of at least 30 days each year.

For intermediate-term or long-term financing, however, satisfactory debt service means the ability to maintain cash flow and financial structure within projected limits. These limits, which may be formally included in the loan agreement as specific terms or *covenants*, are frequently expressed in both dollar amounts and ratios. Minimum dollar limits for working capital, net worth, and net cash income are most often included in such covenants, although upper limits on capital expenditures and officers' compensation may also be specified. Three ratios with which we have become familiar are regularly subject to loan covenants: *Total Liabilities to Net Worth* may have a specified upper limit, while *Current Assets to Current Liabilities* and *Cash and Short-Term Investments plus Accounts Receivable to Current Liabilities* may have minimum values imposed. Failure to adhere to such covenants will result in a condition of default, which allows the bank to take certain actions to assure repayment.

Net Cash Flow

In discussing cash flow, a clear agreement on terminology is critical. The term *net cash flow*—net profit after taxes plus depreciation (and any other noncash charges)—was referenced earlier in connection with the *Debt Coverage Ratio*. Net cash flow (or *cash throw-off*), in theory, provides funds to service debt or replace fixed assets. This net amount, however, does not represent actual additions to cash or a bundle of money sitting idle at the end of the year. A substantial portion of the funds provided by net profit and depreciation may, in fact, be channeled into increased accounts receivable and inventory as fast as those funds are generated by the company. In some cases, accounts receivable and inventory grow so rapidly—through sales expansion, lax asset management, or both—that the net increase in these assets exceeds net cash flow. When that situation occurs, additional borrowing will be required, regardless of profit performance. Projecting cash flow obviously involves more than making an estimate of net income and depreciation from the operating statement. An understanding of cause-and-effect ratio analysis is also required.

Need for Outside Funding

The purpose of cash flow projections, from a management perspective, is to determine the need for outside funding, both long-term and short-term. By anticipating financing requirements well in advance, a business owner or manager is able to seek the most advantageous arrangements at his or her own pace. Borrowing money usually becomes more difficult as the need becomes more urgent.

The banking industry has developed computer software that takes into account the influence of certain key financial ratios—particularly the *Collection Period of Accounts Receivable* and *Cost of Sales to Inventory*—on cash flow. As a result, company owners and managers must be prepared to discuss their business plans in terms of financial ratios, particularly with respect to their credit-and-collection performance and their control of inventory. To serve as a useful decision-making tool, a cash flow projection requires reasonable assumptions about several factors. First of all, management must estimate the rate of sales growth, the percentage of net sales that will be absorbed by cost of sales and other operating expenses (net of depreciation and other noncash charges), the *Collection Period of Accounts Receivable*, *Cost of Sales to Inventory*, and the relationship between cost of sales and accounts payable in order to determine *net cash income*. Net cash income represents the amount of cash added or subtracted from operations, plus changes in current assets and current liabilities, minus interest expense and cash income taxes. A possible increase or decrease in short-term debt is not considered at this point.

Table B3-1 displays highlights from Company D's financial statement for the

Table B3-1.   Projected income statement and pro forma balance sheet for Company D.

	Most recent year	Next year (projected)
Income statement		
Net sales	$50,000,000	$60,000,000
Cost of sales*	40,000,000	45,000,000
Selling & administrative expenses	8,500,000	9,350,000
Net profit before interest expense	1,500,000	5,650,000
Interest expense	550,000	850,000
Net profit before taxes	950,000	4,800,000
Income taxes	300,000	1,600,000
Net profit after taxes	$ 650,000	$ 3,200,000
Balance sheet		
Cash & short-term investments	$ 100,000	$ 500,000
Accounts receivable	2,850,000	4,925,000
Inventory	4,900,000	5,700,000
Other current assets	550,000	300,000
Current assets	8,400,000	11,425,000
Fixed assets	2,450,000	4,000,000
Other noncurrent assets	550,000	250,000
Total assets	$11,400,000	$15,675,000
Current liabilities	$ 5,400,000	$ 5,900,000
Long-term liabilities	4,450,000	5,025,000
Total liabilities	9,850,000	10,925,000
Net worth	1,550,000	4,750,000
Total liabilities & net worth	$11,400,000	$15,675,000

*Including depreciation expense: recent year, $500,000; next year, $900,000.

previous year, together with projected results for the next 12 months. The assumptions required to make financial projections of this kind also apply to cash flow projections. These assumptions about operating performance, asset utilization, and other factors affecting cash flow are shown in Table B3-2. The projection of net cash income is displayed in Table B3-3.

In the real world, net cash income is frequently negative: Accounts receivable and inventory expand by a combined amount larger than the increase in current liabilities plus net cash flow (net profit plus depreciation). Even an extraordinarily profitable company may experience negative net cash income because of rapid sales growth, the need to offer more liberal credit terms, or a strategic move to increase inventory. Poor credit management, inadequate collection procedures, and deficient inventory control can also produce such a result.

Table B3-2. Factors affecting cash flow for Company D.

	Most recent year	Next year (projected)
Net sales	$50,000,000	—
Rate of sales growth[1]	—	+20.0%
Cost of sales		
(% of net sales)[2]	79.000%	73.500%
Selling & administrative expenses		
(% of net sales)[2]	17.000%	15.583%
Nonoperating expenses (net)		
(% of net sales)[2]	0.000%	0.000%
Collection Period of		
Accounts Receivable	20.805 days	29.960 days
Cost of Sales		
to Inventory[3]	8.163 times	7.895 times
Cost of Sales		
to Accounts Payable[2]	9.294 times	12.000 times
Net Sales		
to Fixed Assets	[4]	[4]
Capital expenditures	$500,000	$2,450,000
Income tax rate	31.579%	33.333%
Interest rate on borrowed funds	10.000%	12.000%
Dividend rate	0.000%	0.000%

[1] Based on changes in unit sales and price levels
[2] *Cash* transactions; excluding depreciation
[3] Including depreciation
[4] Not projected by management in this case; capital expenditures estimated instead
Note: Depending on the degree of precision sought, the ratios may be projected with more or fewer decimal places. Ordinarily, only one or two decimal places are used, but the ratios shown above are intended to permit you to derive dollar amounts close to those displayed in Table B3-3 and Table B3-4 while maintaining the dollar format of whole thousands.

As the next step in constructing a cash flow projection, current maturities of long-term debt are subtracted from net cash income to arrive at *discretionary cash flow* available for capital expenditures and dividend payments. For Company D, net cash income is projected as a positive $950,000, but current maturities of long-term debt (anticipated to be $1 million) result in negative discretionary cash flow.

Total financing requirements can be calculated by subtracting capital expenditures and any dividends from discretionary cash flow, as illustrated in Table B3-4. Next, the effect of an increase in net worth through new investment (or a decrease in net worth through stock repurchase) is computed to identify the amount of external financing required. An increase in net worth (shareholders' equity) from additional cash investment will reduce the need for external financing, although a reduction in net worth will require still more financing from sources outside the company. When projected external financing is subtracted from the calculated requirement for outside money, the end result is *effective cash flow*, the amount by which cash and short-term investments are expected to

Table B3-3.   Discretionary cash flow for Company D.

	Most recent year	Next year (projected)
Net sales	$50,000,000	$60,000,000
Cost of sales[1]	−39,500,000	−44,100,000
Selling & administrative expenses[1]	−8,500,000	−9,350,000
Nonoperating expenses (net)[2]	0	0
CASH FROM OPERATIONS	2,000,000	6,550,000
Change in accounts receivable[3]	−150,000	−2,075,000
Change in inventory[3]	−50,000	−800,000
Change in prepaid expenses[3]	0	+250,000
Change in accounts payable[4]	+375,000	−575,000
Change in accrued expenses[4]	+125,000	+50,000
CASH INCOME BEFORE INCOME TAXES AND INTEREST EXPENSE	2,300,000	3,400,000
Interest expense	−550,000	−850,000
CASH BEFORE INCOME TAXES	1,750,000	2,550,000
Cash income taxes	−300,000	−1,600,000
NET CASH INCOME	1,450,000	950,000
Current maturities of long-term debt	−650,000	−1,000,000
DISCRETIONARY CASH FLOW	$ 800,000	$ (50,000)

[1]Excluding depreciation and other noncash charges ($500,000 in most recent year, $900,000 projected for next year)
[2]Excluding interest expense, which is shown below
[3]When this item increases, net cash income is decreased
[4]When this item increases, net cash income is increased

rise or fall during the period. Banks and other commercial lenders ordinarily request projections for the next three to five years, but the abbreviated example in Table B3-3 and Table B3-4 will illustrate the basic principles of cash flow analysis.

Distortions in Cash Flow Projections

Unfortunately, many of the cash flow projections made by business owners and managers, particularly those made on computer spreadsheets, do not specifically include financial ratios in their calculations. The underlying assumptions may be similar; but by failing to tie the cash projections to explicit values for the *Collection Period of Accounts Receivable* and *Cost of Sales to Inventory*, a spreadsheet calculation of cash flow can turn a subtle month-to-month inaccuracy (or bias) into a monumental error in the third-, fourth-, or fifth-year projection. Computation of the key financial ratios, particularly the *Collection Period of Accounts Receivable* and *Cost of Sales to Inventory*, based on projected performance and the company's anticipated financial structure at the end of the period, will quickly reveal any inconsistencies between current results and the cash flow projections.

Table B3-4. Effect on discretionary and effective cash flow for Company D.

	Most recent year	Next year (projected)
DISCRETIONARY CASH FLOW	$800,000	$ (50,000)
Capital expenditures[1]	− 500,000	− 2,450,000
Expenditures for		
miscellaneous assets[2]	0	+ 300,000
Dividends	0	0
FINANCING REQUIREMENTS[3]	300,000	(2,200,000)
Change in owners' equity		
through cash investment	+ 350,000	0
EXTERNAL FINANCING REQUIREMENTS[3]	650,000	(2,200,000)
Change in long-term debt[4]	0	+ 1,575,000
Change in current maturities of		
long-term debt[4]	0	+ 350,000
SHORT-TERM EXTERNAL REQUIREMENTS	650,000	(275,000)
Change in short-term debt[4]	− 800,000	+ 675,000
EFFECTIVE CASH FLOW	$(150,000)	$ 400,000

[1]Negative value indicates capital expenditure
[2]Positive value represents cash generated by reduction of assets
[3]Positive value represents opportunity for payback; negative value indicates need for financing
[4]When this item is negative, debt is repaid and net cash flow is reduced.

If the cumulative projections indicate that the *Collection Period of Accounts Receivable* will decline from 48 days to 42 days during that time, what is the basis for such a change? In the absence of specific plans for improvement of credit policies and collection procedures, this measure should remain essentially constant throughout the projection period. Similarly, suppose that *Cost of Sales to Inventory*, when calculated on operating results for the fifth year and on the pro forma balance sheet at the end of that period, shows a value of 5.3, up from 4.6 during the last year of actual performance. It would be proper to question the reason for this projected improvement in inventory control. In most cases, management will have made no explicit plans for better asset utilization, and the difference between recent results and projected performance will usually be traceable to the compounding of seemingly minor month-to-month rounding or smoothing of the data. Calculating and analyzing the key financial ratios for each projected period will help management to understand the impact of balance sheet changes on cash flow, and also detect any errors that might cause embarrassment in bank negotiations. More importantly, recognizing and correcting unlikely assumptions will enable the company to avoid the financial embarrassment that all too often results from faulty projections.

Basic Principles of Cash Flow Analysis

It is important to note that certain balance sheet items—specifically, accounts receivable, inventory, prepaid expenses, accounts payable, and accrued expenses—affect cash flow through *changes* in year-to-year amounts. On the other hand, the income statement items—cost of sales (net of depreciation and noncash charges), selling and administrative expenses (also net of depreciation and noncash charges), nonoperating expenses (net of nonoperating income), interest expense, and cash income taxes—are, by their nature, summaries of cash activities for the year. Depreciation expense and net profit are not specifically shown, because these items are automatically included in cash from operations.

One balance sheet item, current maturities of long-term debt, requires special attention. This cash flow factor reflects the amount of cash actually paid to meet those obligations during the year, *not* the change in this item on the balance sheet. The net result of the transactions in Table B3-3 is *discretionary cash flow*, the change in the company's cash and short-term investments that would occur if the company planned no capital expenditures, no change in miscellaneous assets, no dividends, no change in owners' equity due to cash investment, and no change in debt (other than the payment of current maturities of long-term debt noted earlier).

Effects of Change in Accounts Receivable and Inventory

Assumptions about the *Collection Period of Accounts Receivable* and *Cost of Sales to Inventory* obviously have a major impact on cash flow. If, for example, management of Company D had determined that the business must permit the *Collection Period of Accounts Receivable* to rise to 45 days in order to meet competitive pressure, projected accounts receivable would have been more than $2,450,000 greater, and discretionary cash flow would have fallen by the same amount. Even with relatively minor differences in the projected ratios, changes in accounts receivable and inventory would have a major impact on Company D's cash flow, largely because of the sales growth planned for the coming year.

Table B3-4 illustrates the factors that affect the often highly significant difference between discretionary cash flow and effective cash flow (the actual change in cash and short-term investments from one period to the next). Examination of Tables B3-3 and B3-4 shows that Company D's projected sales expansion, which is expected to produce cash from operations totaling $6,550,000 during the next year (including an after-tax net profit of $3,200,000, according to the operating statement in Table B3-1), will require an increase of at least $675,000 in short-term bank debt. This additional financing, shown as short-term external requirements, will be needed to meet management's objective of bringing accounts payable in line with common practice in the industry while maintaining the same minimal cash balance at the end of next year. A $675,000 increase in short-term bank borrowing will be needed to boost cash to an adequate level in relation to sales volume. Rapid sales growth, even at a substantial profit percentage, does not necessarily produce a positive cash balance after all factors are considered.

The items in Table B3-4 are often put through several stages of adjustment. Suppose, for example, that the management of Company D had been informed that the bank did not find the proposed increase in debt acceptable. The company's decision makers would then have to study ways to scale down the projected $1,925,000 in additional long-term debt ($350,000 of which would fall due during the next year, boosting current maturities of long-term debt by that amount in the projection) and $675,000 in new short-term debt. In that case, the projected amount of capital expenditures might have to be reduced to stay within available borrowing limits. To remain as close as possible to the original plan, management might decide to operate with the same very low cash the company had at the end of last year, thereby cutting short-term debt requirements by $400,000 to make more funds available for the down payment on capital equipment.

An alternative analysis of this cash flow projection might, on the other hand, cause management to revise its plans for reducing accounts payable by the full $575,000 amount, thereby conserving cash to support the capital expenditure plan. Changes in other factors affecting cash flow, including inventory and accounts receivable, might also be considered. The complete cash flow projection may be adjusted many times before it represents a feasible plan acceptable to both management and outside sources of funds. In studying this example, you will note that the figure shown for capital expenditures on the cash flow projection does not equal the year-to-year change in fixed assets on the balance sheet because of the effect of depreciation during the year.

Important Causal Ratios

Formulating an effective cash flow projection and making a persuasive presentation for financing depend on a sound understanding of the relevant causal ratios, particularly the *Collection Period of Accounts Receivable* and *Cost of Sales to Inventory*. Another causal ratio, *Net Sales to Fixed Assets*, should also be analyzed before and after any proposed capital expenditures. In addition, a projection of the important effect ratios—*Total Liabilities to Net Worth, Current Assets to Current Liabilities*, and *Cash and Short-Term Investments plus Accounts Receivable to Current Liabilities (Quick Ratio)*—will almost certainly play an important role in any analysis of cash flow conducted by a bank or other creditors. Consequently, the company's decision makers should make an effort to anticipate questions and identify possible weaknesses in the company's projected ratios in comparison with industry norms. Whether or not their business currently depends on bank financing, company owners and managers should develop the ability to foresee future borrowing requirements. In some cases, the cash flow projection will show that management should prepare to make best use of a significant cash surplus.

Appendix B4

Gross Margin Return on Inventory

Inventory is ordinarily the single most important financial factor affecting the financial structure of wholesaling/distribution and retailing companies. Inventory management in the broadest sense, from anticipation of customer demand through purchasing, marketing, and selling, is the essence of successful wholesaling and retailing. Other key factors, such as credit and collections, facilities management, and investment adequacy, can also exert a highly important influence on these companies, just as these factors determine the survival and growth of manufacturing and service companies. Nevertheless, inventory management is the foremost element in enterprises formed for the purpose of buying and selling.

As a result, many wholesalers and retailers direct particular attention to a special financial formula, *Gross Margin Return on Inventory* (also known as the *Inventory Turn and Earn Ratio*). It is derived by multiplying one of the causal measures, *Cost of Sales to Inventory*, by *Gross Margin to Net Sales*. Some industries prefer to express *Gross Margin to Net Sales* as a percentage, leading to a *Gross Margin Return on Inventory* of approximately 100 to 200; others prefer to use a decimal fraction, which results in a ratio in the neighborhood of 1.0 to 2.0.

As shown in Table B4-1, Company B reports net sales of $5 million and cost of sales of $3,775,000. Subtracting $3,775,000 from $5 million results in gross margin of $1,225,000. Dividing that amount by $5 million shows that Company B's *Gross Margin to Net Sales* is 24.5% (after converting the decimal fraction, .245, to a percentage). When the cost of sales amount, $3,775,000, is divided by inventory of $750,000, *Cost of Sales to Inventory* is found to be 5.0. Multiplying *Gross Margin to Net Sales* of 24.5% by *Cost of Sales to Inventory* of 5.0 yields *Gross Margin Return on Inventory* of 122.5. Because this derived value does not relate to a specific denominator, it is neither considered a percentage nor properly designated in times; it is simply a reference value.

When High Gross Margin Is Needed

Gross Margin Return on Inventory illustrates the concept that a company needs to achieve a relatively high gross margin if it carries a comparatively high level of

Table B4-1. *Gross Margin Return on Inventory* **for four companies.**

	Company A	Company B	Company C	Company D
Net sales	$1,500,000	$5,000,000	$12,500,000	$50,000,000
Cost of sales	1,110,000	3,775,000	9,750,000	40,000,000
Gross margin	390,000	1,225,000	2,750,000	10,000,000
Inventory	170,000	750,000	2,500,000	4,900,000
Cost of Sales to Inventory				
Company	6.5 times	5.0 times	3.9 times	8.2 times
Industry standard	5.1 times	5.1 times	5.1 times	5.1 times
Gross Margin to Net Sales				
Company	26.0%	24.5%	22.0%	20.0%
Industry standard	21.5%	21.5%	21.5%	21.5%
Gross Margin Return on Inventory				
Company	169.0*	122.5*	85.8*	164.0*
Industry standard	109.7	109.7	109.7	109.7

*This derived value is, strictly speaking, neither a percentage nor a ratio that can be readily expressed as times, since it has no clearly defined denominator. It is simply a reference value which relates inventory turnover to gross margin. As inventory turnover declines (as inventory rises in relation to net sales), a higher gross margin percentage is ordinarily required in order to achieve an adequate net profit percentage.

inventory in relation to sales activity. In general terms, this is certainly true. A retailer of furs or jewelry with *Cost of Sales to Inventory* in the area of 1.5 will surely require higher *Gross Margin to Net Sales* than will a convenience food store with *Cost of Sales to Inventory* of 17.5. Similarly, a meat wholesaler with *Cost of Sales to Inventory* of 25.0 would not expect to earn the same *Gross Margin to Net Sales* as an auto parts distributor with *Cost of Sales to Inventory* of 3.5.

Nevertheless, a furrier or jeweler cannot hope to obtain a gross margin percentage sufficient to produce a *Gross Margin Return on Inventory* equal to that of the convenience store around the corner. While some decision makers in wholesaling and retailing lines of business regard 100 as the minimum acceptable *Gross Margin Return on Inventory* and 125 as a relatively high number, retailers of furs and jewelry typically report a ratio in the area of 65. The owner or manager of a convenience store or meat wholesaling business will normally seek *Gross Margin Return on Inventory* in excess of 350. The mid-range for this measure in wholesaling industries is approximately 140 to 240, while retailing lines commonly fall within the 90 to 100 range. Like all financial measures, *Gross Margin Return on Inventory* must be related to typical industry performance. You cannot rely on simplistic "rules of thumb" to evaluate a company's performance in this or any other area of financial management.

Table B4-1 shows how Companies A, B, C, and D compare with respect to *Gross Margin Return on Inventory*. Although this measure does not apply as well to manufacturing companies as to wholesaling and retailing companies (because the focus in manufacturing is to control the various expense elements in cost of sales and there is not as much emphasis on markup and merchandising), it directs attention to the relationship between inventory turnover and gross margin. Company A once again demonstrates superior performance, reporting relatively high *Gross Margin Return on Inventory* because both components of this measure, *Cost of Sales to Inventory* and *Gross Margin to Net Sales*, are on the high side. Near the middle of the pack, as always, Company B shows a *Gross Margin Return on Inventory* not far above the industry norm. The major influence was *Gross Margin to Net Sales* somewhat higher than the median for the comparison group. Company C trails its competitors as a result of very low *Cost of Sales to Inventory*. Despite *Gross Margin to Net Sales* below the industry norm, Company D achieved very high *Gross Margin Return on Inventory* due to its outstanding *Cost of Sales to Inventory*. The applicability of *Gross Margin Return on Inventory* varies from industry to industry. In many lines of business, however, this measure will remind you that the causal ratio, *Cost of Sales to Inventory*, is closely related to a company's operating cost pattern as well as to the company's basic financial structure.

Appendix B5

The Effect of Value Added

The term "value added," which is occasionally found in industry ratio studies, appears in a variety of business contexts, ranging from financial analysis to marketing to taxation. Value added, in its least specific sense, is the sum of special characteristics (such as exclusive design, reliability, style, or reputation) that enable a company to gain a pricing and profit advantage. In a more narrow context, a so-called value added tax is essentially a tax on sales generated by a company, with credit given for the tax paid on purchases. As applied to ratio analysis, value added is calculated by subtracting purchases of goods and services from net sales. The difference—value added—includes the activities performed by personnel and facilities within the company plus the firm's net profit. Various ratios can be calculated using value added as the numerator (for example, *Value Added to Net Sales* and *Value Added per Employee*) or as the common denominator. The components of value added, such as direct labor and facilities expense, are ordinarily expressed as percentages of the denominator (value added).

A company with net sales of $1 million and outside purchases—including goods for conversion or resale, subcontracting, utilities, supplies, services (from accounting and legal services to repair and maintenance by other parties), rent, and interest—of $610,000 contributes value added of $390,000 through the firm's employees and physical facilities. If the expenses attributable to those employees and facilities are $350,000, then the company's net profit before taxes is $40,000. Value added, at $390,000, is the sum of internal costs and net profit. Although in most industry studies, profit-related measures are calculated on a pre-tax basis, an alternative approach is to consider income taxes as representing outside purchases of services and calculate value added as the sum of internal expenses and after-tax net profit. Using pre-tax net profit as a component of value added in this example, we find that the company's value added of $390,000 divided by net sales of $1 million yields *Value Added to Net Sales* of 39.0% (after converting the decimal fraction, .390, to a percentage).

Higher Value Added in Relation to Sales

Every few years, the idea circulates throughout the business community that higher value added in proportion to sales volume leads to greater profitability.

When value added is defined in its most general sense—as the ability to gain a pricing and profit advantage—the link between value added and profitability leads to a self-fulfilling prophecy. But when the more specific definition of value added is used, does high *Value Added to Net Sales* actually lead to high *Net Profit to Net Sales*? Because net profit is a component of value added, a certain connection necessarily exists. Even beyond that, there appears to be a logical basis for concluding that increasing value added would boost net profit. If the profit earned by subcontractors and suppliers could be incorporated into the company's operations, profit per dollar of net sales would necessarily increase.

Table B5-1 compares the value added and the net profit performance of two manufacturing concerns, Companies I and J. While Company I is essentially an engineering and assembly organization that outsources the production of components and subassemblies, the management of Company J has opted to manufacture the entire product from stock metal with the business's own resources. Is Company J's high value added strategy beneficial? In terms of *Net Profit to Net Sales*, Company J is distinctly superior to Company I. On the other hand, a larger asset base, the acceleration of cash outflow for payroll versus the ability to obtain credit from suppliers, and a consequent increase in interest costs cause Company J's *Net Profit to Net Worth* to lag behind that of Company I, as shown in Table

Table B5-1.   Value added and net profit for two companies.

	Company I	Company J
Net sales	$1,000,000	$1,000,000
Engineering[1]	100,000[2]	100,000[2]
Production: Subcontractor cost	500,000	0
Materials cost	0[2]	100,000
Subcontractor profit	50,000	0
Internal cost[1]	0[2]	400,000[2]
Assembly	150,000[2]	150,000[2]
Sales & administration: Outside purchases	50,000	50,000
Internal[1]	100,000[2]	100,000[2]
Net profit before interest expense	50,000	100,000
Interest expense	10,000	35,000
Net profit before taxes	$ 40,000[2]	$ 65,000[2]
Net Profit to Net Sales	4.0%	6.5%
Value Added to Net Sales	39.0%	81.5%

[1]Expenses attributable to the company's employees and facilities
[2]Value added. Components of value added:

	Company I	Company J
	$100,000	$100,000
Engineering	$100,000	$100,000
Production: Internal cost	0	400,000
Assembly	150,000	150,000
Sales & administration: Internal	100,000	100,000
Net profit before taxes	40,000	65,000
	$390,000	$815,000

[3]Included in subcontractor cost

B5-2. Company J's relatively low *Net Profit to Net Worth* is especially revealing in view of the company's comparatively high *Total Liabilities to Net Worth*.

During a business downturn, Company J would be saddled with comparatively high fixed costs, which would tend to depress net profit. Taking this risk into account, the management of Company J might see, on balance, important compensating advantages in terms of guaranteed flow of production, protection of proprietary designs or processes, quality assurance, or other competitive factors. Consequently, despite its relatively low *Net Profit to Net Worth*, Company J may be the long-term winner in the contest for survival and growth. Only time will tell. Nevertheless, this example suggests that a higher net profit percentage based on higher value added does not necessarily produce higher profitability, at least when measured by *Net Profit to Net Worth*.

An analysis of *Net Cash Flow to Interest-Bearing Debt plus Net Worth*, which more closely parallels the thinking of some professional investors, yields the same result: Company I obtains a higher rate of return than Company J, both because of Company I's lower asset level in relation to net sales (higher *Net Sales to Total Assets*) and because Company I is able to use suppliers' credit to reduce the amount of interest-bearing debt and owners' equity required to support those assets.

Empirical evidence has been advanced by Robert D. Buzzell and Bradley T. Gale, based on the Profit Impact of Market Strategy (PIMS) Program, that higher *Value Added to Net Sales* will produce a higher *Return on Investment* (*Net Profit Before Taxes plus Interest Expense to Long-Term Liabilities plus Net Worth*, in

Table B5-2. Effect of value added on net profit for two companies.

	Company I	*Company J*
Net sales	$1,000,000	$1,000,000
Net profit before taxes	40,000	65,000
Income taxes	13,000	22,000
Net profit after taxes	27,000	43,000
Depreciation	12,000	34,000
Accounts receivable	125,000	125,000
Inventory	50,000	200,000
Fixed assets	100,000	275,000
Total assets	300,000	625,000
Interest-bearing debt	100,000	350,000
Total liabilities	190,000	415,000
Net worth	110,000	210,000
Net Profit to Net Worth	36.4%	31.0%
Total Liabilities to Net Worth	1.7 times	2.0 times
Net Sales to Total Assets	3.3 times	1.6 times
Net Cash Flow to Interest-Bearing Debt plus Net Worth	18.6%	13.8%

the PIMS definition), provided that *Net Sales to Total Assets* is not reduced in the process. With this in mind, a manufacturing firm such as Company I, which now designs and assembles its product, might investigate the feasibility of adding a direct sales force in place of outside distributors before considering the possibility of producing components. Management should analyze such a move very carefully, since the company's distributor relationships might be worth far more in terms of sales effectiveness than the amount that might be saved by developing an in-house sales organization.

Lower Costs Through Specialized Subcontractors

This example has been based on the assumption that Company J can manufacture all components at no higher cost than that incurred by a specialized subcontractor. Subcontractors' profit has been assumed to flow directly to earnings before interest and taxes. In actuality, specialized subcontractors are often capable of producing components at lower total cost than that of an integrated manufacturer. In fact, Company J may well find that subcontractors to the industry are able to develop increasingly cost-effective processes by virtue of a specialized focus in hiring, training, and upgrading of technical skills, as well as the purchase and adaptation of equipment for maximum flexibility and innovation within a narrow range of activity. In addition, such specialized companies often make important production advances by virtue of cumulative experience in meeting the demands of a variety of customers. Under these circumstances, the design and assembly company (Company I) might well surpass Company J with respect to both measures of profitability: *Net Profit to Net Sales* and *Net Profit to Net Worth*. In any case, management can safely assume that value added (in the sense of in-house activities versus purchases and subcontracting) does not necessarily result in a superior strategic position.

Uses of a Specialized Ratio

Some strategic planners have attempted to mix the value added concept with break-even analysis through a specialized ratio, *Fixed Costs to Value Added*. They assert that a company with relatively high *Fixed Costs to Value Added* should consider the price-cutting approach to improving profitability. They theorize that a company in that position would benefit from reducing prices to gain an increase in sales volume—and thereby spread fixed costs over a larger number of net sales dollars, resulting in higher net profit. In effect, they consider *Fixed Costs to Value Added* an indicator of operating leverage.

Determining *Fixed Costs to Value Added* involves a number of definitional problems, particularly with respect to physical assets. If those assets are leased, they are not, strictly speaking, a component of value added, although in every other respect they contribute to the company's operations in a manner identical to assets owned by the firm. Nevertheless, unless all fixed costs are included in value added, the widely circulated admonition that a company will incur a loss if *Fixed Costs to Value Added* exceeds 1.0 does not hold true.

A company with net sales of $1 million, fixed costs of $400,000 (all assumed to represent a portion of value added), purchased variable costs of $300,000, and internal variable costs of $250,000 (also a part of value added) will show a net profit of $50,000 (a third component of value added). When the three elements of value added are summed, the total is $700,000. Dividing fixed costs of $400,000 by value added of $700,000 yields *Fixed Costs to Value Added* of 0.57. Although this ratio is rarely published in industry studies, a reasonable approximation may be derived from certain trade association reports that contain detailed operating statement data through an adaptation of the method for calculating industry standards described in Appendix B2, "Break-Even Analysis."

But what does *Fixed Costs to Value Added* really tell the analyst? This ratio is supposed to alert management to the possible benefits of engaging in price cutting to increase sales, but it often sends the wrong signal. A study of the data in Table B5-3, which displays information on a per $1 million basis for ease of comparison, will indicate one such case.

Companies SP1, SP2, and SP3 are all manufacturers engaged in a consumer goods industry that currently has excess capacity, and each is considering the

Table B5-3. Effect of price-cutting strategy for three companies.

	Company SP1	Company SP2	Company SP3
Net sales	$1,000,000	$1,000,000	$1,000,000
Fixed costs	400,000*	300,000*	280,000*
Variable costs: purchased	200,000	550,000	450,000
Variable costs: internal	350,000*	100,000*	150,000*
Net profit before taxes	50,000*	50,000*	120,000*
Units sold	2,000	2,000	2,000
Unit price	$ 500	$ 500	$ 500
Fixed Costs to Value Added	0.50	0.67	0.51
Fixed Costs to Total Costs	0.42	0.32	0.32
Contribution Margin†	0.45	0.35	0.40
Net Profit to Net Sales	5.0%	5.0%	12.0%

*Value added. Components of value added:

	Company SP1	Company SP2	Company SP3
Fixed costs (all internal in this example)	$400,000	$300,000	$280,000
Variable costs: Internal	350,000	100,000	150,000
Net profit before taxes	50,000	50,000	120,000
	$800,000	$450,000	$550,000

†Net sales minus variable costs equals contribution to overhead and profits; this amount divided by net sales equals Contribution Margin.

possibility of reducing prices to capture a larger share of the market. Let us assume that some management strategists also expect temporary price reductions to stimulate an increase in total industry sales, tending to mitigate the downside risk that a price cut might not achieve a sufficient net sales gain. If the view that a company with high *Fixed Costs to Value Added* is most likely to benefit from a price-cutting strategy is correct, then Company SP2 appears to be the best candidate. A quick look at the comparatively high *Net Profit to Net Sales* of a competitor, Company SP3, suggests that such a move by Company SP2 could be counterproductive, if not disastrous.

Suppose that before Company SP2 can even investigate the potential consequences, Company SP3 acts first, dropping the effective price per unit from $500 to $420 after all cash incentives have been taken into consideration. Companies SP1 and SP2, feeling the need to respond quickly, develop their own financial packages that have the same net result on their price structures, an effective price of $420 per unit.

At this point, we will make the highly optimistic assumption that Companies SP1, SP2, and SP3 all succeed in increasing unit sales by 25%, either by taking market share from other competitors or by stimulating new demand, resulting in a small increase in net sales dollars. The new income statement figures are displayed in Table B5-4. Company SP2, identified by its high *Fixed Costs to Value Added* as the business most likely to benefit from price competition, was actually

Table B5-4. Income statement figures for three companies.

	Company SP1	Company SP2	Company SP3
Net sales	$1,050,000	$1,050,000	$1,050,000
Fixed costs	400,000*	300,000*	280,000*
Variable costs: purchased	250,000	687,500	562,500
Variable costs: internal	437,500*	125,000*	187,500*
Net profit before taxes	(37,500)*	(62,500)*	20,000*
Units sold	2,500	2,500	2,500
Unit price	$ 420	$ 420	$ 420
Fixed Costs to Value Added	0.50	0.83	0.57
Fixed Costs to Total Costs	0.37	0.27	0.27
Contribution Margin†	0.35	0.23	0.29
Net Profit to Net Sales	(3.6)%	(6.0)%	1.9%

*Value added. Components of value added:

	Company SP1	Company SP2	Company SP3
Fixed costs (all internal in this example)	$400,000	$300,000	$280,000
Variable costs: Internal	437,500	125,000	187,500
Net profit before taxes	(37,500)	(62,500)	20,000
	$800,000	$362,500	$487,500

†Net sales minus variable costs equals contribution to overhead and profits; this amount divided by net sales equals Contribution Margin.

the most clear-cut victim of this overly zealous strategic move by Company SP3. Not only did Company SP2 show a substantial loss, but the organization sustained the largest total drop in net profit ($112,500 versus $87,500 for Company SP1 and $100,000 for Company SP3). Because of its outstanding *Net Profit to Net Sales* before the price war began, Company SP3 was still able to turn a small profit and may succeed in forcing some of its weaker competitors to withdraw from the field. Company SP1 was pressured into a net loss by the depth of Company SP3's price cut, but Company SP1 actually suffered the smallest dollar decline because of its comparatively high *Contribution Margin*. This ratio, described in more detail in Appendix B2, is calculated by subtracting variable costs from net sales and then dividing the difference (which represents contribution to overhead and profit) by net sales.

Although *Fixed Costs to Value Added* may perform badly as an indicator of relative benefits when price cutting is too extreme and profit is actually reduced, perhaps it does a better job when the mix of price reduction and unit sales results in higher profit. The figures in Table B5-5, which reflect a 25% rise in unit sales with a price reduction of only $20 per unit, show the same outcome as in Table B5-4: Company SP1 enjoys the largest dollar gain and percentage increase in net profit, while Company SP3 reports the highest *Net Profit to Net Sales*. Company SP2, the business most likely to benefit according to *Fixed Costs to Value Added*,

Table B5-5. Effect of price reduction combined with rise in sales for three companies.

	Company SP1	Company SP2	Company SP3
Net sales	$1,200,000	$1,200,000	$1,200,000
Fixed costs	400,000*	300,000*	280,000*
Variable costs: Purchased	250,000	687,500	562,500
Variable costs: Internal	437,500*	125,000*	187,500*
Net profit before taxes	112,500*	87,500*	170,000*
	950,000	512,500	637,500
Units sold	2,500	2,500	2,500
Unit price	$ 480	$ 480	$ 480
Fixed Costs to Value Added	0.42	0.59	0.44
Fixed Costs to Total Costs	0.37	0.27	0.27
Contribution Margin†	0.43	0.32	0.38
Net Profit to Net Sales	9.4%	7.3%	14.2%

*Value added. Components of value added:

	Company SP1	Company SP2	Company SP3
Fixed costs (all internal in this example)	$400,000	$300,000	$280,000
Variable costs: Internal	437,500	125,000	187,500
Net profit before taxes	112,500	87,500	170,000
	$950,000	$512,500	$637,500

†Net sales minus variable costs equals contribution to overhead and profits; this amount divided by net sales equals Contribution Margin.

finished last again. Clearly, *Fixed Costs to Value Added* has not been a particularly useful indicator of the potential impact of price-cutting strategies for Companies SP1, SP2, and SP3.

An Alternative Ratio

An alternative measure commonly suggested by other strategic planners is *Fixed Costs to Total Costs*. This ratio is also intended to alert management to possible benefits from reducing prices to increase market share or sales volume. Some strategic planners consider it to be the best measure of operating leverage. A company with fixed costs of $300,000 and variable costs of $650,000 has a ratio of 0.32, calculated as follows: Fixed costs of $300,000 plus variable costs of $650,000 equal total costs of $950,000; dividing fixed costs of $300,000 by total costs of $950,000 produces a ratio of 0.32.

Returning to Table B5-3, we find that Company SP1's comparatively high *Fixed Costs to Total Costs* identifies that concern as the one whose management should give first consideration to reducing price in order to increase sales volume and boost net profit. Although, as we found earlier, Company SP1 did enjoy the greatest dollar gain and percentage increase in net profit when the relatively modest price cut produced a 20% gain in net sales, the business suffered a net loss when the price cut was more severe. Interestingly, Company SP2 reported *Fixed Costs to Total Costs* identical to that of Company SP3 before the price war. Consequently, these companies would be expected to fare similarly as price levels changed. As we know, however, Company SP2 was a significantly poorer performer under both conditions with respect to the dollar change in net profit (although the company did show a higher percentage increase in net profit under the relatively favorable circumstances). The difference in outcome is traceable to *Contribution Margin*, which was significantly higher for Company SP3 than for Company SP2. *Fixed Costs to Total Costs* appeared to be a somewhat better indicator of the impact of price-cutting strategies than *Fixed Costs to Value Added*, but both tended to lead to potentially dangerous conclusions.

As this example has demonstrated, you should examine carefully all ratios offered for your consideration. We have seen that no single financial measure can be used as the basis for assessing a company's competitive position and that some special-purpose ratios do not consistently perform as intended.

Appendix B6

Productivity Measures

Almost every discussion of international and interfirm competitiveness revolves around the concept of productivity improvement. How to measure that concept, unfortunately, remains a matter of controversy. In today's relatively unforgiving business environment, a company that enjoys a clear productivity advantage usually finds that fact reflected in a comparatively high *Net Profit to Net Sales*, a relatively high *Net Profit to Net Worth,* and a list of satisfied customers. Likewise, most companies with low productivity already understand the consequences. There is, however, no universal measure of company productivity, although this concept is often defined as *the number of units of output produced per unit of input*.

Financial Ratios Misleading

Some economists attempt to use financial ratios as substitutes for actual physical measures in productivity analysis. All evidence suggests that the conclusions drawn from such studies are, at best, confusing and, at worst, utterly misleading. *Net Sales to Fixed Assets* is, for example, not a good productivity measure, since the book value of fixed assets is greatly affected by the depreciation period allowed and by the age of the assets (which influences both the cumulative amount of depreciation subtracted from original cost and the original cost itself, particularly in times of rapid inflation). In addition, extended business hours or second- and third-shift production also has a major impact on this ratio. *Net Sales to Fixed Assets* is an important causal ratio with respect to a company's operating results and its fundamental financial structure, but it is not intended to measure the productivity of physical facilities. Certainly, comparative analysis of financial ratios to detect company trends and to measure competitive position will often suggest operating areas that should be carefully studied by management. Nevertheless, financial ratios do not directly measure productivity, and it is important for the analyst to understand their limitations and their possible misapplication. Only highly detailed studies of physical inputs (including such items as kilowatt hours of electricity) and physical outputs (such as the number of pounds of bakery products from a certain type of dough, or the number of units of a specific model of bathroom scale) can yield precise measures of productivity. At this stage of business record keeping, such productivity analyses are impractical for many small companies and render useful comparisons between businesses nearly impossible.

Units per Man-Hour

As a compromise between broad generalities and unreasonably detailed approaches, a simple ratio, *Units per Man-hour* (person-hour), would seem to be a basic measure of employee productivity and is often employed. A company producing 2,000 units through the work of 10 individuals during 2,000 hours of employment for each worker in a year would show .10 *Units per Man-hour* (2,000 units divided by 20,000 total man-hours). If each unit sells for $500, the company would report net sales of $1 million for the year. Although the number of units can usually be identified (except in the case of a contract manufacturing company, which produces a variety of products in frequently changing proportions), the number of man-hours may present a problem. As a company acquires new technology, there is often a shift in the balance between direct labor employees (who work directly on the product) and indirect labor employees (who are involved in estimating, software support, supervision/coordination, and maintenance). With increased automation, indirect labor tends to rise rapidly, leading to an artificially great increase in reported productivity if management continues to use direct labor man-hours as the denominator for this ratio. Should *Units per Man-hour* be based on the hours of all employees, including sales, general, and administrative personnel? The answer depends on the purpose of the analysis.

How does the analyst account for changes in the characteristics of the units, which are likely to become different (smaller, faster, lighter, bigger, more durable, perhaps more precise in construction and thereby more reliable over time)? In theory, these differences in the nature and amount of output can be captured in price changes, leading to the use of *Net Sales per Man-hour* (adjusted for inflation) as another measure of employee productivity. If each of the units produced by the company that showed *Units per Man-hour* of .10 sells for $500, then *Net Sales per Man-hour* would be $50 (calculated by multiplying $500 by .10). Alternately, 2,000 units that sell for $500 each yield $1 million in net sales; dividing total sales of $1 million by 20,000 man-hours (10 individuals at 2,000 man-hours each) equals *Net Sales per Man-hour* of $50.

Net Sales per Man-hour may, however, be altered by changes in the company's competitive strategy and operating pattern that are not indicative of any actual productivity differences. Suppose that the business is now characterized by a high degree of "vertical integration," participating in several stages of the manufacturing and distribution chain (for example, producing complete units from a combination of stock metal and parts cast in its own foundry and selling its products through its own sales force). If management has recently decided that the company should become a specialized engineering firm that subcontracts the production of all nonproprietary components and concentrates on design, assembly, and marketing through commissioned sales agents, *Net Sales per Man-hour* will probably rise by virtue of the purchased material (and the shift to outside sales representatives, if all employees are included in the denominator). Achieving the same sales volume with fewer man-hours suggests a productivity increase, but an increase in *Net Sales per Man-Hour* is often traceable to changes in the company's competitive strategy and changes in cost patterns. Under these circumstances, *Net Labor Sales per Man-hour*, calculated by subtracting purchases (including subcontracted services that substitute for direct labor) from net sales before dividing by man-hours, would be a better measure. If the company's cost of material (after any adjustment) is now $200,000, that amount would be subtracted from net sales of $1 million, leaving $800,000 in net labor sales. Dividing net labor sales of $800,000 by 20,000 man-hours produces *Net Labor Sales per Man-hour* of $40.

From another perspective, direct material equals 20.0% of net sales: $200,000 divided by $1 million, expressed as a percentage. That percentage can be translated into $10 per man-hour for the company with *Net Sales per Man-hour* of $50, as follows: 20.0% as a decimal fraction is .20; this fraction multiplied by $50 equals $10, the amount of direct material per man-hour. Consequently, *Net Labor Sales per Man-hour* equals $40: *Net Sales per Man-hour* of $50 minus the $10 attributable to direct material.

Value Added per Man-Hour

A somewhat more narrowly focused ratio designed to measure labor productivity is *Value Added per Man-hour*, which involves subtracting all outside purchases (such as utilities, supplies, and services), as well as direct material, from net sales before dividing by total man-hours for the year. If, for example, the company had purchased $200,000 of such utilities, supplies, and services during the year, its value added would be $600,000: net sales of $1 million minus total outside purchases of $400,000 (direct material of $200,000 plus other outside purchases of $200,000). Value added of $600,000 divided by 20,000 man-hours yields *Value Added per Man-hour* of $30.

What then about possible changes in the production process, which may, as a result of a new company strategy, shift the company's operation from labor-intensive assembly to dependence on a machine that has many man-years of work imbedded in its design, manufacture, and computer software? If the new machine produces units twice as fast as a human being using simple tools, but the machine is only used half the time, has a productivity gain occurred? From a financial point of view, the answer will depend on the cost of the machine, depreciation rates, interest rates, training costs, changes in wage rates as a result of job reclassification, and many other factors. If the interest on a floating-rate loan that was used to finance the machine happens to rise by three percentage points and the company now shows a net loss on this operation, has productivity declined? Can productivity be measured by financial data of this kind? The evidence is not encouraging.

Output-Input Models

Serious practitioners in the field of productivity measurement recognize the problems illustrated by the simplistic examples in the previous paragraphs. Consequently, they have developed elaborate input-output models that attempt to capture every element, from energy usage to employee training costs, in the production process. Yet, no matter now refined the model may be, its success as a measure of productivity is ultimately dependent on a definition and quantification of capacity. A company may be a paragon of productivity on those occasions when the entire plant is working steadily, but it may also appear hopelessly unproductive when sales slacken, particularly if the plant is highly automated. To adjust for such changes in workload, productivity models attempt to relate throughput to capacity utilization. But what is maximum practical capacity? Should a plant operate 24 hours each day, seven days every week? What about the third shift on Christmas Day? In a 40-hour, one-shift work week, should preventive maintenance be performed off-line (on overtime or shift premium hours)? What is the provision for preventive maintenance in a three-shift operation? Can maintenance be dovetailed with changeover and set-up? And what about the quality of items produced?

Once assumptions have been made with respect to capacity, analysts who attempt to measure productivity from financial data will make an estimate of the period costs associated with fixed assets. Is fully depreciated equipment a no-cost input? If a machine is acquired at a bargain price from a dealer in financial difficulty, does it have a lower input value than an identical machine purchased at normal market price? In reality, the analyst rarely has the detailed information to make appropriate adjustments—and would wear himself out attempting to do so. Consequently, most productivity analysts operate under a working assumption that such situations will, on the average, be counterbalanced by transactions of an opposite nature. In actual business practice, that assumption is often false, since depreciated facilities and bargain hunting usually reflect an entire business strategy, not a few isolated incidents. As a result, the financial inputs used in most productivity studies are both arbitrary and unconvincing to management.

Ironically, simple trend analyses and external comparisons of broadbrush ratios—such as *Net Labor Sales per Direct Labor Employee, Direct Labor Payroll Cost per Direct Labor Employee*, and *Facilities Cost per Direct Labor Employee*—often have more practical value in stimulating management thinking than do complex attempts at productivity measurement. These analyses may not be especially accurate, for reasons we have already considered; but, if they cause management to engage in a careful and systematic look at the basic elements of productivity improvement, such rather general measures can serve as useful additions to internal management reports, as well as to industry statistics.

Office and Sales Function

In recent years, there has been increasing interest in applying productivity concepts to office and sales functions. When a physical product is not involved, however, measurement of output and quality becomes even more difficult to define. Does a breathless customer service person rushing through a telephone order represent a higher productivity level than would a slower-paced transaction? How might a productivity measure based on calls handled per hour affect employee performance, customer reaction, and sales volume over a period of several months or years? Is the use of a fax machine to eliminate personal contact with key customers a wise productivity move, even if it results in less employee time per customer? How can top management measure the productivity involved in preparing and distributing 10,000 ineffective sales brochures? Short-sighted assumptions and narrow measurement schemes can lead to highly unfavorable consequences.

This series of inquiries is not intended to discourage the search for improved productivity measures, only to suggest constructive caution. Various broad productivity approximations, such as *Net Sales per Office Employee* or *Gross Margin per Sales Employee*, are useful measures of company conditions and comparative progress. Nevertheless, they are not true productivity standards in the most refined sense, since they do not account for the additional expenses, from automated facilities to car phones, borne by the company to achieve larger sales and gross margin numbers and (in some cases) higher profits. These ratios are, instead, simple reminders to management that there is an important linkage between resources, activities, costs, and financial structure.

Examine Productivity Measures Carefully

The fundamental value of ratio analysis is its ability to direct management attention to basic cause-and-effect relationships. The interactive nature of the 16 key financial ratios produces directly traceable results. As a practical matter, the importance of these fundamental measures of a company's competitive position goes beyond management analysis: Because the key ratios play an important role in major decisions made by bankers and credit grantors—decisions that can have a major impact on the company's growth prospects and competitive position— they have a significance that is as much symbolic as analytical. Most of the so-called productivity measures, on the other hand, are dependent on a variety of specific, yet debatable, assumptions about each company and have little, if any, comparative value. They also do not directly affect the policies of bank loan officers and the credit managers of key suppliers. You should avoid the temptation to calculate a proliferation of ratios that may tend to obscure the fundamental cause-and-effect relationships that make ratio analysis such a useful management tool—and that often have an important effect on the actions of a company's credit grantors.

APPENDIX C

Statistics Displayed in Industry Reports: Meaning and Use of Terms

You must be alert to the effect of statistical methods on industry norms. The percentage or ratio value that represents typical performance (the median) may be substantially different from the dollar-weighted average (which is greatly influenced by the largest companies in the group) or the company-weighted average (which is often strongly affected by a few extremely high or low values in the sample). Detailed knowledge of statistical methods is not required to use industry norms effectively, but you should consider carefully what statistics best serve as benchmarks for evaluating company performance. To assess a company's competitive strengths and weaknesses with confidence, you need a basic understanding of the perspective provided by one statistic versus another.

The Average

The average (called the *arithmetic mean* by statisticians) is found by adding together all the values in a group and dividing by the total number of responses in that group. Two types of averages may be found in industry reports: *company-weighted* (or "unweighted") *averages* and *dollar-weighted* (or "size-weighted") *averages*. *Company-weighted averages* are computed by converting each company's dollar amounts into a ratio, such as *Net Sales to Net Worth*, and then finding the average of those values. *Dollar-weighted averages* are computed by summing the dollar amounts for each financial statement item reported by all companies in the sample (for example, the sum of net sales for all companies in the group) and then dividing one aggregate dollar amount by another (for example, the sum of net worth for all companies in the same group).

In a greatly simplified example, we can see how the different methods of computation affect the resulting standards by considering three firms with the following financial characteristics: (1) Company X, with net sales of $10 million and net profit of $1 million; (2) Company Y, with net sales of $3 million and net profit of $120,000; and (3) Company Z, with net sales of $2 million and net profit of $80,000. Suppose that we are interested in generating comparative statistics for *Net Profit to Net Sales*. There are three steps in calculating the *dollar-weighted average*: First, find the sum of net profit ($1 million plus $120,000 plus $80,000 equals $1.2 million); second, find the sum of net sales ($10 million plus $3 million plus $2 million equals $15 million); third, divide the sum of net profit, $1.2 million, by the sum of net sales, $15 million, to obtain *Net Profit to*

Net Sales: 0.080 or 8.0%. Calculating the *company-weighted average*, on the other hand, begins with finding the ratio for each firm. With respect to *Net Profit to Net Sales*, Company X reports a 10.0% return on sales ($1 million divided by $10 million), while Company Y and Company Z show a 4.0% return ($120,000 divided by $3 million for Company Y and $80,000 divided by $2 million for Company Z). The company-weighted average is calculated by summing these percentages (10.0% plus 4.0% plus 4.0% equals 18.0%) and dividing by the number of firms, three, to obtain *Net Profit to Net Sales*: 0.060 or 6.0% Because the largest firm, Company X, reported the highest profit percentage, its relatively great dollar amount for both components (net profit and net sales) influences the dollar-weighted average upward. At 8.0%, the dollar-weighted average was significantly above the 6.0% company-weighted average, which treated all three percentages equally. These two methods are further illustrated and compared with the median in Table C-1.

Dollar-Weighted Average

Dollar-weighted averages are appropriate for charting major economic trends or evaluating the performance of publicly traded companies that have a significant share of a definable market, but they are less useful for assessing the competitive position of small and medium-size companies. By summing all dollar amounts for ratio components and then dividing one total (e.g., for net sales) by another (e.g., for total assets) to determine the industry standard, the dollar-weighted average gives a company with net sales of $100 million two hundred times the influence of a company generating a $500,000 annual sales volume. While dollar-weighted averages may be an appropriate representation of general industry characteristics, they tend to diminish comparative value for relatively small companies whose management undoubtedly recognizes that they are operating on a different plane from the largest 1,000 companies that dominate these statistics. Separating industry data into size classifications helps to overcome the problem of submerging smaller companies in the dollar pool. Nevertheless, a $1 million–$10 million classification will still permit some companies to exercise nearly 10 times the influence of other companies within the same

Table C-1.   Company-weighted and dollar-weighted averages for a group of five companies.

	Company AA	Company BB	Company CC	Company DD	Company EE	Total
Net sales	$1,200,000	$2,400,000	$3,600,000	$4,800,000	$9,600,000	$21,600,000
Fixed assets	100,000	90,000	375,000	470,000	1,900,000	2,935,000
Net Sales to Fixed Assets	12.0	26.7	9.6	10.2	5.1	63.6

Median = 10.2 (the middle value from the array of ratios: 5.1, 9.6, 10.2, 12.0, 26.7)

Company-weighted average = 12.7 (the average derived from the sum of ratios divided by the number of companies: 12.0 + 26.7 + 9.6 + 10.2 + 5.1 = 63.6; 63.6 ÷ 5 = 12.7)

Dollar-weighted average = 7.4 (the sum of net sales divided by the sum of fixed assets: 21,600,000 ÷ 2,935,000 = 7.4)

group. In addition, the group containing the largest companies is usually open-ended, allowing even greater potential impact in that category by the giants of the industry. The smallest companies in a particular business line may also find themselves virtually unrepresented in dollar-weighted averages for companies with total assets of $1 to $1 million. For that reason, most industry reports and the leading sources of multi-industry data use company-weighted averages for operating statement percentages and medians for the key financial ratios.

Company-Weighted Average

When an average of any kind is deemed an appropriate statistic, the *company-weighted average* is ordinarily superior to the dollar-weighted average for the purpose of comparing an individual company to performance by its peers. By giving the percentage of every company in the sample an equal influence, the company-weighted average eliminates the possibility that two or three very large concerns will determine the outcome for an entire category. Nevertheless, the company-weighted average may be strongly influenced by a small number of extreme values. If seven companies report the following percentages— 2.0%, 3.0%, 4.0%, 5.0%, 6.0%, 8.0%, and 16.0%—then the total for the group is 44.0%. Dividing this figure by 7 gives a company-weighted average of 6.3%. In this case, the average (6.3%) is higher than the individual percentages reported by five of the seven companies in the group. Because the average can be distorted by a few extremely high or low percentages, this statistic may not always be entirely representative of the typical company in a particular group. Nevertheless, the average is the statistic most familiar to the majority of businesspeople, and it is used in the vast majority of industry reports, primarily in presenting expense and profit percentages.

The Median

The *median* is the middle value in a set of numbers arrayed from the lowest value to the highest. For the seven companies with the following ratios—2.0, 3.0, 4.0, 5.0, 6.0, 8.0, and 16.0—the median is 5.0, the middle ratio. Three of the companies reported ratios higher than the median, while the ratios shown by another three of the companies were lower than the median, making the median a good measure of typical performance for companies in this group. Using the median in this case is similar to asking the top executive from each of these seven companies to compute his concern's ratio and then selecting the middle ratio as representative of the group. (When the number of values is evenly divisible by 2, the median is the average of the middle two numbers.) The median is the preferred statistic for displaying financial ratios, because it eliminates the effect of extremely high or low values that can occur when certain ratios are calculated.

Net Sales to Net Worth, for example, is less than 1.0 for some companies with extremely strong owners' equity in relation to sales volume (ordinarily the result of a rapid drop in sales experienced by a well-capitalized firm in a highly cyclical industry). On the other hand, this ratio can be more than 1,000.0 for companies with a very small amount of net worth. In fact, a business that has only $100 of net worth as a result of operating losses will exhibit extraordinarily high *Net Sales to Net Worth* at almost any level of sales activity. Such a value would seriously distort the company-weighted average (and possibly the dollar-weighted average, as well), but it would have only a minimal effect on the median.

Negative Numbers

The situation, however, can be even more difficult for the compiler of statistics, since net worth will become a negative number if the erosion of owners' equity causes total liabilities to exceed total assets. In that case, the ratio is infinitely high (represented as a negative value through ordinary algebraic computation). Specific numerical values are no longer meaningful for companies with deficit net worth, and an average of positive and negative values would be entirely useless. Nevertheless, the negative values should not simply be thrown away, since every response in the survey sample is equally important. By converting the negative values (which indicate deficit net worth) to very high positive ratios, placing them in the array of responses, and selecting the middle value as the median, a representative measure of typical performance can be found. If more than 50% of all companies in the group report a negative net worth (an actual occurrence in samples of small firms within a highly cyclical industry such as petroleum production and oil field support), the report should plainly state that fact.

Net Sales to Working Capital is subject to the same difficulty involving a negative denominator (working capital), since current liabilities exceed current assets for a small but significant proportion of companies in numerous industries. In a few capital-intensive service lines, such as cable television, a majority of companies in the entire national sample have reported deficit working capital.

The greatest challenge in data handling and statistical presentation is *Net Profit to Net Worth*, which may have a negative numerator (net profit) or a negative denominator (net worth), or, in some cases, both. Following ordinary algebraic rules, a computer will take the two negative numbers reported by a company in financial difficulty—a business showing both a net loss and deficit net worth—and routinely convert that company into a profitable enterprise, since one negative divided by another negative equals a positive value. A loss on deficit net worth, however, actually represents an infinitely large negative ratio and should be placed at the lowest end of the array. Similarly, a net profit on deficit net worth is considered an infinitely large positive ratio and properly belongs at the highest end of the sample values. Then the median is found by identifying the middle value. Unfortunately, not all industry reports follow this methodology, but software designed to address the problems inherent in certain key financial ratios is now available on microcomputers, enabling accurate calculation and presentation of industry statistics.

Inconsistent Relationships

As a result of neutralizing the effect of extreme percentages, medians do not maintain a consistent relationship to one another, as averages do. Consequently, the median figure for the total (for example, selling and administrative expenses) of a group of individual expense items (telephone, office compensation, and so forth) will be equal to the figure obtained by adding together the medians for those individual items only by coincidence. In fact, owing to the characteristics of the median, it is not unusual for a company to have expense percentages equal to, or even somewhat above, the median for each individual expense item and yet have a total expense percentage below the median. Table C-2 illustrates the reason for this occurrence. Company AA's expenses are somewhat higher, as a percentage of sales, than the median for each individual item. In the aggregate, however, Company AA's expenses are somewhat lower than the median. This apparently contradictory result stems from the fact that Company AA did not incur any extremely high expense percentages, while each of the other four companies reported one item well above the group norm. A close examination of detailed industry data has revealed that many expenses are subject to considerable variation and that most companies report at least one cost item that is extremely high. These unusually high percentages may be planned (such as an extensive advertising campaign or extraordinarily generous fringe benefits), or they may result from inadequate cost control. Most expense items cannot be reduced beyond a certain level, but they can increase almost without limit. As a result, the median will ordinarily be lower than the average, which is frequently pulled upward by a few extremely high values.

The Most Representative Measure for Expense Items

All factors considered, the median is generally the most representative measure of the typical company with respect to any specific expense item. In the example above, the median for Expense Item 1 was, at 1.2%, identical to the percentage reported by two companies, while two companies indicated a higher figure and one reported a lower percentage. It is likely that five executives exchanging information about this expense area would conclude that the typical percentage was somewhere in the 1.2–1.3% area. By comparison, the average, at 1.6%, was higher than the expense percentage reported by four of the five companies in this hypothetical group. Using an average that has been influenced by one or more extremely high percentages can easily result in misleading conclusions. Nevertheless, most business-people and their accountants feel more comfortable with averages, rather than medians, for operating expenses, because they can identify all variances. Not only does the sum of the averages for expense items equal the average for the total item, but the sum of the company's differences from the group average for the various expense items will explain the company's difference from the average with respect to net profit. If the industry report restricts operating statement percentages to a single statistic, the company-weighted average is most often selected. Financial management reports published by national trade associations frequently include both the average and the median. Through the display of both statistics, the analyst

Table C-2. **Median and average: The effect of expense percentages for a group of five companies.**

Expense item	Company AA	Company BB	Company CC	Company DD	Company EE	Median	Average
Item 1	1.4%	1.2%	1.0%	1.2%	3.2%	1.2%	1.6%
Item 2	1.4	1.2	1.2	3.2	1.0	1.2	1.6
Item 3	1.4	3.2	1.2	1.2	1.0	1.2	1.6
Item 4	1.4	1.0	1.2	1.2	1.7	1.2	1.3
Item 5	1.4	1.2	3.2	1.0	1.2	1.2	1.6
Total	7.0%	7.8%	7.8%	7.8%	8.1%	7.8%	7.7%

can determine the influence of extreme values on the average relative to the typical response represented by the median. Both the median and the average can be very useful in assessing the operating strengths and weaknesses of a company or division, but the limitations of each measure should be well understood.

The Range of the Middle 50% of Participants

The *range of the middle 50% of participants* (commonly known as the *mid-range*) helps the analyst to compare a company with the *range of common experience* for similar organizations in its line of business. The lower end of the mid-range is known as the *lower quartile*, the value that separates the lowest one-fourth of responses from the remaining three-fourths. The *upper quartile*, conversely, is the value that divides the highest one-fourth of responses from the other three-fourths. The mid-range, which is the range between the lower quartile and the upper quartile, shows the middle half of values with respect to each key financial ratio, providing a framework for understanding a company's competitive strengths and weaknesses. If, for example, a company's *Net Profit to Net Worth* is 12.5%, and the analyst finds that the median for this ratio is 17.5%, he can tell immediately that the company's return on shareholders' equity is relatively low. But how serious is this difference in comparison with the general experience of competing companies? Reference to the range of the middle 50% of participants will help to judge the importance of the variance. If the lower end of the range is 14.0%, the analyst would know that the company's 12.5% figure falls into the lowest one-fourth of companies represented in that particular category. In other words, *Net Profit to Net Worth* would be lower than the values reported by three-fourths of all companies in that group. Such a finding would deserve careful attention. If, however, the analyst learned that the lower end of the range is 6.8%, he would realize that the 12.5% value is well within the "range of common experience." In that case, the difference between the company's 12.5% return and the 17.5% median would still warrant further investigation, but the analyst should direct initial attention to any ratios that fall outside the range of the middle 50% of participants. The mid-range is not displayed in all industry reports. When it is available, however, you will find it useful in putting a company's performance in perspective.

Index